HIGHROAD GUIDE
— TO THE —

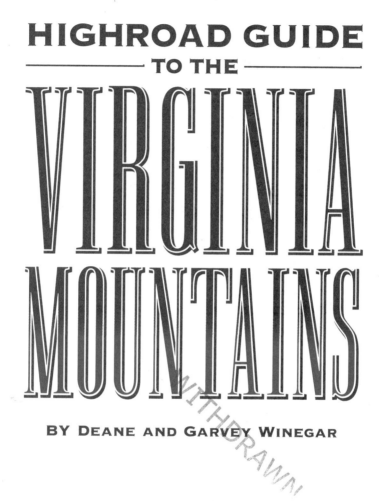

BY DEANE AND GARVEY WINEGAR

LONGSTREET
ATLANTA, GEORGIA

Published by
LONGSTREET PRESS, INC.
a subsidiary of Cox Newspapers,
a subsidiary of Cox Enterprises, Inc.
2140 Newmarket Parkway
Suite 122
Marietta, Georgia 30067

Printed by RR Donnelley & Sons, Harrisonburg, VA

1st printing 1998

Library of Congress Catalog Number 97-76536

ISBN: 1-56352-462-7

Book editing, design, and cartography
by Lenz Design & Communications, Inc., Decatur, Georgia

Cover illustration by W.L. Sheppard, *Picturesque America*, 1872.

Cover design by Richard J. Lenz, Decatur, Georgia

Illustrations by Danny Woodard, Loganville, Georgia

The publisher would like to thank Fulcrum Publishing for permission to reprint an excerpt from *Mountains of the Heart* by Scott Weidsensaul. Copyright © 1994 by Scott Weidensaul. Used by permission of Fulcrum Publishing, 350 Indiana Street, Golden, Colorado.

The Appalachians captured me as a child, and they have never released their hold. I am not unusual in this; mountains in general seem to exert an especially profound grip on the human imagination. Whatever the reason, I get twitchy when I spend too much time in a place where the highest point on the horizon is a telephone pole or a grain silo. I need to be able to look into the hills and know that I could disappear into them when the tame world gets to be too much, like a promise of refuge always waiting on the doorstep.

— Scott Weidsensaul, *Mountains of the Heart*

Contents

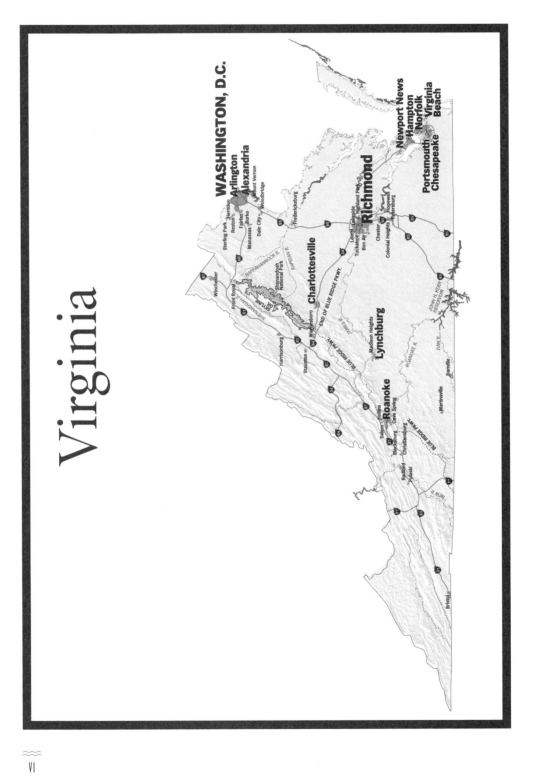

Virginia

How to Use Your Highroad Guide

The *Highroad Guide to the Virginia* Mountains includes a wealth of detailed information about the best of what the Virginia mountains have to offer, including hiking, camping, fishing, canoeing, mountain biking, and horseback riding. The *Highroad Guide* also presents information on the natural history of the mountains, plus interesting facts about Virginia's flora and fauna, giving the reader a starting point to learn more about what makes the mountains so special.

This book is divided into seven major sections using Virginia's physiographic regions, plus two additional sections. One is an introduction to the natural history of the mountains, and the other details long trails and river valleys that cut across these provinces. Virginia's major mountain provinces include the Appalachian Plateau, the Valley and Ridge, and the Blue Ridge. Because of the volume of information, the Valley and Ridge province is divided into three sections to help the reader.

The maps in the book are keyed by figure number and referenced in the text. These maps are intended to help orient both the casual and expert mountains enthusiast. Below is a legend to explain symbols used on the maps. Remember, hiking trails frequently change as they fall into disuse or new trails are created. Serious hikers may want to purchase additional maps from the U.S. Geological Service before they set out on a long hike. Sources are listed on the maps, in the text, and in the appendix.

A word of caution: The mountains can be dangerous. Weather can change suddenly, rocks can be slippery, and wild animals can act in unexpected ways. Use common sense when in the mountains so all your memories will be happy ones.

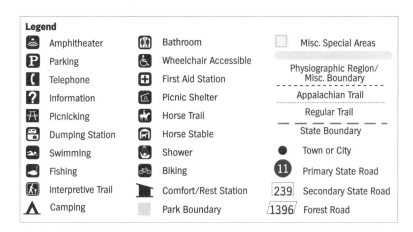

Legend

Amphitheater	Bathroom	Misc. Special Areas
Parking	Wheelchair Accessible	Physiographic Region/ Misc. Boundary
Telephone	First Aid Station	
Information	Picnic Shelter	Appalachian Trail
Picnicking	Horse Trail	Regular Trail
Dumping Station	Horse Stable	State Boundary
Swimming	Shower	Town or City
Fishing	Biking	11 Primary State Road
Interpretive Trail	Comfort/Rest Station	239 Secondary State Road
Camping	Park Boundary	1396 Forest Road

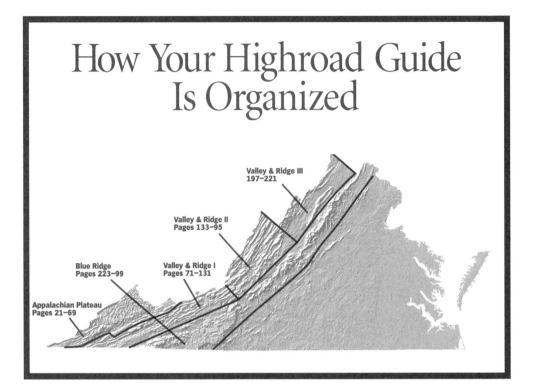

How Your Highroad Guide Is Organized

Valley & Ridge III
197–221

Valley & Ridge II
Pages 133–95

Valley & Ridge I
Pages 71–131

Blue Ridge
Pages 223–99

Appalachian Plateau
Pages 21–69

Preface

The layout of this book follows nature's arrangement of the mountains. The goal was to provide easy access to information on various sites and attractions, while letting the story of western Virginia unfold in sequence. The major divisions are Virginia's mountain provinces, taken from west to east—the Plateau, the Valley and Ridge, and the Blue Ridge. A final chapter covers long trails and river valleys that ignore boundaries as they meander from one province into another. The 33.4-mile Virginia Creeper Trail, for instance, is about half in the Valley and Ridge, half in the Blue Ridge.

Generally, the book follows each province, in turn, from south to north. A visitor to Shenandoah National Park in the Blue Ridge can glance at the table of contents or flip to the preceding and following chapters to see that Wintergreen and Sky Meadows State Park are nearby.

The book is broad in scope—more than a guide on where to go and what to do. Just as a cookbook and a recipe are the beginning of enjoying a meal, finding a state park or driving into a national forest is the beginning of adventure. What's special here? Can you see bears or bobcats? When is the hawk migration? What is this rock? Why the cedars? Are there waterfalls? Fossils? Caves? Good fishing?

We've loaded the chapters with extras—the stuff of these venerable old hills. Tips a ranger, botanist, or biologist passed along. Discoveries made only after several visits to a park or preserve.

Feel free to personalize this guide with your own thoughts and observations. Mark it up, highlight the text, write in the margins, add notes: *Push jewelweed leaves under water—silver! Photographed blurry upside-down reflection of full moon at Sherando Lake. Seven frogs identified by sound at Peaks of Otter.* Our blessings.

The mountains smell good and the backroads beckon. We're shutting down the computer. Happy trails.

Deane and Garvey Winegar

Acknowledgments

Readers of this book have at their fingertips far more than the work of two writers. Fascinating information came from earth scientists, ecologists, biologists, and botanists endowed with endless curiosity about how the mountains came to be and how ecosystems work. Site managers, foresters, fisheries managers, local guides, conservationists, volunteers, cartographers, college professors, and many others eagerly shared their knowledge. Our families allowed quiet time to write.

Our warmest thanks to Marge McDonald, project director for the series of mountain books at Longstreet Press. Not only did she entrust us with the Virginia book and grant extra time for research, but she also found editors worth their weight in quill pens. Richard Lenz and Pam Holliday provided gentle encouragement, guidance, a safety net for our copy, and their own expertise on the Southern Appalachians.

We're indebted to Gary Waugh with the Virginia Department of Conservation and Recreation (DCR) and Steve Carter-Lovejoy, Lesa Berlinghoff, and Tom Rawinski at the DCRs Division of Natural Heritage. Updating us with the latest information on state parks were Craig Seaver at Natural Tunnel State Park, Jim Kelly at Hungry Mother State Park, Eric Hougland at New River Trail State Park, Janet Blevins at Southwest Virginia Museum and Karlan State Park, Richard Johnson at Claytor Lake State Park, Christine Humphrey and Frances Simmons at Douthat State Park, Jess Lowry from Sky Meadows State Park, Andy R. Guest from Shenandoah River State Park, Phil Koury at Grayson Highlands State Park, John Grooms at Fairy Stone State Park, and Carl Mullins, superintendent of Breaks Interstate Park.

For information on federal lands, we depended on David Olson, public relations officer, Al McPherson, recreation assistant, and Tom Collins, geologist for the George Washington and Jefferson National Forests; Bob McKinney, interpretive specialist with Mount Rogers National Recreation Area; and Brad Williams, information specialist with the Highlands Gateway Visitor Center.

Assistance from the busy staffs at the national forest ranger districts came from Lisa Nutt, wildlife biologist, and Lois Boggs, interpreter, Clinch Ranger District; Beth Lament and other staff, Blacksburg Ranger District; Debbie Hawkins, public affairs program manager at Wythe Ranger District; Cynthia Snow, district ranger, Elizabeth Higgins, receptionist, and the late Jenifer Shoemaker, creator of an extensive trail guide, James River Ranger District; Dawn Coulson, forestry technician, Warm Springs Ranger District; Dale Huff, assistant ranger, New Castle Ranger District; David Rhodes, district ranger, Deerfield Ranger District; Steve Parsons, district ranger, and Bob Tennyson, forester, Dry River Ranger District; John Coleman, district ranger, Stephanie Bushong, interpretive specialist, and Kay Hand, senior citizen enrollee/receptionist, Lee Ranger District; Pat Eagan, district ranger, Glenwood Ranger District; and Kathy Hall, forester, Pedlar Ranger District.

Helpful staff at the Wildlife Management Areas (WMA) of the Virginia Department of Game and Inland Fisheries includes Scott Whitcomb, wildlife biology assistant at Clinch and Hidden Valley WMAs, and Jay Jeffreys, wildlife biologist at Havens WMA.

Expert help on the origin of Virginia's mountains came from Dr. James Beard, curator of earth sciences for the Virginia Museum of Natural History; from geologist and author Keith Frye of Tyro, Virginia; and from Alan Penick and Jack Nolde with the Virginia Division of Mineral Resources.

At national parks, thanks to Jack Collier, chief ranger and acting superintendent and Carol Borneman, chief interpreter, Cumberland Gap National Historical Park; to Karen Michaud, interpretive specialist and Greta Miller, executive director, Shenandoah Natural History Association, Shenandoah National Park; and to Peter Givens, Blue Ridge Parkway, Virginia specialist, National Park Service.

Kudos to Geneva Varner for help with North Fork of Pound Lake, Russell Artrip and Tanya Hall for help with John W. Flannagan Dam and Reservoir, Bill Sullivan at the Jonesville District of the Virginia Department of Transportation for information on the Wilderness Road Trail, and Joyce Lane at the Upper Valley Regional Park Authority for help with Grand Caverns and Natural Chimneys.

A tip of the writers' hat to the Virginia Chapter of The Nature Conservancy—especially Robert Riordan, director of communications, and Don Gowan, conservation program specialist at the Conservancy's Clinch Valley Bioreserve.

We're also indebted to Michele Wright with the Alleghany Highlands Chamber of Commerce, Judy Watkins and Martha Steger with the Virginia Division of Tourism, Geraldine Wilmer at Natural Bridge, Mark Glickman at Wintergreen, Betty Scott at the Grayson County Tourist Information Center, F. William Ravlin, gypsy moth researcher in the Department of Entomology at Virginia Polytechnic Institute and State University, and Nancy Hugo with the Virginia Native Plant Society who supplied information on the wildflowers of Thompson Wildlife Management Area.

And we can't forget Wesley Baugher, the always-on-time driver for Federal Express.

Virginia Physiographic Regions

Virginia has five distinct physiographic regions

The Natural History of the Virginia Mountains

T he desire to move mountains is a dream as old as the human spirit. Mountain moving, however—or mountain building, for that matter—is best left to nature and time. Take Virginia's gentle mountains. The soft, blue-green folds on the horizon, shrouded in morning mist, appear to have been here forever. In human terms, they have existed for a very long time. In fact, at approximately 250 million years old—100 million more than the Rockies—they've seen their share of birthdays. But there was a time when no forested slopes graced the granite and gneiss bedrock that would someday support Virginia. Eons ago, when Planet Earth was young, events were taking place that would set the stage for present-day life in the

[*Above*: The Blue Ridge mountains on a frosty morning]

mountains of the Old Dominion.

The environment that now supports the white-tailed deer browsing beechnuts on Cumberland Mountain is intrinsically tied to the algae, giant insects, and lungfish that made a home on the planet millions of years ago.

And the ruffed grouse that flushes in a startling whirr on Shenandoah Mountain? Its existence is as closely linked to the first amphibian that crawled from the primordial ooze of the Devonian Period over 400 millions years ago as to the highbush blueberries the grouse ate this morning.

A simple but profound clue to the moving past of Virginia's mountains is in the fossilized seashell embedded in rock at a high mountain pass near the West Virginia line. How did it get there? And why there, and not in the Blue Ridge on Mount Rogers, Big Stony Man, or Old Rag? The answers stagger the imagination.

From Speculation to Understanding

When geology was a young discipline, scientists studying the earth were intrigued with uncanny similarities in the coastlines of Africa and North America. Like two pieces of a puzzle, the continents appeared as though one would snug neatly into the curvatures of the other.

Speculation began. Could it be? Was it possible that the earth's crust was not fixed in place, but fluid? The idea of continental drift—or plate tectonics—was born.

If giant crustal plates moved slowly across the earth's surface, that would explain a lot of things. Opposing continents also had coastlines with contours that seemed to match up. Rocks on opposite shorelines had a similar composition and similar fossils. Mountains along the edges of some continents looked for all the world like wrinkles from a monumental fender-bender. Deep ocean canyons or trenches off the coasts could be the point where one plate was sliding beneath another. The idea was tempting, but skeptics were many. In North America, the theory became material for jokes. Finally, modern instrumentation lent credibility. Imagine the reaction as scientists began to prove what had lain so simply before their eyes, too fantastic to believe.

Radioactive analysis determined amazing similarities in chunks of rocks on the two seemingly disparate continents. Magnetic analysis gave clues about the original orientation of rock strata in relation to present positions. Analysis of seismic waves revealed the nature of the earth at great depths. Gradually, geologists pieced together some events with reasonable certainty, and formed the basis for making good guesses at others.

Most scientists now believe the world's continents have, inch by inch, drifted together, then broken apart—more than once. At a rate of no more than 5 inches per year, the earth's plates would never win the Indy 500. But these colliding land masses caused unimaginable heat and pressure, torturing and twisting the earth's crust, and crushing or metamorphosing one form of rock into another. Mountains that were pushed up one time would be destroyed the next. From time to time during the earth's restless heaving, shallow oceans would flow in over the land, then withdraw.

Three of these events, or *orogenies* as they are called, played a part in building the southern Appalachians. The bedrock that underlies today's Appalachians was mostly created during the Grenville Orogeny that began 1.1 billion years ago. Subsequent lava flows from volcanoes that erupted as the continents pulled apart also contributed.

For the most part, the bedrock is invisible, far beneath the sedimentary layers of rock that formed above it after life began. The notable exception is the rock along the eastern edge of the Appalachians. Because it was closest to the point of impact, the bedrock was shoved up and over rock to the west as the plates drifted together again, millions of years after the Grenville event.

This lifeless bedrock, born of fire and crushing force, is there for humans to see and touch. Today, families cast blankets upon it for their picnics. Wildflowers grow in soil pockets on its slopes, and ravens build nests in its crevasses. Climbers cling to its sheer vertical surfaces, bodies pressed against cool granite boulders as hands search for purchase in a niche or indentation. Hikers walk upon this rocky link with ages long past. Hang gliders leap from its upthrust edges, and drift away like feathers to the valley below.

Virginia's Mountain Inheritance

[Fig. 3] Virginia's claim to this Appalachian inheritance includes these four distinct physiographic regions, from west to east:

The **Appalachian Plateau** rises across the state's extreme southwest corner. Layered sedimentary rock remains for the most part in its original horizontal position. The tough sandstone tabletop has severely eroded over the ages, forming deep, narrow ravines and hollows. The weathering exposes fossils of early marine life in a timeline that goes back through the ages from the top down. Also exposed are seams of coal deposited from the Pennsylvanian Period of the Paleozoic era.

The **Valley and Ridge** makes up most of Virginia's western province. Folds and blocks of layered rock were turned on their side during the Paleozoic era. The landscape then eroded at varying rates of speed, depending on the composition of the rock, to form the linear mountains and parallel valleys we see today, trending southeast/northwest. Thick deposits of highly erodible limestone from ancient marine life in the Mississippian Period left a heritage of caverns, caves, and sinkholes.

The weathered mountain wall of the **Blue Ridge** to the east broadens to a plateau in southern Virginia. The Blue Ridge has the state's oldest rock and highest peaks. Here, billion-year-old granite from basement rock was forced up over much younger rock to the west. As the continents pulled apart, the rift action caused volcanoes to

Geologic Time Scale

Era	System & Period	Series & Epoch	Some Distinctive Features	Years Before Present
CENOZOIC	Quaternary	Recent	Modern man.	11,000
		Pleistocene	Early man; northern glaciation.	1/2 to 2 million
	Tertiary	Pliocene	Large carnivores.	13 ± 1 million
		Miocene	First abundant grazing mammals.	25 ± 1 million
		Oligocene	Large running mammals.	36 ± 2 million
		Eocene	Many modern types of mammals.	58 ± 2 million
		Paleocene	First placental mammals.	63 ± 2 million
MESOZOIC	Cretaceous		First flowering plants; climax of dinosaurs and ammonites, followed by Cretaceous-Tertiary extinction.	135 ± 5 million
	Jurassic		First birds, first mammals; dinosaurs and ammonites abundant.	181 ± 5 million
	Triassic		First dinosaurs. Abundant cycads and conifers.	230 ± 10 million
PALEOZOIC	Permian		Extinction of most kinds of marine animals, including trilobites. Southern glaciation.	280 ± 10 million
	Carboniferous	Pennsylvanian	Great coal forests, conifers. First reptiles.	310 ± 10 million
		Mississippian	Sharks and amphibians abundant. Large and numerous scale trees and seed ferns.	345 ± 10 million
	Devonian		First amphibians and ammonites; Fishes abundant.	405 ± 10 million
	Silurian		First terrestrial plants and animals.	425 ± 10 million
	Ordovician		First fishes; invertebrates dominant.	500 ± 10 million
	Cambrian		First abundant record of marine life; trilobites dominant.	600 ± 50 million
	Precambrian		Fossils extremely rare, consisting of primitive aquatic plants. Evidence of glaciation. Oldest dated algae, over 2,600 million years; oldest dated meteorites 4,500 million years.	

spew forth successive lava flows in both southern and northern sections of the Blue Ridge, covering all but the highest peaks.

The rolling foothills called **Piedmont** have only a few prominent mountains. Mountain-building processes are evident, nonetheless, in the western Piedmont in underlying cracked granites and transformed greenstones.

Life Begins

[Fig. 4] Despite the age of the Precambrian basement rock, the oldest rocks in Virginia formed nearly two billion years after the first one-celled bacterium cloned itself by simple division in some ancient ocean. Life on earth began about 3.5 billion years ago when primitive algae created pond scum. However, most major groups of plants and animals did not evolve until much later Precambrian times about 2,200 million years ago, as the climate moderated and shallow seas washed over the region that would one day be called Virginia.

By the Cambrian Period (about 480 to 600 million years ago), deposits of the first insectlike animals called trilobites began settling to the ocean floor. Then tiny animals called graptolites added their remains to the flooded deltas of the next period—the Ordovician (about 435 to 480 million years ago). Decomposing Ordovician gases led to the formation of oil, lead, and zinc in layers of limestone, sandstone, and shale.

Then came spore-bearing land plants and coral reefs from the Silurian Period. In subsequent ages, remains of great varieties of Devonian fishes, then Mississippian mosses and Pennsylvanian reptiles, settled on top of earlier sediments, much the way colored sands stratify in a jar.

As life was taking on more complex forms, massive collisions occurred again, crushing the sedimentary layers with increasing intensity nearest the point of impact. To the west, however, the layers remained intact.

About 450 million years ago, the Taconic Orogeny crumpled the eastern edge of the North American plate, forming granite at the edges. Mountains began to build, only to be destroyed by the next crushing event. A hundred million years later, the eastern edge of North America felt the impact from another slow-motion event called the Acadian Orogeny. Most geologists believe the latest collision occurred near the end of the Paleozoic Era, about 250 million years ago, and pushed the southern Appalachians into being. A mass called Laurussia, composed of North America, Greenland, and Europe, drifted together over a period of 50 million years with another supercontinent called Gondwana, composed of Africa, South America, and India.

Faults, or fractures, appeared toward the east coast, and great blocks of layered rock thrust themselves up and over other blocks, or were crumpled into folds. For a time, earth's continents existed as one large mass called Pangaea.

About 220 million years ago, say scientists, this supercontinent began to break up. As the breach grew wider, the Atlantic Ocean was born.

The sea waters rolled back over time to reveal the Appalachian Mountain system. The new range stretched from central Alabama 1,500 miles northeastward to the Gaspe Peninsula in Quebec, Canada. Many geologists take the range even farther, to the Labrador Sea, where the ridge disappears into the ocean about 15 miles north of Newfoundland. Before the weathering effects of wind and rain subdued our nation's oldest mountains, the Appalachians possibly soared to the dizzying heights of the modern Himalayas. Although erosion and time would change their appearance, the groundwork was laid.

Mountains as History Makers

Now the stage was set. Decayed Paleozoic marine life and newly formed mountains provided the script for the nature of things to come. The direction of a single drop of rain in Virginia, for instance, is determined by the aged Appalachians. On eastern slopes, a falling raindrop will end up in the Atlantic. But to the west, it will take a much longer route, transported by several river systems to spill finally into the Gulf of Mexico.

The residue of rich marine life, lifted high above the valleys on budding mountains over the millennia, came to support complex ecosystems of various natural environments with diverse collections of plants and animals. Examples of these environments are boulderfields, hardwood forests, hemlock and heath forests, bogs, and limesinks.

Not only have Virginia's mountains been a key player in determining natural history, but they've shaped the course of human events as well. In the Valley and Ridge province, farmers found lush deltas. Layers upon layers of plants and animals deposited by early seas put corn and cabbage on their tables. The chance orientation of layered rock beneath the surface, however, could result in poor soil in an adjacent valley, where families would struggle to survive.

The coal that formed mostly from decaying woody plants crushed in Appalachian Plateau sandstone markedly influenced human settlement in southwest Virginia, where coal was king for many years. In fact, coal is still the most valuable mineral resource in the state.

Mountains born of continental drift partitioned Indian tribes and hunting grounds and delayed westward expansion of pioneers. These nearly impenetrable ranges funneled farmers and settlers from the North southward to fertile valleys, and became the scene of bloody Civil War battles. They inspired sonnets from the British and made Scots-Irish farmers homesick for their own highlands.

Today these seemingly eternal hills provide recreation for the city-weary, solace for the troubled, and a home for things wild and free. The stuff of our mountains—from inanimate rocks to vibrant life forces—flows from one eon to another in an ever-changing tapestry. From the oceans came life, developing from microscopic, one-celled simplicity to a creature equipped with backbone and lungs and able to crawl ashore, to an upright being that can devise a spaceship capable of riding a tail of fire to other planets.

The prescription for this life contains a simple rule—that every living thing must die, to decay and return its minerals to form the rocks of the earth. Nowhere have the threads of this natural cloth been more intricately woven, more beautifully blended, than in the primeval mountains of Virginia.

The Mountain Ecosystem

The forests of Virginia's mountains are in transition. Like a patient brought out of intensive care, the condition is guarded. The trouble, it seems, stems from the forests' very desirability. Even before white settlers arrived, Native Americans manipulated the forests and its wildlife. The Shenandoah Valley—a popular hunting ground for various nomadic tribes—was repeatedly burned to provide grasslands for herds of bison and elk. Big Meadows in Shenandoah National Park was probably kept open with regular burnings to provide forage for elk and deer and to simplify the gathering of chestnuts.

For a time, forested slopes, where soil was thin and poor, were left for the most part with their cover of magnificent chestnuts and oaks. As early settlers claimed the lush farmlands in the valley, however, newcomers were forced to stake out less-desirable sites on mountains. They cleared land for crops and pasture, but the steep slopes quickly eroded and became too poor to farm. Families would abandon the depleted soil and move higher up the mountains. The demand for iron, copper, and manganese during the Civil War further stressed the resources. Iron and manganese furnaces sprang up throughout the forests, and operators cut every usable tree within dragging distance to keep the fires stoked. Many trees not removed for mining were hauled away by railroad for lumber.

Finally, visitors to the mountains became alarmed at the devastation. A preservation

NORTHERN RED OAK
(Quercus rubra)
Red oaks can be identified by tiny bristles on the tip of each leaf.

Persecution and habitat destruction have led to the demise of the mountain lion or cougar, Felis concolor, *which in turn has played a role in the population explosion of white-tailed deer* (Odocoileus virginianus). *The mountain lion is the natural predator of deer. Reports of sightings of the cougar may be a sign that the animal is making a quiet comeback in the Virginia mountains.*

movement got under way at the eloquent urging of such naturalists as Henry David Thoreau, author of *Walden,* and John Muir, founder of the Sierra Club.

An early champion of the conservationist movement was Gifford Pinchot, who became the first chief of the U.S. Forest Service. In 1911, Pinchot wrote: "No one can really know the forest without feeling the gentle influences of one of the kindliest and strongest parts of nature. From every point of view it is one of the most helpful friends of man. Perhaps no other natural agent has done so much for the human race and has been recklessly used and so little understood."

Pinchot and President Theodore Roosevelt worked to bring wounded and abandoned lands under the protection of the federal government. In 1917, the George Washington National Forest was established, as the federal government bought and set aside "the lands nobody wanted."

Among the devastating effects of logging the mountainsides without restraint were massive flooding and erosion in the Tennessee Valley drainage west of Virginia's Plateau province. In 1936, the U.S. Forest Service bought land for the Jefferson National Forest's Clinch Ranger District in southwest Virginia, largely to protect the headwaters of the Tennessee River from the disastrous effects of denuding the land of trees. In the same year, Shenandoah National Park was opened in the Blue Ridge Mountains. Wildlife also suffered greatly from the removal of tree cover, from silted streams, burnings, and unconstrained killing. Indians, after acquiring firearms, killed off the last woodland bison in the southern Appalachians by 1760. Elk disappeared in the mid-1800s. Settlers quickly extirpated gray wolves, red wolves, and cougar without a second thought.

With no restraints, they also shot black bear, white-tailed deer, wild turkey, and bobcat, and trapped otter, beaver, and other furbearers. Elk, wolves, and bison never recovered. Though no concrete evidence proves the return of cougar (mountain lion), reliable sightings continue to trickle in, especially from high, remote areas of the Blue Ridge. The Peaks of Otter on the Blue Ridge Parkway is a frequently named locale. White-tailed deer, wild turkey, and black bear have been restored to much of their former range—success stories for wildlife management. Ironically, the return of these animals has been funded almost solely by hunters and anglers. Modern wildlife management has also enabled bobcat, beaver, and otter to make a comeback at some locations. Improving habitat for game animals has coincidentally benefitted many other species.

The American Chestnut

The American chestnut (*Castanea dentata*) once made up 40 to 50 percent of southern Appalachian forests. Nearly pure stands covered some forest slopes. The tree is a fast grower, and will grow most anywhere except in a swamp. The reddish-brown wood is lightweight, straight-grained, and easy to split. The trees grew 120 feet high and 10 feet across—trunks wide enough to fill most people's guest bedroom. Today's basketball players could stretch out on a stump and not touch the sides.

Chestnut wood was almost impervious to rot. Consequently, the tree was perfect for homes, barns, rail fences—anything that had to withstand sun, wind, and rain. Woody debris from downed chestnuts would last for decades, and added stability to the headwaters of streams. Both people and wildlife relished the sweet nut. Indians boiled the nuts to make stew, and colonists from England pickled them, used them in stuffings, and ground them into flour.

However, a fungus, *Cyphonectria parasitica*, introduced into New York from China in 1906 quickly spread throughout the chestnut's domain, ravaging the forest giants. None was immune. In Virginia, the tree was wiped out between 1910 and 1934. In 40 years, the chestnut blight killed 3.5 billion trees. The loss of the tremendous annual mast crops had a severe effect on mammals that depended on the tree for food. Especially hard hit by the demise of the chestnut were residents of the Appalachians, already besieged by hardships of the Great Depression. Resourceful mountaineers had found uses for every part of the tree—the wood, the nuts, even the bark. They also lost a prime source of income derived from hauling the wood and wagonloads of nuts to market.

The blight does not damage the tree's root system, and hope stays alive in new shoots that spring from old roots beside decaying stumps. Saplings appear healthy at first. As the trunk attains a 3-to-5-inch diameter, the rusty-red blight is evident on the bark. The tree sometimes becomes large enough to produce the tasty nuts in their prickly burrs before succumbing to disease. In fact, the chestnut is still a common understory tree. Unless scientists can develop a blight-resistant strain, though, the once-mighty chestnut is relegated to the status of underling.

More than a half century since the last tree succumbed to blight, the loss of the American chestnut from the forest continues to have an impact. Watersheds of the Appalachians are in the process of reestablishing an equilibrium. Woody debris that once stabilized streams is missing. Other riparian shade trees that might have replaced the chestnut as a stream stabilizer are fighting their own battles with disease. The Eastern hemlock, under assault by the wooly adelgid, is the most notable example.

The health of a watershed is important, among other reasons, for its natural response to large floods that sometimes accompany hurricanes. A healthy watershed is resilient and can recover rapidly, but a watershed under stress from past or current land use may suffer disproportionately with longer periods of recovery.

Public Lands in Virginia

Many of Virginia's mountainous areas are now public lands. The George Washington National Forest [Fig. 25], established in 1917, covers more than a million acres. The GW extends for 140 miles along the Appalachian Mountains of northwestern Virginia and spills over into West Virginia. Four wilderness areas protect 32,000 acres from development.

The U.S. Forest Service created the Jefferson National Forest [Fig. 15] in 1936 on the southern end of the George Washington. The 705,192 acres of the Jefferson spread across the mountains of southwest Virginia. A small portion also spills across state lines into West Virginia and Kentucky. The Jefferson has 11 wilderness areas with a total of 57,000 acres.

Although legislatively considered two separate forests, the George Washington and Jefferson were combined in March 1995, for administrative purposes. Headquarters for both are located in Roanoke under the name George Washington and Jefferson National Forests. The National Forests are managed for multiple use, including timber production, recreation, hunting, and fishing.

Mount Rogers National Recreation Area (NRA) [Fig. 34], in Virginia's southern Blue Ridge Mountains, is a 115,000-acre area of the Jefferson designated expressly for public enjoyment.

The National Park Service administers three areas in Virginia mountains—Shenandoah National Park [Fig. 43] and the Blue Ridge Parkway [Fig. 37, Fig. 38], both in the Blue Ridge Mountains [Fig. 32], and Cumberland Gap National Historical Park [Fig. 7] in Virginia's southwestern tip.

The state has eight state parks in the mountains and foothills. These include Hungry Mother [Fig. 19], New River Trail [Fig. 50], Grayson Highlands [Fig. 33], Claytor Lake [Fig. 51], Fairy Stone [Fig. 36], Smith Mountain Lake [Fig. 39], Douthat [Fig. 28], and Sky Meadows [Fig. 45]. In addition, Breaks Interstate Park [Fig. 11] on the Kentucky border is shared by Virginia and Kentucky.

The Virginia Department of Conservation and Recreation (DCR) administers the parks and an ever-increasing number of Natural Area Preserves. The preserves, under the DCR's Natural Heritage Program, are designed to protect the habitat of rare, threatened, and endangered plant and animal species and rare communities and ecosystems. Most do not have facilities for public access.

The Virginia Department of Game and Inland Fisheries operates 29 Wildlife Management Areas (WMA) for wildlife habitat, hunting and fishing, wildlife viewing, hiking, and protection of unique plant communities. Of 180,000 total WMA acres, 123,000 are in the mountains. In addition, the Appalachian Trail and other long trails [Fig. 46] provide hikes through scenic portions of the state. Several navigable rivers and scenic byways add more options for enjoying the outdoors in the mountains of the Old Dominion.

The Health of the Forest

Ghost forests. What's eating the trees? The question is a common one, say park rangers and forest rangers. Usually the curiosity stems from sights of large areas of gray, bare trees—a "ghost forest" in the midst of summer's greenery. The answer, most often, is the gypsy moth.

Although this exotic pest is the most destructive at present, the forest must deal with many other diseases and pests, both native and exotic. These include the hemlock wooly adelgid, pine beetle, dogwood anthracnose, fall cankerworm, and balsam wooly adelgid, all discussed below. A disturbing decline in the health of oak trees is also under study. In addition, butternut is under attack by the butternut canker, American elms are killed by Dutch elm disease, and table mountain pines—dependent on fire for restoration—are declining because of damage by bark beetles and the absence of fire for recovery. Foresters note the successful reforestation of cutover land and former agricultural land, watershed improvement, erosion control, fire protection, and expansion of wildlife populations that were priorities during the first half of the 1900s. Following an intensive study by state and federal agencies called the Southern Appalachian Assessment, new focuses include the possible development of gene conservation to protect declining tree species and improve the resistance of Eastern and Carolina hemlock, American chestnut, and butternut to insects and diseases.

Gypsy moth. Defoliated mountainsides have become an increasingly familiar scene over the past decade. Just as forest trees are leafing out in spring, hungry gypsy moth caterpillars are hatching and going to work on them. In heavily infested areas, entire slopes are denuded of foliage. Caterpillar droppings (frass) rain from the trees and cause an overwhelming stench. The trees usually leaf out again, although the leaves are lighter and smaller. Repeated defoliation stresses trees and eventually will kill them.

The gypsy moth made its way to America in 1869 courtesy of Etienne Leopold Trouvelot, who was attempting to find a better silk moth and make a few bucks. The moth escaped into the New England countryside where it had no natural enemies. It took more than a century to make its way to Virginia. But between its first appearance in 1980 and today, it has become a household word in the Commonwealth.

The pest crept southward, county by county, despite extensive attempts to halt its progress with sprays, pheromone (chemical attractant) traps, burlap rings applied to trunks to trap the caterpillars—everything short of incantations and magic potions. But in 1996 and again in 1997, an amazing occurrence gave the forests—and homeowners—a break. A fungus (*Entomophaga maimaiga*), first introduced in the early 1900s, mysteriously reappeared and devastated the gypsy moth population in Virginia. Incredibly, no areas experienced defoliation.

For the moment, the gypsy moth is no more abundant than other moths. However, entomologists warn that the fungus may have its own boom and bust years, just as the gypsy moth does. Although subdued, the moth lives on and the Virginia Department of Agriculture and Consumer Services notes the continual spread southward.

Oak decline. The health of oak trees is declining in the southern Appalachians, even in areas not yet affected by the gypsy moth. State and federal agencies studying the problems attribute the decline to many factors, including drought, disease, advancing tree age, and insect damage.

Oak decline causes reduced growth, crown dieback, and, after several years, mortality. Members of the red oak group (northern red, black, and scarlet oaks) are more susceptible than those in the white oak group (white and chestnut). Damage is more common in areas of poor, thin soil. Oaks stressed by drought, gypsy moth defoliation, or other factors may then become susceptible to shoestring root rot, a fungus root-decay pathogen native to North America and found throughout eastern forests. The oak is the tree that largely filled the vacuum after the demise of the American chestnut. The tree contributes to many complex ecosystem processes including the cycling of nutrients, the dynamics as a dominant canopy tree in a stand, and forest succession. Acorns are eaten by many wildlife species and are a staple in the diet of white-tailed deer, wild turkey, black bear, and gray squirrel. A black bear study, however, indicated these opportunistic animals would turn to grapes that grow in the sunlight under a destroyed oak canopy.

Oak is also a prime tree for the timber industry. Obviously, its decline has serious implications for the forests.

Hemlock wooly adelgid. The hemlock wooly adelgid, a major exotic pest in the Glenwood and New Castle ranger districts of the Jefferson National Forest [Fig. 14] for several years, is expanding its range in the national forest. Virtually all major stands of hemlock on the Glenwood are infested, and the adelgid is progressing south. To the north, Shenandoah National Park [Fig. 43] also has infestations.

While feeding, the insect injects a toxic saliva into hemlock foliage. The needles turn brown and drop from the tree. Over the years, the tree loses its foliage from bottom to top. After hatching from an egg, the insect is easily spread by wind, birds, deer, and other forest animals. This pest introduced from Asia has no natural enemies and has the potential of killing all hemlocks in the forest. Several varieties of foreign ladybird-beetles are under consideration for release as a biological control.

Hemlock, which grows along streams in sheltered hollows, is valuable as a shade tree for cold-water fisheries and for wildlife cover. The tree is the main component in several beautiful stands of old growth forests. Some hemlocks in the Limberlost of Shenandoah National Park are 350 to 400 years old.

Southern pine beetle. The southern pine beetle prefers hard pines, particularly loblolly, pitch, shortleaf, table mountain, and Virginia pines. A serious outbreak of the pest between 1991 and 1993 on the Glenwood Ranger District of the Jefferson National Forest [Fig. 15] affected even white pines, which are normally resistant. The outbreak ended following extremely cold temperatures during the winter of 1993–94, which killed most of the beetles.

Cutting the effected trees can stop infestations of southern pine beetles. Biological control methods include making the habitat suitable for parasites and predators of the beetles. Insecticide sprays are another option.

Dogwood anthracnose. Dogwood anthracnose is a fungal disease that causes leaf spots and stem cankers and can kill shoots and stems of flowering dogwood. Since it was first reported in the late 1970s, the fungus has become widespread in the eastern United States. It has been found in every county within the southern Appalachians.

Dogwoods at high elevation in shaded sites are at greatest risk and have little resistance. Anthracnose has no known natural enemies, and there are no practical methods for its control. In some areas, all the dogwoods have already been killed. Flowering dogwood—with its welcome sprinkling of white blossoms in the drab forest understory in early spring—is an important source of soft mast for wildlife.

Fall cankerworm. Fall cankerworm is one of the more common and injurious of the many species of loopers, spanworms, and inchworms that attack eastern forests.

The species will typically hatch in late April or early May, when leaf buds begin to open. Young larvae then feed on the buds and unfolding leaves. Hikers may notice defoliation and hear the sound of raining frass, or excrement, from the larvae. These larvae drop from the leaves on silk strands. Wind often detaches them and blows them great distances. Four to five weeks after hatching, they enter the soil to pupate, usually in early June.

An infestation in the Pedlar Ranger District [Fig. 25] of the National Forest on the east slope of the Blue Ridge Mountains is being monitored by the U.S. Forest Service.

Balsam wooly adelgid. The balsam wooly adelgid is attacking all but a few stands of Fraser fir in boreal forests on high summits in the southern Appalachians. The insect injects a deadly secretion as it feeds below the bark. The nearly pure stands of Fraser fir in Mount Rogers National Recreation Area [Fig. 34] are unaffected, while firs elsewhere are being decimated. Foresters have recently discovered that the Mount Rogers fir produces outer bark at a higher rate than fir elsewhere.

Scientists are studying the phenomenon, trying to develop resistant strains. Cones of seeds from Mount Rogers trees are sought by Christmas tree growers for their resistance to the adelgid.

Other Disturbances

Visitors to Virginia's parks and forests may also notice areas of severe destruction caused by both nature and humans. Examples are eroded areas, blow-downs, washed-out ravines, and standing deadwood. Such scenes may result from past logging operations (erosion), hurricane-force winds (blow-downs), ice storms (stands of broken and dead trees), or flooding rains (debris-strewn ravines, streams, and river valleys).

Fire—used by Native Americans and European settlers—may have altered forest dynamics for hundreds of years, according to a study called the Southern Appalachian Assessment. Fire prevention and suppression in the twentieth century, therefore, has changed a long-term pattern, and there are ecological consequences.

Fire—or its suppression—is probably the most common form of natural disturbance in the southern Appalachians. Its effects on southern yellow pines are well understood. It was probably a major factor in the development of oak forests on upland sites, but its ecological effects need further study.

Historically, forests with healthy ecosystems respond well to natural disturbances—even depend on them sometimes. A healthy watershed, for instance, is resilient and can rapidly recover from the effects of a large flood. Trees killed by lightning or downed by wind are used by various birds, animals, and insects for shelter or food.

But disturbances not built into the dynamics of the ecosystem may result in a much slower recovery. Besides the use or suppression of fire, other examples of disturbances include the many logging and tram roads pushed into the forest during the 1800s and early 1900s, strip mining, unmanaged tree removal, and the practice of bulldozing streams to straighten and widen them (channelization). Streams carrying water from steep mountainsides normally run clear until they pass areas where the soil has been disturbed. Only then do they pick up a cloudy green or brown tint.

Nature produces an extremely tough forest floor, full of nutrients and nearly impervious to erosion, no matter how severe the storm. But soil-building takes time. At one inch every 50 to 100 years, the process is often too slow relative to the needs of humans for forest products.

The U.S. Forest Service must continually weigh human needs against the needs of the forest for recovery.

Diversity in the Southern Appalachians

The southern Appalachians harbor the most diverse plant life in the temperate region of the world. More than 130 species of trees and 2,250 vascular plants grow in the region. Field scientists have identified 175 species of terrestrial birds, 65 species of mammals, and an estimated 25,000 species of invertebrates.

The diversity of crayfish, snails, and freshwater mussels in the Southeast is greater than in any other part of the world, and much of the diversity is in the southern Appalachians. The region also has more species of fish than any other place in the country. The watershed for the Tennessee River—much of which lies in Southwest Virginia—has especially high concentrations of these aquatic species.

A combination of factors contributes.

First, the abundance of plant life is partly attributable to mild climate and plentiful rain. The southern Appalachians receive the second highest amount of rainfall in the country, topped only by the rain forest of the Pacific Northwest.

Species richness is also a result of overlapping northern and southern habitats. Many southern species—Carolina hemlock (*Tsuga caroliniana*), Fraser fir, persimmon, pawpaw, mud salamander, and narrowmouth toad, to name a few—reach the northern extent of their range in the mountains of the southeastern United States.

Conversely, numerous plant and animal species native to New England and Canada extend their range southward down a fingerlike corridor of the Appalachians. Examples of Virginia's high-country species borrowed from northern climes are northern wood sorrel, bigtooth aspen, mountain-ash, red squirrel, red-breasted nuthatch, saw-whet owl, and golden-crowned kinglet.

Actually, northern species had a bit of help. During the last ice age of the Pleistocene epoch some 10,000 years ago, glaciers reached only into Pennsylvania, stopping short of Virginia. Northern species of plants and animals migrated south with colder temperatures, ahead of the ice sheets. The southern Appalachians served as a refuge until the glaciers finally began to melt, retreating north. Certain forest communities found the high altitudes in the mountains hospitable even after the ice age was over, and they remain today.

An example of the effects of glacier-induced species migration are the boreal forests in the rarified atmosphere of summits above 5,000 feet. In Virginia, such forests cover the summits of high peaks in Mount Rogers NRA [Fig. 34] in the southern Blue Ridge [Fig. 32] and peaks in the Laurel Fork area [Fig. 25] (Warm Springs Ranger District) of western Highland County.

The endangered northern flying squirrel (*Glaucomys sabrinus fuscus*) inhabits the forests in both areas. At Laurel Fork, the diminutive, nocturnal mammal leaps and glides from bough to bough in the isolated patches of red spruce and northern hardwoods that rode the ice flows southward. The rich, decaying soil beneath the conifers produces fungi, mushrooms, lichens—the diet of the northern flying squirrel. Sharing the same forest are other remnants from the ice age—the snowshoe hare, the fisher, and the paper birch (*Betula papyrifera*).

Extremes in altitude also enhance species diversity. Each 1,000 feet in elevation is accompanied by a 3.6-degree Fahrenheit decrease in temperature. A 6,000-foot increase in altitude is similar to driving 1,000 miles north. A trip from the James River, at an altitude of 650 feet, to the 5,729-foot summit of Mount Rogers in Virginia's southern Blue Ridge is the rough ecological equivalent of a drive from the James River to the shores of Canada's Hudson Bay.

Depending on the route to Mount Rogers, the traveler would pass through a variety of forest communities. These might include a silty lower floodplain, wetlands and bogs, cove hardwoods, shale barrens, oak-hickory forest, oak-pine forest, northern hardwoods, grassy balds, boulderfields, and muskegs, ending in an alpine spruce-fir forest. Each community has plant and animal species especially adapted for survival.

A key component for determining which species are found in various communities—but certainly not the only determining factor—is elevation. Other criteria are orientation to the sun, moisture, competing species, soil nutrients and textures, and pure luck. The fate of a seed eaten by a blue jay or a berry eaten by a cedar waxwing is dependent on the bird's itinerary for dispersal.

Salamanders. So many species of salamanders occur in the southern Appalachians—34 at last count—that many scientists now believe the region is the center for salamander evolution. Shenandoah National Park [Fig. 43] has 17 species. The Mount Rogers NRA has 26. In the Mount Rogers/Whitetop area, 20 species live on approximately 2,000 acres—the greatest known diversity of salamanders in an area of this size on earth. Several varieties are found nowhere else in the world.

One explanation for the diversity is the region's high precipitation. Salamanders must stay moist to keep their sensitive skin from drying out.

The isolating effect of the mountains also contributes to the variety and rarity of species. As temperatures warmed following the last ice age, salamanders probably migrated gradually up the mountainsides to find cooler habitat. Finally, separated from one another on various summits by now-inhospitable valleys, salamanders evolved into many distinct species. The Shenandoah salamander lives at just three sites on the north and northwest-facing talus slopes above 2,900 feet in Shenandoah National Park. Because *Plethodon shenandoah* cannot survive at lower altitudes, and cannot compete with the red-backed salamander (*Plethedon cinereus*) in woodlands surrounding the talus, it has no way—short of sprouting wings—to migrate to other talus slopes on other mountains.

RED SALAMANDER
(*Pseudotriton ruber*)

So specific are many of the habitats where various members of these caudates have evolved, the salamanders have been named for particular mountains or summits. Examples are the Peaks of Otter salamander, the Cow Knob salamander, and the Roanoke Mountain salamander.

Forest Types

A complex eastern deciduous forest covers 70 percent of the Southern Appalachians. Approximately 30 percent is unforested. Common trees are oak, beech, birch, hickory, walnut, maple, basswood, elm, ash, tulip, and hornbeam. Most of the forest has been cut over several times since white settlers arrived.

The deciduous forest includes several major forest types with many combinations, variations, and mixes of successional stages. Basic to the Appalachians in Virginia are oak-hickory, cove hardwood, northern hardwood, spruce-fir, and oak-pine. Fallow fields, woodland edge communities, streams, marshes, swamps, bogs, glades, grassy balds, boulderfields, and shale barrens add variety. Many of these communities—some listed as rare—are discussed throughout the book. Two of the most common forests in Virginia—oak-hickory and cove—are described below.

Oak-hickory forest. The thin soils on the majority of forested dry mountain slopes of the southern Appalachians are dominated by an oak-hickory forest. The canopy is composed of northern red, white, black, scarlet, and chestnut oaks, along with white pine, pignut hickory, shagbark hickory, mockernut hickory, bitternut hickory, sourwood, and black walnut. Oak-hickory forests have replaced the former chestnut-oak forests. Though forest canopies are often dominated by just two nut-producing tree groups—oaks and hickories—a rich variety of other species grow in the understory. Some of the more common understory trees and shrubs include flowering dogwood, mountain laurel, red maple, witch-hazel, redbud, shadbush, highbush blueberry, deerberry, and azalea.

Nuts produced by oak-hickory canopies—or hard mast, as they're called collectively—support black bears, white-tailed deer, wild turkeys, blue jays, gray squirrels, Eastern chipmunks, and raccoons.

Cove hardwood forest. A forest community unique to the region is the Appalachian cove hardwood forest. In the rich, moist soil of sheltered coves and bottomlands are stands of lush hardwood forests where towering white or American basswoods, tulip poplars, Eastern hemlocks, and yellow buckeyes gradually rise to heights of 80 to 120 feet.

Songbirds, wildlife, ferns, wildflowers, understory trees, and shrubs are diverse and abundant in cove forests. Unlike the oak-hickory forest prevalent throughout most of the Appalachians, the cove forest may have six to eight tree species that share dominance.

High in the canopy, a brilliant scarlet tanager sings, and the great-crested flycatcher darts out from a snag to snatch an insect from midair. A slanting ray of sun piercing the thick canopy in a mature cove forest might briefly reflect the red crest and black-and-white wings of the wide-ranging pileated woodpecker. The pileated may defend an area of 150 to 200 acres, dependent on large trees of mature forests for a continual supply of carpenter ants.

SCARLET TANAGER
(Piranga olivacea)

This bird has a distinctive "chick-burr" call.

Before the canopy of a cove forest grows too thick, a dense understory houses another array of birds, including the colorful hooded warbler. Close to the complex, multilayered, spongy soil are the often-overlooked smaller creatures such as mice, salamanders, lizards, frogs, snakes, and insects.

Cove forests, valued for timber production, are rarely left undisturbed. However, occasional stands of this type are in nearly inaccessible places such as pockets of remote wilderness areas or rich bottomlands between high ridges. Some cove forests that escaped the logger's axe in the 1800s and early 1900s remain untouched today. Outstanding old growth forests are the result.

Huge, widely spaced trunks of virgin timber disappear into a thick, layered canopy. In the dimly lit understory lie decaying hulks of former giants of the forest, their dark outlines softened by carpets of ferns and mosses. Mushrooms and fungi sprout from softened bark; ants and beetles work busily in the interior.

Old growth—formerly considered a forest past its prime and with little value for wildlife—is coming under closer scrutiny. The importance of woody debris to aquatic ecosystems is one area of study. The debris provides a slow release of nutrients to both soil and stream and stabilizes streambeds during periods of high water.

High levels of important nutrients—nitrates, sulfate, phosphate, calcium, magnesium, and organic carbon—are available for new growth.

Summer temperatures on a hot day can be 10 degrees cooler in the naturally air-conditioned old growth forest. When soils are saturated, a single large oak can draw 3,000 gallons of water from the ground in a day. The value of these and other benefits of old growth are being weighed against the demand for timber and the philosophy of forest renewal through periodic harvesting. Old growth cove forests are complex factories with hundreds of years of experience at filtering water and air, harnessing solar energy, building soil, recycling waste, and providing a controlled release of minerals from the underlying rock base.

In Virginia, examples of these rare stands of cathedral-like forests still exist in Rich Hole [Fig. 23(6)] and Ramsey's Draft wilderness areas and in Shenandoah National Park [Fig. 43].

Scarlet Tanager

A common summer resident at the park and throughout Virginia's pine and oak forests, *Piranga olivacea* is the only North American red bird with black wings and a black tail. Females are yellow-green. During nesting season, the striking male may sing his repetitive robinlike warble from the top of a dead tree.

Mountain Magic

It's difficult to speak of mountains without superlatives. In human reckoning, everything about them—their age, their size, the forces required to create them—is grandiose.

The immensity and scope of mountains, of course, are part of their appeal. Like the forces that created the universe, we speak of mountains in time frames with little relevance to anything human. Words and phrases such as eons, millennia, billions of years, continental drift, and orogenies are our best efforts to describe what perhaps can only be comprehended in relative terms, even by scientists themselves.

Yet unlike the heavens, mountains are touchable. We walk upon them, sift their living soil through our fingers. We feel the wind they create on a ridgetop or the cool air that sinks down a ravine. We hear the hollows play with a roll of thunder.

Maybe what mountains do best for their human admirers is to create a physical bond with forces too great to comprehend with the mind. With our feet on the ground, they lead our eyes to the stars and link us with the primeval grandeur of the universe.

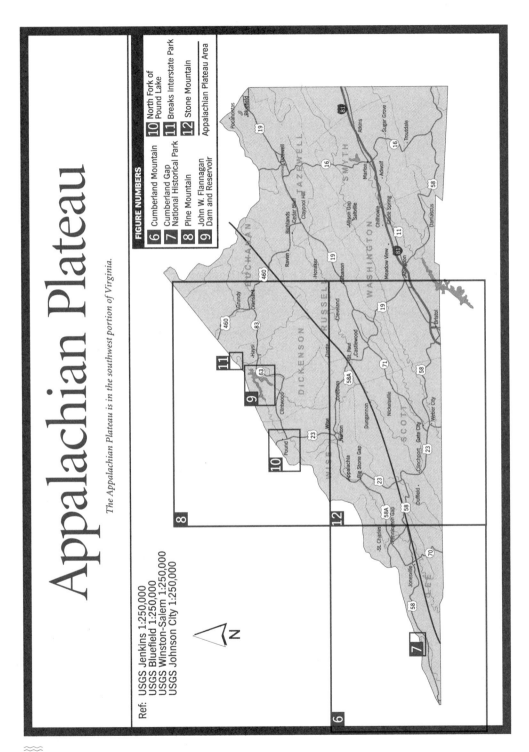

Appalachian Plateau

The Appalachian Plateau is in the southwest portion of Virginia.

Ref: USGS Jenkins 1:250,000
      USGS Bluefield 1:250,000
      USGS Winston-Salem 1:250,000
      USGS Johnson City 1:250,000

FIGURE NUMBERS

6 Cumberland Mountain	10 North Fork of Pound Lake
7 Cumberland Gap National Historical Park	11 Breaks Interstate Park
8 Pine Mountain	12 Stone Mountain
9 John W. Flannagan Dam and Reservoir	Appalachian Plateau Area

The Appalachian Plateau

The Appalachian Plateau is the westernmost physiographic region of the great Appalachians. Various forces have eroded sections of the once flat-topped Plateau. Glaciers rounded off the ridges of the Plateau in Pennsylvania and New Jersey. Wind, rain, and rivers scoured deep ravines in a southern portion of the Plateau sometimes called the Cumberland Mountains.

The Cumberlands include the Plateau from northwest of Knoxville, Tennessee, up into Kentucky, Virginia, and West Virginia. The Plateau consists of gray sandstone, underlain by softer Greenbrier limestone and shales. Highest elevations in the Virginia portion of the Plateau are around 4,200 feet. Unlike the tilted upthrusts of rock in the Valley and Ridge province to the east, the Plateau sandstone is layered horizontally, as is evident in road cuts and rocky cliffs in river gorges. Virginia claims only a bit of the Appalachian Plateau where it swipes the southwestern corner of the

[*Above:* Hay-scented ferns in the Appalachian Plateau]

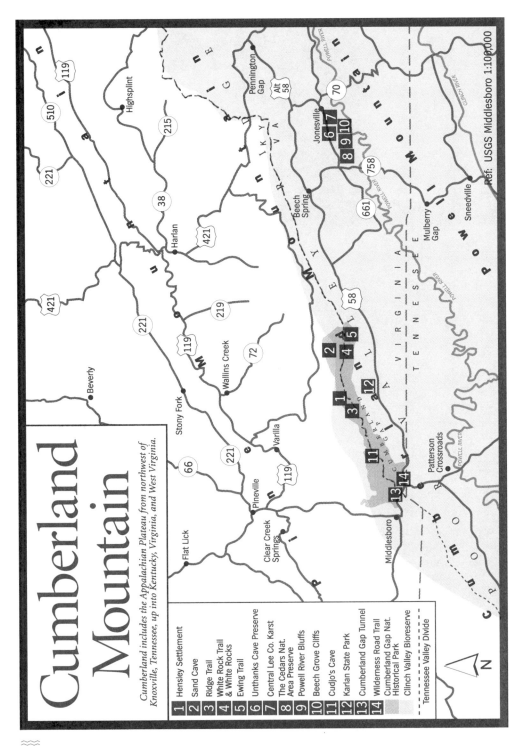

Cumberland Mountain

Cumberland includes the Appalachian Plateau from northwest of Knoxville, Tennessee, up into Kentucky, Virginia, and West Virginia.

1. Hensley Settlement
2. Sand Cave
3. Ridge Trail
4. White Rock Trail & White Rocks
5. Ewing Trail
6. Unthanks Cave Preserve
7. Central Lee Co. Karst
8. The Cedars Nat. Area Preserve
9. Powell River Bluffs
10. Beech Grove Cliffs
11. Cudjo's Cave
12. Karlan State Park
13. Cumberland Gap Tunnel
14. Wilderness Road Trail

Cumberland Gap Nat. Historical Park

Clinch Valley Bioreserve

Tennessee Valley Divide

Ref: USGS Middlesboro 1:100,000

state in Wise, Dickenson, Buchanan, northern Scott, and western Lee counties. But that little bit has made a world of difference in the state's history. For it is in the sandstone of the Plateau that seams of coal were discovered as early settlers explored the unmapped, rugged sections of southwest Virginia. The coal turned out to be high quality, and mining began in the late 1800s. Coal-generated power is one of the least expensive sources of electricity, and coal still generates nearly 60 percent of the country's electricity.

The tenacious nature of those whose lifework is tied to coal is evident in a ride through coal country, where houses perch on any scrap of flat land—land so steep and rocky from erosion that the two ends of a ranch home seem to hang over the edge. Family gardens curve around hillsides. V-shaped gorges formed by gradual erosion of the extremely hard sandstone cause backroads to wind and twist like spaghetti.

A complex, eastern deciduous forest, dominated by northern hardwoods and interspersed with pines and other conifers, covers most of the Plateau province. In fact, more plant species can be found in the southern Appalachians as a whole than anywhere else in North America. The mountains served as refuges when glaciers covered the north. Big game was extirpated until modern game management brought back the black bear, white-tailed deer, and wild turkey. In Wise and Dickenson counties, bear and deer hunting are still limited while the species continue to recover. Early timber industries and mining companies stripped whole mountains of their trees, causing massive erosion and flooding in the Tennessee Valley drainage to the west. The U.S. Forest Service bought the Clinch Ranger District land in 1936, largely to protect the headwaters of the Tennessee River from the disastrous effects of deforestation.

Cumberland Mountain

[Fig. 5(6), Fig. 6] The name comes from England's duke of Cumberland. But this long and narrow mountain in Virginia's southwest corner has a history that goes back much further in time than any English duke. Cumberland Mountain is part of a huge, four-sided block of the earth's crust forced upward in ancient times. Today, it defines the eastern edge of the Appalachian Plateau in Virginia.

Its twin, Pine Mountain [Fig. 5(8), Fig. 8], is 25 miles west, on the other side of the block. The two are mirror images of each other for most of their length. Pine Mountain's steepest slope is on its northwest side, while Cumberland's is on its southeast side. Pine Mountain has exposed limestone on its northwest slope and sandstone on its southeast slope. Cumberland Mountain is just the opposite.

Cumberland Mountain has an extensive limestone cave system on the Virginia side. But one of its most prominent features, Sand Cave [Fig. 6(2)] on the Kentucky side, is sculpted from sandstone. How these mountains were created affects everything from geological formations to the color of hepatica. The flower is a delicate pink in limestone soil on the Virginia side, but it is generally white in sandstone and shales on the Kentucky side.

In springtime, on rocky slopes at higher elevations, stands of Catawba rhododendron (*Rhododendron*) display stunning purple blossoms. Birds typical of eastern deciduous forests are abundant here: the wood thrush (*Hylocichla mustelina*), hermit thrush (*Hylocichla guttata faxoni*), veery (*Hylocichla fuscescens*), red-eyed vireo (*Vireo olivaceus*), scarlet tanager (*Piranga olivacea*), and many varieties of warblers, to name a few.

The southern end of the mountain begins at Cove Lake State Park at Caryville, Tennessee. With one exception—where Big Creek comes through at Ivydell, Tennessee—Cumberland Mountain remains unbroken until it arrives in Virginia. At the Virginia/Tennessee/Kentucky border is Cumberland Gap, carved out in the mountain's infancy by Yellow Creek. Originally, the creek flowed east into the Powell River. For awhile the creek continued to flow east, carving through the new mountain. But Cumberland Mountain rose too fast, and Yellow Creek was diverted westward to the Kentucky side, where it remains today.

Cumberland Mountain continues its journey to the northeast, defining the Virginia/Kentucky border with its ridgeline. On its northern end, the same mountain is called Stone Mountain. Once the Kentucky border veered off to the west, Virginians claimed the rest of the mountain for their own with a different name. The lines of Cumberland's northeast end are more blurred than those of its Pine Mountain twin. What started as Cumberland ends as Stone, gradually losing its identity where the Plateau bulges into Virginia.

CUMBERLAND GAP

[Fig. 7] What a sight it must have been. Standing at the narrow, 2-mile-wide notch, or gap, on Cumberland Mountain, a visitor with lots of time—say, a couple of centuries—would have had the privilege of watching one of America's most unusual animal and human migrations. First it was woodland bison (*Bison bison pennsylvania*), elk (*Cervus canadensis*), and white-tailed deer (*Odocoileus virginianus*) that trampled a trail through this natural doorway to the salt licks and ample food of bluegrass Kentucky beyond the mountain barrier. Bands of Shawnee and Cherokee indians followed the animals to the rich hunting grounds, and sometimes raiding parties followed one another.

So many bleached bones of rival Indian tribes littered the trail from the Potomac River south through Cumberland Gap then north to the Ohio River that the route came to be called Warrior's Path. Then in 1750, white explorers led by Dr. Thomas Walker found this narrow pass through the Appalachian Mountains, of which the Cumberland range is a part. With only primitive transportation, restless colonists along the eastern seaboard had been stymied all along the mountain wall. Also, French settlers and allied tribes of the Iroquois Confederacy made the western frontier beyond the mountains dangerous to explore. Shawnees, distressed at encroachment on their rich Kentucky hunting grounds by white trappers and settlers, became increasingly belligerent.

In 1774, at Point Pleasant, Kentucky, the Shawnees and a confederacy of Delaware, Wyandot, Cayuga, and other Indian tribes led by Cornstalk lost a bloody battle with Virginia settlers and militia. To save their families, the Shawnees gave up rights to their hunting grounds by signing the Treaty of Camp Charlotte in 1774. The 1775 Treaty of Sycamore Shoals ended most troubles with the Iroquois Confederacy. Then Daniel Boone and 30 men marked and cleared the Wilderness Trail through Cumberland Gap into Kentucky.

Hunters began crossing the mountain through the gap, and they were followed by waves of land-hungry immigrants. By the end of the Revolutionary War in 1783, an impressive stream of 12,000 people had crossed into the new territory. The stream became a river, then a torrent. By 1792, the population west of the gap was more than 100,000, and Kentucky was invited to join the Union. As the century came to a close, traffic on the Wilderness Road continued day and night. The curses of oxen drivers and the bawl of cattle mingled with the jingle of horse harnesses and the groans of loaded wagons struggling across Cumberland Gap. By 1800, just 50 years after it was

WHITE OAK (Quercus alba)
The leaves on a single oak tree
 may have different shapes, making
 identification a challenge. White
oak leaves have deep or shallow clefts between lobes.

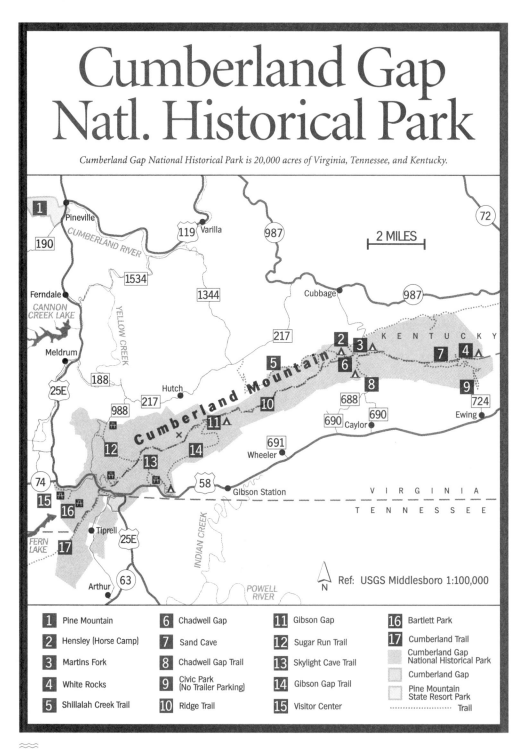

Cumberland Gap
Natl. Historical Park

Cumberland Gap National Historical Park is 20,000 acres of Virginia, Tennessee, and Kentucky.

2 MILES

Ref: USGS Middlesboro 1:100,000

1 Pine Mountain	**6** Chadwell Gap	**11** Gibson Gap	**16** Bartlett Park
2 Hensley (Horse Camp)	**7** Sand Cave	**12** Sugar Run Trail	**17** Cumberland Trail
3 Martins Fork	**8** Chadwell Gap Trail	**13** Skylight Cave Trail	Cumberland Gap National Historical Park
4 White Rocks	**9** Civic Park (No Trailer Parking)	**14** Gibson Gap Trail	Cumberland Gap
5 Shillalah Creek Trail	**10** Ridge Trail	**15** Visitor Center	Pine Mountain State Resort Park
			.... Trail

discovered by Walker, the famous gap had funneled more than a third of a million people from the East to the new lands of the West.

Very soon, those headed west were met by thousands of head of cattle, pigs, sheep, and turkeys being driven east through the gap as the first settlers moved their cash crops to coastal markets. Cumberland Gap declined in importance only after easier routes were established in the 1820s and 1830s by dredging canals such as the Erie, Pennsylvania Main Line, and Chesapeake and Ohio.

CUMBERLAND GAP NATIONAL HISTORICAL PARK

[Fig. 5(7), Fig. 6, Fig. 7] The National Park Service provides the perfect way to become immersed in the rich human and natural history of Cumberland Mountain. Occupying 20,000 acres of Virginia, Tennessee, and Kentucky, Cumberland Gap National Historical Park straddles the mountain for 20 miles along Virginia's southwest border. No words on a page can demonstrate as well as the view along the historic Wilderness Road (US 58 from the Virginia side) what a formidable barrier this mountain wall presented to the early settlers.

At the visitor center [Fig. 7(15)] on US 25E at Middlesboro, Kentucky, a brochure and trail map are available. Most visitors to the park take the winding mountain road from the visitor center up to Pinnacle Overlook. There they are treated to spectacular views into Virginia, Kentucky, and Tennessee—a panoramic landscape where cascading ridgelines fade from deep blue up close to soft lavender in the distance. In autumn, local bird watchers gather at the Pinnacle. Migrant birds and butterflies use the Cumberland's updrafts to soar or flutter their way to the balmy Gulf states and beyond. Early on an October morning, as many as 50 to 100 hawks and other birds of prey lift off at the gap. The raptors catch a thermal, rising in ascending circles high above, then coasting out of sight on another day's journey to the southwest.

Frequent visitors have come to appreciate the interpretive programs on subjects as varied as meteor showers, autumn hawk migration, and geologic formations. For a summer program called Pioneer Camp, park rangers dress as early pioneers called long hunters. They fire black-powder long rifles, tan hides, and cook stew over an open fire. For children, the park has a program called Kids Explore Cumberland Gap. Children are taught how to use a compass and map, identify birds by sound, and survey a stream by wading in to search for aquatic insects, crayfish, and snails.

One way people appreciate Cumberland Gap National Historical Park is by hiking its 50 miles of trails. The park's best features take time to enjoy. These include the Skylight Cave [Fig. 7(13)], Hensley Settlement [Fig. 6(1)], Sand Cave [Fig. 6(2)], and White Rocks [Fig. 6(4), Fig. 7(4)], not to mention the wildflowers, wildlife, tumbling streams, talus slopes (boulderfields), and scenic views open only to the hiker or horseback rider. On the Virginia side of the mountain, 1.3 miles east of the Kentucky line, a road leads off US 58 to the park's Wilderness Road Campground [Fig. 6(14)], where 160 forested, spacious sites offer privacy. Around the campground are the

Virginia pine (*Pinus virginiana*), dogwood (*Cornus florida*), yellow poplar (*Liriodendron tulipifera*), and red maple (*Acer rubrum*) characteristic of intermediate succession. Severe windstorms around the vulnerable border of this cleared area have blown down the oaks, hickories, and beech typical of the northern hardwood forest that covers most of the mountain.

A mile-long trail from the picnic area adjacent to the campground leads to Skylight Cave [Fig. 7(13)]. The 200-foot-long limestone cavern is safe to explore. One-quarter mile past the cave, this trail intersects the Ridge Trail [Fig. 7(10) Fig. 6(13)].

Directions: The visitor center and road to the Pinnacle Overlook are on US 25E, just east of Middlesboro, KY. The Wilderness Road campground and picnic area are on US 58 in Virginia's southwest tip. From the visitor center, go 3 miles east on US 25E, through the Cumberland Gap Tunnel [Fig. 6(13)] to US 58, and continue 1.3 miles to the campground and picnic area on the left. Continue east on US 58 in Virginia to access trailheads on the park's southeast slope.

Activities: Hiking, including self-guided nature trails and overnight trails. Camping, picnicking, interpretive programs, fishing for children only in Little Yellow Creek (no license required), bicycling, horseback riding, horse camping. Caving in Cudjo's Cave will resume when Cumberland Gap is restored in several years.

Facilities: Visitor center at Middlesboro, KY. Campground with 160 sites on US 58 in Virginia with picnic tables, grills, and paved pull-ins, including some that will accommodate large trailers and RVs (no hookups). Restrooms have hot showers. Four primitive campgrounds on Ridge Trail are accessible by foot only (permit required at visitor center). Amphitheater for seasonal music and craft demonstrations and interpretive programs. Bicycling (.75-mile trail). Horseback riding on many trails (brochure available) and horse camping by permit near Hensley Settlement.

Dates: Open year-round; hours for visitor center and shuttle are seasonal.

Fees: There is no charge for admission or backcountry camping; a fee is charged for camping at the main campground.

Closest town: Middlesboro, KY, is just west of visitor center. Cumberland Gap, TN, is on east side of tunnel.

For more information: Superintendent, Cumberland Gap NHP, Box 1848, Middlesboro,

LITTLE BROWN BAT
(*Myotis lucifugus*)
Probably the most abundant bat in North America, this bat is also seen in cities.

KY 40965. Phone (606) 248-2817.

HENSLEY SETTLEMENT

[Fig. 6(1)] Still standing on a plateau in a remote clearing, high atop Cumberland Mountain, are houses, barns, and fences of several restored farmsteads from the early 1900s. Established by Sherman Hensley in approximately 1904, the little community of about 12 families constructed buildings from hand-hewn chestnut logs and topped them with shake roofs. Isolated from civilization, community members survived through their own cunning and skill.

Hundreds of people assemble at the Hensley Settlement on a Saturday night around August 12 each year for a program called Shooting Star Spectacular. The evening is set to coincide with the literally stellar performance of the Perseid Meteor Shower, an annual heavenly phenomenon. On this occasion, private vehicles are allowed on the road to the Hensley Settlement. The clearing is located along the Ridge Trail 12 miles from the Pinnacle and just west of Chadwell Gap [Fig. 7(7)] at 3,358 feet. Shuttles, when they are running, offer an easy journey along the Shillalah Creek Trail [Fig. 7(5)] from the Kentucky side of Cumberland Mountain to the settlement.

Dates: If funded, open June–mid-Aug.

Fees: A fee is charged for the shuttle.

CUDJO'S CAVE

[Fig. 6(11)] Temporarily closed to tourism, this cave is located on the Virginia side of the gap on a portion of US 25E no longer in use since the completion of the tunnel through the mountain in 1996. Rising from the cave's limestone floor is the largest known stalagmite—a giant that brings to mind California's sequoias.

Left to a consistently cool silence punctuated only by slow limestone drips are several species of bats. Unimpressed by Cudjo's monstrous stalagmite, these nocturnal mammals spend much of their lives suspended upside-down among the stalactites of the cave ceiling. Included is the endangered Indiana bat (*Myotis sodalis*).

When the gap is restored to resemble the Wilderness Road as it was in the late 1700s, wild cave expeditions will begin. The path will be lighted from lanterns attached to cavers' heads rather than from the colored lights that wash the walls of commercial caves.

SAND CAVE

[Fig. 6(2)] This giant overhang of sandstone (40 to 80 feet high and approximate-

Indiana Bat

The federally endangered Indiana bat (*Myotis sodalis*), can only benefit from the restrictions on human traffic at Cudjo's Cave. For hibernation, the small brown bats with mouselike ears need undisturbed limestone caverns, where they hang in compact clusters of 500 to 1,000 or more.

ly 150 feet wide) is easily the most outstanding geological feature in the park. Sand Cave, carved by the weathering effects of wind and rain, is an example of "headward erosion." In another few million years the park superintendent predicts there will be "a jim-dandy arch." Headward erosion may take its time, but the result will be an impressive natural tunnel.

The cave, located on the Kentucky side of Cumberland Mountain ridge, is a carrot on a stick to hikers along the Ridge Trail. The trail to the cave leads off the Ridge Trail 16 miles northeast of the Pinnacle Overlook. Sand Cave is also accessible by a strenuous climb up the Ewing Trail at the park's east end. This route is 8 miles round-trip. But timing a trek to coincide with spring wildflowers will double the reward for a hiker's effort.

HIKING TRAILS AT CUMBERLAND GAP NATIONAL HISTORICAL PARK

Fifty miles of well-maintained hiking trails provide the best opportunity to become familiar with Cumberland Mountain. These trails range from short, paved paths accessing overlooks to rugged climbs over sandstone boulders as big as houses. Skylight Cave [Fig. 7(13)], Sand Cave [Fig. 6(2)], and White Rocks [Fig. 6(4), Fig. 7(4)] are accessible by trail spurs off the main Ridge Trail [Fig. 7(10)].

At present, biking is allowed only on the .75-mile trail at the visitor center [Fig. 7(15)] and on the old highway through the gap, until restoration begins. Construction of a multiuse trail will add variety for mountain bikers in the near future. Around the campground, the park service has added wood chips to the natural forest floor of the hiking trails. Trails are not blazed, but are easy to follow, with handrails and bridges along the way.

Though mountainous and strenuous at times, the park trails are not difficult, except for the Chadwell Gap Trail [Fig. 7(8)]. Allow yourself extra time to rest along this 1.5-mile steep ascent up the south slope of Cumberland Mountain. From the trailhead at VA 688 north of Caylor, you'll climb to 3,385 feet at the summit. Also, the last 2 miles of the 5-mile Gibson Gap Trail [Fig. 7(14)] are moderately strenuous, as it winds its way from the main campground up to the backcountry campground at Gibson Gap [Fig. 7(11)].

Spring wildflowers are especially picturesque on the Virginia side of the mountain along the short Skylight Cave Trail [Fig. 7(13)], the 5-mile Gibson Gap Trail [Fig. 7(14)], and the 4-mile Ewing Trail [Fig. 6(5)]. On the Kentucky side, the Sugar Run Trail [Fig. 7(12)] supports a hemlock and rhododendron forest,

Turk's Cap Lily

At heights of 3 to 7 feet, this showiest member of the lily family lives along the trail in the Sand Cave area. *Lilium superbum* likes wet meadows and swampy woods. Its many drooping, red-spotted, orange flowers must have reminded its namer of a kind of cap once worn by Turks.

growing in soil left from the Pennsylvanian deposits. Look for tiny fossils embedded in rocks in the higher elevations, especially at the top of the Ewing Trail.

Park officials advise not to hike this wild area alone. **Watch your footing near cliffs and rock outcroppings.** Plan for the possibility that fires may be prohibited in the backcountry during dry spells. Carry an alternative fuel source. Backcountry camping is allowed (by permit from the visitor center) at four areas along the Ridge Trail [Fig. 6(3)]—Gibson Gap [Fig. 7(11)], Chadwell Gap [Fig. 7(7)], Martin's Fork [Fig. 7(3)], and White Rocks [Fig. 6(4), Fig. 7(4)]. Pit toilets are the only improvements. Camping outside these areas is not allowed. A one-room primitive cabin with fireplace and six bunks at Martin's Fork (near the Hensley Settlement) also requires a permit.

RIDGE TRAIL. [Fig. 6(3)] This moderate trail on the Virginia/Kentucky line along Cumberland Mountain ridge starts at Pinnacle Overlook and runs 16.6 miles east to White Rocks. It connects to all major park trails and to four primitive backcountry campgrounds (permit required). It leads 11.7 miles from the Pinnacle to the Hensley Settlement [Fig. 6(1)]. Other side trips from the Ridge Trail include Skylight Cave, Sand Cave, and White Rocks.

Trail: 16.6-mile linear path along Cumberland Mountain ridge, accessible from the Pinnacle Overlook and by other trails at both ends.

Elevation: 2,440 feet at Pinnacle Overlook to 3,513 feet just west of White Rocks.

Degree of difficulty: Moderate, with many ups and downs.

Surface: Natural forest floor and rock.

EWING TRAIL. [Fig. 6(5)] On the shortest but steepest path to Sand Cave and White Rocks the payoffs are many, especially in the spring. Hikers who take time and smell the flowers along the switchbacks will not be disappointed. Explorers should also look for painted trillium (*Trillium undulatum*), bloodroot (*Sanguinaria canadensis*), hepatica of varying hues, spring beauty (*Claytonia virginica*), and large patches of nodding trillium (*Trillium cernuum*). Rocks at the top of Ewing Trail provide the best opportunity in the park for discovering embedded fossils of ancient marine shellfish. To get to the trailhead at Civic Park [Fig. 7(9)], go east on US 58 from

SPRING PEEPER (Hyla crucifer) This treefrog is identified by an "X" on its back.

Wilderness Road campground and picnic area 12 miles. At Ewing, go left (north) on VA 724 1 mile to Civic Park.

Trail: 3.8-mile ascent to Ridge Trail.

Elevation: From 1,550 feet at Civic Parking Lot on VA 724 to 3,500 feet at junction with Ridge Trail.

Degree of difficulty: Moderate, with steep areas and several switchbacks.

Surface: Natural forest floor and rock.

WHITE ROCKS TRAIL AND WHITE ROCKS. [Fig. 6(4), Fig. 7(4)] For pure scenic enjoyment, take this 1-mile cutoff from the Ewing Trail, across the Ridge Trail, to White Rocks and White Rocks backcountry campground. The path is not difficult once it intersects with the Ridge Trail. Cross it to get to the campground, or go east .5 mile on the Ridge Trail to see the 600-foot-high sheer cliffs that are the White Rocks.

From the lookout at 3,500 feet, the views of Harlan County, Kentucky, on one side and Lee County, Virginia, on the other are spectacular. But visitors who spend a bit of time examining the rocks up close will find quartz pebbles embedded in limestone which tell a strange story. There are deeper areas of limestone and shales, below younger, more shallow layers of Pennsylvanian sandstone. At these high elevations, it is overwhelming to think of the lap of oceans that deposited these layers more than 290 million years ago and ponder the upheaval that brought the deposits to these heights.

SUGAR MAPLE
(*Acer saccharum*)
Sugar maple's sap is the source of maple syrup and sugar.

White Rocks, prominent from the Wilderness Road in Virginia, served as a marker for early travelers in the valley below as they labored west toward Cumberland Gap. When the cliffs came into view atop Cumberland Mountain, shining in the afternoon sunlight, travelers knew they had one more day to Gibson Station. There they would assemble in large groups for protection against Indians during the treacherous journey through the gap.

Trail: 1-mile trail from Ewing Trail to White Rocks, intersecting Ridge Trail.

Elevation: 3,500 feet at highest point.

Difficulty: Difficult from Ewing Trail up to Ridge Trail, moderate from Ridge Trail to White Rocks.

Surface: Natural forest floor and rock.

THE CUMBERLAND GAP TUNNEL

[Fig. 6(13)] Imagine the relief of pioneers, had they discovered such a wonder. A modern, four-lane highway through the mountain. Completed in 1996, this pair of two-lane tunnels opened to carry travelers under instead of over the gap that has seen so much history. The massive engineering project of carving twin tunnels through nearly 1 mile of solid rock was a joint effort by the National Park Service and the Federal Highway Administration. Layers of sandstone, shale, limestone, and chert laid down through millennia were drilled, analyzed, exposed with pilot tunnels, excavated, blasted, supported, and waterproofed in preparation for the new highway. Begun in 1985, the project took 10 years before autos could use it.

The old portion of US 25E above the tunnel is abandoned today. The Park Service intends eventually to restore the Wilderness Road through the gap to give visitors an appreciation of the path early pioneers used in the late 1700s. Meanwhile, the road that felt the march of history is quiet—left again to birdsong, the tinkle of tiny mountain rills, and the pale wash of moonlight on Cumberland Mountain.

CUMBERLAND GAP TOURS

A tour bus operating twice daily picks up visitors at motels, bed and breakfasts, or restaurants for two- or three-hour tours of the Cumberland Gap area. Guide Tom Shattuck is a Daniel Boone fan, and has written a Cumberland Gap guidebook.

Other half-day or full-day offerings include a Wilderness Road Adventure Tour, Great Smoky Mountains Tour (Dollywood, Pigeon Forge, and Gatlinburg), and Big Stone Gap Tour (*Trail of the Lonesome Pine* outdoor drama, coal museum, and Southwest Virginia Museum). Tours are flexible and can be adjusted to suit individual desires. Service area includes Middlesboro, Kentucky, Pineville, Kentucky, and Cumberland Gap, Tennessee. The service is approved by the Department of Transportation and Interstate Commerce Commission.

Dates: Open year-round.

Fees: A fee is charged for the gap tour.

For more information: Wilderness Road Tours, 224 Greenwood Road, Middlesboro, KY 40965. Phone (606) 248-2626.

TENNESSEE VALLEY DIVIDE

Rain falling on the Virginia side of Cumberland Mountain will eventually end up in the Tennessee River. Rain that falls on the Kentucky side winds its way to the Cumberland River. Both rivers are heavily controlled with dams, but the Tennessee River, under the management of the Tennessee Valley Authority, has achieved fame as one of the most managed river valleys in the world. The imaginary line marking the separation of the Tennessee River watershed from others is called the Tennessee Valley Divide. The beginnings of river watersheds don't always follow boundaries between states as the Tennessee Valley Divide does here along Cumberland Mountain. For watershed management, however, it's convenient when they do.

Virginia's Dickenson County, for instance, also borders Kentucky, a bit farther to the north. But the divide runs along the east side of Dickenson instead of the west. Water in Dickenson County flows west into Kentucky and north into the Ohio River instead of south into Tennessee. A mother in Cincinnati, Ohio, gives her child a glass of water at bedtime. The mother has a vested interest in what happens to that water on Fryingpan Creek in Dickenson County, hundreds of miles away in Virginia.

KARLAN STATE PARK

[Fig. 6(12)] Visitors will enjoy a stroll beneath century-old ash and maple trees on the grounds of one of Virginia's newest state parks. In 1993, the state purchased 200 acres that were part of an old farm originally owned by Robert M. Ely. Several of Ely's descendants lived in a mansion that still stands on the property. The mansion was constructed in the late 1870s and renovated several times in the 1900s. It stands empty now and closed to the public, awaiting restoration work. (The mansion may be rented for weddings or other functions.) The grounds, however, are open for picnicking and exploration. The rolling countryside and woodlands at Karlan offer tempting subjects for photography in any season.

Along a wooded path in spring, hikers may find columbine (*Aquilegia*) with its nodding red and yellow blossoms, and hear the plaintive, gentle call of bluebirds from an adjacent field. Bobwhite quail (*Colinus virginianus*) call their own names from the hedgerows.

Another delicate, nodding plant—spotted wintergreen (*Chimaphila maculata*)—emerges in dry woods here and displays its white blooms in summer. White-tailed deer quietly appear at the edge of woods at dusk to browse the open fields. In autumn, the great variety of plants and trees of Karlan turn yellow, red, gold, and rust. The sheer cliffs of White Rocks gleam at their 3,500-foot perch atop Cumberland Mountain in the background. Blue jays (*Cyanocitta cristata*), quiet and secretive in the early summer nesting season, now gather in raucous gangs. A great horned owl (*Bubo virginianus*), attempting to sleep out the day high in one of the old maples, finds itself the target of the blue jays' restless excitement. A snowy winter day is also a lovely time to visit this old farm, when the bright red of a cardinal (*Cardinalis cardinalis*) huddled against the cold in a dark evergreen has its own wild appeal.

A self-guided loop trail leading to Cave Hill on park property is under construction. The trail will explain the history of the park, which was on the Wilderness Road explored by Daniel Boone. Vegetation and geology of the area will also be featured. (Karlan sits at the eastern edge of the Appalachian Plateau in a transition karst zone, full of limestone caves and sink holes.) The trailhead is located on the east side of 690, about .75 mile north of US 58. The old L&N (Louisville and Nashville) Railroad splits Karlan in half. Visitors can hike, bike, or ride horses on the easy Wilderness Road Trail that has replaced the railroad.

Directions: From Cumberland Gap at the junction of US 25E and US 58, go 7 miles east on US 58. Park is on left. Or, from Ewing in Lee County, go west 4 miles on US 58, and turn right into park just past second junction with VA 690 (both junctions on right side, as VA 690 makes a loop).

Activities: Hiking, biking, horseback riding, picnicking.

Facilities: Hiking/biking/equestrian trail, picnic tables, self-guided loop trail. Plans include a village, refurbished mansion, and visitor center.

Dates: Open year-round.

Fees: None.

Closest town: Ewing, 4 miles east.

For more information: Karlan State Park, Route 2, Box 78, Ewing, VA 24248. Phone (540) 445-3065.

WILDERNESS ROAD TRAIL

[Fig. 6(14)] The Virginia Department of Transportation (VDOT) purchased the old L&N (Louisville and Nashville) railroad bed in the southwest tip of Lee County for possible use when US 58 was widened to four lanes. Now, in cooperation with local jurisdictions, VDOT is turning the railroad bed into a trail for those who would like to hike, bike, or ride horseback on the same path the early settlers took on their way to Cumberland Gap. Ten miles have been completed so far.

The trailhead on the eastern end is at a parking lot on the north side of US 58, 3 miles west of Ewing. The wide, easy path heads westward, through Karlan State Park [Fig. 6(12)]. Then it passes Gibson Station, once the assembly point for pioneers preparing to cross through Cumberland Gap on their way west to the bluegrass of Kentucky. On the west end, the trail leaves the railroad bed and the grade becomes steeper as it ascends to its temporary end at the Wilderness Road Campground of Cumberland Gap National Historical Park. West of the packed gravel trail toward the gap, the trail passes through open farmland and woodlands and crosses small tributaries of Indian Creek. VDOT built sturdy bridges across streams and developed access to streams for watering horses.

Instead of rumbling trains of the past, the bubbly voice of the wood thrush, the cooing of the mourning dove, and the sharp bark of a gray fox fill the air.

Black-eyed susan (*Rudbekia hirta*) and Queen Anne's lace (*Daucus carota*) sway among the trail-side grasses on a summer afternoon. Other sites along the trail could include a groundhog (*Marmota monax*) munching clover near his burrow or a red-eft, the subadult stage of the red-spotted newt (*Notophthalmus viridescens*). This is prime territory for

Red-eyed Vireo

Even in the doldrums of a hot summer day, the musical, robinlike song of the red-eyed vireo can bring the woods to life. This common woodland bird is found not only on the Wilderness Road Trail, but throughout Virginia's hardwood forests. The sparrow-sized vireo is olive-green above and whitish below, and it has a distinguishing red eye.

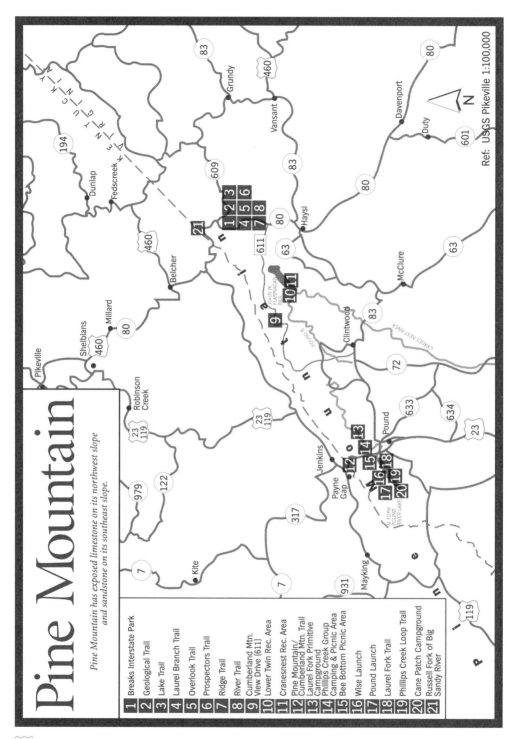

Pine Mountain

Pine Mountain has exposed limestone on its northwest slope and sandstone on its southeast slope.

1 Breaks Interstate Park
2 Geological Trail
3 Lake Trail
4 Laurel Branch Trail
5 Overlook Trail
6 Prospectors Trail
7 Ridge Trail
8 River Trail
9 Cumberland Mtn. View Drive [611]
10 Lower Twin Rec. Area
11 Cranesnest Rec. Area
12 Pine Mountain/ Cumberland Mtn. Trail
13 Laurel Fork Primitive Campground
14 Phillips Creek Group
15 Camping & Picnic Area
16 Bee Bottom Picnic Area
16 Wise Launch
17 Pound Launch
18 Laurel Fork Trail
19 Phillips Creek Loop Trail
20 Cane Patch Campground
21 Russell Fork of Big Sandy River

Ref: USGS Pikeville 1:100,000

the rusty-yellow eastern fox squirrel (*Sciurus niger*), a rather large squirrel found in the woodlands. To the north is the steep, south-facing slope of Cumberland Mountain that dictated the path this railroad and the Wilderness Road took.

Plans are to involve Tennessee and Virginia localities in extending the trail along the old railroad bed at both ends. On the southwest end, the Wilderness Road Trail will follow the old train route south into Claiborne County, Tennessee. The present path that leads away from the railroad bed, ending in the National Historical Park campground, will become a spur of the extended trail. Also, VDOT has plans for wildflower plantings and plans for an asphalt surface for hikers and bikers on one side of the path, leaving the other side for horses.

Trail: 10-mile linear path with plans to extend both ends along old railroad bed.

Elevation: 1,200 to 1,300 feet with no more than 10 percent grade except at temporary west end where trail rises to about 1,400 feet.

Degree of difficulty: Easy, with some steep sections on temporary west end.

Surface: Packed fine gravel.

Directions: East-end trailhead at parking lot in Caylor on north side of Route 58 near the middle intersection (there are 3 intersections of Route 684 and Route 58), next to Wheeler's store, 3 miles west of Ewing in Lee County. West-end trailhead in Gibson Station on north side of Route 58, .25 mile west of the intersection of Route 693 and Route 58. There is also a trailhead at Wilderness Road Campground at Cumberland Gap National Historical Park. Campground is on US 25E in southwestern tip of Lee County, 1.3 miles east of junction with US 58. Access also available where railroad bed comes through Karlan State Park, about 4 miles west of Ewing.

For more information: Jonesville Residency Office, VDOT, PO Box 704, Jonesville, VA 24263. Phone (540) 346-1911.

Pine Mountain

[Fig. 8, Fig. 5(8)] This 125-mile-long mountain teamed up with the parallel ridge of Cumberland Mountain to the east to bar early explorers and pioneers from traveling west. Together, the two mountains, like side-by-side folds in a blanket, march northeast from east Tennessee into east Kentucky and southwest Virginia in a duo jointly called the Cumberland Mountains.

Near Jellico, in east Tennessee, a stream called Clear Fork breaks through the ridge to define the southern end of Pine Mountain. About 35 miles northeast, the Cumberland River only briefly interrupts the ridgeline where it breaks through at Pineville, Kentucky. The Russell Fork of the Big Sandy River [Fig. 8(21)] in Virginia defines the northern end of Pine Mountain in dramatic fashion as the river circles 600 feet below a pyramidal sandstone formation called The Towers. The Russell Fork almost comes back to touch itself as it carves its way through the mountains, then takes off for the Kentucky border to the west. Through the same gorge passes the CSX Railroad, visible testimony to the Herculean task engineers and work crews faced in the early 1900s. In a feat that involved cutting four tunnels and two bridges through the nearly impenetrable sandstone, they opened the mountains to coal mining and connected the Ohio Valley and Midwest to the Atlantic seaboard.

Pine Mountain was formed when tremendous pressure from sliding plates beneath the earth's crust forced the rocks on the Virginia side up over those on the Kentucky side along the Pine Mountain fault. Though the mountain was formed at the same time as the rest of the Plateau province, its long, linear shape is more characteristic of the mountains of the Valley and Ridge province to the east. The Pennsylvanian sandstone of its upper layer, however, gives its origin away.

When hiking the trails on the southeast slope, visitors may come abruptly to harsh fields of sandstone boulders, where plant life claims a tenuous foothold. Where piles of these rocks form caves, Indians and wildlife found shelter. Mixed Appalachian hardwoods interspersed with pines cover the mountain. Private landowners on the steeper Kentucky side, however, are familiar with the large patches of exposed Greenbrier limestone. This Mississippian Greenbrier limestone is younger than the Cambrian-age limestone of the Valley and Ridge by at least 140 million years.

The public land on the Virginia side of Pine Mountain in Wise and Dickenson counties is a well-kept secret. In this remote section of southwest Virginia are thousands of acres of national forest, an interstate park, drives with incredible scenery, and two immense lakes inviting those who enjoy water sports.

Whether they're speaking of the hiking trail, the scenic drive, or the mountain itself, many local residents refer to Pine Mountain as Cumberland Mountain. Indeed, Pine Mountain resembles the long, parallel ridge of Cumberland Mountain. Pine Mountain also defines the Virginia border with Kentucky in Wise and Dickenson counties, just as Cumberland Mountain defines the Virginia/Kentucky border in Lee County in Virginia's southwest corner.

With modern maps and satellite photographs, it's easy to see that Cumberland and Pine mountains are distinct and separate. But early settlers in Wise and Dickenson counties had little way of knowing the ridge between themselves and Kentucky was not Cumberland Mountain, but was actually a parallel

*The red fox (*Vulpes vulpes*) is a shy, small, doglike animal that is distinguished from the gray fox by the white tip at the end of its tail. Gray foxes have dark tails with no white tip.*

ridge 25 miles west of Cumberland. Once a name is used for centuries, it sticks.

▓ PINE MOUNTAIN/CUMBERLAND MOUNTAIN TRAIL

[Fig. 8(12)] Whether it's called Pine Mountain Trail (official U.S. Forest Service name) or Cumberland Mountain Trail (used by local residents), the 22.8-mile scenic path along the rugged spine of Pine Mountain attracts hikers who enjoy solitude and a challenge. The trail connects Pound Gap where US 23 crosses Pine Mountain in Wise County with Breaks Interstate Park in northern Dickenson County.

The hiker will travel beneath a hardwood forest canopy, passing many rocky outcroppings with panoramic views of Kentucky and Virginia. In fall, not only is the foliage spectacular, but this ridge is a fine vantage point for watching the annual migration of hawks and other birds of prey. Horseback riders can use the trail, but there are rocky sections on both ends too treacherous for a horse. Many riders make a 9.5-mile loop hike by combining VA 611, FR 2071, and FR 616 with Pine Mountain Trail. A newly developed parking area at Counts Cabin (junction of VA 611 and FR 2071) has room for horse trailers. To find the parking area, from Clintwood in northwestern Dickenson County, go 2.5 miles north on VA 631 to Isom. Then go northeast on VA 611 about 4 miles to parking area.

All of the loop is public property. However, many other parts of Pine Mountain Trail pass through private tracts, often with no posted signs or boundary markers. Hikers should respect the rights of property owners and carry trail maps, which can be obtained at the Clinch Ranger District office. Also, because of the isolation of the area, be sure to carry adequate water, extra clothing, and a first aid kit.

Mountain Ash

This small deciduous tree grows in open meadows and in the woods on Pine Mountain. Its flat-topped clusters of small white flowers bloom after the leaves appear. In fall, clusters of red berries develop. *Sorbus americana* has a more extensive range in northern climes, but in Virginia it is found only in the mountains.

For more information: Clinch Ranger District, 9416 Darden Drive, Wise, VA 24293. Phone (540) 328-2931.

Trail: 22.8-mile linear path along the crest of Pine Mountain.

Elevation: 870 feet at Russell Fork River at north trailhead to 3,137 feet near Dutton Gap.

Degree of difficulty: Moderate, with difficult and strenuous sections.

Surface: Natural forest floor and rocky sections.

The Big Sandy River Watershed

Dickenson County and the Pine Mountain section of Wise County, rimmed by mountains, can be compared to a tray tilted toward one corner. Rain falling here from the southeastern slope of Pine Mountain east to Russell County eventually finds its way out a crack on Dickenson's northeast corner and into West Virginia. That crack is called Breaks Gorge. The last chute funneling the water out of the crack is Russell Fork. Hundreds of streams empty the plateau of Dickenson, winding down through sandstone hollows where homes perch on the sides of steep hillsides. On its way to The Breaks, the water supplies three major rivers (Pound, Cranes Nest, and Russell Fork) and two reservoirs (North Fork of Pound [Fig. 10] and John W. Flannagan [Fig. 9]). Before the water leaves the state, Virginians dam it twice, fish it, ride boats over it, swim in it, hike and camp on its borders, and enjoy the scenery around it. Then, released from Dickenson County, the Russell Fork heads northwest into Kentucky for the Big Sandy River.

Most of the Big Sandy watershed that drains Pine Mountain in Virginia is protected by national forest land. April and May warmth encourages the buds of oaks, hickories, and tulip poplar (*Liriodendron tulipifera*) to sprout. The understory attracts pollinators with splashes of white from flowering dogwoods, purple from redbuds, and rose pink from rhododendrons. Emerging from the leaf litter is the abundant large-flowered trillium (*Trillium grandiflorum*), with sepals and white petals in threes.

In October, the lakes and rivers of the Big Sandy watershed paint an upside-down watercolor reflection from a fiery palette. Red maples, glowing yellow poplars, and rusty-red pin oaks (*Quercus palustris*) are set off by the patchy beige and white bark of sycamores (*Ficus sycomorus*) leaning out over the water. While black bear, white-tailed deer, and wild turkey are native to the area, they were hunted out in the early 1900s. The Virginia Department of Game and Inland Fisheries is currently restocking all three animals. At present, hunters are more likely to have success with small game such as squirrel, rabbit (*Oryctolagus cuniculus*), and ruffed grouse (*Bonasa umbellus*). Beaver (*Castor canadensis*), raccoon (*Procyon lotor*), muskrat (*Ondata zibethicus*), and mink (*Mustela vison*) are active around the waterways. The long-legged bird with a slate-blue body fishing the shallows of the reservoirs is the great blue heron (*Ardea herodias*). Great blues usually migrate south in the fall. The occasional bird that stays behind may fall victim to severe weather.

The excellent fishing available in the Pine Mountain drainage is well known to locals but largely undiscovered by the rest of the world. To take advantage of this uncrowded angler's and boater's mecca, anglers should grab their fishing license and rod and reel, and stop by a tackle shop for tips on what's biting where. Licenses and trout stamps are available at marinas at both reservoirs and at area stores.

RUSSELL FORK OF BIG SANDY RIVER

[Fig. 8(21)] The Russell Fork of the Big Sandy River begins along VA 80 in southern Buchanan County. The river gains strength as it collects tributaries on its journey northwest into Dickenson County. In northern Dickenson, waters from the Pound and Cranes Nest rivers are dumped into the Russell Fork below John W. Flannagan Reservoir. It is here that the Russell Fork earns its national reputation for ferocity and great natural beauty.

With miles of churning whitewater, thundering drops, and immense boulder gardens, Russell Fork cuts an impressive hole through the northeastern end of Pine Mountain, the location of Breaks Interstate Park. Over millennia, the river has carved its twisting and tumultuous route out of subtly colorful Pennsylvanian sandstone in Virginia's Dickenson County, as it heads inexorably northwestward. The river then continues its plunge into adjoining Kentucky.

Loggers once used the Russell Fork to float timber that had been cut and hauled to the river during winter. When spring floods came, the logs were released to race their way to Elkhorn City, Kentucky, to be sold. The VA 611 bridge near the confluence of the Russell Fork and Pound rivers at the small community of Bartlick played an important role. Gates forming a dam to back up massive log rafts once hung from the bridge piers. Russell Fork is visible from the high overlooks of Breaks Interstate Park, and from several roads crisscrossing the area. Among them are VA 80, VA 611, and VA 739. The latter crosses Flannagan Dam. At several points along Russell Fork's route, the Virginia Department of Game and Inland Fisheries stocks trout for fishermen.

RAFTING AND BOATING THE RUSSELL FORK. Rafters, canoeists, and kayakers travel great distances to run the Russell Fork, but the river can be very unkind to all but expert paddlers. In the 5-mile-long gorge section, which flows through the park, paddlers may find themselves twisting through intense and dangerous Class V rapids while trying to glance upward at vertical cliff walls more than 1,600 feet high.

This is world-class whitewater, and it is best to run it with an experienced guide or outfitter during the first four full weekends in October, when large amounts of water are being released at Flannagan Reservoir. Only then is flow great enough to cover the boulder gardens. Call the dam at (540) 835-9544 for release times. The gradient, or drop, of the Russell Fork ranges from an occasional, gentle 5 feet per mile all the way to a white-knuckle 180 feet per mile. One violent 75-foot stretch, called "El Horrendo," is considered one of the wildest in the East.

The list of commercial companies that run the Russell Fork varies from year to year. Some outfitters that once ran the river have concluded it was too dangerous. The current list is as follows: Russell Fork Expeditions, (800) THE-FORK; Upper Yough Whitewater Expeditions, (800) 248-1893; Russell Fork Whitewater Adventures, (540) 530-7044; Cherokee Adventures, (800) 445-7238; Sheltowee Trace Outfitters, (800) 541-RAFT; American Whitewater, (800) 837-3022.

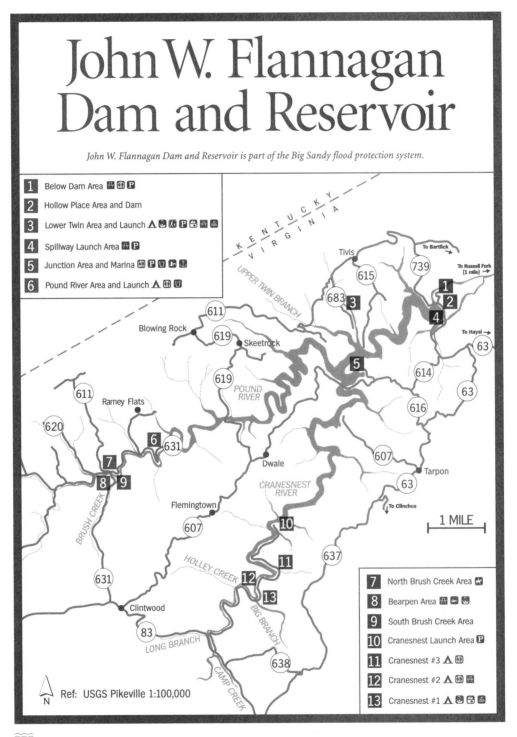

John W. Flannagan Dam and Reservoir

John W. Flannagan Dam and Reservoir is part of the Big Sandy flood protection system.

1 Below Dam Area

2 Hollow Place Area and Dam

3 Lower Twin Area and Launch

4 Spillway Launch Area

5 Junction Area and Marina

6 Pound River Area and Launch

7 North Brush Creek Area

8 Bearpen Area

9 South Brush Creek Area

10 Cranesnest Launch Area

11 Cranesnest #3

12 Cranesnest #2

13 Cranesnest #1

Ref: USGS Pikeville 1:100,000

1 MILE

N

☷ JOHN W. FLANNAGAN DAM AND RESERVOIR

[Fig. 9, Fig. 5(9)] Built in 1964 as part of the Big Sandy River flood control complex, John W. Flannagan Dam and Reservoir became, as did many U.S. Army Corps of Engineer lakes, much more than just a way of storing vast amounts of water in the mountains. The blue-water lake—considered one of the cleanest in the United States—threads its way into many narrow coves and hollows. The 250-foot-high dam impounds 1,145 acres with 40 miles of shoreline. The water is deep (175 feet at the dam intake), and the sheer sandstone cliffs along its banks provide ideal hiding places for cold-water species of fish such as walleye and trout. In fact, this 13-mile-long lake is one of the premier walleye lakes in the state, second only to Lake Moomaw in Alleghany County. McConaughy rainbow and Crawford brown trout are stocked yearly by the state. Keepers must be at least 16 inches in the lake, with a creel limit of two fish daily. In the Pound and Cranes Nest rivers, keepers must be 7 inches, with a creel limit of six. Anglers are permitted to keep five Flannagan bass of 1 foot or more in size daily. For other restrictions, check state fishing regulations, available at the lake office and area stores.

Periodically, lake waters are released through a 16-foot-diameter outlet tunnel drilled through a mountain at the dam site. The purpose of the water releases is to increase the late-summer river flow below the dam, and to make room for winter snow melt and spring floods. The largest amounts are let go on the first four full weekends in October, an event whitewater rafters, canoeists, and kayakers eagerly anticipate. Several outfitters in the area take people down the Russell Fork River through Breaks Interstate Park for a turbulent but scenic fall ride (*See* Rafting and Boating the Russell Fork, p. 41).

Flannagan has three campgrounds—Lower Twin [Fig. 9(3)], Pound [Fig. 9(6)], and Cranesnest [Fig. 9(11, 12, 13)]—in addition to five boat ramps, several picnic areas, play areas, two amphitheaters, and a marina. The development of hiking trails has not been a priority here. Girl Scouts established a .75-mile guided loop trail at Lower Twin area [Fig. 9(3)] called Trail of Trees. Another .75-mile trail and a 2-mile trail connect Lower Twin to other areas. Other paths have formed from the feet of many fishermen and even wildlife walking the lake edge. Many of these paths are steep in places and need work to be called hiking trails. Elevations begin at 1,400 feet, and surfaces are hard-packed dirt.

Those who enjoy recreational boating but don't like competing for space should try Flannagan, where most of the fishermen are back in coves and hollows. An osprey catching its fishy lunch from the lake may provide entertainment when the fish aren't biting. Watch the banks for a mink taking its young to the water's edge for a drink or a multicolored wood duck (*Aix sponsa*) sticking its head out of a hollow in a nesting tree. Both red and gray foxes hunt the lake's perimeter for mice and voles.

Directions: Lower Twin Recreation Area and Campground [Fig. 9(3)]: From Haysi in northern Dickenson County, follow US 80 3 miles north, turn left on VA 611, travel about 7 miles, and follow signs to the campground. Pound River Campground [Fig. 9(6)]: From Norton in Wise County, take US 23 north to Pound, then take VA 83, 8 miles east to Clintwood, turn left on VA 631 at light, and follow signs. Cranesnest Recreation Area and

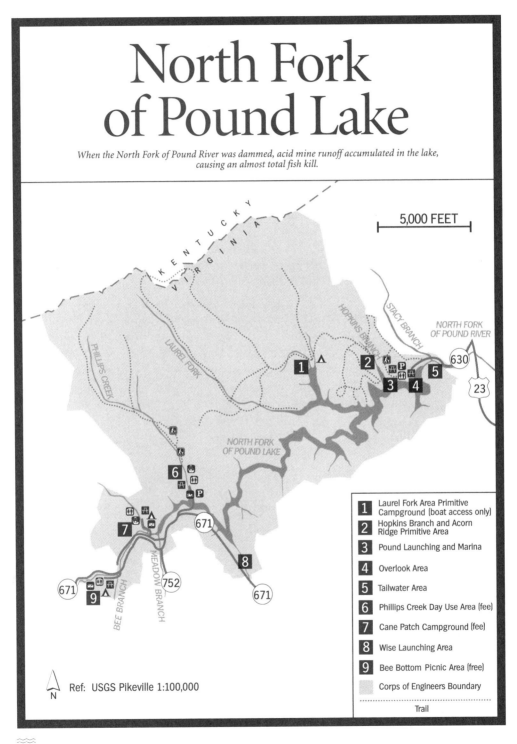

North Fork of Pound Lake

When the North Fork of Pound River was dammed, acid mine runoff accumulated in the lake, causing an almost total fish kill.

5,000 FEET

KENTUCKY
VIRGINIA

HOPKINS BRANCH
STACY BRANCH
NORTH FORK OF POUND RIVER

PHILLIPS CREEK
LAUREL FORK

630

23

NORTH FORK OF POUND LAKE

671

752

MEADOW BRANCH
BEE BRANCH

671

671

1 Laurel Fork Area Primitive Campground (boat access only)
2 Hopkins Branch and Acorn Ridge Primitive Area
3 Pound Launching and Marina
4 Overlook Area
5 Tailwater Area
6 Phillips Creek Day Use Area (fee)
7 Cane Patch Campground (fee)
8 Wise Launching Area
9 Bee Bottom Picnic Area (free)
   Corps of Engineers Boundary
   Trail

Ref: USGS Pikeville 1:100,000

N

Campgrounds [Fig. 9 (11, 12, 13)]: From Norton in Wise County, take US 23 north to Pound, then take VA 83, 8 miles to Clintwood, continue through Clintwood about 2.5 miles, and follow signs on the left onto VA 747 access road.

Activities: Swimming, fishing, picnicking, recreational boating, seasonal hunting, hiking. World-class white water rafting, kayaking, and canoeing below the dam (October weekends and sometimes in spring).

Facilities: Boat ramps, campgrounds (electric hookups at Lower Twin), picnic shelters, restrooms, hiking trails, showers, trailer sites and sanitary stations, marina, amphitheaters, play areas for children. Grocery stores, phones, and gas stations are nearby.

Dates: Recreation areas and marina boat ramp, open year-round. Campgrounds and campground boat ramps, open mid Apr.–mid-Oct.

Fees: Fees are charged for launch ramp and camping.

For more information: Resource Manager, Corps of Engineers, John W. Flannagan Dam and Reservoir, Route 1, Box 268, Haysi, VA 24256-9736. Phone (540) 835-9544.

CAMPGROUNDS AT FLANNAGAN RESERVOIR. At this uncrowded facility, visitors can usually choose between open and shady sites, some lakeside, and some in woods. Pets must be leashed. Loaded firearms and fireworks are prohibited. Fires are permitted only in grills or designated places. Complete camping rules are available from any ranger, the lake office, or the gate attendant at the campground.

LOWER TWIN. [Fig. 9(3)] 33 sites, restroom and showers, hiking trails, picnic area, play area, amphitheater, boat ramp.

POUND RIVER. [Fig. 9(6)] 23 lakeside sites with boat access, boat ramp, restrooms, drinking water. Nearby, Dickenson County provides areas for ball fields, a swimming pool, and a show ring for horses.

CRANESNEST. [Fig. 9(11, 12, 13)] 37 sites in three areas, some with concrete or gravel base, picnic area and picnic shelter, amphitheater, restrooms and showers, play area, trailer dump station.

NORTH FORK OF POUND LAKE

[Fig. 10, Fig. 5(10)] By damming the North Fork of Pound River in 1966, the U.S. Army Corps of Engineers created North Fork of Pound Lake, a long, thin, pristine body of water in the secluded mountains of southwest Virginia. At only 154 acres, the lake is neither broad nor large. It threads, instead, into scores of secluded coves and narrow

Virginia Spiraea

Flannagan Reservoir is a sanctuary for one of Virginia's endangered plants, Virginia spiraea (*Spiraea virginiana*). With its tough horizontal root system, the 3- to 10-foot-high shrub clings to life on eroded stream banks where its competition has been washed away. Ruffed grouse eat the buds. Flat-topped, white-flower clusters appear in mid-summer.

hollows created by the steep terrain. As a result, 13.5 scenic miles of wooded shoreline encircle the lake, much of it accessible by walking trails (*see* Hiking at North Fork of Pound Lake, p. 48) or state roads (VA 630, VA 671, and VA 752).

North Fork of Pound Lake got off to an unpromising start. When the river was dammed, acid mine runoff accumulated in the lake, causing an almost total fish kill. Lime was added to the incoming upper end of the lake to bring the pH level back to normal. Then the lake was restocked with both native and exotic fish. Today spotted bass are abundant, a 26-pound muskellunge was caught in the lake in 1993, and the North Fork of Pound River below the dam is stocked with trout by the state Department of Game and Inland Fisheries (*see* Fishing North Fork of Pound Lake, p. 49).

The lake is especially attractive for a day or a weekend of canoe cruising. Since the whole lake is a no-wake zone, this is not the place for high-powered bass boats. Land around the lake is part of the Clinch Ranger District of the Jefferson National Forest. The Ranger District has also taken over operations of lake facilities from the Corps of Engineers.

Camping in the area around the lake ranges from uncrowded backcountry to car camping in a meadow campground. Hikers also enjoy a selection of walking trails that include old roads and abandoned railroad beds and wind past small waterfalls and interesting rock formations, and through hemlock and rhododendron thickets. Other recreational facilities include two launch ramps, and picnic areas.

Directions: Pound launch and picnic area: Take US 23 to Pound, turn west off the bypass on VA 630 at junction with Business US 23 into Pound, follow VA 630 .9 mile to launch.

Activities: Fishing, boating (no-wake), canoeing, kayaking, camping, picnicking, swimming, hiking, mountain biking, seasonal hunting in surrounding national forest, volleyball, basketball, interpretive programs.

Facilities: Launch ramps, campgrounds (developed, primitive, or backcountry), swimming beach, picnic area with tables and grills, volleyball and basketball courts,

JACK-IN-THE-PULPIT

(*Arisaema triphyllum*) This common biennial grows to 3 feet tall and produces bright red clusters of berries.

hiking trails including self-guided trail, bathhouse, flush toilets, water fountains, trailer waste disposal, playground, amphitheater.

Dates: Pound launch, open year-round. Wise launch, open Apr. 1–Nov. 15. Cane Patch Campground, open Memorial Day–Labor Day. Bee Bottom Picnic Area, open Apr. 1–Nov. 15. Hiking trails, open year-round.

Closest town: Pound, 1 mile east on VA 630.

Fees: Fees are charged for camping and launch ramps.

For more information: Clinch Ranger District, 9416 Darden Drive, Wise, VA 24293. Phone (540) 328-2931.

Jack-in-the-pulpit

Keep a sharp eye out along the banks of tributary streams at North Fork of Pound Lake for jack-in-the-pulpit. The green and purplish-brown striped flower, which resembles a preacher in an elaborate covered pulpit, hides beneath three large leaves. Though sometimes hard to spot, *Arisaema triphyllum* is abundant in the damp woods of the Appalachians.

CAMPING AND RECREATION AT NORTH FORK OF POUND LAKE

Three types of camping are available—backcountry camping with no facilities, primitive camping accessible only by foot or boat, and camping at a developed campground. Picnicking is available at Bee Bottom Picnic Area [Fig. 10(9)], Pound Launch Overlook [Fig. 10(3)], and Laurel Fork Camping and Picnic Area [Fig. 10(1)].

CANE PATCH CAMPGROUND. [Fig. 10(7)] This is the only developed campground at North Fork of Pound Lake. It's on a flat area at the southwestern end of the lake, with play areas for children, basketball and volleyball courts, and fields for ball games. Use is light on weekdays, and moderate to heavy on weekends.

Directions: Follow US 23 to Pound, in northern Wise County. Go west on VA 671 and continue 6.5 miles to campground.

Facilities: 34 camping units (can accommodate vehicle up to 32 feet) with picnic table, and fireplace or grill; bathhouse with flush toilets and showers; central water fountains; trailer disposal station; amphitheater.

Dates: Open mid-May–Sept.

Fees: A fee is charged for camping.

LAUREL FORK PRIMITIVE CAMPGROUND. [Fig. 10(1)] For a quiet setting in the Jefferson National Forest, hike or boat to this spot on a cove in the upper lake. Facilities include primitive campsites, picnic areas with cooking grills, and boat tie rings. The Laurel Fork Trail, which begins at the Pound launch, leads to the campground.

BACKCOUNTRY CAMPING. The Jefferson National Forest surrounding the lake is completely open for camping. Visitors should check on possible restrictions on campfires, carry water along, pack all litter, and leave no trace of a visit to this wild country.

PHILLIPS CREEK GROUP CAMPING AND PICNIC AREA. [Fig. 10(6)] By reservation only. Located near the southwestern end of the lake, this area also features a well-placed interpretive trail.

Directions: Take US 23 to Pound Lake, turn west 1 mile south of Pound Lake on VA 671, and continue about 5.5 miles to recreation area.

Facilities: 6 picnic sites and shelters, large open field for camping, vault toilets, interpretive trail. No water or electric.

BEE BOTTOM PICNIC AREA. [Fig. 10(9)] Bee Bottom is maintained with families and recreation in mind. Mowed open areas invite children to run and offer a place for ball games. Hardwood trees surround the open area.

Directions: Take US 23 to Pound Lake, in northern Wise County. Turn west on VA 671 1 mile south of Pound and continue 7.2 miles to picnic area.

Facilities: 31 picnic units (each with parking spur, picnic table, grill), pit toilets, water fountains, playground.

Dates: Open Apr. 1–Oct. 31.

Fees: A fee is charged per vehicle.

HIKING AT NORTH FORK OF POUND LAKE

PHILLIPS CREEK LOOP TRAIL. [Fig. 10(6)] This easy, self-guided nature trail leads hikers first along an abandoned railroad bed and then to an old homestead where apple and peach trees planted by the owners still provide food for deer.

Wildlife food plantings of lespedeza, persimmon (*Diospyros virginiana*), and black walnut (*Juglans nigra*) line the trail. An Indian grave is one highlight. Waterfalls have carved beautiful patterns in sandstone rock, and footbridges across streams lead to the remnants of a whiskey still.

Directions: Take US 23 to Pound Lake. Turn west on VA 671 1 mile south of Pound and continue about 5.5 miles to recreation area.

Trail: 1.3-mile loop from Phillips Creek Group Camping and Picnic Area.

Elevation: 1,600 feet.

Degree of difficulty: Easy, with slopes less than 20 percent.

Surface: Natural forest floor, with footbridges.

LAUREL FORK TRAIL. [Fig. 10(1)] Though difficult, the rock formations and variety of plant life and wildlife make this trail worth the effort. It begins at the Pound launch parking lot and takes off up a steep slope for approximately .5 mile. The Laurel Fork Trail connects to old logging roads and other trails on Pine Mountain. Follow signs to Laurel Fork.

Trail: 1.5 miles from Pound launch to Laurel Fork Primitive Campground.

Elevation: 1,600 feet at base climbing to about 2,050 feet on ridge.

Degree of difficulty: Difficult, with steep slopes that can become slippery.

Surface: Natural forest floor, with rocky places.

FISHING AT NORTH FORK OF POUND LAKE

Spotted bass are abundant but small in the lake. Crappie and bluegill fishing is good. Channel catfish and muskie have been stocked. A fair population of smallmouth bass and redbreast sunfish also find the cool lake water to their liking. Below the dam, the North Fork of Pound River is a medium-size stream with shallow runs and riffles.

The state stocks trout in the river on a regular basis. A state fishing license and a trout stamp are required. Normally, a national forest stamp is required if fishing on federal property, but one is not required at North Fork of Pound Reservoir. The river passes through the town of Pound, where parking and licenses are available. Best times to fish for trout are October through early summer.

Directions: Pound launch: Take US 23 bypass at Pound, turn west off the bypass on VA 630 at the junction with Business US 23 into Pound and follow VA 630 .9 mile to launch. Wise launch: Take US 23 bypass at Pound, turn west on VA 671, and continue 5.1 miles to launch.

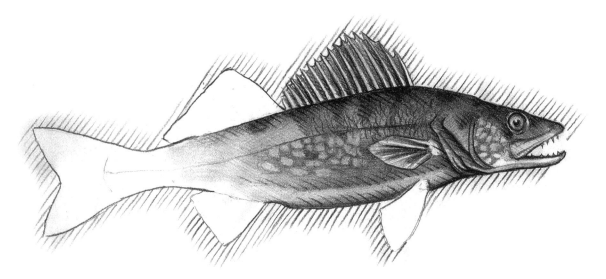

WALLEYE
(Stizostedion vitreum)
With a common name stemming from its large eye, the walleye is sometimes erroneously called a "walleyed pike." Walleye can grow to 2 feet long and up to 20 pounds.

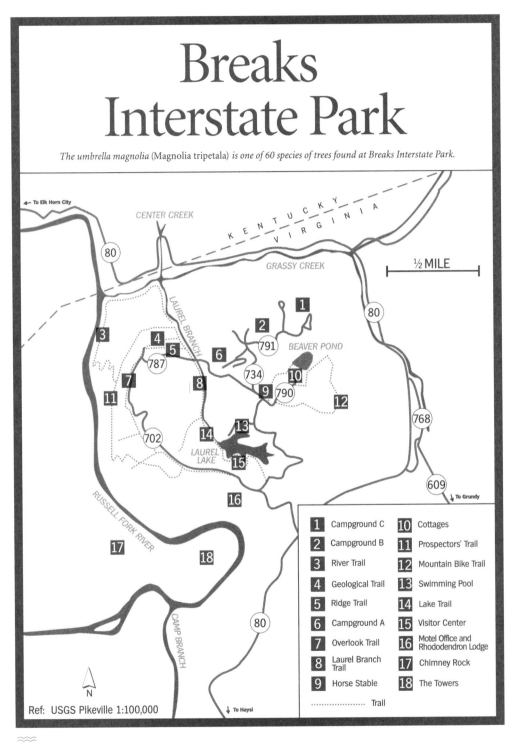

Breaks Interstate Park

The umbrella magnolia (Magnolia tripetala) *is one of 60 species of trees found at Breaks Interstate Park.*

← To Elk Horn City

CENTER CREEK

KENTUCKY
VIRGINIA

80

GRASSY CREEK

½ MILE

80

LAUREL BRANCH

1

2

791

BEAVER POND

3

4

5

787

6

734

10

7

8

9 790

11

12

768

702

13

14

LAUREL LAKE

15

609
↓ To Grundy

16

RUSSELL FORK RIVER

17

18

80

CAMP BRANCH

N

↓ To Haysi

Ref: USGS Pikeville 1:100,000

1 Campground C	10 Cottages
2 Campground B	11 Prospectors' Trail
3 River Trail	12 Mountain Bike Trail
4 Geological Trail	13 Swimming Pool
5 Ridge Trail	14 Lake Trail
6 Campground A	15 Visitor Center
7 Overlook Trail	16 Motel Office and Rhododendron Lodge
8 Laurel Branch Trail	17 Chimney Rock
9 Horse Stable	18 The Towers
·········· Trail	

Breaks Interstate Park

[Fig. 11, Fig. 5(11)] Breaks Interstate Park is often called "The Grand Canyon of the South." Perhaps the scale of the 5-mile-long, .25-mile-deep gorge that forms the park's centerpiece cannot rival that of the Grand Canyon, but the canyon is among the longest and deepest east of the Mississippi River. A better title might be "The Grand Canyon with Clothes On." Where the raging Russell Fork of the Big Sandy River has carved the solid sandstone over millions of years to break through Pine Mountain, nature has dressed the canyon walls in some of Virginia's most spectacular scenery.

Remote and formerly inaccessible, the area now known as Breaks Interstate Park was virtually undiscovered by the traveling public until after World War II, when two-lane roads were built into the coal-rich mountains. Black seams of coal are visible still in the roadside cliffs throughout the area. John Fox Jr., author of *The Trail of the Lonesome Pine*, traveled three days in 1900 in a horse-drawn buckboard to reach The Breaks from Big Stone Gap, 70 miles distant. His subsequent article in *Scribner's* magazine caused a flurry of interest in what he called "the most isolated spot this side of the Rockies." Daniel Boone is credited with discovering The Breaks in 1767 as he attempted to find ever-improved trails into Kentucky and the Ohio River Valley beyond. Passes through these rugged mountains were called "breaks" by early settlers. The Breaks was one of only a handful of narrow passageways through 125-mile-long Pine Mountain. Even today, no more than half a dozen roads cross Pine Mountain. Dickenson County, where The Breaks is located, is one of the few counties in Virginia that does not have a U.S. highway within its borders.

The Breaks was too much for Boone and his two companions. When they tried to navigate this awesome gorge by foot, they encountered copperheads and rattlesnakes, as well as the Russell Fork of the Big Sandy River as it crashed through a constricted canyon with 1,000-foot sheer walls. They were overwhelmed by impenetrable tangles of rhododendron and mountain laurel and a forest of towering trees, some of which were 7 feet thick. The three men pitched camp nearby, sat out the winter of 1768, then turned back to their homes on North Carolina's more peaceful Yadkin River.

Today, 4,600-acre Breaks Interstate Park—so called because it sits astride the state line shared by both Kentucky and Virginia and offers a view into Tennessee on clear days—attracts more than a third of a million visitors annually.

They come to fish the still pools, to raft the Class IV–Class VI rapids of the Russell Fork River, to stand at panoramic overlooks, to camp in the park's wooded campsites, to walk the miles of meandering hiking trails, and to see the beauty of Catawba rhododendron in lavender bloom in early May.

The modern, glass-walled Rhododendron Restaurant and Breaks Motor Lodge [Fig. 11(16)] seem to hang over the gorge rim. Visitors savor memorable meals and sunsets while listening to the roar of the river far below. Though the park is open

Breaks Interstate Park features a gorge which many call the "Grand Canyon of the South." The park sits astride the Virginia-Kentucky state border.

year-round, the lodge and restaurant season is April 1 through December 21. Several cottages with split-level floor plans are available year-round, but they must be rented by the week. Motels are also located nearby. The Breaks' visitor center [Fig. 11(15)] is a combined information center and comfort station. It houses mountain photographs, wildlife specimens, maps and books, an explanation of the park's unusual geological features, and an excellent coal exhibit. The coal exhibit shows how "black gold" was formed through natural processes some 200 million years ago and how miners risk their lives even today to bring the precious fuel to the surface.

The woods ring with old-time gospel sings each Memorial Day, Father's Day, and Labor Day weekend as up to 20,000 people pour into the park to hear professional and amateur groups give free concerts. A freewill offering is taken and divided among the singers.

No mountain park would be complete without a display regarding the mountaineer's most important crop (corn) which he both ate and drank. A working mill grinds corn into meal at the visitor center, and there's a moonshine still (not operational) that shows how the early settlers mixed work and recreation.

More than 60 species of trees can be found here, including northern hardwoods such as walnut (*Juglans* sp.), chestnut oak (*Quercus prinus*), black oak (*Quercus velutina*), red oak (*Quercus borealis*), white oak (*Quercus alba*), locust (*Robinia pseudoacacia*), and beech (*Fagus grandifolia*). In spring, blossoms of white flowering dogwood, redbud (*Cercis canadensis*), cherry (*Prunus serotina*), and two varieties of magnolia sprinkle the woods with color and fragrance.

A wildflower field guide is helpful for identifying the herb robert (*Geranium robertianium*), showy orchis (*Orchis spectabilis*), bird's-foot violet (*Viola pedata*), Virginia bluebell (*Mertensia virginica*), cardinal flower (*Lobelia cardinalis*), and wood lily (*Lilium philadelphicum*). For variety, visitors might search the edges of rock outcrops, deep woods, stream edges, and river habitats.

Directions: The park is located in northern Dickenson County, where Dickenson/Buchanan County, VA, and Pike County, KY, converge. From Haysi in northern Dickenson County, take VA 80 8 miles north to the park entrance, on the left.

Activities: Swimming, hiking, boating, whitewater rafting (seasonal), whitewater canoeing and kayaking (with your own craft), and horseback riding. Pond fishing for bass and bluegill, and river fishing for bass, trout, and walleye.

Facilities: Visitor center, campground (electric, water, and sewer available; alcohol not allowed), restaurant, gift shop, housekeeping cottages, motor lodge, pool and snack bar, hiking trails, bike trail and rental bikes, boat dock and rental boats, stable and rental horses, fishing lake (license may be purchased at visitor center), picnic shelters. Primitive camping allowed in backcountry by permit.

Dates: Gates: open year-round. Visitor center: open Apr. 1–Dec. 21. Campground: open Apr. 1–Oct. 31. Restaurant and gift shop: open Apr. 1–Dec. 21. Cottages: open year-round. Motor lodge: open Apr. 1–Dec. 21. Pool and snack bar: open Memorial Day weekend–Labor Day. Boat dock: open seasonally. Riding stable: open seasonally.

Fees: A fee is charged for admission, and for campsites, cottages, motor lodge, picnic shelters, pool, pedal boats.

Closest town: Elkhorn City, KY, is on KY 80 in Pike County, 5 miles west of the park entrance. Haysi, VA, is on VA 80 in Dickenson County, 8 miles south of the entrance.

For more information: Breaks Interstate Park, PO Box 100, Breaks, VA 24607-0100. Phone (540) 865-4413 or 4414. Call (800) 982-5122 for motor lodge reservations.

TRAILS AT BREAKS INTERSTATE PARK

More than 13 miles of hiking trails lace the park, varying from easy to difficult. Most are less than 1 mile long, but interconnected trails provide longer hikes over varying terrain. Maps with descriptions of each trail are available at the park office. Trail names describe the outstanding physical features of each: Cold Spring, Geological, Grassy Creek, Grassy Overlook, Lake, Loop, Overlook, Prospectors', Ridge, River, Towers, and Tower Tunnel trails. The Ridge and Geological trails are self-guided, with booklets available.

Elevations vary from 870 feet at Russell Fork in the canyon bottom to 1,978 feet at Clinchfield Overlook where the Overlook Trail begins. Surfaces are hard-packed dirt and rock, and are well maintained, with steps, handrails, and benches along the way. All are marked with colored blazes, with no intersecting trails having the same color. Pets must be leashed. Register at the visitor center for backcountry overnight camping. Stay away from exposed overlooks during thunderstorms. Bicycles are permitted only on the Mountain Bike Trail.

GEOLOGICAL TRAIL. [Fig. 11(4)] This half-hour, self-guided nature trail takes its name from the interesting rock formations and faults along its way. The path varies from smooth to rocky, and it changes grade frequently. On hot days hikers enjoy the cool air along the rock face. This trail can be combined with the Ridge Trail for a loop back to the Stateline Overlook.

Trail: .35 mile, self-guided.

Degree of difficulty: Moderate.

Blaze: White.

LAKE TRAIL. [Fig. 11(14)] This easy walking trail, popular with wildlife watchers, takes visitors along the undeveloped side of Laurel Lake past marshes and inlets. This trail joins the Laurel Branch Trail and also connects with the pool and dock areas. Entry points are at Potter's Knoll, the visitor center, and the dam.

Trail: .5 mile.

Degree of difficulty: Easy.

Blaze: Orange.

LAUREL BRANCH TRAIL. [Fig. 11(8)] Named for the stream it follows its entire length, this trail extends from the lower end of Laurel Lake to Grassy Creek. From the lake to a rock formation called The Notches, the terrain is flat and easy. The last .5 mile through a mixed forest of hemlock and hardwoods, the climb becomes steep, rocky, and uneven. Rhododendron thickets reward the hiker with their showy pink booms in June and July.

Trail: 1.25 miles.

Degree of difficulty: Easy at first, becoming difficult the last .5 mile.

Blaze: Red.

OVERLOOK TRAIL. [Fig. 11(7)] Frequent grade changes characterize this scenic path that leads along the edge of cliffs to provide an almost continuous canyon view. The hike is spectacular in spring and fall. **Protect children from edges where there are no railings.**

Trail: .75 mile.

Degree of difficulty: Difficult.

Blaze: Green.

PROSPECTORS' TRAIL. [Fig. 11(11)] This hike follows the base of the cliffs about 350 feet beneath the major overlooks, following the contours of the land until it becomes rocky the last .5 mile. It offers a different perspective on the rock cliffs, overlooks above, and canyon below.

Trail: 1.5 miles.

Degree of difficulty: Moderate.

Blaze: Orange.

RIDGE TRAIL. [Fig. 11(5)] Bird watchers favor this self-guided nature hike across the top of a ridge covered with hardwoods and mountain laurel. After an easy, level

DUTCHMAN'S BREECHES (Dicentra cucullaria) White, waxy petals shaped like baggy trousers give this plant its name.

beginning, the trail becomes steep near The Notches.

Trail: .5 mile, self-guided.

Degree of difficulty: Easy at first, then difficult.

Blaze: Blue.

RIVER TRAIL. [Fig. 11(3)] Hikers are advised to wear sturdy shoes, take water, and travel with a companion on this extremely steep and rugged trail with many switchbacks, descending to a gentler grade along the river. Outstanding views.

Trail: 1 mile.

Degree of difficulty: Difficult.

Blaze: Blue.

Dutchman's Breeches

The sheltered gorge of Breaks Interstate Park has become home to this yellow-tipped, white spring flower *Dicentra cucularia* that suggests tiny pantaloons hung upside-down to dry. It has pale green, fernlike leaves and grows only 6 to 12 inches tall.

CUMBERLAND MOUNTAIN VIEW DRIVE

[Fig. 8(9)] Half a day is needed to explore this winding stretch of rural Appalachia and national forest. The Cumberland Mountain View Trail is a 19-mile drive into America's past as mountainous Dickenson County unfolds alongside VA 611 between Clintwood, VA and Breaks Interstate Park.

The unpretentious yet scenic back road even retains an unpaved 3-mile stretch as a memento to the roads of yesteryear. This is authentic Appalachia with all its sweeping natural beauty on display—the beauty that caused early Scots-Irish settlers to come, to see, to stay. Along the Cumberland Mountain View Drive are sharp turns and sheer drop-offs, quiet fishing coves and weathered log barns, swinging bridges and roadside overlooks where wild geraniums and trillium provide a colorful foreground for Pine Mountain. This is ruffed grouse and wild turkey country.

Visitors shouldn't be surprised to see either bird walking across the road. Deer aren't numerous in Dickenson County, but after years of restocking by state officials, it is possible that visitors might catch the bright eyes of a doe and fawn peering from the hardwood groves and rhododendron thickets of the Jefferson National Forest. Though rural and remote, the road is safe and well maintained. At the Old Ranger's Cabin near Clintwood, visitors can examine the foundation of one of the area's earliest settlement homes. And at Splash Dam Bridge near Flannagan Dam, they can inspect the ingenious, turn-of-the-century locks built on the Russell Fork River to aid in floating logs downstream during spring floods.

Directions: About 5 miles south of Breaks Interstate Park on VA 80 in northern Dickenson County, go west on VA 611. Or from Clintwood, go 2.5 miles north on VA 631 to join VA 611 at Isom.

For more information: Breaks Interstate Park, phone (540) 865-4413.

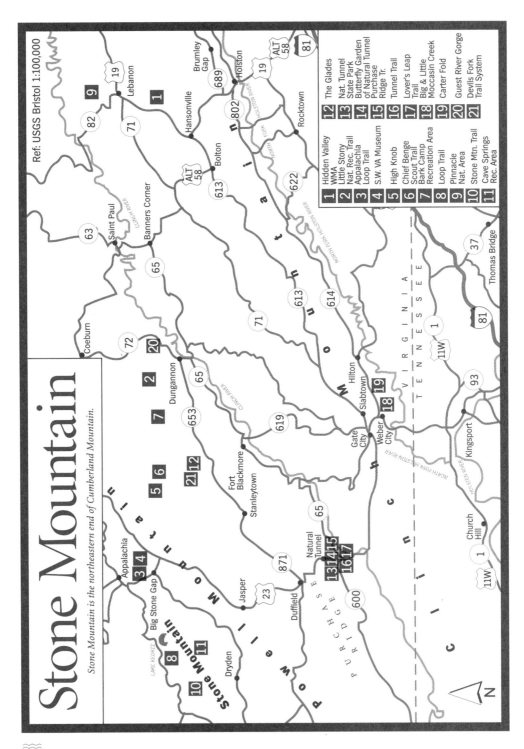

Ref: USGS Bristol 1:100,000

Stone Mountain

Stone Mountain is the northeastern end of Cumberland Mountain.

1 Hidden Valley WMA	**8** Loop Trail	**15** Purchase Ridge Tr.
2 Little Stony Nat. Rec. Trail	**9** Pinnacle Nat. Area	**16** Tunnel Trail
3 Appalachia Loop Trail	**10** Stone Mtn. Trail	**17** Lover's Leap Trail
4 S.W. VA Museum	**11** Cave Springs Rec. Area	**18** Big & Little Moccasin Creek
5 High Knob	**12** The Glades	**19** Carter Fold
6 Chief Benge Scout Trail	**13** Nat. Tunnel State Park	**20** Guest River Gorge
7 Bark Camp Recreation Area	**14** Butterfly Garden of Natural Tunnel	**21** Devils Fork Trail System

Stone Mountain

[Fig. 12] Stone Mountain is actually the mauled and contorted northeastern end of magnificent Cumberland Mountain that defines Virginia's southwestern border with Kentucky. Six miles below Pennington Gap in Lee County, the Kentucky/Virginia line veers off from Cumberland Mountain toward the west. At that point, where the mountain belongs to Virginia on both sides, it first becomes Stone Mountain, then Little Stone Mountain, stretching its stalwart ridgeline some 28 miles more, past Big Stone Gap, to Norton in Wise County.

Then the mountain that ages ago rivaled the 125-mile-long Pine Mountain to the west becomes jammed and confused. After Stone Mountain formed, continuing pressures caused by the collision of the African and North American continents crushed the part now called Little Stone Mountain. It pushed it up against Powell Mountain, and folded it into a boomerang shape around Powell Valley. Its eastern and southern borders are marked by the Guest and Clinch rivers.

Road cuts on the north side of Little Stone Mountain offer a great comparison between the nearly horizontal rock formations of the Appalachian Plateau and the steeply tilted layers of the Valley and Ridge province. Take US 23, which runs parallel to the Powell River, for this look back to the violent end of the Paleozoic era some 250 to 300 million years ago. In the Pennsylvanian and Permian periods of this era, tremendous pressure from the earth's shifting plates gradually buckled the earth's crust. A road cut often reveals stratifications turned nearly sideways.

Today, the Clinch Ranger District of the Jefferson National Forest offers access to a diverse potpourri of habitats and scenery on Stone Mountain. These include northern hardwood forests, southern hardwoods, cove forests, pine forests, old growth forests, rhododendron thickets, beaver ponds, marshes, bogs, hemlock-lined stony creeks, deep gorges, sheer cliffs, and rocky outcrops. All this variety remains relatively unassaulted by tourist-season crowds.

Stone Mountain & Little Stone Mountain

A long, narrow strip of national forest runs along Stone Mountain from about 8 miles west of the Lee County line to Norton, squeezing between Big Stone Gap and Appalachia.

🌄 CAVE SPRINGS RECREATION AREA

[Fig. 12(11)] Cave Springs may be used as a base camp to explore rhododendron-lined hiking trails through a mostly hardwood forest dotted with large boulders and steep cliffs. One trail leads to a scenic overlook and cave where a spring begins. The west end of the 14-mile Stone Mountain Trail starts here. The picnic area has a small

Eastern Hemlock

The graceful hemlock (*Tsuga candensis*) is a shade-loving tree of cool, moist ravines and stream banks. The slow-growing evergreen takes 20 to 40 years to begin producing seeds and may reach immense proportions. The 300-year-old trees on Stone Mountain Trail could live to be as old as 1,000 years.

swimming lake. Campsites are shaded with hardwoods and offer privacy. The elevation at the recreation area is 1,500 feet, with trails climbing Stone Mountain to 2,750 feet above the campground.

Directions: From Big Stone Gap in southern Wise County, take Alternate US 58 west 2.5 miles to right turn on VA 621. Continue 6.1 miles to campground entrance.

Activities: Camping, picnicking, hiking, swimming, and seasonal hunting in surrounding national forest.

Facilities: Camping area has 41 camping units with picnic tables and spaces for RVs up to 22 feet, central water, flush toilets, warm showers, and a trailer disposal station. Picnic area has a small lake for swimming, 10 tables and grills, and a drinking fountain.

Dates: Open May 14–Oct. 15.

Fees: A fee is charged for day use, and for camping.

Closest town: Big Stone Gap, 9 miles east.

KEOKEE LAKE

[Fig. 12] This hidden jewel of the Clinch Ranger District features a picturesque 92-acre lake with secluded coves surrounded by marsh grasses and hardwood forests of red oaks, white oaks, and hickories. With no gasoline-powered motors allowed, the lake attracts only those who enjoy quietly probing the shoreline by canoe or casting from a john boat for largemouth bass and sunfish around the dead trees emerging from the shallows. Early and late in the day, a raccoon, muskrat, or fox may come for a drink at the lake's edge. The lake can also be explored by foot on the encircling trail. A spur connects to the middle of the more challenging Stone Mountain Trail.

Directions: From Appalachia in western Wise County, take Alternate US 58 southwest 1 mile to right turn on VA 68. Follow VA 68 west for 7 miles. In Lee County, VA 68 becomes VA 606. Continue on VA 606 for 2 miles to left turn on VA 623 and go 1 mile to lake.

Activities: Fishing for bass, tiger muskie, sunfish, and catfish. Boating (electric motors only), hiking, picnicking, and seasonal hunting in surrounding national forest.

Facilities: 92-acre lake, paved launch ramp, 4 picnic tables and grills, vault toilets, hiking trails.

Dates: Open year-round.

Fees: None.

Closest town: Appalachia, in western Wise County, 11 miles east.

LAKE KEOKEE LOOP TRAIL. [Fig. 12(8)] Beyond the edges of this easy trail around Lake Keokee, an occasional frog plops in the water. The turquoise wings of a dragonfly clinging to marsh grass are iridescent in the afternoon sunlight. Indian pipe (*Monotropa uniflora*) pokes its white flower out of the leaf litter under the oaks. From the other side of the lake, a spur leads in less than 1 mile to Stone Mountain Trail at Olinger Gap. After crossing Stone Mountain Trail and continuing along this spur another .5 mile down the south side of Stone Mountain, this trail connects with VA 622 at Old Still Hollow.

Trail: 4-mile loop around lake.
Elevation: 2,200 feet.
Degree of difficulty: Easy.

STONE MOUNTAIN TRAIL

[Fig. 12(10)] This rugged, 14.3-mile trail, straight as a Kansas highway, follows the crest of Stone Mountain between Big Stone Gap and Cave Springs Recreation Area. Visitors who don't have a day or two set aside to hike it should take at least part of a morning or afternoon to explore the eastern end of the trail. After walking up a series of rock stairs built in the 1970s by the Youth Conservation Corps, hikers will enter a deep hemlock forest lining the banks of Roaring Branch. Miniature waterfalls among the sculpted sandstone boulders are picture perfect.

A stand of old growth hemlocks that has evaded the woodsman's axe for more than 300 years is on this section of the trail. Then, at 3.5 miles, hikers can catch their breath at High Butte, a scenic rock outcrop with the Powell River to the south, and

EASTERN HEMLOCK
(Tsuga canadensis)
Long-lived hemlocks develop slowly in the shade. Their bark was once a commercial source of tannin in the production of leather.

Black Mountain and Kentucky to the north.

Directions: East end access is 1.4 miles north of Big Stone Gap on the left side of Alternate US 58. Parking is available .2 mile farther beside dumpsters. The trail also connects at the middle with a spur to Lake Keokee and at the west end to Cave Springs Recreation Area.

Trail: 14.3-mile straight path along crest of Stone Mountain between Alternate US 58 at Big Stone Gap and Cave Springs Recreation Area.

Elevation: 1,500 feet at beginning to 3,000 feet at High Butte.

Degree of difficulty: Difficult.

Surface: Natural forest floor, with rocky sections.

APPALACHIA LOOP TRAIL

[Fig. 12(3)] A challenging trail if you take it fast, it is negotiable for the average hiker who has time to rest along the way. The Appalachia Loop Trail is on Little Stone Mountain, typical Appalachian Plateau country, with profuse boulderfields and sand-loving rhododendron thickets.

Directions: From Appalachia, take Alternate US 58 southwest for .5 mile to left turn onto Town Route 1321. Go to end of road, turn left on Town Route 1319, travel the length of a city block, and go right on Town Route 1322. Trailhead is at end of road on right.

Trail: 4-mile loop.

Elevation: 1,500 feet to 2,560 feet.

Degree of difficulty: Difficult, with steep, rocky sections.

SOUTHWEST VIRGINIA MUSEUM

[Fig. 12(4)] Located on US 23 at Big Stone Gap, 18 miles north of Natural Tunnel State Park [Fig. 12(13), Fig. 16] near Duffield, the museum tells the story of exploration and development of southwest Virginia. The transformation of Big Stone Gap into a vital cultural area after coal and iron ore were discovered in the area in the late 1870s is featured in the main gallery on the first floor.

Second-floor exhibits tell of local people at the turn of the century. The outside world was having a profound influence as mail-order catalogs, photographs, radios, and railroads ended the people's isolation. The flow of early settlers into and through southwest Virginia as the Wilderness Road was opened through Cumberland Gap is chronicled on the third floor.

The museum is administered by the Virginia Department of Conservation and Recreation, which operates the state parks. Information on one of the state's newest parks, Karlan, is available here. Karlan is located off US 58 in Lee County, about 10 miles east of Cumberland Gap, Tennessee (*see* Karlan State Park, p. 34). Other attractions in the town of Big Stone Gap include the June Tolliver Playhouse, home of the seasonal outdoor performance of the musical *Trail of the Lonesome Pine*, based on the book by John Fox Jr.; the John Fox Jr. Museum, the author's home which is now a Virginia Historical Landmark; and the Harry W. Meador Jr. Coal Museum.

Directions: The museum is located in Big Stone Gap at the corner of West First Street and Wood Avenue (US Alternate 58), just off US 23 in Wise County. If you take US 23 into town, go west at the intersection with Wood Avenue.

Dates: Open year-round, hours are seasonal.

Fees: A fee is charged for admission.

For more information: Southwest Virginia Museum, Box 742, Big Stone Gap, VA 24219. Phone (540) 523-1322.

North End of Stone Mountain

[Fig. 12] South of Norton, on either side of the Wise and Scott county lines, Stone Mountain surges to a height of almost 4,200 feet at High Knob—the highest point of Virginia's Appalachian Plateau—before plunging toward the Clinch River to disappear in the earth at the edge of the Valley and Ridge province. Most of the mountain belongs to the Clinch Ranger District of the Jefferson National Forest. Three recreation areas, several disparate hiking trails, and wide-ranging natural environments give outdoor lovers plenty to do. Offerings include stunning views at High Knob [Fig. 12(5)], lakes to fish, shady mountain campgrounds, a new rails-to-trails hike through dramatic Guest River Gorge, a beaver-controlled wetland to explore, and another long trail that links many of the sites. Mountain bikers can patch together trails on the forest service roads and old logging roads that crisscross the mountain.

A little-known backroad, VA 653, stretches some 18 miles along the southern border of Stone Mountain between Sunbright and Dungannon. Spring wildflowers put on a show here, where the roadside and fields are spread with trillium, Dutchman's breeches, bleeding heart (*Dicentra spectabilis*), wild geranium (*Geraniaceae maculatum*), and trout lily (*Erythronium americanum*). To get to the North End of Stone Mountain from Dungannon, in northeastern Scott County, go north on VA 72 less than 1 mile and turn left on VA 653.

For more information: Clinch Ranger District, 9416 Darden Drive, Wise, VA 24293. Phone (540) 328-2931.

▨ HIGH KNOB

[Fig. 12(5)] At 4,162 feet (close to .8 mile high), the peak called High Knob is one of the highest points in mountainous southwest Virginia—or anywhere else in the state, for that matter. From the third story of the stone-and-timber, octagonal observation tower atop High Knob, a visitor can look into five states on a clear day. High Knob is a profoundly beautiful place, surrounded by mountains growing progressively smaller in the distance in Virginia, Kentucky, Tennessee, West Virginia,

Broad-winged Hawk

The crow-size broadwing (*Buteo platypterus*), living in canopied woods, may go unnoticed until its fall migration. Then hundreds fill the sky over High Knob and at other mountain lookouts, sometimes forming "kettles" of circling birds using warm updrafts to gain altitude.

and North Carolina. Though off the beaten path, High Knob is readily accessible by VA 619 from Norton.

The road to the top, though, is a true anachronism—as tight and tortuous as any in Virginia today. Leave your motor home at the bottom. This road, with its frequent twists, switchbacks, and steep grades, is more suited to horse and wagon or perhaps stubby Model A coupes. The surface is narrow blacktop. The scenic road threads its way through dense hemlock and southern hardwood forests, as well as rhododendron thickets that bloom into early July at this high elevation.

Modern cars will experience no problems navigating the steep, 5-mile trip to the High Knob parking lot, but drivers may want to consider coming off the mountain in low gear to keep brakes from overheating. In winter, when ice and snow cover the old highway, it is best to forget the imposing mountain altogether. On a clear day, even a short trip to High Knob will reward visitors with panoramic views. Visitors who have more time will discover developed campgrounds; stocked, pristine streams and lakes for fishing or wading; a national forest with deer and turkey to hunt or photograph; a 4-acre lake for swimming; and a choice of hiking trails from 1.5 miles to 22 miles long. The High Knob observation tower is also a prime viewing area for the annual hawk migration in September and October.

Depression-era craftsmen employed by the Civilian Conservation Corps (CCC) built High Knob Recreation Area. Tight log buildings still stand, as does stonework of a beauty and mastery seldom seen today. Sturdy footbridges cross cascading mountain streams. The entire project, though more than half a century old, wears that gracefully aged and weathered look so typical of CCC undertakings in the Appalachian Mountains.

Directions: From Norton in south-central Wise County, take VA 619 south up the mountain 3.7 miles. Go left on FS 238 and continue east for 1.6 miles to campground entrance road.

Activities: Camping, swimming, picnicking, hiking, fishing, mountain biking, interpretive programs, scenic views, and seasonal hunting in surrounding national forest.

Facilities: 13 single and 1 double camping units with picnic table and fireplace, central water, flush toilets, and trailer disposal station. 300-foot swimming beach on 4-acre cold-water lake. Bathhouse with warm showers and flush toilets. 14 picnic tables with grills. Hiking trails. Amphitheater.

Dates: Camping, open mid-May–end of Sept. Picnicking, open mid-May–Oct. 31.

Swimming, open Memorial Day–Labor Day.

Fees: A fee is charged for day use and for camping.

Closest town: Norton, 7 miles north.

CHIEF BENGE SCOUT TRAIL

[Fig. 12(6)] The Chief Benge Scout Trail is a fairly difficult and mountainous 19.6 miles, but it offers more than ample rewards. It takes off from the High Knob observation tower through lush, waist-high carpets of jewelweed. The Scout Trail winds across knobs and through hollows, beside rushing streams and along canopied paths of Catawba rhododendron and mountain laurel. The lower end connects with Little Stony National Recreation Trail [Fig. 12(2)], and continues 3 miles to Hanging Rock at Dungannon. The trail provides an excellent opportunity for a two- or three-day backpacking trip. Anglers should pack a rod if they would like to catch stocked trout from Mountain Fork or Little Stony Creek. Or hikers can approach the trail in sections by leaving a second car at one of several access roads.

Chief Benge was a fierce Indian leader who terrorized southwest Virginia's early white settlers. He took savage umbrage at those who wanted to shove his people from their ancestral mountains west into flat, hot Oklahoma territory.

Trail: 19.6-mile winding path.

Elevation: 4,200 feet at High Knob to 2,350 feet at lower trailhead.

Degree of difficulty: Difficult because of length and uneven terrain.

LITTLE STONY NATIONAL RECREATION TRAIL

[Fig. 12(2)] This 2.8-mile path through the deep gorge follows Little Stony Creek through a 400-foot-deep and 1,700-foot-wide gorge, before Little Stony flows into the Clinch River northeast of Dungannon. It also connects the long Chief Benge Scout Trail [Fig. 12(6)] with Hanging Rock Picnic Area, at the southeast corner of Stone Mountain. Little Stony follows a narrow gauge railroad bed constructed in the early 1900s for logging. Most of it is wide, with a grade of only 4 to 5 percent, but hikers should be prepared to climb large rocks and boulders in places. Mountain laurel and rhododendron decorate the trail with white, pink, and purple in May and June. Cove hardwoods and hemlock have repaired the devastation done to the gorge itself by the logging operation in the 1920s. Rocky outcroppings and ledges tower high

Catawba Rhododendron

Many travelers time their mountain visits to coincide with the May and early-June blossoming of *Rhododendron catawbiense*. The flower clusters on this eye-catching rhododendron range from pinkish purple to purple. The evergreen thickets grow on mountain slopes and along stream banks, forming shady canopies over hiking trails. The higher the altitude, the later the bloom.

above the sheer sides of the gorge, while two waterfalls and numerous cascades tumble over boulders below.

Near the lower trailhead is Hanging Rock, the rocky upthrust caused by the Hunter Valley Fault. This fault line marks the northeastern border of the Appalachian Plateau's hold on Virginia.

Directions: To reach the upper trailhead from Coeburn, in eastern Wise County, go south on VA 72 about 3.5 miles, then west on VA 664 1 mile to left on FR 700. Continue on FR 700 to intersection with FR 701. Go 1 mile south on FR 701 to parking lot. The lower trailhead is at Hanging Rock Picnic Area parking lot, about 7 miles south of Coeburn off VA 72.

Trail: 2.8-mile path through deep gorge.

Elevation: 2,350 feet at upper trailhead to 1,750 feet at Hanging Rock.

Degree of difficulty: Moderate.

Surface: Natural forest floor interspersed with areas of rocks and boulders.

CHRISTMAS FERN
(Polystichum acrostichoides)

BARK CAMP RECREATION AREA

[Fig. 12(7)] Located in northern Scott County at 2,700 feet, Bark Camp makes a pleasant stopover for hikers on Chief Benge Scout Trail [Fig. 12(6)], between High Knob [Fig. 12(5)] and the junction with Little Stony National Recreation Trail [Fig. 12(2)]. They can camp in large wooded sites, fish for bass, trout, sunfish, and northern pike in the 60-acre, warm-water lake, or paddle the quiet waters with a canoe or kayak. Hikers can walk the lake perimeter on an easy 3.7-mile loop, a stroll beneath hemlocks where slanting rays of sunlight catch the yellow-green leaves of ferns covering the forest floor. The lake trail connects with Chief Benge Scout Trail.

Directions: From Norton, take Alternate US 58 6 miles east to Tacoma, turn right on VA 706, and travel 4.1 miles. Turn left on VA 699 and travel .3 mile. Go right on gravel VA 822, and drive 1.7 miles to the recreation area.

Activities: Warm-water fishing, boating (electric motors only), picnicking, camping, hiking.

Facilities: Day use area: fishing lake with piers for the handicapped, picnic tables and grills, vault toilets, trails. Campground: 19 sites with picnic table, flush toilets, central water.

Dates: Day-use: open last Saturday in Mar.–mid-Oct. Campground: open mid-May–end of Sept.

Fees: A fee is charged for day use and for camping.

Closest town: Norton, 12 miles to the northwest.

THE GLADES

[Fig. 12(12)] Here's a well-kept secret not found in the national forest handouts. Deep in the Clinch Ranger District, between High Knob and Bark Camp Lake, is a boggy meadow called The Glades. Here, nature's architect, the beaver, has taken advantage of typical Plateau topography on Stone Mountain to create his favorite habitat—a wetland. At an elevation of about 3,000 feet, beavers have felled trees to slow Glady Fork to a meandering, marshy series of pools and bogs before it tumbles down to Stony Creek. Consequently, seeds that cannot take hold under the hardwood canopies that cover most of Stone Mountain take a liking to the sunny, wet meadows. The pink, steeple-shaped flower clusters of steeplebush (*Spirea tomentosa*) appear in late summer. Red-winged blackbirds (*Agelaius phoeniceus*) find protection among the clumps of soft rush (*Juncus effusus*), and muskrats feed on its stalks. The bur reed (*Sparganium americanum*) feeds not only the muskrat, but also marsh birds and waterfowl such as the colorful wood duck, which eat its seeds.

Other wetland-loving plants playing their part in the complex ecosystem include cinnamon fern (*Osmunda cinnamonea*), manna grass (*Glyceria striata*), and a variety of sedges, rushes, and sphagnum mosses. The marsh is interspersed with shrubby patches of rhododendron and mountain laurel.

By flooding woodlands, the beavers have caused tall oaks and hickories to die. The stark, dead trunks of these trees still emerge from the marsh, or lie in the ooze, attracting turtles, blacksnakes, and garter snakes. The flashy, black-and-white pileated woodpecker (*Dryocopus pileatus*) stays busy extracting grubs and insects from the decaying bark. Birds normally associated with more northern climes, such as the magnolia warbler (*Dendroica magnolia*) and Canada warbler (*Wilsonia canadensis*), make their home here. The red-shouldered hawk (*Buteo lineatus*) finds easy prey among the grasses. Spring peepers, leopard frogs, tree frogs, and cricket frogs keep up a riotous chorus in spring and summer. The Glades is accessible by car or from the Chief Benge Scout Trail [Fig. 12(6)].

Directions: The Glades lies atop Stone Mountain just southwest of Edith Gap at the Scott County line between High Knob and Hanging Rock. From the Chief Benge Scout Trail at Edith Gap, go south on VA 706 a short distance and turn right on FR 291. Walk 1 mile to end of road. By car, from Dungannon on the Clinch River (5 miles west of Russell County line), take VA 72 north .5 mile to left turn on VA 653. Go 1.5 miles west on VA 653, turn right on VA 706, travel about 5 miles, turn left on FR 291, and go 1 mile to end of road.

GUEST RIVER GORGE

[Fig. 12(20)] To carve Guest River Gorge through the east end of Stone Mountain, the Guest River over the ages sliced a ragged, serpentine gash through the Pennsylvanian sandstone of rural Wise County. The sheer cliffs that rise 400 feet above the tumbling mountain river are estimated to be more than 300 million years old. The gorge lies near the southeastern edge of the Appalachian Plateau. The oldest rock, called the Lee Formation (323 million years old), lies in the bedrock. Rock of the Norton Formation in the sides is younger, estimated to be about 317 million years of age near the top. The Guest River—designated a Virginia Scenic River—begins above Norton on Indian Mountain. The 30-mile river flows past Coeburn, enters the gorge, and cascades over ledges and around huge boulders beneath sheer canyon walls.

The Guest flows out of the gorge and empties into the Clinch River where Wise, Scott, and Russell counties meet.

Before the first white settlers arrived, Native Americans used the Guest River and gorge area for hunting, fishing, and tool making. Indians walked beneath the towering hardwoods and hemlocks and speared fish in the river as early as 9000 B.C. and as late as the mid-eighteenth century. Both coal and saltpeter were mined in the area. The coal was used for heating. Saltpeter was used to make explosives. In 1922, workers carved and blasted a short tunnel through the hard sandstone. A railroad was laid so that steam and later diesel locomotives could haul the coal and saltpeter through the

CHESTNUT OAK (Quercus prinus)
This is also called rock oak because of its preference for a rocky habitat.

gorge. In a few places, the cliffs were cut away for the railroad. For the most part, though, the gorge remains as nature created it.

After the train was no longer needed, Norfolk-Southern Railroad donated the abandoned railroad to Wise County which, in turn, donated it to the Jefferson National Forest. Rails and ties were taken up and trestles over the river were repaired by Flatwoods Job Corps students. Turning the railroad into a trail took the cooperation of the U.S. Forest Service, the Wise County Board of Supervisors, the Norfolk-Southern Railroad, the Virginia General Assembly and community activists. In 1994, the new Guest River Gorge Trail was dedicated.

Directions: From US 58 at Coeburn in Wise County, go south 2.3 miles on VA 72. Just past Flatwoods picnic area (on right), go left on paved FR 2477, and travel 1.4 miles to trailhead parking. More access points are in plans.

Activities: Biking, hiking, running. No hunting or camping permitted in the gorge. Anglers, kayakers, and canoeists may also access and use the river through the gorge.

Facilities: Vault toilets and information station at trailhead. Don't count on using the nearby picnic tables and toilets at Flatwoods picnic area. Current plans are to lock the gate and convert this area to reservations only. Additional trailheads with modern restrooms, picnic facilities, and pay phones are in the plans for the Guest River Gorge.

Closest town: Coeburn, 4 miles north of trailhead.

For more information: Clinch Ranger District, Jefferson National Forest, 9416 Darden Drive, Wise, VA 24293. Phone (540) 328-2931. Office located on VA 646 at Wise, across road from Clinch Valley College.

THE GUEST RIVER GORGE TRAIL. [Fig. 12(20)] Today the old railroad bed, a rails-to-trails conversion, provides a level, broad, 5.8-mile passageway through the scenic gorge where, as late as the 1980s, access was almost entirely limited to trains. A brochure on this self-guided trail is available at the trailhead or by writing the address above. Much of the trail will seem isolated from the rest of the world, but expect occasional heavy day use in the first .5 mile down to the railroad trestle across the Guest River. Local groups plan to build an exploratorium and hands-on museum, perhaps on one of the high cliffs overlooking the Guest River. Also in the plans are more access points and visitor conveniences such as restrooms and pay phones.

River and trail meander through forests of hardwoods and hemlock, above rapids and waterfalls, and past ancient rock formations carved by wind and water. At one point, the Guest River Gorge Trail goes though the old train tunnel, named Swede Tunnel. Three rebuilt wooden railroad trestles safely span the Guest River and Crab Orchard Creek and offer unique views. Along the trail, devil's walking stick (*Aralia spinosa*) is abundant. This large shrub has spines on both leaves and stems. A member of the ginseng family, it produces white flower heads in July and August. A moist streamside under hardwood canopy is its favorite habitat. The round trip to the

The gray squirrel (Sciurus carolinensis), *is one of the most commonly seen mammals of the southern Appalachians. It feeds primarily on nuts and serves an important role in propagating new trees because of its habit of burying nuts in the ground.*

Guest River's confluence with the Clinch and back to the trailhead takes about a half day, allowing time to stop and wet a lure or catch a crayfish.

Trail: 5.8 miles along abandoned railroad bed through a gorge 400 feet deep. The gentle path follows the twists and turns of the Guest River, a Virginia Scenic River.

Elevation: 1,500 to 2,000 feet. Although the trail and adjacent river drop only 500 feet, the massive boulders in the rushing water offer a challenge to kayakers and canoeists.

Degree of difficulty: Easy, since the trail follows an old railroad bed where grades were, of necessity, limited. From the trailhead near Coeburn to the trail's end where the Guest River flows into the Clinch River, the trip is a gentle, downhill trek. Coming back, of course, the grade is slightly uphill.

Surface: Gravel. Trail is wide and smooth. The first .5 mile, which goes through Swede Tunnel to the first trestle, is accessible to the handicapped.

DEVILS FORK TRAIL SYSTEM. [Fig. 12(21)] The soothing sound of water cascading over rocks. Quiet pools beneath virgin hemlocks. Expansive vistas from remote overlooks on Little Mountain. Rewards such as these await those who tackle the tough hikes of this trail system southwest of High Knob.

The Devils Bathtub Trail goes up Devils Fork along an old railroad grade once used for carrying logs and coal from the slopes of Little Mountain. As hikers cross back and forth across the stream, they pass through old growth hemlock stands, see a rusting, abandoned railroad car, and watch water racing down rock chutes and swirling through the rock tub that gives the trail its name.

After 1.5 miles, at the Devils Bathtub, the hiker can double back to the parking lot or continue westward, following the Devils Fork Loop Trail up Corder Hollow to a 20-foot waterfall, passing many hollows and beautiful views. After 4.2 miles (5.7 miles from the start), the loop trail connects with Straight Fork Ridge Trail. The hiker can go left on this trail for 1.8 miles up Little Mountain to the upper trailhead at FR 237, or go right 1.6 miles down the mountain to finish the loop at the parking lot.

The lack of facilities and the rugged terrain make this an ideal trail for those who like a more remote experience. Two primitive camping areas (no water) are available on the loop trail, one at the lower west end and one about .7 mile west of the connection with the Straight Fork Ridge Trail.

Directions: From Fort Blackmore, in central Scott County, go north on VA 619 for 2.9 miles to junction with VA 653. Continue north on VA 619 for 1.1 miles and turn left on FR 619 at white house with fenced yard and go .3 mile to trailhead parking. To access northern trailhead for Straight Fork Ridge Trail from VA 619 at High Knob, go southwest on FR 237 for 4 miles to trailhead.

Trails: Devils Bathtub Trail is 1.5-mile (one-way) path along old railroad grade, with 10 crossings of Devil Fork. Devils Loop combines Devils Bathtub Trail with 6-mile rigorous climb and descent on Little Mountain back to trailhead at parking lot. Straight Fork Ridge Trail leads from northeast point of Devils Fork Loop 2 miles up scenic ridge to FR 237 on Little Mountain.

Elevation: Lower trailhead is at 1,550 feet. Highest points are 2,000 feet on Devils Bathtub Trail, 2,800 feet on Devils Loop Trail, and 3,350 feet where Straight Fork Ridge Trail connects with FR 237.

Degree of difficulty: Moderate, with many stream crossings (which may be treacherous) on Devils Bathtub Trail, and moderate to difficult (because of steep sections) on Devils Loop and Straight Fork Ridge trails.

Surface: Natural forest floor with many stream crossings.

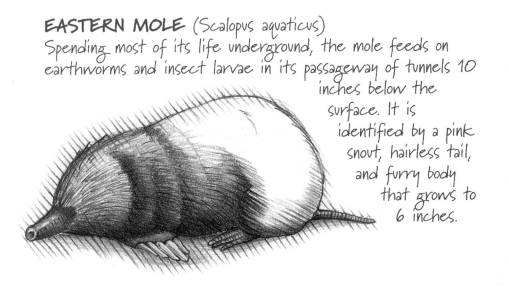

EASTERN MOLE (Scalopus aquaticus)
Spending most of its life underground, the mole feeds on earthworms and insect larvae in its passageway of tunnels 10 inches below the surface. It is identified by a pink snout, hairless tail, and furry body that grows to 6 inches.

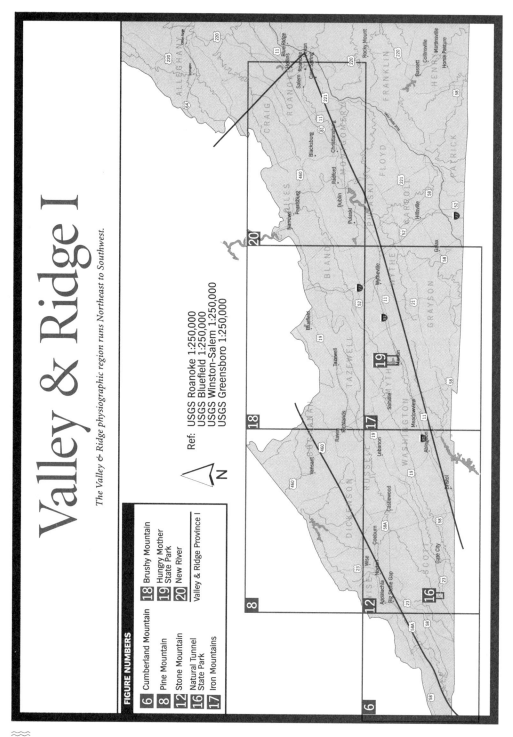

Valley & Ridge I

The Valley & Ridge physiographic region runs Northeast to Southwest.

Ref: USGS Roanoke 1:250,000
     USGS Bluefield 1:250,000
     USGS Winston-Salem 1:250,000
     USGS Greensboro 1:250,000

N

FIGURE NUMBERS

6	Cumberland Mountain	18	Brushy Mountain
8	Pine Mountain	19	Hungry Mother State Park
12	Stone Mountain	20	New River
16	Natural Tunnel State Park		Valley & Ridge Province I
17	Iron Mountains		

Valley and Ridge Province I

The Valley and Ridge physiographic region of Virginia is characterized by long, narrow mountain ranges running northeast/southwest, separated by river valleys. The province lies between the Appalachian Plateau to the west and the Blue Ridge Mountains to the east. Where the sedimentary layers of rock are exposed in the Valley and Ridge, they are often tilted and folded, unlike the horizontally stacked layers of the Plateau. However, visitors to the area about 450 million years ago might not have been able to tell the difference between the two provinces.

Layers of decaying marine life of ancient oceans were deposited uniformly over the basement granites and gneisses. When the African continental plate drifted into the North American plate, geologists theorize, land to the east—closer to the point of impact—buckled, forming waves of rock called anticlines and synclines. Sometimes, a stratified layer would break—or fault—creating a thrust fault, and rise over anoth-

[*Above*: Black bears are native to the Valley and Ridge Province]

er, leaving complex patterns of older rock on top of younger rock, and leaving geologists scratching their heads. Even after the passage of millennia, topo maps and aerial photos tell the story of long ridges suddenly curved into horseshoe shapes, or crumpled by adjacent mountains.

To further compound the puzzle, eroding winds and water acted on the layers at varying speeds, wearing away softer rock on mountaintops and depositing it in the valleys. Exposed ridges of erosion-resistant sandstone remain atop Clinch Mountain in southwest Virginia and Massanutten Mountain in the Shenandoah Valley. More easily erodible limestone soils settled in the valleys where they pro-

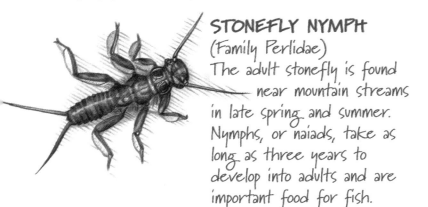

STONEFLY NYMPH
(Family Perlidae)
The adult stonefly is found near mountain streams in late spring and summer. Nymphs, or naiads, take as long as three years to develop into adults and are important food for fish.

duced fertile soils for farming. Slightly acidic water seeping through the limestone carved an estimated 2,500 underground caverns. Today, a handful of these caverns in the Shenandoah Valley offer guided tours. Caving groups explore the noncommercial, or "wild" caves.

Hikers on the trails in the Valley and Ridge may come upon fields of boulders at the base of slopes, if vegetation hasn't covered them over the years. As a result of the cooler temperatures of the last ice age, wedges of ice formed between sedimentary layers of rock. With repeated freezing and thawing, expanding and contracting, cracks formed. Finally, boulders split and tumbled from cliffs, creating boulderfields or, as geologists call them, talus slopes.

Along steep, rocky, south-facing slopes in the Valley and Ridge province are shale barrens. Often found where a meandering river has eaten into the hillside, these hostile environments support only the hardiest of plants, such as tenacious varieties of rock-cress (*Arabis*). (For more on shale barrens, see Johnson Creek Natural Area Preserve, page 150.) Northern hardwoods such as sugar maple (*Acer saccharum*), red maple, and yellow birch (*Betula lutea*) grow in higher elevations.

Only a few places in the Valley and Ridge of Virginia are high enough for an occasional patch of red spruce (*Picea rubens*), balsam fir (*Abies balsamea*), and other vegetation and wildlife more familiar to Canadians. Southern hardwoods, dominated by oak and hickory, forest the relatively dry lower slopes. In moist, dark hollows, lacy hemlock foliage shades rocky streams and rhododendron and wildflowers attract hikers. More open lowland streams, rivers, and wet areas are lined with sycamores, cottonwoods (*Populus deltoides*), silver maple (*Acer saccharinum*), and sweet gum (*Liquidambar styraciflua*).

Before early settlers hunted these forests, bison, elk, wolves, and mountain lions roamed the wilderness. Their memory lives in place names such as Elkhorn Lake, Buffalo Gap, and Wolf Creek. Now, larger wildlife include the black bear, white-tailed deer, wild turkey, and great blue heron.

When larger animals are nowhere to be seen, the forests are still full of smaller life. Crayfish hide beneath rocks in the streams. Salamanders are in damp areas under leaves and rocks. Flying squirrels, opossums, and raccoons visit campgrounds at night. By day, chipmunks skitter back and forth from their dens in the woods, and groundhogs grow fat and sassy in fields and on roadsides. Where vegetation is dense, the variety of morning birdsong can be astounding.

Totaling 1.8 million acres, the George Washington and Jefferson National Forests occupy parts of several major mountain ranges in the Valley and Ridge province. Owned by the public, most areas of the forest are open for hiking, camping, wading, wildlife watching, wildflower identification, photography, cross-country skiing, picnicking, and seasonal hunting and fishing.

Several state parks, natural areas, and wilderness areas provide their own unique windows to the Valley and Ridge. Highways and byways offer scenic drives, including many that have never received official scenic designation. Some of the best drives are the hairline county roads on maps, or forest service roads that skirt a wilderness or snake their way back and forth up one side of a mountain and down the other.

Local people enjoy being asked how little communities got their names—places such as Lick Skillet, Silent Dell, and Cracker Neck, or streams such as Alone Mill Creek and Purgatory Creek. The possibilities for becoming acquainted with Virginia's Valley and Ridge are everywhere. The only bounds are imagination and time.

In this book, the Valley and Ridge province is divided into three sections: Valley and Ridge I, Valley and Ridge II, and Valley and Ridge III. Valley and Ridge I is the southern portion of the province, beginning in the southwest corner of the state. It extends northeastward roughly along the same course as Interstate 81. Following the natural trend of the mountains through the Blacksburg Ranger District and Havens Wildlife Management Area, it ends at Roanoke and in the western corner of Craig County.

EASTERN WHITE PINE
(*Pinus strobus*)

Powell River Valley

The Powell River Valley spreads 30 miles across Virginia's southwestern corner. Defined by Cumberland and Stone mountains to the west, and Wallen Ridge and Powell Mountain to the east, the valley narrows as it stretches 60 miles northeast from the Tennessee border of Scott County into southern and western Wise County.

▓ POWELL RIVER

The Powell River, which helped carve the Powell River Valley, takes a leisurely trip through some of the most remote and rugged mountain country in Virginia. Beginning modestly at an altitude of 3,500 feet in the Plateau sandstone of western Wise County, the river gains strength and authority as it passes the coal towns of Norton and Appalachia. Then it churns through the pass it has carved between Stone and Little Stone mountains at Big Stone Gap [Fig. 12]. The Powell enters the Valley and Ridge province to make its own contribution to picturesque Powell Valley.

Paddlefish

Perhaps the strangest looking critter on the Powell's threatened list is the paddlefish (*Polyodon spathula*). The blue-gray to olive-gray fish grows to a length of 44 to 64 inches, and gets its name from a long, paddle-shaped snout. The paddlefish depends on clean gravel and clean water for spawning. It feeds by straining plankton and aquatic insects through its gills.

The shoving and jostling of land masses 250 to 300 million years ago created a curious fold at the northeastern end of Powell Valley that almost shut it off from the rest of the world. Framed by Little Stone Mountain on the northwest, Powell Mountain on the southeast, and Wallen Ridge to the south, the pastoral valley has an arrowhead shape, pointed toward Norton. So striking is the view, an overlook was created on the northbound side of US 23, 4 miles south of Norton.

At Big Stone Gap, the South Fork of the Powell River, emptying Big Cherry Reservoir from atop Powell Mountain, joins forces with the Powell River proper. The larger river squeezes between Stone Mountain and Wallen Ridge to enter Lee County and heads for the Tennessee line in the southwestern corner of Virginia, eventually to join the Tennessee River. Opportunities for recreation on public land lie in the navigable part of the Powell River and in the mountains that frame the valley (*see* Appalachian Plateau, p. 21). Also, a new natural area in Lee County is helping to protect a critical watershed.

▓ FISHING AND BOATING THE POWELL RIVER

Between Norton and Appalachia, look for signs along US 23 and Alternate 58 indicating where the Virginia Department of Game and Inland Fisheries has stocked trout. The trout fishing signs are white, and are posted to trees beside stocked streams and lakes in the mountains. A mining-related fish kill in 1996 drastically reduced fish populations in the North Fork of the Powell, which drains Stone Mountain and the Plateau area north of Pennington Gap. The game department will resume stocking when water quality is restored.

Below Big Stone Gap, the river becomes wide and slow enough for canoeing and kayaking. Anglers wade, fish from the bank, and put boats in at road crossings during the early spring spawning runs of the native sauger and walleye. Once this season is over, they revert to smallmouth bass, rock bass (redeye), and channel and flathead catfish. Most of the Powell is considered public waters, especially below Big Stone Gap, but public canoe and boat ramps do not exist.

A bridge crossing a river where a canoe or small boat can be slid into the water is a public access, and anglers and floaters do launch and take out at crossings such as US 58, Alternate 58, and VA 421, as well as several secondary roads. Above Big Stone Gap, wading is the preferred method of fishing. Below the city, on the 90-mile trip to the Tennessee state line, the Powell is well suited to floating. A good topo map may be necessary to locate launch sites.

Clinch River Valley, Clinch Mountain, and North Fork of Holston

The Clinch River gets its start near Tazewell, in Tazewell County. Helping it gain strength are many small tributaries draining steep hollows and ravines of coal country in the Appalachian Plateau of northwestern Tazewell County and northwestern Russell County.

Equally important, however, are the little streams and rivulets coming from the part of Tazewell County that's in the Valley and Ridge province—places such as the east slope of Burkes Garden, Thompson Valley, Paint Lick Mountain, and Knob Mountain. Born a hybrid—part Plateau coal country, part Valley and Ridge farming country—the Clinch then slows its pace. In Russell County, it comes into its own and begins the serious work of transporting to the Tennessee River the waters from northern Russell County, Scott County, and the southeastern slopes of Stone Mountain, Little Mountain, and Powell Mountain. South of Clinchport, in southern Scott County, Copper Creek adds clear, cold water to the Clinch from the eastern side of Copper Ridge and the western side of Moccasin Ridge.

Big Moccasin Creek and Little Moccasin Creek [Fig. 12(18)] drain the east side of Moccasin Ridge and the west slope of Clinch Mountain. The two creeks meet north of Gate City and cut through Clinch Mountain at Moccasin Gap, to join the languid North Fork of the Holston on its way into Tennessee and the Tennessee River.

Jefferson National Forest

Jefferson National Forest covers 690,000 acres.

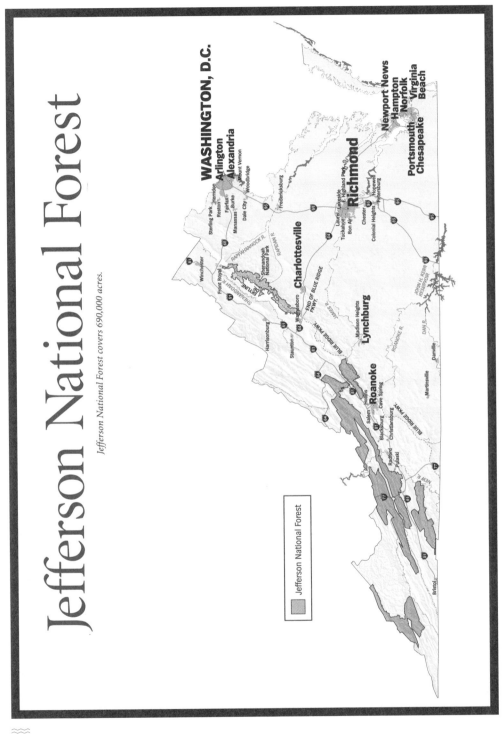

Jefferson National Forest

Ranger Districts in Jefferson National Forest

Jefferson National Forest has five ranger districts.

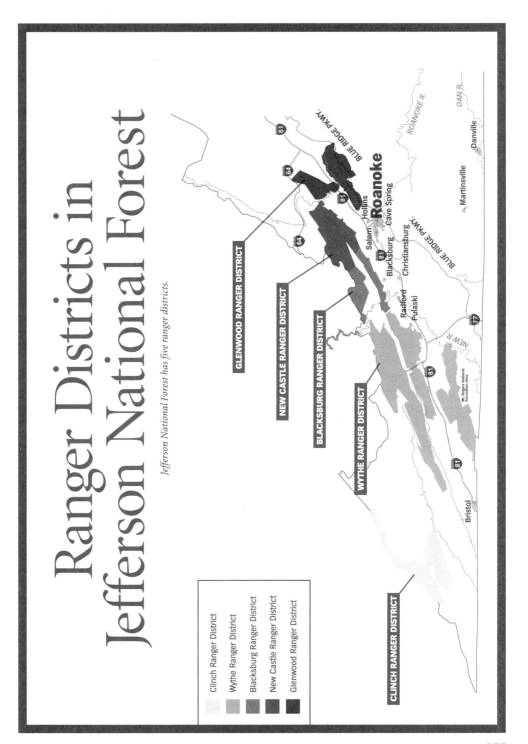

GLENWOOD RANGER DISTRICT

NEW CASTLE RANGER DISTRICT

BLACKSBURG RANGER DISTRICT

WYTHE RANGER DISTRICT

CLINCH RANGER DISTRICT

Clinch Ranger District
Wythe Ranger District
Blacksburg Ranger District
New Castle Ranger District
Glenwood Ranger District

FISHING AND FLOATING THE CLINCH RIVER

Known primarily for its stocked muskie (*Esox masquinongy*), the Clinch is also gaining a reputation for its stocked walleye (*Stizostedion vitreum*). Fish up to 9 pounds are showing up at scales. With an 11-inch to 14-inch slot limit, the river is improving as a smallmouth fishery.

The Clinch is considered navigable from the town of Richlands in Tazewell County to the Virginia/Tennessee line in Scott County. Therefore, boating is legal in that stretch, and the river is becoming popular with float fishermen and canoeists. The uppermost access point is on VA 80 at Blackford in Russell County. Boats may also be put in at Cleveland, Carterton, and St. Paul in Russell County; at Dungannon, Clinch River, and Clinchport in Scott County; and from VA 727 just north of the Tennessee line. Two of the put-ins—Dungannon and Clinchport—have launch ramps.

CLINCH MOUNTAIN

A landmark of southwest Virginia is the stiff backbone of Clinch Mountain. It enters Virginia from Tennessee in western Scott County, turns east briefly, then takes off to the northwest. From Moccasin Gap at Gate City, the ridgeline rises to 3,020 feet and is unbroken for its entire march to Tazewell County.

Clinch Mountain curves around Brumley Mountain, which abruptly rises from the valley floor on the Washington/Russell county border. The once straight-as-an-arrow ridge also bends like an anvil around Laurel Bed Lake. But from Gate City northward, Clinch Mountain allows no breach and doesn't lose its identity until it bumps into the strange bowl of Garden Mountain some 90 miles to the northeast in Tazewell County.

NORTH FORK OF THE HOLSTON RIVER

[Fig. 12] For its entire length in Virginia, Clinch Mountain has company. Starting as nothing more than a ditch in a Bland County field, the North Fork of the Holston River winds a sinewy path that roughly parallels Clinch Mountain all the way to Tennessee, as both river and mountain grow in strength.

FISHING THE NORTH FORK OF THE HOLSTON. Smallmouth bass anglers are in heaven floating the quiet, green waters of the North Fork of the Holston. The river routinely produces smallmouth up to 5 pounds in weight. Channel catfish keep fishermen down on the river at night, lanterns glowing. However, mercury contamination from a salt-mining operation upriver at Saltville in the early 1970s still has the river under a health advisory. Fishing is allowed, but fish should not be eaten.

CLINCH VALLEY BIORESERVE

[Fig. 6] The upper Tennessee River system of southwest Virginia and northeast Tennessee is, according to The Nature Conservancy, "one of the world's last great places." The private, nonprofit Conservancy has defined a 2,200-square-mile area across seven southwest Virginia counties and four northeast Tennessee counties as the Clinch Valley Bioreserve. Included are the watersheds of the Clinch, Powell, and Holston rivers, which form the headwaters of the major Tennessee River system. In Virginia, the boundaries stretch from Mount Rogers, in the Blue Ridge Mountains of eastern Smyth County, west to Cumberland Gap, where Virginia, Kentucky, and Tennessee meet. The defined area runs northeast into Tazewell and Bland counties to, but not including, Burkes Garden.

BROAD-WINGED KATYDID
(Microcentrum rhombifolium)
Heard more often than seen, these insects are named for their shrill song.

Such bioreserves contain outstanding examples of rare ecosystems, natural communities, and species deserving of protection. The focus differs from that of traditional nature preserves. Rather than attempting to protect endangered species at a specific site, the bioreserve has the broader goal of protecting an entire ecosystem.

In a bioreserve, the Conservancy identifies two areas: 1) core areas with habitat critical for rare species and 2) buffer areas, where water pollution, land development, invasion by non-native species, and other factors affect the health of the core area. Core areas may be set aside by traditional methods of purchasing land. In buffer areas, the Conservancy works in partnership with local people, businesses, governments, and agencies to meet human and economic needs while protecting fragile environmental areas such as watersheds.

The Virginia sections of the Clinch and Powell rivers are vital to the health of the Tennessee River system because the two rivers are the system's only undammed, unspoiled headwaters. Called "the most ecologically diverse region of Virginia," by the Conservancy, the river valleys contain more than 400 species of rare plants and animals, 22 of which are listed under the federal Endangered Species Act. The diversity is unmatched in the mid-Atlantic and northeastern United States.

Dependent on the swift waters of the Powell and Clinch are 16 species of rare fish such as the yellowfin madtom (*Noturus flavipinnis*), along with one of the world's richest concentrations of freshwater mussels. The number of mussel species identified here has dwindled from 60 to about 40. Of those, 26 are listed by the Conservancy as globally rare. At least 50 globally rare cave organisms, including beetles, spiders, flies, and other uncelebrated insects inhabit a network of some 1,250 caves beneath the rocky, porous

Freshwater Mussels

Most freshwater mussels live in runs and riffles on beds of cobble, gravel, sand, and silt, their existence dependent on water quality. But mussels themselves make a contribution to the water's purity with their method of filter-feeding. Adults spend their lives straining out silt, one-cell algae, microscopic animals, and debris. The combined work of entire beds of mussels can be significant downstream.

surface of the bioreserve. The endangered gray bat, Indiana bat (*Myotis sodalis*), and Virginia big-eared bat hang from the ceilings of various caves. So far, landowners have voluntarily agreed to register 16 biologically significant caves for some level of protection.

Past industrial mercury contamination on the North Fork of the Holston and cattle farming along the Middle Fork have degraded the Holston River's waters significantly. The river is included in the bioreserve not because of its current diversity, but for its potential for recovery and for its importance as part of the Tennessee Valley watershed.

The Natural Heritage Division of the Virginia Department of Conservation and Recreation (DCR) performs an important first step in the establishment of such bioreserves with an intensive inventory of the region's most significant natural elements. Both state and federal game and fish agencies also assist, boosted with research by academic and amateur naturalists. To protect the bioreserve, the Conservancy must come up with creative solutions to degradation from agriculture, mining, and other economic mainstays of the region. An example is the effort to restore riparian (stream bank) damage done by grazing cattle. Unfortunately, cattle are rough on stream banks. When native vegetation is trampled, banks erode and sediment and animal wastes wash downstream. Water quality deteriorates and stream life is threatened. In mountainous areas, such as the headwaters for Copper Creek, swift running waters can erode unprotected streambanks quickly. In porous areas such as the Central Lee County Karst, contaminated water goes underground and flows downstream unfiltered and unpurified, finding its way into wells and rivers. Funding from the U.S. Fish and Wildlife Service and the DCR Division of Soil and Water Conservation enables the Conservancy to work with farmers to build fences to keep livestock out of rivers, find alternate water sources for cattle, and restore native vegetation to stream banks.

The Conservancy has acquired six preserves in core areas of the Clinch Valley Bioreserve. The first acquired (1983) was Pendleton Island, a 35-acre preserve on the Clinch River in central Scott County, a couple of miles southwest of Fort Blackmore. With 40 species of mussels in the waters around three wooded isles, this stretch is called the richest 300 yards of mussel diversity on the planet. It is illegal to pocket so much as a single mussel shell from these waters.

Since 1983, five more preserves have been purchased. Gray's Island Preserve, just outside Dungannon in northern Scott County, includes 300 acres of prime farmland

and a stretch of the Clinch River with a significant mussel population. The Conservancy is selling farmland back to local farmers with restrictions to protect the river.

Four preserves, including one transferred to the state in 1997 as a Natural Area Preserve, are in the Central Lee County Karst (*see below*). In the karst is the last intact cedar limestone glades community in Virginia—a key component of the bioreserve. The Conservancy also worked with Russell County officials and the state DCR to set aside a rugged 200-acre tract called The Pinnacle as another Natural Area Preserve, now administered by the DCR. (*See* Pinnacle Natural Area Preserve, page 88.)

For more information: The Nature Conservancy, Clinch Valley Bioreserve, 102 South Court Street, Abingdon, VA 24210. Phone (540) 676-2209.

CENTRAL LEE COUNTY KARST

[Fig. 6(7)] Before the Powell River leaves the state, it dawdles its way through a limestone seepage called the Central Lee County Karst. Karsts are characterized by porous limestone with deep fissures, sinkholes, underground caves, and streams. Because of the networking of underground water, any stream or river pollution can be devastating to fragile stream and cave life in the entire area.

A portion of the karst called The Cedars lies in a type of pavementlike limestone called Hurricane Bridge. This part of the Clinch Valley Bioreserve is about 3 miles wide and extends from Jonesville some 10 miles southwest to the Tennessee line. Shallow, drought-prone soil on the rocky ground creates an opening in the forest called a limestone glade where specialized plant and animal life survive.

Running glade clover (*Trifolium calcaricum*) was found in the limestone glade eight years ago. The only other site where it is known to exist in the world is 200 miles away in Tennessee. Producing creamy-white blossoms with wine-colored veins in May, the running glade clover resembles common white lawn clover, though it is not closely related. It has long, trailing stems, or stolons, which run along the ground and put down additional roots. The endangered herbaceous plant prefers thinly wooded to open areas, and has been located in 24 places over a 5-square-mile area.

The Lee County cave isopod (*Lirceus usdagalun*), an endangered crustacean resembling a grain of rice with legs, is found in two caves in The Cedars and nowhere else in the world. The tiny, eyeless, unpigmented troglobyte, or cave-dweller, kept plans for a federal prison and a county airport at bay for two years until the projects were moved to other sites.

As it flows through the glade area, the Powell River offers protection to the threatened spiny riversnail (*Io fluvialis*), and three threatened species of fish, each only inches long. These include the slender chub (*Erimystax cahni*), emerald shiner (*Notropis atherinoides*), and western sand darter (*Ammocrypta clara*). The Conservancy acquired the following four preserves with habitat critical to rare and endangered species in the karst area.

None is developed for public access at this time.

THE CEDARS NATURAL AREA PRESERVE [Fig. 6(8)], a 50-acre tract at the northern end of the karst, was first purchased as a Nature Conservancy preserve in 1996. It was transferred by the Conservancy to the state in 1997 to become a Natural Area Preserve. This purchase is a good example of cooperation between agencies to protect such treasures. A bond referendum passed by voters for the acquisition of natural areas and state parks is providing the funds. Eventually, the Department of Conservation and Recreation which administers the preserve will buy additional land for interpretive trails and public parking.

The scrubby, rocky barrens and glades of the state's newest Natural Area Preserve lie on the southern side of US 58 west of Jonesville. From a distance, the stand of red cedars, which often serve as a marker for limestone soil, may seem unremarkable. But the same poor, shallow soil in which the cedars thrive, along with a few Virginia pine and chinquapin oak, also supports 16 rare plant species and provides habitat for the loggerhead shrike (*Lanium ludovicianus*). Once common in Virginia, the shrike is rare to uncommon in the state and declining rapidly. Insects are the shrike's main diet, but it will eat small birds, mammals, and amphibians when insects are scarce. Lacking talons, the shrike is known for sometimes impaling its victim on thorny plants or barbed wire.

UNTHANKS CAVE PRESERVE [Fig. 6(6)] is one of Virginia's largest and most biologically significant caves. It has an underground stream and 13 miles of mapped passageways that contain several rare cave organisms.

POWELL RIVER BLUFFS PRESERVE [Fig. 6(9)] consists of towering limestone bluffs harboring rare plants such as false aloe (*Manfreda virginica*) and pitcher's stitchwort (*Arenaria patula*). The preserve is doubly valuable for its frontage on the most productive mussel shoals of the Powell River.

EASTERN REDCEDAR
(*Juniperus virginiana*)
Cedar chests are made from the fragrant wood of this tree.

BEECH GROVE CLIFFS PRESERVE [Fig. 6(10)] includes 100 acres of open woodland interspersed with limestone glades. Five rare plants grow on the cliffs above the panorama of the Powell River Valley.

SNORKELING IN THE CLINCH RIVER VALLEY

Perhaps underrated as an outdoor activity, freshwater snorkeling is a wonderful way to cool off on a hot summer day while exploring the unfamiliar underwater world of mountain streams. Go to a sports or outfitting store. Spend at least $25 or $30 for a good mask that won't leak, and buy a snorkel. Locate a mountain stream or river that is fairly clear. Where highway bridges cross the water, public rights-of-way allow legal access. If the river is considered navigable, the entire riverbed is public land, so you can wade upriver or downriver without getting on someone's private property. Pick a place where the current is not too swift and the water no deeper than your arms are long. Wade out into the current, face upstream, and lie face down in the water, letting it support your body while you breathe through the snorkel. Use your hands on the bottom to pull yourself along. You'll be amazed at what you find.

Snorkeling will open a window to the fascinating life in the stream and among the rocks on the bottom. Some rocks may be covered with several varieties of snails. Various freshwater mussels may line the bottom. Minnows will rest in the eddies on the downstream side of rocks and boulders. A crayfish may pump itself backward from you with its powerful tail. Before long, you'll find yourself in a bookstore, looking for field guides to identify the plant life and critters that inhabit a stream. Snorkeling is a perfect outlet for a child's energy and natural curiosity. The importance of protecting streams from pollution and siltation will be obvious when they see firsthand how a mussel feeds.

Before you take any mussels home for a meal, check local restrictions. Collecting rare or endangered mussels from the Tennessee Valley watershed is illegal. Game wardens will not hesitate to ticket anyone violating the law.

NATURAL TUNNEL STATE PARK

[Fig. 16, Fig. 12(13), Fig. 13(16)] When William Jennings Bryan stood on a high cliff above Natural Tunnel more than 100 years ago, he declared in his finest stentorian voice that the 850-foot-long tunnel, carved by a cascading stream though limestone and dolomitic bedrock, ought to qualify as "the eighth wonder of the world."

More than 100 years earlier, Daniel Boone also came upon Natural Tunnel while scouting a route for his Wilderness Road to the frontier lands west of the Allegheny Mountains. But Boone, an unlettered and pragmatic man, left no Bryanesque pronouncements. Boone was looking for passes, or gaps, through the mountains, not evidence of a million years of natural water erosion and geologic plate grinding, impressive though such evidence might be.

Natural Tunnel today is the centerpiece of Virginia's Natural Tunnel State Park.

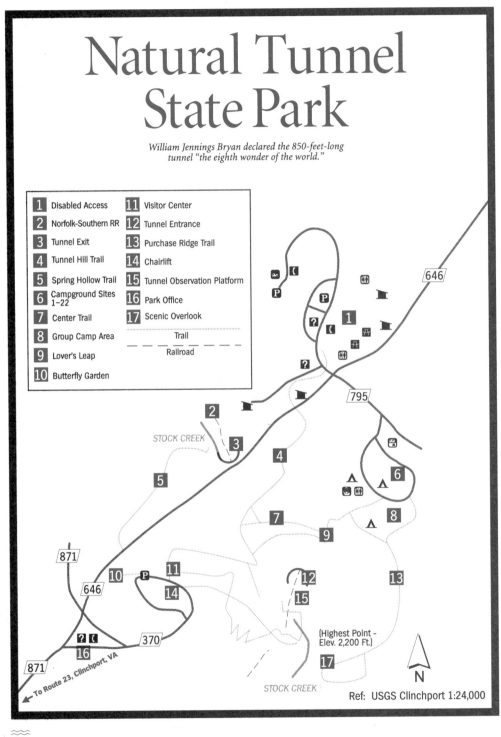

Natural Tunnel State Park

William Jennings Bryan declared the 850-feet-long tunnel "the eighth wonder of the world."

1	Disabled Access	11	Visitor Center
2	Norfolk-Southern RR	12	Tunnel Entrance
3	Tunnel Exit	13	Purchase Ridge Trail
4	Tunnel Hill Trail	14	Chairlift
5	Spring Hollow Trail	15	Tunnel Observation Platform
6	Campground Sites 1–22	16	Park Office
7	Center Trail	17	Scenic Overlook
8	Group Camp Area		Trail
9	Lover's Leap		Railroad
10	Butterfly Garden		

STOCK CREEK

646

795

871

646

370

871

To Route 23, Clinchport, VA

(Highest Point - Elev. 2,200 Ft.)

N

STOCK CREEK

Ref: USGS Clinchport 1:24,000

Though half hidden in the rugged mountain folds of southwest Virginia in Scott County, the tunnel and its surroundings have stirred the imaginations of naturalists, geologists, and other visitors since the area was first visited and described by Lt. Col. Stephen H. Long in 1831. The 850-acre park surrounding Natural Tunnel today is designed to help visitors savor the relentless power of natural forces. Seven hiking trails, some with breathtaking views, crisscross the area. A modern, suspended chair ride, similar to a ski lift, does away with the need for a 530-foot climb down a foot trail to the tunnel entrance. The chair lift and observation deck above Stock Creek, which helped carve the tunnel from surrounding limestone, also accommodate the handicapped. Watch as many as 20 Norfolk Southern trains rumble through Natural Tunnel daily, still hauling coal to power plants of the Southeast.

In spring, a variety of wildflowers such as columbine (*Aquilegia canadensis*), jack-in-the-pulpit (*Arisaematriphyllum*), and fire pink (*Silene virginica*) bloom throughout the park. American beech (*Fagus grandiolia*) and tulip poplar shade the forest floor in summer. Autumn is a blaze of color as hardwoods turn rust, red, yellow, and gold. Canby's mountain lover (*Pachistima canbyi*), a rare wildflower, grows on the park grounds.

Natural Tunnel State Park is also one of the premier karst areas of the state, according to Craig Seaver, park manager. An untold number of holes, caves, and underground caverns lie in the sedimentary carbonate dolostone (similar to limestone, but with a magnesium component) and siliciclastic (comprised mostly of clay and quartz) rocks in the area. Even on the drive to the park from Gate City along US 23, road cuts have exposed fault lines and layers of twisted rock that were once an ocean floor. Seaver compares the mounded shape of some rocks to the appearance of sand mounded up on a beach by wave action.

The park vicinity is pocked with sink holes. A sink hole is a circular hole, from a couple of feet to a mile across, where an underground cavern has collapsed. Residents of the area used to try to fill these "sinks" with everything from garbage to junk cars until they learned they were despoiling their own springs, wells, and water supplies. A new hiking trail will soon lead to a sink hole at Rye Cove at the park's upper end.

Interpreting the area's natural history is a focus of guided hikes and tours to the mouth of the tunnel for a firsthand look at how an underground river can sculpt solid rock over hundreds of thousands of years. The stratified rock of Natural Tunnel belongs to what is called the Knox group (named for rock first exposed at Knoxville, Tennessee). It was laid down during the early Paleozoic Era, during the Ordovician and Cambrian periods. The Knox group carbonates contain fossils of algae that were plentiful 500 million years ago—some 270 million years before dinosaurs walked the earth.

The tunnel was once thought to be the uncollapsed remains of a large cave system. Modern geologic evidence, however, does not support this theory. The tunnel and creek are positioned along what is called the Glenita fault, a zone of structural weakness between the gently folded Rye Cove syncline, or downfold, on the east, and the more tightly folded Purchase Ridge syncline to the southwest.

The Glenita fault is evident a few feet above the north opening into the tunnel, and it is visible to the west and south through the wooded bluffs between the tunnel and VA 871. Because of the many fractures along the fault zone, circulating ground waters are better able to dissolve the deformed rocks. The gradual erosion (wearing away) and solution (dissolving) of rock that resulted in the formation of Natural Tunnel is a long and complex process. Geologists with the Virginia Division of Mineral Resources now believe a large sink developed in the ground above the present tunnel near the north portal. The waters of Stock Creek seeped from above into the sink, descending underground to about the current level of the creek. The water then flowed southward and rose from the depths to emerge as a spring near the south portal. Because the rock strata happened to be relatively horizontal here, it could support the great weight of the span that developed.

As the sink gradually grew larger, the cascading waters of Stock Creek, laced with abrasive grains of quartz sand and gravel, carved a steep valley below the tunnel. Visitors today can witness the spectacular result—a semicircular amphitheater, comprised almost entirely of sedimentary carbonate rock, that towers above Stock Creek. The park also has a 2,000-seat, man-made amphitheater, which is the setting not only for programs about the park, but for traveling troupes and entertainment groups as well.

Wild caving is another new offering at Natural Tunnel. Visitors with a thirst for adventure can don hard hats, coveralls, boots, and head lamps such as those used by miners. Park naturalists lead the way beneath the surface to a limestone cave with stalactites and stalagmites.

The modern visitor center [Fig. 16(11)] houses wildlife displays, exhibits on the formation of Natural Tunnel, samples of fossilized marine life from the tunnel walls, and relics from the early days of the tunnel railroad.

Directions: From Gate City in southern Scott County, travel 13 miles north on US 23/58. Or from Big Stone Gap in southern Wise County, travel 15 miles south on US 23. Then go east on VA 871 1 mile to park entrance.

Activities: Hiking, camping, picnicking, swimming, caving, guided hikes, interpretive programs, swimming, canoe trips.

Facilities: 7 hiking trails, 29 tent or RV campsites with grills and tables, restrooms, hot showers, dump station, large picnic area with grills, 4 picnic shelters, large amphitheater, visitor center, gift shop, chairlift, 5,400-square-foot swimming pool with bath house and concession, playground. No alcoholic beverages or firearms allowed. Pets permitted, but must be on leash or kept in enclosed area. Park plans to build an outdoor center in the future.

Dates: Open year-round. Pool: open Memorial Day–Labor Day. Campground: open Mar.–Dec. Chairlift: open weekends only May, Sept., Oct.; Memorial Day–Labor Day, daily.

Fees: A fee is charged for parking, tent sites, chairlift, swimming.

For more information: Superintendent, Natural Tunnel State Park, Route 3, Box 250, Duffield, VA 24244. Phone (540) 940-2674.

Closest town: Duffield is 5 miles north on US 23 (limited services). Gate City is 13 miles south on US 23, and offers grocery stores, laundromat, service stations, restaurants, motels, and churches.

BUTTERFLY GARDEN OF NATURAL TUNNEL STATE PARK. [Fig. 12(14), Fig. 16(10)] Sweet smells wafting by visitors' noses at Natural Tunnel are likely from the butterfly garden started in 1996. Guests may follow their noses—or perhaps a spicebush swallowtail—to the colorful area at the end of the parking lot adjacent to the visitor center. There, the southwest Virginia Master Gardeners surprise even the park superintendent with the success of the flowers they planted to attract butterflies. Among the 35 varieties are sweet alyssum (*Lobularia*), butterfly-weed (*Asclepias*), blanket flower (*Giallardia*), larkspur (*Delphinium*), day-lily (*Hemerocallis*), bee-balm (*Monarda*), catnip (*Nepeta*), and lavender (*Lavandula*).

Volunteer groups such as the Master Gardeners are responsible for a great deal of landscaping, trail building and clearing, and other work at Virginia's state parks.

HIKING TRAILS OF NATURAL TUNNEL STATE PARK. The park's seven trails are not long, but by interconnecting them, hikers can manage a 3- or 4-mile hike with several views of the tunnel and precipitous gorge. The trails have been improved with paved walkways, railings, steps, and benches.

Five trails are basically level, as mountain trails go. The Purchase Ridge Trail [Fig. 12(15), Fig. 16(13)] however, climbs 1.1 miles to 2,200 feet, the park's highest point. The climb is strenuous at times, but the reward is a scenic overlook of the tunnel from afar. The .3-mile Tunnel Trail [Fig. 12(16), Fig. 16(4)] is easy as it leads down into the gorge for a close view. However, if the tunnel doesn't take guests' breath away, the short but steep climb back up will. The .4-mile Lover's Leap Trail [Fig. 12(17), Fig. 16(9)] has an accompanying brochure to guide you through the area's history as you walk the woods above the tunnel.

TIGER SWALLOWTAIL

(*Papilio glaucus*)
This butterfly takes its name from its yellow wings with black tigerlike stripes. The female's wings are brownish-black in its dark phase.

PINNACLE NATURAL AREA PRESERVE

[Fig. 12(9)] This place is a naturalist's dream. It has a little bit of everything. Towering above Big Cedar Creek are dramatic cliffs and ledges. As background music to the drilling of a pileated woodpecker, the creek glides across gentle riffles, hesitates in smooth pools, and tumbles over an impressive cascade as it searches out the Clinch River.

The 200 acres of Pinnacle Natural Area Preserve are home to a rich assortment of natural communities—cove woodlands, riverine plants, limestone cliff vegetation, ridgetop glades, and high-gradient streams. Nine rare animal species and 12 rare plants have been identified at the preserve. The paths you walk at the Pinnacle very likely were the same paths walked by Indians who once lived here, say archeologists.

The Pinnacle was formerly managed by Russell County as Big Cedar Creek Park. Recognizing the fragile nature of the area, county supervisors conveyed the property to The Nature Conservancy in 1989 for temporary protection until the site was taken into the state's system of natural area preserves. It is now managed by the Department of Conservation and Recreation as a satellite of Hungry Mother State Park. The DCR has recently acquired more land surrounding the Pinnacle to allow for recreation and to provide a buffer to the preserve's more sensitive areas.

The calcium-rich bedrock of Pinnacle Natural Area Preserve has eroded to produce fertile soils on slopes below dolomite and limestone ledges. The presence in the soil of magnesium, the component in dolomite that differentiates it from limestone, has a subtle though significant effect on the vegetation. Unusual ferns and wildflowers—the kind you won't find in most identification books—thrive in these conditions. Smooth cliff-brake (*Pellaea atropurpurea*), northern prickly ash (*Zanthoxylum americanum*), and Carey's saxifrage (*Saxifraga careyana*) are among the varieties. Saxifrage, a relative of the rose family, is a plant of cool mountains and rocky places. Its leaves often form a rosette or cluster at the base. Dolomite glades such as the one at the Pinnacle usually grow on steep, south-facing slopes, and frequently contain one or more globally rare plant species. The federally endangered glade spurge (*Euphorbia* sp.) and Canby's mountain lover grow here.

The waters of Big Cedar Creek, which drain the northwest slope of Clinch Mountain Wildlife Management Area and part of Moccasin

HELLBENDER
(*Cryptobranchus alleganiensis*)

The hellbender grows to 29 inches.

Ridge, are cold enough to support a trout fishery and are in the state's regular trout stocking program. Beneath the creek surface, however, lies magic beyond beautiful trout. This relatively pristine stream makes its own contribution to the rare mussels of the Clinch and other southwest Virginia rivers that are part of the upper Tennessee River drainage.

The endangered birdwing pearlymussel (*Lemiox rimosus*) dwells in shallow riffles of fast-flowing streams such as this one. The impact of coal mining on water quality and the invasion of foreign zebra mussels threaten its existence, even here. This mollusk grows to about 2 inches long and has a dark green outer shell.

With a mask and snorkel, a person wading Big Cedar can peek beneath the surface for a possible encounter with the locally rare spiny soft-shell turtle (*Trionyx spiniferus*), the globally rare spiny riversnail, or the hellbender (*Cryptobranchus alleganiensis*). At 18 inches long, the hellbender is one of the largest salamanders in the world. Though it would never win a beauty contest, this resident of clear Appalachian streams is harmless to man. Fishermen may occasionally curse it for stealing bait, but the hellbender feeds mainly on crayfish.

A foraging skunk may nose into a rotten log to send the Big Cedar Creek millipede (*Brachoria falcifera*) scurrying for cover. Unlike centipedes, which have one pair of legs on each body segment, the slower-moving and smaller millipedes have two pairs of legs on each segment. If the skunk is quick enough, he'll have this globally rare millipede for lunch. Protection of rare and endangered species is of prime importance at Pinnacle Natural Area Preserve. Stay on trails and keep pets on a leash to avoid damaging fragile wildflowers and plants. All plant and wildlife species here are protected by law and should not be disturbed.

Be careful of slippery rocks, especially around waterfalls. Diving in unfamiliar water is very dangerous.

Directions: From Lebanon, in south-central Russell County, take VA 82 north about 1 mile and turn right on VA 640. Go 4 miles and turn left on gravel road VA 721, which leads across a low-water bridge to the parking lot (and waterfall) at Big Cedar Creek. There are times of high water when you won't be able to cross the low-water bridge to enter the Pinnacle area. If in doubt, check with rangers at Hungry Mother State Park (*see* Hungry Mother State Park, p. 105).

Activities: Hiking, swimming, snorkeling, fishing, picnicking.

Facilities: None.

Dates: Open year-round. High water and winter snow and ice may make access impossible.

Fees: None.

Closest town: Lebanon is 7 miles southwest.

For more information: Hungry Mother State Park, Route 5, Box 109, Marion, VA 24354. Phone (540) 783-3422.

HIKING TRAILS AT PINNACLE NATURAL AREA PRESERVE. [Fig. 12(9)] Since protection of rare communities of plants and animals is the focus here, trails have not been a priority. However, a network of nameless trails was built by the Young Adult Conservation Corps in 1978. The trails run along the banks of Big Cedar Creek and the Clinch River and climb to a scenic overlook atop Copper Ridge, where there is a view of the Pinnacle and below, the stream.

As hikers ascend, they will pass through a ridgetop glade community of rare, fragile plants with unusual names such as American harebell (*Campanula rotundifolia*), tufted hair grass (*Deschampsia caespitosa*), Canby's mountain lover, and white camas (*Zigadenus glaucus*).

Trails: Network of paths along creek and river and ascending to the Pinnacle.

Elevation: 1,600 feet at river to 2,400 feet at the Pinnacle.

Degree of difficulty: Easy to moderate.

CARTER FOLD

[Fig. 12(19)] Tucked into the shadow of Clinch Mountain at Hiltons is a rustic building called the Carter Fold, where old-time acoustic mountain music still rings down the hollows every Saturday night. The weekly event is sponsored by the family of Mother Maybelle Carter and June Carter Cash of country music fame. Shows begin at 7:30 p.m.

Directions: Hiltons is on US 58 in southeastern Scott County, about 5 miles north of Weber City.

Fees: A fee is charged for admission.

For more information: The Carter Family, PO Box 111, Hiltons, VA 24258. Phone (540) 386-9480.

HIDDEN VALLEY WILDLIFE MANAGEMENT AREA

[Fig. 12(1)] Discovering a forest-green fishing lake atop steep and wild Brumley Mountain is akin to finding an emerald in a haystack. Brumley abruptly rises from the valley floor, interrupting the northwest/southeast line cut by Clinch Mountain. On the mountain's flat top, the Virginia Department of Game and Inland Fisheries manages 6,400 acres for wildlife. Brumley Creek has been dammed in narrow Hidden Valley to form a high-country lake that harbors walleye, smallmouth bass, rock bass, and bluegill. A boat ramp on the north side provides access, but the open banks make casting easy for the angler without a boat.

Area fishermen and hunters use the area, but largely undiscovered is its potential as a place to watch wildlife, identify songbirds, and photograph spectacular scenery in a setting far from the crowds that prefer more developed areas. Migrating hawks and other birds of prey sometimes settle in the protected high valley overnight, but fall-migrating, southbound birds of prey are more visible at Clinch Mountain Wildlife Management Area 25 miles to the northeast (*see* Clinch Mountain Wildlife

Management Area, p. 93).

Visitors should wear blaze orange during fall or winter hunting seasons and bring clothes suitable to the cooler temperatures and unpredictable weather changes of high elevations. Elevations at Hidden Valley exceed 4,000 feet. Topo maps and a compass are helpful when exploring the estimated 10 miles of trails in the unmarked backcountry. Two of the more popular trails lead out of the parking lot at the Wildlife Management Area (WMA) entrance. They provide panoramic views of the Clinch Mountain ridge to the southeast. No developed campgrounds are available, but camping is allowed throughout the forest, as long as campsites are 100 yards away from the lake. Stays are limited to 14 consecutive days.

Beaver

The sudden slap on the water is probably the resident beaver (*Castor canadensis*) sounding a warning with its broad, flat tail. This large, nocturnal rodent, prized for its fur, was once trapped out of much of its former range. With protection, the beaver is staging a comeback in Virginia.

The cover of mixed hardwoods, including white and red oaks, yellow birch, American beech, and hickory is home to white-tailed deer, black bear, wild turkey, ruffed grouse, gray squirrel, and cottontail rabbit. Hunters should check the Virginia Department of Game and Inland Fisheries for regulations, which change yearly, and may vary from those of surrounding Washington County.

Evergreen hemlocks and rhododendron thickets shade the moist, deep ravines and hang over the lake on the south side. In places, including a patch along the road on the far end of the lake, just before you get to the dam, the rhododendrons have grown quite large. Profuse running cedar adds its own carpet of green throughout the year. Ducks and waterfowl are attracted to the boggy upper end of the lake where aquatic vegetation and stumps of flooded trees offer food and cover. Beaver sign is often visible here, too.

Directions: From Abingdon, in Washington County, follow US 19/Alternate US 58 approximately 8 miles north, and turn to right on VA 690. Go 2.4 miles on VA 690 to parking area at a fork in the road. To reach the lake, go 1 mile on the left fork and turn right.

Activities: Fishing, boating, hunting, hiking.

Facilities: Lake with launch ramp. Hiking trails.

Dates: Open year-round unless inaccessible due to bad weather.

Closest town: Abingdon is approximately 8 miles away.

For more information: WMA work station (early and late in day), phone (540) 944-3434. Virginia Department of Game and Inland Fisheries, Region III Office, Route 1, Box 107, Marion, VA 24354. Phone (540) 782-9051. Or, VDGIF Headquarters, 4010 West Broad Street, Richmond, VA 23230. Phone (804) 367-1000. For questions about boating or law enforcement, phone (540) 783-4860.

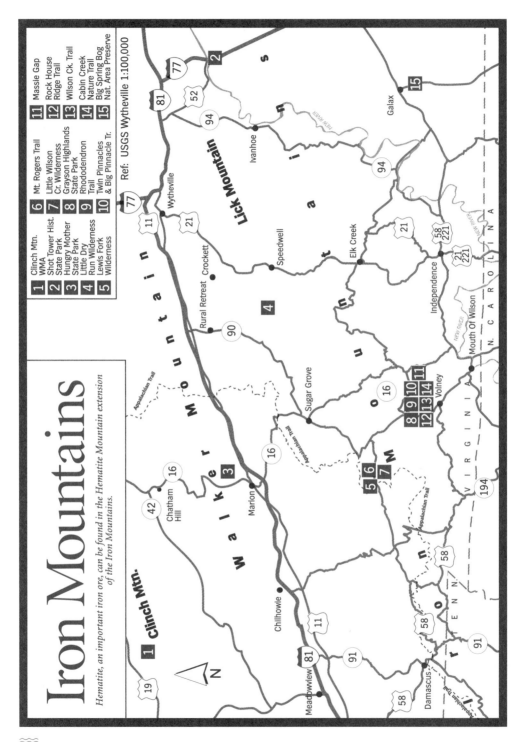

Iron Mountains

Hematite, an important iron ore, can be found in the Hematite Mountain extension of the Iron Mountains.

N

1 Clinch Mtn.

Ref: USGS Wytheville 1:100,000

1	Clinch Mtn. WMA	**6**	Mt. Rogers Trail
2	Shot Tower Hist. State Park	**7**	Little Wilson Cr. Wilderness
3	Hungry Mother State Park	**8**	Grayson Highlands State Park
4	Little Dry Run Wilderness	**9**	Rhododendron Trail
5	Lewis Fork Wilderness	**10**	Twin Pinnacles & Big Pinnacle Tr.
11	Massie Gap		
12	Rock House Ridge Trail		
13	Wilson Ck. Trail		
14	Cabin Creek Nature Trail		
15	Big Spring Bog Nat. Area Preserve		

SCENIC DRIVES

Getting from Hidden Valley Wildlife Management Area (WMA) to Clinch Mountain WMA has its own rewards.

Take VA 689, VA 80, and VA 613 through Poor Valley, which lies on the southeastern flank of Clinch Mountain and is separated from Rich Valley (to the south) by Little Mountain. The pleasant drive through this tiny, picturesque valley follows the West Fork then the East Fork of Wolf Creek.

Parallel backroads on the south side of Little Mountain (VA 611, then VA 91 and VA 42) in the Holston River watershed are also recommended. None is an official scenic byway. Maybe the valley was too pretty to pick just one.

Directions: From VA 690 at Hidden Valley WMA, turn left (south) onto US 19 and go 1.5 miles. Turn right on VA 689 and go about 4 miles to Hayters Gap. Go left (north) on VA 80 about 1.75 miles and take VA 613 northeast 4 miles. Go left on VA 790 to ascend Clinch Mountain.

CLINCH MOUNTAIN WILDLIFE MANAGEMENT AREA

[Fig. 17(1)] Clinch Mountain Wildlife Management Area (WMA), the second largest WMA in Virginia, is also the state's most biologically diverse. The steep rise from the valley floor at 1,600 feet to the highest peak of 4,700 feet is the primary reason for the diversity. At lower elevations, southern hardwoods—trees more typical of north Georgia—prevail, along with related bird and animal life. These trees include white oak, American beech, sweet gum, black gum, sourwood, and various hickories. At higher elevations, look for the peeling, pale-yellow bark of abundant yellow birch. Also, there's Eastern hemlock, sugar maple (which turns bright red in fall), American beech, pitch pine, table mountain pine, Virginia pine, and northern red oak.

Four counties—Washington, Russell, Tazewell, and Smyth—lay claim to parts of the WMA's 25,477 acres. The entrance road on Short Mountain along Big Tumbling Creek lies in the northern tip of Washington County. Big Tumbling Creek, two smaller creeks, and Laurel Bed Lake are popular with area anglers for good reason. During a fee-fishing season, the Virginia Department of Game and Inland Fisheries (VDGIF) stocks them daily (except Sunday) with hatchery-raised trout. Fishing permits are on sale at the concession stand on the entrance road.

Fisherman cast nightcrawlers, meal worms, flies, or spinners for trout along these canopied streambanks, where icy water cascades over ledges and forms clear pools. Big Tumbling Creek is a tempting place to pull over on a warm spring afternoon and introduce a youngster to the pleasures of wading a cold stream in pursuit of the colorful rainbow trout.

Northeast of the entrance road, in Russell County, Clinch Mountain has a butterfly-shaped plateau called Beartown Mountain. At 4,700 feet, Beartown is the WMA's highest point, rising more than 3,000 feet above the valley floor. Southern hardwoods give way to northern hardwoods here, even patches of red spruce. The picturesque evergreen with its ragged dark green spires is a favorite subject in paintings of alpine meadows. On a lower plateau, to the east of Beartown and still in Russell County, the waters of Laurel Bed Creek have been dammed to form 300-acre Laurel Bed Lake. Although more than 1,000 feet lower than Beartown Mountain, the lake is plenty high enough to be suitable temporary cold-water habitat for the brook trout that are stocked. The season extends from mid-March to Labor Day, but the fishing is best in spring, when limits of six trout are common.

Like many mountain lakes and streams, the waters of Laurel Bed Lake gradually became too acidic to support trout on a long-term basis. In 1996, biologists worked to raise the pH levels with a liming project, which included using a helicopter to place limestone sand into the stream above the lake. After restoring the proper balance, biologists continue to stock catchable-size trout for current seasons. In addition, they are stocking fingerling brook trout in the lake each year (beginning in fall of 1997). The biologists hope the fish will feed naturally on lake forage and grow to trophy size, returning Laurel Bed to the premier fishery it was in the past.

Gasoline motors are not allowed, but a big-muscled bass boat would be an overstatement on quiet Laurel Bed Lake anyway. There are two launch ramps for putting in canoes, kayaks, or john boats for a quiet paddle along the shoreline.

Visitors may have to throw a branch out of the trail or climb over a fallen tree now and then to hike the narrow footpaths of the rugged mountain country. Old logging roads and a narrow gauge railroad bed also provide good access to hunters, hikers, mountain bikers, and horseback riders. Hikes may lead visitors into the backcountry of Tazewell or Smyth counties. By their very nature, WMAs are more primitive than state parks, but they offer a fine place to see a variety of habitats and wildlife. A topo map and compass are helpful guides in this undeveloped country.

Black bear, white-tailed deer, wild turkey, gray squirrel, cottontail rabbit, ruffed grouse, groundhog, raccoon, waterfowl, and nongame species as well, benefit from the state's management activities at Clinch Mountain. These management activities include mowing and burning over 500 acres of clearings and trails; planting shrubs to provide edge cover; thinning thick growths of trees and shrubs to allow food-producing types such as oak, apple, thornapple, and walnut to grow; planting strips of native warm-season grasses; and regenerating forests through firewood cuttings and saw timber harvest.

Crayfish

This diminutive and tasty relative of the lobster feeds at night. Its diet consists mostly of plants and occasionally animal life that it tears apart with its pincers. During the day, the crayfish hides beneath river rocks or in a burrow. In soft ground beside the river, a chimney of tiny mudballs gives away the presence of such a burrow.

Beavers have cut trees in many places, damming creeks and opening the forest canopy to increased sunlight. The creation of ponds and wetlands has attracted aquatic wildlife such as waterfowl, muskrats, frogs, turtles, water snakes, and the animals that prey on them. Rushes, sedges, and shrubby growth have replaced the hardwoods. Fifty wood duck nesting boxes are maintained by the Virginia Department of Game and Inland Fisheries. Plans include an ambitious bluebird box program and the refurbishing of tree swallow houses along Laurel Bed Lake.

The tree swallow (*Iridoprocne bicolor*) has an unusual habit that resembles play. The agile bird with blue-green back, forked tail, and white underparts seems to enjoy carrying a feather into the air, dropping it, and diving to catch it as it falls. The great blue heron and solitary sandpiper fish the shallows. Pied-billed grebes, black ducks, and buffleheads may stop to restock the larder on their fall migrations.

Directions: From junction of VA 107 and VA 91 in Saltville, in northwestern Smyth County, go south on VA 91 .25 mile. Turn right (north) on VA 634. Go about 1 mile and bear left on VA 613 and continue 3.5 miles. Go right on VA 747 and follow this road into the WMA.

Activities: Fishing, boating, hunting, archery, hiking, camping, horseback riding, mountain biking.

Facilities: Trout-stocked streams and 300-acre lake, two boat ramps, archery targets, and access roads and rough trails for hiking and horseback riding. For camping, 22 open sites with tables, grills, hand water pump, and pit toilets. Seasonal snack bar.

Dates: Foot travel, open year-round. Main access gate closed to vehicular traffic annually, second Sat. in Sept.–first Sat. in Apr. Fee fishing first Sat. in Apr.–Sept. Hunting seasons vary annually and according to species, but most occur in fall. Check VDGIF for dates. Camping permitted year-round (up to 14 consecutive days). Only backcountry camping permitted during hunting season.

Fees: Admission is free; a fee is charged for trout fishing (during fee period, state license required during nonfee period) and camping.

Closest town: Saltville, 7 miles southeast.

For more information: WMA work station (early and late in day), phone (540) 944-3434. Virginia Department of

EASTERN CRAYFISH

Game and Inland Fisheries, Region III Office, Route 1, Box 107, Marion, VA 24354. Phone (540) 782-9051. Or, VDGIF Headquarters, 4010 West Broad Street, Richmond, VA 23230. Phone (804) 367-1000.

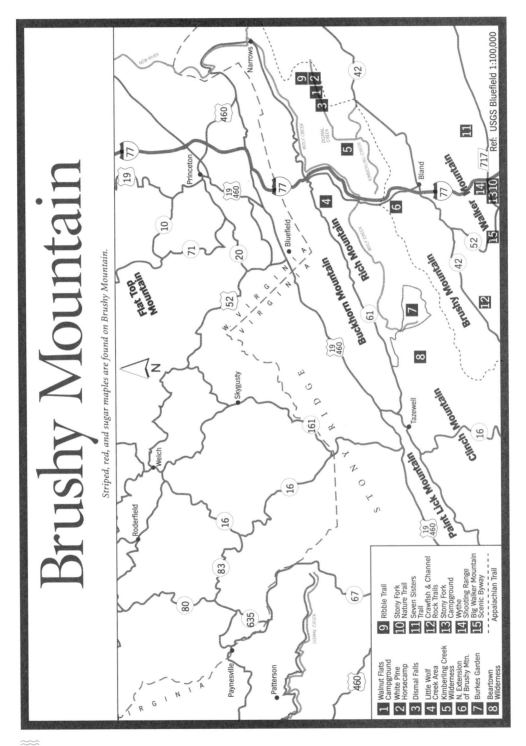

Brushy Mountain

Striped, red, and sugar maples are found on Brushy Mountain.

Ref: USGS Bluefield 1:100,000

Legend:

1. Walnut Flats Campground
2. White Pine Horsecamp
3. Dismal Falls
4. Little Wolf Creek Area
5. Kimberling Creek Wilderness
6. N. Extension of Brushy Mtn.
7. Burkes Garden
8. Beartown Wilderness
9. Ribble Trail
10. Stony Fork Nature Trail
11. Seven Sisters Trail
12. Crawfish & Channel Rock Trails
13. Stony Fork Campground
14. Wythe Shooting Range
15. Big Walker Mountain Scenic Byway
- - - Appalachian Trail

Burkes Garden Area

▓ BURKES GARDEN

[Fig. 18(7)] Few people ever stumble upon Burkes Garden by accident. A topo map or relief map will make clear the reason why. The pastoral community—10 miles long and 4.5 miles wide—is surrounded by bowl-shaped Garden Mountain.

Several other mountains butt up against Garden Mountain, making access even more difficult. Contributing to seal off Burkes Garden from the rest of the world are Rich, Clinch, Little Brushy, Brushy, and Round mountains. At 3,100 feet, the elevation of Burkes Garden gives it claim to the title "highest valley in Virginia." The mountains around it rise to 4,408 feet on the ridge of Beartown Wilderness. If a visit brings you here on a sweltering July day, you may think fall has come when you feel temperatures in the valley as much as 15 degrees Fahrenheit lower than outside.

The ridges of Garden Mountain are made of erosion-resistant sandstone, while the material that once filled the valley was highly erodible limestone and shale. Much of the limestone and shale, eroding over the millennia, gradually disappeared through a canyon on the north side, and some has dissolved in the waters that sink beneath the porous base. The same canyon that drained material from the bowl is almost blocked by Rich Mountain. Burkes Garden Creek, carrying water from the many mountain springs that nourish the valley, manages to thread its way through the canyon, turning right at Rich Mountain. There it joins Little Creek to form Wolf Creek, part of the New River drainage.

Burkes Garden lies within the boundaries of southern Tazewell County, but to keep the community in the county, the Tazewell boundary has to bulge into Bland County. In fact, the Bland County line traces a line around the ridges for about two-thirds of the distance. Hikers on the Appalachian Trail, which runs along the Garden Mountain ridge on the south side, are walking the county line—and enjoying incredible views. If engineers should get the notion to convert this giant thumbprint in the topography into the world's biggest stadium, they can forget it. Most of the surrounding mountains fall within the Jefferson National Forest's Wythe Ranger District, and Beartown Wilderness snuggles up against the southwest flank of the basin. Besides, in Burkes Garden, nobody's selling.

Farms in the community have been owned by the same families for generations. George Washington Vanderbilt, who built America's largest private home in Asheville, North Carolina (Biltmore Estate), first tried to buy land here in the late 1800s for his dream home. The locals were unimpressed with the money being offered. No one parted with a single acre.

Despite the difficulty in crossing the mountains to see this unusual bowl, it's worth the effort. A good time to visit and meet the people who live here is during the Burkes Garden Fall Festival, held annually on the last Saturday in September.

The northern entrance is paved and easier to drive than the southern entrance. The southern entrance is closer for most traveling up and down the valleys of Virginia, and offers the best view from the top. However, in winter the dirt road may be impassable and even in spring, the deep hollows may still be iced over. Whatever the route of entry, those who negotiate the many switchbacks in the mountain roads on the north or south entrances are amazed as they descend into the giant bowl.

At the bottom, they find fields of cattle and sheep, mailboxes with nothing on them but a name, the state's smallest telephone company, and two stores. One is run by the Amish, who farm, make crafts, and operate several other businesses. The Amish sell baked goods and garden-fresh vegetables. An elementary school is here, but high school students are bused out of the valley to Tazewell. On a prominent knoll is a Lutheran cemetery, with German headstones from the 1700s.

Directions: Northern entrance (paved): from I-77, in northern Bland County, take Exit 64 (Rocky Gap) and go west on VA 61, toward Tazewell. Drive 19 miles and turn left on VA 623, which leads over Rich and Garden mountains to Burkes Garden. Southern entrance (dirt): from I-77 at Bland, in south-central Bland County, take Exit 52 and go west on US 42 about 10.5 miles and turn right on VA 623. Follow the winding road with many switchbacks approximately 5 miles, first over Brushy Mountain, then over Garden Mountain and into Burkes Garden.

For more information: Tazewell County Tourism, Route 1, Box 194, Tazewell, VA 24651. Phone (800) 588-9401. Also, Tazewell Area Chamber of Commerce, Tazewell Mall Box 6, Tazewell, VA 24651.

BEARTOWN WILDERNESS
[Fig. 18(8)] As the old saying goes, you can't get there from here. Beartown Wilderness, encompassing 6,375 steep, rugged acres west of Burkes Garden, has no roads and only one primitive hiking trail leading into it. Vehicles with a high wheel base can take a rough road from the lower parking area of the wilderness to Chestnut Ridge on the southern border of the wilderness. The well-maintained Appalachian Trail (AT), blazed with white bars, also runs along this ridge for 3 miles.

The northern border of the wilderness is the equally formidable Clinch Mountain. A few old logging roads are fast being reclaimed by the forest. Blow-downs, fallen limbs, and new growth make even foot travel a challenge. For those who enjoy wilderness, however, the difficulty of access is a plus. Exploring streams, hollows, and slopes is a solitary venture, where the eyes of wild animals rather than other people watch visitors curiously.

Few people take the trouble to follow Roaring Fork, a native trout stream, to its beginnings on the Tennessee Valley Divide on Garden Mountain, where a stunning view of Burkes Garden opens up below. Fewer still have identified rare plants that exist here, or found the beaver ponds or the sphagnum bog where Cove Branch begins. Those hardy souls who become familiar with Beartown know it for its diversity. Elevations vary from 2,300 feet at Roaring Forks's confluence with Laurel Creek to 4,408 feet on the ridgetops. A northern spruce-fir forest grows at high elevations. Red oak, chestnut oak, white oak, and varieties of hickory dominate the dry slopes. Hemlocks and heavy thickets of rhododendron hug the protected hollows. An angler wading Roaring Fork in spring to fish for native brookies may hear wild turkey gobbling in the forest. A bobcat may slip through the undergrowth, unnoticed. In summer, resident warblers flit through the heath thickets where white-tailed fawns lay hidden. Blue jays flock in the tops of white oaks in fall while, below, a chipmunk with bulging cheek pouches scoots back and forth, storing a cache of nuts in its burrow for winter. The "yank-yank" of a nuthatch or bell-like whistle of a tufted titmouse keeps the woods alive during winter's icy grip.

Camping is available at an AT shelter on the southeast corner of the wilderness. Because the wilderness is part of the Jefferson National Forest, visitors can also camp anywhere within it. Visitors need their topo map, compass, and a water supply before starting out.

Directions: From I-77 in south-central Bland County, take Exit 52 and turn left onto US 52/VA 42. Go 14.4 miles west on VA 42 and go right on VA 625. Bear right when road forks after .5 mile. Go 7.3 miles from fork to lower parking area, .2 mile past AT crossing. Hike 2 miles north on the AT to get to Chestnut Ridge and the wilderness border.

Activities: Hiking, fishing, camping, hunting.

Facilities: None.

Dates: Open year-round.

Fees: None.

Closest town: Tazewell is approximately 20 miles to the northwest. Wytheville is 20 miles southeast.

For more information: Wythe Ranger District, 1625 West Lee Highway, Wytheville, VA 24382. Phone (540) 228-5551.

THE LITTLE WOLF CREEK AREA

A pair of trails, combined with the Appalachian Trail (AT), give hikers two loop hikes of 6.75 miles and 3 miles on Brushy Mountain and Little Wolf Creek [Fig. 18(4)] (not to be confused with Wolf Creek to the north). The area is located just southeast of Garden Mountain, which surrounds Burkes Garden, and is west of I-77 at Bland. These trails and a picnic area are among the few developed portions of this area of the Jefferson National Forest.

High Water Trail and Trail Boss both begin on VA 615 at a parking area on Laurel Creek. Both are blue-blazed trails used as alternate routes by AT hikers during periods of heavy rain. High Water Trail is on the west side of the road. The lower section of the loop follows the white-blazed AT up pretty Little Wolf Creek, crossing the creek often. The upper, blue-blazed portion returns along the top of Brushy

PILEATED
WOODPECKER
(Dryocopus pileatus)

Mountain. A short walk along VA 615 returns you to the parking area.

The Trail Boss loop is on the east side of VA 615, combining with the AT for a hike that includes crossing a bridge over a stream that flows around boulders, walking along the stream, and touring the upland hardwoods on the dry slopes of Brushy Mountain.

Directions: From I-77 at Bland, go west on US 52 for 3.25 miles to VA 615. Take right fork (north) and go 2.75 miles to parking lot on left, near a bridge.

Trails: 6.75-mile loop on west side of road and 3-mile loop on the east.

Elevation: 2,400 to 3,100 feet.

Degree of difficulty: Moderate.

Closest town: Bland is 7 miles east.

For more information: Wythe Ranger District, 1625 West Lee Highway, Wytheville, VA 24382. Phone (540) 228-5551.

PICNICKING AND HIKING AT WOLF CREEK

On the banks of Wolf Creek (not to be confused with Little Wolf Creek to the south), just a bit over 3 miles from I-77, there's a place for a picnic on the wide banks of an attractive, free-flowing trout stream. A shelter here accommodates 32 people, with additional sites scattered throughout the woods. A scenic ramp/bridge leads to three loop trails of about 2 miles each in the Jefferson National Forest. Look for impressions of rail timbers still visible on the grade of an old tram line.

Directions: From I-77 at Bastian in Bland County, take Exit 58 and go west about .25 mile, then turn left (south) on US 52. Go .1 mile and go right on VA 614. Follow VA 614 for 3 miles to picnic area.

Activities: Picnicking, hiking, fishing, hunting in surrounding national forest.

Facilities: 14 picnic tables and grills; shelter with 4 tables, 4 grills, and a serving table. 3 loop trails, trout-stocked creek, vault toilets.

Closest town: Bastian is 5 miles to the southeast.

For more information: Wythe Ranger District, 1625 West Lee Highway, Wytheville, VA 24382. Phone (540) 228-5551.

KIMBERLING CREEK WILDERNESS

[Fig. 18(5)] When spring comes, visitors standing on the crest of Hogback Mountain in eastern Bland County at the edge of this remote national forest wilderness might ask themselves, Who could be trying, every few minutes, to start a chain saw? The sound comes from far down the hollow of Sulphur Spring Fork, on the southeast slope of the mountain. Then a realization hits. A male ruffed grouse is drumming on a decaying log. The rapid-fire sound of a revving motor is made by staccato beats of cupped wings against his body. There it is again—a slow thump-thump-thump that gradually speeds to a crescendo and fades off. Perhaps a female, impressed with the sound, is answering him with soft clucks.

At 3,200 feet, Hogback Mountain is the highest point of Kimberling Creek Wilderness. From here, the wilderness drops to the southeast down several hollows of North Fork and Sulphur Spring Fork, which are tributaries of Kimberling Creek. Just one finger of the wilderness reaches out at the bottom to touch Kimberling Creek, at 2,282 feet.

Hardwoods, interspersed with white and yellow pine, forest the slopes. In the understory are dogwood, sourwood, red maple, mountain laurel, and rhododendron. A few abandoned logging roads and an old railroad grade are all that remain of man's former presence here. Left undisturbed, trillium, pipsissewa (*Chimaphila umbellata*), and Indian pipe (*Monotropa uniflora*) now poke their heads through leaf litter where trucks once rumbled, carrying out giant chestnut trees from the mountainside. A visitor standing on the mountaintop may be the only human in the area.

Directions: From I-77, take Exit 52 and go east on US 52 into Bland. In Bland, turn left (north), staying on US 52, and continue 3.9 miles. Turn right on VA 612. Go .3 mile and turn left on FR 640 (rough road). After 4.6 miles, stop at parking area on right.

Activities: Camping and hunting.

Facilities: None.

Closest town: Bland, in central Bland County, is about 5 miles south.

For more information: Wythe Ranger District, 1625 West Lee Highway, Wytheville, VA 24382. Phone (540) 228-5551.

HIKING AT KIMBERLING CREEK WILDERNESS. There are no designated trails in the area. However, about 3 miles of old logging roads and a 3-mile railroad bed (on North Fork) offer limited access for those who enjoy the isolation and don't mind negotiating fallen trees, detouring around thickets, and shuffling through leaf cover. Hiking can be very difficult at times, where storms have blown down giant tulip poplars and pin oaks or ice coverings accompanied by high winds have snapped trees like matchsticks.

A topo map, a compass, and a companion are necessary before heading into this backcountry. Backcountry camping is permitted anywhere within the wilderness. Campers are asked to practice leave-no-trace ethics when cleaning up a campsite.

Walker Mountain and Brushy Mountain

[Fig. 18] Walker Mountain is hardly mountain enough to divert a road as it rises gently above the valley floor north of Bristol. Its neighbor to the west, Clinch Mountain, dwarfs it. In fact, Walker all but disappears as it passes by Abingdon. But as the ridge enters Smyth County, it comes into its own, helping to define the western edge of the Great Valley as it runs northeast to the New River. North of the New River, the ridge becomes Sinking Creek Mountain. Flanking Walker on both sides are ridges with a confusing array of similar names. Don't try to apply logic to the designations. Roughly paralleling Walker across Rich Valley to the west is Little Mountain, which becomes Brushy Mountain as it progresses northeast.

East of Walker Mountain, a completely different ridge is also called first Little Brushy Mountain, then Brushy Mountain, then Little Brushy again, then Brushy, then Little Walker, and finally, beyond the break by the New River, it becomes Brush Mountain. Students of Virginia Polytechnic Institute and State University at Blacksburg know Brush Mountain well as the scenic backdrop of their campus.

Whatever the names, these mountains evoke compliments from travelers on Interstate 81. Those with time to stop find plenty of opportunities to explore Walker and its Brush/Brushy neighbor to the east. A state park, part of the Appalachian Trail, and the Wythe Ranger District of the Jefferson National Forest all make contributions. Hidden within a mountain fold north of Marion is a state park which has its own unusual name, Hungry Mother. The Appalachian Trail crosses the range about 11 miles to the north of the park and intertwines with two of the mountains' own footpaths, the Crawfish and Channel Back trails.

WYTHE RANGER DISTRICT

[Fig. 15] The Wythe Ranger District of the Jefferson National Forest contains scenic byways, dramatic overlooks, a campground, two picnic areas, hiking trails (including a 60-mile stretch of the Appalachian Trail), two wilderness areas, and a shooting range. Even so, many of the forested slopes of the Wythe's 173,400 acres have no inroads. The single campground and two picnic areas lie along the Big Walker Mountain Scenic Byway north of Wytheville.

The lack of developed areas is tantalizing to those who enjoy bushwhacking into places where few feet have gone before. And there is always plenty to do in nearby Mount Rogers National Recreation Area, just across the valley to the southeast (*see* Mount Rogers National Recreation Area, p. 237). However, during peak seasons, people who enjoy a more solitary outdoors experience may find it on the limited but lesser-known trails of the Wythe District. For help in planning an outing, stop by or call the Wythe Ranger District office at Wytheville or the Highlands Gateway Visitor Center at Fort Chiswell.

Directions: The Wythe Ranger District office is located on the northbound side of US 11 west of Wytheville, in central Wythe County. Highlands Gateway Visitor Center is at Factory Merchants Mall in Fort Chiswell, east of Wytheville. From I-81, take Exit 80 to the service road and follow signs. The visitor center is on the far side of the mall.

For more information: Wythe Ranger District, 1555 Sherwood Forest Road, Wytheville, VA 24382. Phone (540) 228-5551. Highlands Gateway Visitor Center, Factory Merchants Mall, Fort Chiswell, VA 24360. Phone (540) 637-6766.

The views from Big Walker Scenic Byway are some of the best in Virginia. The byway passes through both public and private land on the Wythe and Bland county line north of Wytheville. The public land belongs to the Wythe Ranger District of the Jefferson National Forest.

Hungry Mother State Park

Hungry Mother State Park is named for the words spoken by a child found near the park, according to a popular legend.

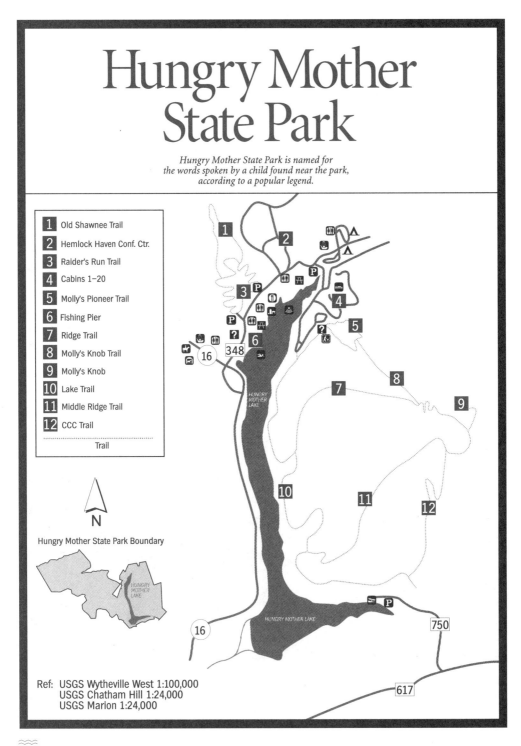

1 Old Shawnee Trail
2 Hemlock Haven Conf. Ctr.
3 Raider's Run Trail
4 Cabins 1–20
5 Molly's Pioneer Trail
6 Fishing Pier
7 Ridge Trail
8 Molly's Knob Trail
9 Molly's Knob
10 Lake Trail
11 Middle Ridge Trail
12 CCC Trail
·········· Trail

N

Hungry Mother State Park Boundary

Ref: USGS Wytheville West 1:100,000
USGS Chatham Hill 1:24,000
USGS Marion 1:24,000

HUNGRY MOTHER STATE PARK

[Fig. 19, Fig. 13(19), Fig. 34(1)] First, consider the legend of Hungry Mother State Park, the creek by the same name that winds through these gentle mountains, and the strenuous hiking trail with the same name that leaves the park, then threads through hemlock and hardwood to Molly's Knob.

Legends are elusive, yet the state of Virginia gives its imprimatur to the Hungry Mother story on a plaque at the park office. Legend has it that Indians attacked and wiped out several settlements along the New River south of the park as westward migration began. That part is verifiable. On one raid, Indians supposedly captured a settler named Molly Marley, along with her small child. Mother and daughter were carried off to a camp on a mountaintop north of the park. In time, Molly and child escaped. With only wild berries for food, they began the long trek out of the mountains, searching for the settlement.

Molly collapsed from exhaustion near the foot of a mountain. The child continued to wander down a small creek. When searchers found the child, the only words she could say were, "Hungry. Mother." Searchers retraced the child's steps and found Molly Marley dead where she had collapsed. Today the mountain where the Indian camp was believed to have been located is called Molly's Knob. The stream the mother and daughter followed is called Hungry Mother Creek. When the 2,180-acre park opened in 1936, a dam was built on the creek to form Hungry Mother Lake, the centerpiece of Hungry Mother State Park.

Today, the park facilities and trails hide among the Appalachian hardwoods and conifers, so that visitors' first and everlasting impression is the pristine-looking, 108-acre lake, framed by steep mountain shoreline. Inside the park office is a collection of Indian projectile points gathered from the area. This region, after all, was home to the Cherokee and the Iroquois thousands of years before European eyes ever saw its beauty.

Five log, eight frame, and seven wood-sided cabins are available for rent from March through November. Maple trees and rhododendron thickets provide sylvan privacy. If visitors prefer to camp, there are three loops with a total of 43 sites. Loop C has the only elevated wood platforms in the state park system. An oak-hickory-pine canopy provides shade. Crowding is usually not a problem. Warm summer days attract families to the swimming beach where children build sand castles while their parents sun themselves on towels. Twelve miles of trails lead away from the sounds of splashing children through oak, hickory, and tulip poplar forest cover, opening on lake views from Little Brush Mountain and Walker Mountain.

In spring, migrating and resident warblers fill the mornings with bird song in Hungry Mother State Park woodlands. Many of these birds flit among the treetops, and are more easily identified by their song than by their appearance. The black-throated blue warbler (*Dendroica caerulescens*), for instance, has a buzzy, rising "zwee ZWEE zwee" that the interpreter might suggest sounds like "please SQUEEZE me."

Wood Warblers

The tiny size and quick movements of various wood warblers (*Parulidae*) make them difficult to tell apart, even with binoculars. However, similar species can often be ruled out by observing behavior, examining habitat, and listening for the distinctive songs. The worm-eating warbler (*Helmitheros vermivorus*), for example, prefers dry, wooded hillsides and has a buzzy, insectlike song. But the gaily colored hooded warbler (*Wilsonia citrina*) is more often found in the luxuriant undergrowth of moist woods. It has a clear, ringing, melodious voice. The worm-eating warbler pokes about in the leaf litter for insect larvae while the hooded warbler darts about the understory, often catching insects on the fly.

The happy, melodic song of the chestnut-sided warbler (*Dendroica pensylvanica*) may be easier to remember by its resemblance to "very pleased to MEETCHA!" This warbler builds its nest of grass and bark in undergrowth just a few feet off the ground, but the nesting female's secretive nature makes the nest next to impossible to find. The hooded warbler (*Wilsonia citrina*), northern parula (*Parula americana*), and black-and-white warbler (*Dendroica magnolia*) have also made appearances.

Fishing has improved with game-management practices, so that Hungry Mother Lake now has good largemouth bass, bluegill, crappie, muskellunge, and walleye fishing. Channel catfish of 15 to 30 pounds are hauled in occasionally. The lake has produced two state-record northern pike. Anglers familiar with the lake find the best fishing by probing the wooded coves by boat. The prohibition against gasoline-powered motors ensures a quiet outing. A state fishing license is required.

Here's an agenda that could easily fill a weekend: Check out the information center and pick up a trail brochure. Learn about the area's plants and animals on the interpretive trail. Rent a paddleboat. Take a swim. Grab a dog with the works at the snack bar. Saddle old Dusty and Duke for a placid half-hour ride on the horse trail behind the stable. Hike to Molly's Knob [Fig. 19(9)]. Dine on fried chicken and mashed potatoes at the restaurant. Sit under a starlit sky at the amphitheater as a park interpreter points out the constellations. Drift off to sleep as a gentle rain patters on your tent.

Rise before dawn for an early-morning bird walk. Watch a group of children launch leaf boats in Hungry Mother Creek. Rent a rowboat and photograph a pair of Canada geese with seven goslings bobbing between them. Thread a hook through a piece of cut bait and haul in a channel cat. Identify Christmas fern (*Polystichum acrostichoides*), trailing arbutus (*Epigaea repens*), and Indian pipe (*Monotropaceae*) on the Old Shawnee Trail. Flush a ruffed grouse. Close out the weekend with an evening campfire sing.

Directions: From US 11 at Marion, go north on VA 16 4 miles to park.

Activities: Camping, picnicking, hiking, horseback riding, mountain biking, cross-country skiing, swimming, seasonal hunting and fishing, boating (no gasoline motors), interpretive programs, July arts and crafts festival, other special events.

Facilities: 43 campsites (water and electric at 32 sites) with central bathhouses; picnic areas with drinking water, grills, and restrooms; 20 rental cabins; restaurant and gift shop; 3 picnic shelters; swimming beach with bathhouse and concession; 12 miles of hiking trails; horse rental and guided horse trail; 108-acre fishing lake; rowboat and paddleboat rental; launch ramp; fishing platform for the handicapped; amphitheater; information center. Also, rental conference center with meeting rooms, cabins, pool, sports complex, and picnic area.

Dates: Park open year-round. Camping and cabins: open Mar. 1–Dec. 1. Swimming: open in the summer. Boat and horse rental: open daily in the summer and weekends only after Labor Day.

Fees: A fee is charged for parking, camping, cabins, horse rental. Launch ramp is free (plus parking fee).

Closest town: Marion is 4 miles south.

For more information: Hungry Mother State Park, Route 5, Box 109, Marion, VA 24354. Phone (540) 783-3422. Reservations, phone (800) 933-PARK.

HIKING AT HUNGRY MOTHER STATE PARK. Most of the 12 miles of trails are across the lake, on the western end of Little Brushy Mountain. Two smaller trails are behind the restaurant and picnic area. All are easy to moderate, well marked, and have signs at trailheads and at junctions.

The larger network of trails on Little Brushy Mountain consists of three connected loops. Beginning near the cabins, white blazes on Molly's Knob Trail [Fig. 19(8)] lead 1.6 miles to the summit at 3,270 feet. On a clear day, Virginia's highest peak, Mount Rogers, is visible to the southwest. Hikers can return along the orange CCC Trail [Fig. 19(12)] or the yellow Middle Ridge Trail [Fig. 19(11)], or backtrack to take the Ridge Trail (gold blaze) [Fig. 19(7)]. All these are connected by the 3.1-mile Lake Trail (navy-blue blaze) [Fig. 19(10)] at the bottom.

Along the Lake Trail, the green heron might be visible. Though awkward-looking, the feeding heron slips easily on orange legs though the branches of a fallen tree, poking about in the shallows for minnows or tadpoles. A well-camouflaged dusky salamander slithers quickly out of harm's way.

On the bank above a fallen tree is a plant with long spires of white blossoms. The plant—a black cohosh (*Cimicifuga racemosa*)—has an unpleasant odor. The smell, which repels bugs, gives the plant its other name—bugbane. At dusk, watching from near the boat ramp, you may see a muskrat—or is it a beaver?—trailing a V behind itself as it crosses a corner of the lake. Both animals are residents at Hungry Mother.

Raider's Run Trail (royal-blue blaze) [Fig. 19(3)] is a good place to find spring wildflowers. Raiders Run Trail is a .9-mile loop that climbs gradually to the Old Shawnee Trail (green blaze) [Fig. 19(1)]. Old Shawnee is more narrow and climbs to views of Walker Mountain before descending through rhododendron and mountain laurel thickets. Combining the two trails makes a 1.8-mile loop.

Ask the park staff where visitors might find some of the flowers they've recorded. These include interesting or showy varieties such as yellow lady slipper (*Cypripedium calceolus*), fringed polygala—also called gaywings and bird-on-the-wing—(*Polygala paucifolia*), jack-in-the-pulpit (*Arisaema triphyllum*), wild geranium (*Geranium maculatum*), meadow rue (*Thalictrum*), and bowman's root (*Gillenia trifoliata*). Also, see if they'll point out the resident albino squirrel for you.

Trails: Over 12 miles of interconnecting trails in 2 separate networks.

Elevation: 2,220 feet at lake level to 3,270 feet at Molly's Knob.

Degree of difficulty: Easy to moderate with some steep sections.

HUNGRY MOTHER ARTS AND CRAFTS FESTIVAL. Held annually the third weekend of July, this juried event is the longest-running state park arts and crafts festival in Virginia. Area artisans erect their booths in a grassy clearing and under the park trees. Stained glass, pottery, basketry, leather work, acrylics, and photography are among the exhibits.

For more information: Smyth County Chamber of Commerce, 200 Main Street, Marion, VA 24354. Phone (540) 783-3161.

HIKING BRUSHY MOUNTAIN AND CRAWFISH VALLEY

CRAWFISH AND CHANNEL ROCK TRAILS. Between Marion and Wytheville on the north side of Interstate 81 is a little-known, 10-mile loop in the Wythe Ranger District of the Jefferson National Forest. The loop, marked with orange, diamond-shaped blazes, is formed by two hiking trails, the Crawfish Trail and the Channel Rock Trail [Fig. 18(12)].

The trail begins in Crawfish Valley, between Walker and Brushy mountains. After crossing Bear Creek and climbing to the top of Brushy Mountain, it follows the ridgeline along the Tennessee Valley Divide about 4 miles. The footpath then descends through Channel Rock Hollow, back into Crawfish Valley, and returns to the parking lot.

Because of the trail's remote location, with no developed recreation areas nearby, human impact is light. When walking quietly, the chances of surprising a deer, turkey, or ruffed grouse are good. There are changes in vegetation as the trail courses through open fields of wildflowers and climbs from moist, protected creek bottom to dry ridgetop. The orange-blazed loop catches the Appalachian Trail (AT) on its journey north across the Great Valley of Virginia. The AT cuts across the loop, providing two access points and opportunities for extended hikes. Local volunteers work hard to keep such trails as these clear of debris.

Directions: From I-81 at Rural Retreat, west of Wytheville, take Exit 60 and go northeast on VA 680 2.5 miles to VA 625. Turn right and continue 4 miles to FR 727-2. Follow this road 2 miles to gate and parking.

Activities: Hiking, mountain biking, horseback riding.
Trail: 10-mile loop dissected by the Appalachian Trail.
Elevation: 2,500 to 3,300 feet.
Degree of difficulty: Moderate.

BIG WALKER MOUNTAIN SCENIC BYWAY

[Fig. 18(15)] Travelers along Interstate 81 or Interstate 77 who don't mind taking an extra half hour to get to the perfect picnic spot—one with quite a view—should turn onto the Big Walker Mountain Scenic Byway and drive to the top. The Byway passes through both public and private land on the Wythe and Bland county line north of Wytheville. The public land belongs to the Wythe Ranger District of the Jefferson National Forest, and it includes several attractions.

On the crest of Walker Mountain, at 3,405 feet, is an overlook with Rich Valley, Brush Mountain, and Garden Mountain spread out to the northwest. In the foreground is the yellow and green patchwork of farms. A tiny silo or farmhouse here and there glints in the sun. In the background is Garden Mountain, a bowl-shaped mountain with the tiny community of Burkes Garden hidden inside, and Beartown Wilderness [Fig. 18(8)] lies toward the west.

A .75-mile trail leads from the lookout parking lot to a large rock outcrop called Monster Rock, with the same view. The short trail climbs from 3,500 to 3,800 feet.

For an equally panoramic vista in the opposite direction—and for a stunning place to eat lunch—take the road across the highway from the parking lot 4 miles to Big Bend Picnic Area. At 3,950 feet, seven tables with grills and fireplaces sit under a canopy of oaks, among boulders and orchard grass. In June, rhododendrons attract butterflies and honeybees. On a clear day, Mount Rogers, Virginia's highest point (5,729 feet), is visible in the distance from the overlooks. The long, linear structure of the Ridge and Valley province is evident from both Monster Rock and Big Bend. Another picnic area, Dark Horse Hollow, is located on the banks of Stony Fork Creek off US 52, 2.3 miles south of the junction with VA 717. Stony Fork is a stocked trout stream.

Other attractions include a pleasant national forest campground, two more hiking trails, access to the Appalachian Trail, a shooting range, and several historical markers. A privately run gift shop (seasonal) at the Big Walker Mountain Overlook has a 100-foot tower to climb if the mountain's height of 3,405 feet isn't enough.

HEADWATERS HUNTING. The view from Big Walker Mountain Overlook includes headwaters of two mighty river systems. Below, in the field of one Bland County farm, lies the beginning of the North Fork of the Holston River, headwaters of the famous Tennessee River, and Walker Creek, headwaters of the ancient New River.

Raindrops falling on that field will either drain to the south or to the north. All will eventually flow into the Gulf of Mexico. But the northbound runoff will head for West Virginia and Ohio. Water in the southbound rivulet will make it all the way to Alabama before heading back to find the Ohio in western Kentucky, where thoroughbreds graze on bluegrass.

Driving along VA 42 in the valley, this field of opposite headwaters is near the place VA 622 crosses VA 42. To get there, continue north along the US 52 byway to the junction with VA 42 and turn left. Go south about 5 miles to the junction with 622. This is the Tennessee Valley Divide, where precipitation may go either way. The actual beginning of the South Fork of the Holston is another 1.5 miles south, where VA 623 comes in from the north and two creeks converge on the east side of VA 42 (VA 623 is also the back entrance to Burkes Garden; *see* p. 97). Finding headwaters can lead you to some interesting places. A good map, a bit of curiosity, and time to hike, bike, or drive Virginia backroads are all that's necessary to get started.

BIG WALKER MOUNTAIN SCENIC BYWAY MILE MARKERS: 500 yards from turn off of I-77 onto VA 717 (right)—Access road to Wythe Shooting Range.

Mile 1.1 (on left, VA 717)—Access road to Stony Fork Creek.

Mile 1.25 (on left)—Seven Sisters Trail (east trailhead).

Mile 1.5 (on left)—Astin homesite and access to Stony Fork Creek.

Mile 3.8 (on left)—Stony Fork Campground, Stony Fork Creek, Stony Fork Nature Trail, Seven Sisters Trail.

Mile 4.3—Byway junction with US 52. Go right. (Or go left 2.3 miles to Dark Horse Hollow Picnic Area.)

Mile 7.8—Big Walker Lookout and access (on right) to Big Bend Picnic Area (4-mile drive).

Mile 12.7 (left)—Access road to Appalachian Trail.

ROSEBAY
RHODODENDRON
(Rhododendron
maximum)
With evergreen leaves
and clusters of
white to pink
flowers, this
rhododendron grows on slopes.

Mile 12.8 (right)—Picnic table.

Mile 15.6—End of byway at I-77.

Directions: At Exit 47 on I-77, 5 miles north of Wytheville, take VA 717 west. Look at odometer to follow sites along the way. Go 4.3 miles to US 52 and turn right (north). Stay on US 52 for 11 miles, going over Walker Mountain and connecting with I-77 at Exit 52.

Activities: Picnicking, hiking, camping, seasonal hunting and fishing in national forest.

Facilities: Scenic overlook and tower, campground, 2 picnic areas (no water), 3 hiking trails, access to Appalachian Trail, stocked trout stream.

Dates: Byway and Big Bend Picnic Area, open year-round. Dark Horse Hollow Picnic Area, open Apr.–Nov. Gift shop, open Apr.–Oct.

Fees: Byway and Big Bend Picnic Area, free; a fee is charged for Dark Horse Hollow Picnic Area.

Closest town: Wytheville is 5 miles south.

For more information: Wythe Ranger District, 1625 West Lee Highway, Wytheville, VA 24382. Phone (540) 228-5551.

CAMPING AT WALKER MOUNTAIN

Stony Fork Campground [Fig. 18(13)] is located on the southern end of the Big Walker Mountain Scenic Byway, about 9 miles north of Wytheville. The 53 sites are spread under the dappled sunlight of a hardwood forest. Each site has a picnic table, fireplace, and lantern post. The East Fork of Stony Fork Creek winds through the campground, drawing children like a magnet to set leaf boats a-sail or hunt for tadpoles and salamanders.

Directions: From I-77, 5 miles north of Wytheville, take Exit 47 and go west on VA 717 3.8 miles to campground entrance on left.

Activities: Camping, hiking, fishing.

Facilities: 53 campsites with table, fireplace, and lantern post; nature trail; fishing stream.

Dates: Open Apr.–Nov.

Fees: A fee is charged for single-unit and double-unit campsites. Dump station is free for campers staying at Stony Fork Campground. A dump station fee is charged for campers staying elsewhere.

Closest town: Wytheville is 9 miles south.

For more information: Wythe Ranger District, 1625 West Lee Highway, Wytheville, VA 24382. Phone (540) 228-5551.

WYTHE SHOOTING RANGE

[Fig. 18(14)] A 10-lane range next to Stony Fork Campground offers a safe place to practice target shooting and sight a gun, free of charge. The range includes target frames

The purple trillium, Trillium erectum, *is one of the most common eastern trilliums. It has three maroon or reddish-brown petals.*

in six 25-yard lanes and four 100-yard lanes. Targets can be set at 7, 15, and 25 yards on the 25-yard lanes, and 7, 15, 50, and 100 yards on the 100-yard lanes.

Directions: From I-77 5 miles north of Wytheville, take Exit 47 and go west on VA 717 500 yards to right turn on maintenance road. Before reaching maintenance building, turn left and drive .5 mile.

For more information: Wythe Ranger District, 1625 West Lee Highway, Wytheville, VA 24382. Phone (540) 228-5551.

HIKING AT WALKER MOUNTAIN

STONY FORK NATURE TRAIL. [Fig. 18(10)] This yellow-blazed path leads 1 mile through an oak-hickory-pine forest. An understory of rhododendron and mountain laurel blooms in early summer and stays green through winter, though temperatures below 28 degrees Fahrenheit make their leaves fold down.

Trail: 1-mile, horseshoe-shaped nature trail looping back to campground.

Elevation: 2,400 to 2,500 feet.

Degree of difficulty: Easy.

SEVEN SISTERS TRAIL. [Fig. 18(11)] Branching off from the Stony Fork Nature Trail, this orange-blazed, 4.8-mile trail climbs from 2,500 feet to a height of 3,300 feet on Little Walker Mountain. Hikers will notice the variation in growth as they climb from streamside vegetation and giant, old-growth pines to a dry, ridgetop oak-hickory forest.

Summer views are limited because of leaf cover, but visitors can see long distances in winter. The trail parallels the East Fork of Stony Fork Creek below as it heads northeast about 3.5 miles before descending to the creek and the parking area on VA 717, 2.5 miles east of the campground.

Trail: 4.8-mile hike along ridge of Little Walker Mountain.

Elevation: 2,500 to 3,300 feet.

Degree of difficulty: Moderate.

HIKING AT LITTLE WALKER AND TRACT MOUNTAIN

TRACT FORK AND POLECAT TRAILS. [Fig. 20(19, 20)] Northwest of Pulaski, crossing the Wythe and Pulaski county line, is a duo of trails connecting Little

Walker Mountain and Tract Mountain. Tract Fork Trail is a wide, easy, 4-mile path along Tract Fork Creek, with parking lots on both ends. Yellow, diamond-shaped blazes mark the path. Polecat Trail, marked with orange, diamond-shaped blazes, leads 1.5 miles up a Peak Creek tributary, upstream from Gatewood Reservoir.

Directions: To access Tract Fork Trail, take VA 99 north from Pulaski to VA 738 (Robinson Tract Road). Follow VA 738 4 miles to left on VA 641. Go 2.5 miles to end of road and beginning of FR 692. Go 1.5 miles to end of FR 692 at trailhead. To access Polecat Trail, take VA 603 north from Wytheville 4 miles. Turn right (east) on VA 600 and go 7 miles to right on FR 707. Go 2.75 miles to trail-hiker sign on roadside. Trail is on north (left) side of road.

Trails: Tract Fork is a 4-mile path along Tract Fork Creek. Polecat is a 1.5-mile path up a tributary creek.

Elevation: Tract Fork varies from 2,400 to 3,000 feet. Polecat varies from 2,300 to 2,500 feet.

Degree of difficulty: Tract Fork is easy. Polecat is moderate.

Surface and Blaze: Natural. Polecat Trail: orange, diamond-shaped blaze. Tract Fork Trail: yellow, diamond-shaped blaze.

Brook Trout

In Virginia, the term "native trout" refers to the brook trout—the only trout native to the region. Biologists have been encouraged to learn that brook trout (*Salvelinus fontinalus*) still account for 80 percent of the wild trout in the state's 2,300 miles of wild trout streams. The brook trout is one of several species of trout found in the cold, well-oxygenated waters of national forest streams and lakes. A native of northeastern North America, the species has been widely transplanted. Highly esteemed as game fish, brookies can be taken on artificial flies, spinning lures, and with live bait (where permitted). These colorful members of the char family will eat just about anything. Aquatic insects, worms, leeches, and crustaceans are favored, but larger trout will eat other fish, frogs, and even small mice.

Brook trout rarely exceed 5 pounds, though an occasional fish up to 10 pounds rewards a patient angler. Rainbow trout from the western United States have taken over most of the brook-trout habitat in other southeastern states. In fact, Virginia currently has more native brook trout streams than all other southeastern states combined. The very colorful "brookie " is dark olive green with light wavy or "wormy" markings. Its sides are lighter, sometimes with a bluish cast, and covered with pale yellow spots and a sprinkling of red spots encircled by blue halos. Bright orange fins on the outer edges help with identification. Brook trout are intolerant of water exceeding 70 degrees Fahrenheit.

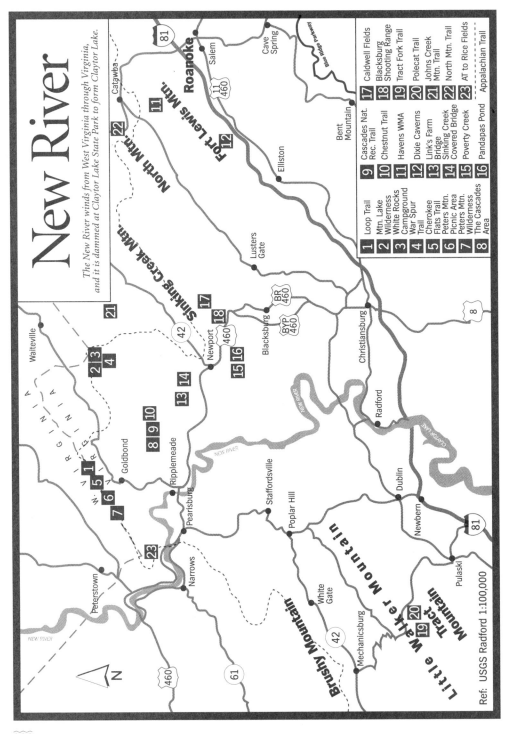

New River

The New River winds from West Virginia through Virginia, and it is dammed at Claytor Lake State Park to form Claytor Lake.

1	Loop Trail	9	Cascades Nat. Rec. Trail	17	Caldwell Fields
2	Mtn. Lake Wilderness	10	Chestnut Trail	18	Blacksburg Shooting Range
3	White Rocks Campground	11	Havens WMA	19	Tract Fork Trail
4	War Spur Trail	12	Dixie Caverns	20	Polecat Trail
5	Cherokee Flats Trail	13	Link's Farm Bridge	21	Johns Creek Mtn. Trail
6	Peters Mtn. Picnic Area	14	Sinking Creek Covered Bridge	22	North Mtn. Trail
7	Peters Mtn. Wilderness	15	Poverty Creek	23	AT to Rice Fields
8	The Cascades Area	16	Pandapas Pond		Appalachian Trail

Ref: USGS Radford 1:100,000

Blacksburg Ranger District

[Fig. 15] Many who have lived in Virginia all their lives—even vacationed in the mountains—are unaware of the wealth that nature has to offer in and around the national forest west of Blacksburg. Recreation in the Jefferson National Forest here is centered in three areas. The first area, from Blacksburg heading northwest on US 460, is a long, skinny gorge between the joined-at-the-hip ridges of Brushy Mountain and Sinking Creek Mountain. The highway crosses the parallel mountains on the Eastern Continental Divide. Stocked trout streams lead away from the highway here in opposite directions.

To the left, Poverty Creek runs to the New River and ultimately the Gulf of Mexico. The upper end of this creek has been dammed to form Pandapas Pond [Fig. 20(16)]. To the right, Craig Creek leads past the Blacksburg Shooting Range [Fig. 20(18)] and the Caldwell Fields Recreation Area [Fig. 20(17)], and northeastward to the James River, the Chesapeake Bay, and the Atlantic Ocean.

After crossing these two mountains, US 460 passes the second cluster of outdoor attractions, which lies in the mountains to the north. On a jumble of mountain ridges and plateaus are two wilderness areas, a well-maintained recreation area, one of the state's most beautiful waterfalls, rock outcroppings with panoramic views, spruce bogs, stands of old-growth forests, a tremendous variety of flora and fauna, a developed campground, and a large network of trails to explore it all. In addition, cameras click when visitors discover covered bridges at Pembroke and at Newport.

The third area is in the mountains across the New River to the south, in a portion of the Walker Creek and New River watershed in southeastern Giles County. Located on the west side of Brushy Mountain's northern end are another pretty waterfall, a stocked trout stream, hiking trails, and primitive campgrounds.

Because of the variation in elevation in the Blacksburg Ranger District (1,700 to 4,200 feet), many species of plants and animals exist here. The area marks the northern boundary of many southern species and the southern limit of northern species. At the ranger district office in Blacksburg, brochures and a district map are available. The staff can answer questions and give visitors information such as where wildflowers are blooming and which unusual trees to look for. There is also a bookshelf full of excellent field guides and outdoor references. Networks of trails are available for hikers, joggers, mountain bikers, and equestrians.

Directions: The Blacksburg Ranger District Office is housed in a modern brick building on Business US 460 on the south side of town. As you enter Blacksburg on South Main Street from the south (Business 460 west), the office is on the left about halfway down a long hill. The address is 110 Southpark Drive, but this is just a loop off the main highway.

For more information: Blacksburg Ranger District, 110 Southpark Drive, Blacksburg, VA 24060. Phone (540) 552-4641.

Brushy Mountain and Sinking Creek Mountain

PANDAPAS POND

[Fig. 20(16)] Pandapas Pond is a pleasant little 8-acre lake, easy to reach off US 460. In addition to a measure of solitude, it offers fishing, a walking trail around the lake, and picnicking, and it is well suited for a morning of leisurely, flat-water canoeing. Pandapas is in the headwaters of Poverty Creek [Fig. 20(15)] in northwest Montgomery County, just minutes west of Blacksburg. An easy 1-mile loop trail at an elevation of 2,200 feet skirts the pond's edge. At the northeast end is a wetland environment. Surrounding the pond are Appalachian hardwoods and pines.

A butternut tree (*Juglans cinerea*)—sometimes called white walnut—grows about midway between US 460 and Poverty Creek on the northwest side of the pond. The wood of this tree is much lighter brown than its cousin, the black walnut. The greenish nut has a sticky surface and is oval rather than round, as the black walnut is. In the colorful understory in spring are redbud, flame azalea, pinkster, Catawba rhododendron, and mountain laurel.

Where the lake trail crosses a little bridge at the lower end of the pond, the brilliant red spires of cardinal flower (*Lobelia cardinalis*) grow. Somewhere back in the woods, a yellow-billed cuckoo (*Coccyzus americanus*) calls. (Like ovenbirds, they're never in sight.) Because the cuckoo is inclined to sound off when a storm is approaching, mountain people call the bird a "rain crow."

District naturalists know which of the wildflowers at Pandapas Pond are in bloom. Colonies of rare fringed polygala (*Polygala paucifolia*)—also known as gaywings and bird-on-the-wing—find conditions perfect in the moist woodlands. This tiny purplish flower grows only 2 to 6 inches tall. Depending on the time of year, visitors can also find fire pinks (*Silene virginica*), several varieties of bird's-foot violet (*Viola pedata*), liverwort (*hepatica*), wandflower (*Galax*), and yellow lady slipper (*Cypripedium calceolus*).

Due to environmental concerns, the area around the parking lot and Pandapas Pond are off-limits to bikers, equestrians, and campers. Foot travel is welcome. Primitive camping is allowed along Poverty Creek below the lake on national forest land, and there are fire rings alongside the creek. An annual children's fishing day attracts families to the Blacksburg Ranger District in early May. Call for exact dates.

Directions: Take US 460 west from Blacksburg for 3 miles. Turn left across from VA 621 (which goes to the right) on newly constructed FR 708, which may not show on your map.

Activities: Hiking, fishing, boating (no motors), picnicking, backcountry camping, seasonal hunting in surrounding national forest.

Facilities: 8-acre fishing lake, easy hiking loop and other trails, picnic tables.

Dates: Open year-round.

Fees: None.

Closest town: Blacksburg is 3 miles east.

For more information: Blacksburg Ranger District, 110 Southpark Drive, Blacksburg, VA 24060. Phone (540) 552-4641.

POVERTY CREEK AND CRAIG CREEK

[Fig. 20(15)] Below Pandapas Pond, Poverty Creek threads its way southwest through the mountain pass to the New River. On the other side of US 460, Craig Creek takes off for the James River. Both streams are stocked by the state with feisty rainbow, brook, and brown trout from an area hatchery. In summer, the water level in the two streams gets low, and stocking is suspended until the creeks refill. Trout fishing is best in late fall, winter, and early to late spring.

On these streams, morning fog hangs in the treetops like a gossamer canopy. Even in summer, an occasional leftover trout and several minnows flash in the gin-clear water. Outside the cool dimness created by overarching hemlocks, fish dart for cover beneath undercut banks.

Poverty Creek below the pond leads to an old logging road, and along the path are beaver cuttings where the secretive animals have dammed the stream to form more wetlands. Wildflowers and moisture-loving plants thrive here. Off the trail a bit, many varieties of mushrooms spring from decaying organic matter.

Directions: Take US 460 west from Blacksburg for 3 miles. Turn left on FR 708 (across from VA 621) for Poverty Creek, or right on VA 621 for Craig Creek.

Dates: Open year-round.

Fees: None.

Closest town: Blacksburg is 3 miles east.

For more information: Blacksburg Ranger District, 110 Southpark Drive, Blacksburg, VA 24060. Phone (540) 552-4641.

BLACKSBURG SHOOTING RANGE

[Fig. 20(18)] An 18-position rifle and pistol range and a single-position trap shooting range are available for the public just 3 miles west of Blacksburg. The rifle/pistol range is designed for firing at a stationary target at 25, 50, and 100 yards and at 100 meters. Clay pigeons may be used on the trap range.

Directions: Take US 460 west from Blacksburg for 3 miles. Turn right on VA 621. Range is on left.

Activities: Target and trap shooting.

Facilities: 18-position rifle/pistol range with target frames, single-position trap range, parking for handicapped.

Dates: Open year-round.

Fees: None.

Closest town: Blacksburg is 3 miles east.

For more information: Blacksburg Ranger District, 110 Southpark Drive, Blacksburg, VA 24060. Phone (540) 552-4641.

CALDWELL FIELDS

[Fig. 20(17)] A campground consisting of three fields on Craig Creek is available for groups year-round. Rates vary from $25 to $50, depending on group size. Reservations are required. The largest field is set aside for day use only. Having been left in a more or less natural state, it is a good place to study wildflowers or watch wildlife, especially early and late in the day.

The other two smaller fields can be rented for overnight events. They have been cleared and landscaped, and have group fire rings.

Directions: Go west from Blacksburg on US 460 3 miles. Turn right on VA 621 and go about 10 miles.

Activities: Group camping.

Facilities: Group fire rings, handicapped-accessible restroom, vault toilet (no water).

Dates: Available by reservation year-round.

Fees: A fee is charged for admission.

Closest town: Blacksburg is 3 miles east.

For more information: Blacksburg Ranger District, 110 Southpark Drive, Blacksburg, VA 24060. Phone (540) 552-4641.

TULIPTREE OR YELLOW-POPLAR

(Liriodendron tulipifera)
Of eastern broadleaved trees, the tuliptree is one of the straightest and tallest and has one of the largest diameter tree trunks. Wind-borne seeds of the tulip poplar make their way into the openings in mountain forests to take over in areas denuded by heavy logging or disease.

The Cascades Area

[Fig. 20(8)] Hikers who make the 2-mile journey up to the Cascades, a much-photographed, 66-foot waterfall on Little Stony Creek, find that getting there is half the fun. Little Stony—a native trout stream—tumbles down a dramatic, narrow gorge from the same plateau that holds one of only two natural lakes in Virginia, Mountain Lake. After the initial precipitous drop over steep cliffs into a deep pool, the stream winds and gurgles around boulders, creates more pools, and flows out into a wide valley northeast of Pembroke on its way to the New River.

Cool air sifts down the gorge from the high plateau, keeping temperatures down even in midsummer. The frozen falls are equally beautiful in winter. In the grassy valley of Little Stony Creek sits a beautiful picnic area with 15 tables and grills. Shading the area are apple and pear trees, native buckeyes, box elders, and walnut trees. Stream banks grow lush in late summer with the gold-orange blossoms of spotted jewelweed (*Impatiens capensis*).

In the parking lot, look for summer colonies of dame's rocket (*Hesperis matronalis*). The small, four-petaled blooms of pinkish purple grow on spires up to 4 feet tall. To fish for the native brook trout in Little Stony, use single barbed hooks and artificial lures only. Also needed are a fishing license, a trout stamp, and a national forest stamp.

Directions: From Blacksburg, follow US 460 west to Pembroke. Turn right on VA 623 and go 4 miles to parking lot. Total distance is 19.5 miles.

Activities: Hiking, picnicking, fishing.

Facilities: 15 picnic tables with grills; toilets; water fountains.

Dates: Open year-round.

Fees: None.

Closest town: Pembroke is 4 miles south.

For more information: Blacksburg Ranger District, 110 Southpark Drive, Blacksburg, VA 24060. Phone (540) 552-4641.

MOUNTAIN LAKE WILDERNESS

[Fig. 20(2)] This 11,113-acre wilderness area, which lies in three counties and two states, is the largest roadless area on the Blacksburg Ranger District of the Jefferson National Forest. Roadless, however, does not mean inaccessible. Unlike some wilderness areas, this one has ample hiking opportunities, including a stretch of the Appalachian Trail (AT) which crosses the area, and a loop hike through an old-growth forest. Motorized travel and bicycles on the wilderness area are prohibited. Access is limited to foot and horseback.

No question that Mountain Lake Wilderness is remote. It's located north of Blacksburg on the West Virginia border. The southwestern side is on a high plateau, which makes for easy walking, atop Salt Pond Mountain and Big Mountain in eastern

Giles County. On the southeastern side, the terrain drops steeply down Salt Pond Mountain. The northeast border of the wilderness catches the northwest corner of Craig County and a piece of Potts Mountain. The northern section spills over into Monroe County, West Virginia. This area of splendid natural diversity is just a half hour's drive north of the college town of Blacksburg. Visitors who like their wilderness mixed with comfort and good food can stay at a retreat on Mountain Lake, for which both the wilderness and resort are named.

Incredible though it may seem, this deep, cold lake sitting on a mountain plateau is the only natural lake in Virginia's mountains and one of only two lakes in the state that aren't man-made. (Lake Drummond, in the Great Dismal Swamp in southeastern Virginia, is the other.) Most of the world's natural lakes were formed by the scouring action of glaciers. However, in the last Ice Age, glaciers did not reach as far south as Virginia. Instead, a rock slide, perhaps several thousand years ago, dammed a narrow valley to form Mountain Lake. Debris gradually plugged holes in the slide as cold mountain springs filled the lake to the current depth of 100 feet. Water temperatures rarely exceed 72 degrees. Records show fluctuations in the depth over the past 200 years that could be caused by drought or by underground leaks through the talus forming the dam.

Snowshoe Hare

Very large back feet help support the snowshoe hare (*Lepus americanus*) on soft winter snow. Another name for this nocturnal mammal, "varying hare," refers to its camouflaging color change from white in winter to dark brown in summer. Hunters make use of the snowshoe's habit of running in wide circles before dogs. Once beagles are on the chase, hunters—rather than following after the dogs—wait for the hare to circle back to them.

Resort guests tell of beautiful stocked trout caught from the lake's waters.

Mountain Lake is not part of the Jefferson National Forest or Mountain Lake Wilderness, but the resort conducts hikes and bike rides onto the surrounding national forest. If the cabins and lake look familiar, it's because the movie *Dirty Dancing*, starring Patrick Swayze, was filmed at Mountain Lake Resort. The wilderness lies squarely on the Eastern Continental Divide. Rain or snow falling on the western edge seeks out streams that carry runoff to the New River, then the Ohio River, then the Mississippi River, and eventually the Gulf of Mexico. Precipitation falling on the eastern slope rushes away in the opposite direction to join water in the James River headed for the Chesapeake Bay.

Because of its position on mountaintops, Mountain Lake Wilderness provides an unpolluted beginning for several streams, including White Rock Branch of Stony Creek, Little Stony Creek, and several branches of Johns Creek and Potts Creek. Elevations at Mountain Lake Wilderness range from 2,200 to 4,100 feet. The variation encourages diverse flora and fauna.

For example, a wetland called Manns Bog produces sphagnum moss. Sphagnum moss is used by gardeners for packing and planting, and was once sought by physicians who used it to dress wounds. A tiny summer flower with five white petals, on a stem rising above a rosette of reddish, sticky basal leaves is also found here. It's the round-leaved sundew (*Drosera rotundifolia*)—a carnivorous plant that supplements its diet with an occasional insect. Sundew thrive in nutrient-poor soils and acidic bogs.

Patches of bluets (*Houstonia caerulea*) grow at overlooks, in the open woods, and on streamsides. Other flora to look for along the trails and streams include wood anemone (*Anemone quinquefolia*), galax (*Galax aphylla*), jack-in-the-pulpit (*Arisaema triphyllum*), and fire pink (*Silene virginica*). Stands of virgin red spruce, fir, and hemlock—all high-country trees—coexist with moss-covered boulders and carpets of fern in a moist hollow where War Spur Branch drops off the plateau and heads down to Johns Creek. The hemlocks in particular are massive in comparison to other trees in the surrounding oak-hickory climax forest. This stand is an easy walk along the War Spur and Chestnut trails.

In this and other stands of old-growth forest, many varieties of ferns grow. A pocket guide will help visitors identify which ferns they've found. Here at Mountain Lake Wilderness, slanting rays of sunlight sift through the thick canopy and catch the lacy fronds of cinnamon fern (*Osmunda cinnamomea*), bracken (*Pteridium aquilinum*), and hay-scented fern (*Dennstaedtia punctilobula*).

Perhaps because they were in so remote a location, the ancient trees somehow missed the scorched-earth logging practices of the early 1900s. To sit for awhile on a fallen log and soak up the immense peace among some of the largest and oldest trees in the East is well worth the walk along a 2.5-mile loop trail that begins and ends in the wilderness parking lot. Come in spring or early summer to catch the understory of rhododendron, mountain laurel, azalea, and blueberry in bloom. Or come to experience the near silence of an old-growth forest during a winter snowfall. During such a snowfall, a large, white rabbit with big feet may hop across the path. Snowshoe hares, creatures of Canadian provinces and Alaska, survive in high pockets of the Appalachians as far south as North Carolina. Snows that are only a couple of inches deep in the valley below can accumulate quickly on the plateau.

White Rocks is a remote campground on the northwest border of the wilderness in Giles County, near the West Virginia line. A 1.5-mile, easy, nature trail loop, called Virginia's Walk, begins and ends in the campground, offering an excellent place to see area wildlife, including white-tailed deer, gray fox, raccoon, opossum, wild turkey, ruffed grouse, and woodcock. Black bear and bobcat, though rarely seen, also live here.

Directions: West side of wilderness: from the junction of US 460 and US 460 bypass on the west side of Blacksburg, go west 6.6 miles and turn right on VA 700.

Go 6.9 miles to Mountain Lake Resort where VA 700 ends and VA 613 comes in from the left and heads north. Continue north on VA 613, which becomes a dirt road. In 3 miles, you'll see wilderness boundary signs on your right, and in another half mile you'll find the parking area for the War Spur and Chestnut trails. VA 613 traces the left flank of the wilderness for about the next 3.5 miles. The AT crosses this stretch of road.

East side of wilderness: from the junction of US 460 and US 460 bypass on the west side of Blacksburg, go west 5 miles and turn right on VA 42. Go .1 mile and turn left on VA 601. After about 1 mile, bear right at Y intersection and go 7.2 miles. Go left on VA 632. Parking area for AT, which leads into wilderness, is .7 mile on left.

WHITE ROCKS CAMPGROUND

[Fig. 20(3)] At the junction of US 460 and US 460 bypass west of Blacksburg, go 16 miles west and turn right on VA 635. Continue for 17 miles past Goldbond. Turn right on VA 613 (gravel). Go .8 mile to entrance on left and drive 1 mile to campground.

Activities: Hiking, horseback riding, backcountry camping, fishing, seasonal hunting.

Facilities: 25 miles of maintained hiking trails, AT shelter, ranger district office at Blacksburg. White Rocks Campground: 49 sites with lantern post, fireplace, and table; central water; trailer disposal station; toilets.

Dates: Wilderness open year-round. Campground open Apr. 1–Dec. 1.

Fees: A fee is charged for campsites.

Closest town: Blacksburg is 17 miles south.

For more information: Blacksburg Ranger District, 110 Southpark Drive, Blacksburg, VA 24060. Phone (540) 552-4641. Mountain Lake Resort, phone (800) 346-3334 or (540) 626-7121.

PETERS MOUNTAIN WILDERNESS

[Fig. 20(7)] This small wilderness, on the West Virginia border 19 miles west of Blacksburg, requires a bit of effort to explore. The 3,326 acres are on the southeast slope of steep-sided Peters Mountain, with elevations ranging from 3,000 feet on Stony Creek to 3,956 acres on the crest. No roads enter the wilderness, and most trails go straight up the hollows.

Southern Appalachian hardwoods cover the slopes, while hemlocks and a heath understory grow in protected ravines. An old-growth hemlock and red spruce forest remains on the area near the ridge. Stony Creek, which skirts the bottom edge of the wilderness (and is easily accessible along VA 635), is a stocked trout stream. Here, the big tooth aspen (*Populus grandidentata*), which grows in small patches along VA 635 in the Stony Creek drainage, is at the southern extremity of its range in Northeast America. The leaves range in size from 2 to 3.5 inches, they are oval to nearly round, and they have rounded teeth that are coarser than those of the quaking aspen.

Also scattered throughout the drainage are Fraser magnolia (*Magnolia fraseri*), a southern species. This magnolia has huge, fragrant white flowers in May. It's also called "earleaf magnolia," for the earlobe-shaped base of its waxy leaves.

The Interior Picnic Area, shaded by white pines, is located at the grassy edge of rhododendron-lined Stony Creek near the Appalachian Trail.

Directions: At the junction of US 460 and US 460 bypass west of Blacksburg, go 16 miles west and turn right on VA 635. About 2 miles past Goldbond, look for wilderness signs on trees on the left side. The road borders the wilderness for about 3 miles. To find Interior Picnic Area, after right turn on VA 635, go 9 miles and look on left.

Activities: Hiking, horseback riding, backcountry camping, fishing, hunting.

Facilities: Hiking trails, ranger district office at Blacksburg. Interior Picnic Area: 4 tables, grills, water (hand pumped).

Dates: Wilderness and picnic area open year-round.

Fees: None.

Closest town: Pembroke is about 11 miles southeast.

For more information: Blacksburg Ranger District, 110 Southpark Drive, Blacksburg, VA 24060. Phone (540) 552-4641.

Peters Mountain Mallow

An endangered wildflower, Peters Mountain mallow (*Iliamna corei*), grows in pockets of shallow soil on a sandstone outcrop on the northwest slope. The Nature Conservancy protects this single remaining population with fencing, artificial watering, and removal of encroaching vegetation.

PETERS MOUNTAIN WILDERNESS TRAILS

Most trails here follow streambeds up the steep hollows. The Appalachian Trail (AT) travels the wilderness boundary along the ridgeline of Peters Mountain, beginning at the very steep southern end of Peters Mountain, traveling 11 miles north, then descending Pine Swamp Branch to Stony Creek.

AT TRAIL TO RICE FIELDS. [Fig. 20(23)] The Rice Fields are extensive open pastures with rock outcroppings near the southern end of Peters Mountain. About a third of the hike consists of the very steep climb up the rocky southern end of Peters Mountain. The white-blazed AT then follows the saddles and peaks northeast along the ridge, with many expansive views into West Virginia to reward the hiker along the way.

With a map from the Ranger District Office, hikers can choose other trails, such as a four-wheel-drive path, to descend Peters Mountain for a loop hike. Hikers should bring extra clothing in case of sudden weather changes.

Directions: Follow US 460 west from Blacksburg, crossing the Senator Shumate

Bridge just west of Pearisburg. Go right on VA 641 (Stillhouse Branch Road). Parking lot is .5 mile ahead where AT crosses VA 641. Driving distance from Blacksburg is 23 miles.

Trail: 5-mile hike (one-way) up Peters Mountain and along ridge on edge of wilderness.

Elevation: 1,700 feet to 3,400 feet.

Degree of difficulty: Moderate with very steep beginning.

Surface: Part rocky, part natural forest floor.

CHEROKEE FLATS TRAIL. [Fig. 20(5)] Located just past the Interior Picnic Area on the banks of Stony Creek, Cherokee Flats is a handicapped- and stroller-accessible fishing trail. It provides access to fishing holes with stocked trout. The Cherokee Flats Trail gradually becomes more challenging as it goes along the creek.

Directions: At the junction of US 460 and US 460 bypass west of Blacksburg, go 16 miles west and turn right on VA 635. Go 10 miles to parking, on left.

Trail: Short, handicapped- and stroller-accessible fishing trail.

Elevation: 2,600 feet.

Degree of difficulty: Easy to moderate.

Surface: Paved and hard-packed forest floor (all handicapped accessible).

LOOP TRAIL. [Fig. 20(1)] This easy-to-moderate, 8-mile trail follows several small streams and offers an excellent opportunity to discover the variety of vegetation that can exist at varying elevations.

Directions: From US 460 west of Blacksburg, go 16 miles west and turn right on VA 635. Cherokee Flats Trail is 10 miles ahead (1 mile past the Interior Picnic Area), on left. For Loop Trail, go 11.4 miles (2.4 miles past Interior Picnic Area), turn left on VA 722, and go to red gate. Trailhead is .5 mile past gate.

Trail: 8-mile loop following streams.

Elevation: 2,600 to 3,300 feet.

Degree of difficulty: Easy to moderate.

Surface: Natural forest floor, grassy in places.

JOHNS CREEK MOUNTAIN TRAIL. [Fig. 20(21)] Located on Johns Creek Mountain, due north of Blacksburg, this trail offers a fine chance to see wildlife and stand on rock outcroppings, enjoying sweeping views of valleys below. From the western trailhead, the hike begins with a vigorous, .5-mile climb on the AT to the summit, and the rest of the hike is basically downhill. From the high point, the Johns Creek Mountain Trail extends out the ridgeline, crossing saddles and peaks, gradually descending for 3.5 miles to the parking area on VA 658. Combining this hike with the AT makes part of a circuit that will lead back to the highway within 3 or 4 miles of the parking area. Shelters are located along the AT. Maps of the ranger district are available in Blacksburg.

Directions: Western trailhead (.5-mile climb to summit): from US 460 west of Blacksburg, go about 5 miles west and turn right on VA 42 at Newport. Go 1 mile and turn left on VA 601. Go 7 miles to AT crossing. Eastern trailhead: after turning right on VA 42 at Newport, drive 9.5 miles to VA 658. Turn left. Trailhead is at crest of mountain.

Trail: 4-mile path that quickly climbs, then gradually descends Johns Creek Mountain.

Elevation: 2,755 to 3,600 feet.

Degree of difficulty: Easy to moderate.

Surface: Natural forest floor with rocky sections.

HIKING THE CASCADES AREA

If you enjoy wildflowers, a guidebook will be worth its weight in your backpack. Many varieties of wildflowers bloom at the falls and at various elevations on both the lower and upper trail here. Among them are cut-leaved toothwort (*Dentaria laciniata*), bloodroot (*Sanguinaria canadensis*), Dutchman's breeches (*Dicentra cucullaria*), jack-in-the-pulpit (*Arisaema triphyllum*), chickweed (*Stellaria media*), wild blue phlox (*Phlox divaricata*), wild ginger (*Asarum canadense*), Dutchman's pipe (*Aristolochia durior*), ginseng (*Panax quinquefolium*), Canada lily—also called meadow lily and wild yellow lily—(*Lilium canadense*), and spotted wintergreen (*Chimaphila maculata*). Look for violets in five different colors.

Jeffersonian twin-leaf (*Jeffersonia dyphylla*) was named for Thomas Jefferson by his friend, William Bartram. The limestone-loving plant looks a bit like bloodroot and mayapple. It's one of only two species of twin-leaf known in the world. Walking fern (*Camptosorus rhizophyllus*), which grows on rocky ledges, has blades with a long, pointed tip that reach to the ground and form new plants.

CASCADES NATIONAL RECREATION TRAIL. [Fig. 20(9)] The easy, 2-mile hike up Little Stony Creek to the Cascades is well worth the effort. The spirited mountain creek—a native trout stream—is shaded by dark hemlocks and rhododendron thickets that lean over the water. The 66-foot falls have carved a pool in the rocks below.

Trail: 2-mile climb up Little Stony Creek to 66-foot waterfall (4 miles round-trip).

Elevation: 2,140 to 2,810 feet.

Degree of difficulty: Easy.

Surface: Natural forest floor, rocks interspersed with old fire road.

THE APPALACHIAN TRAIL (AT). [Fig. 20] The AT has a strong presence in the Cascades Area. After crossing the New River west of Pearisburg, the AT ascends Peters Mountain going from 1,700 feet to 3,400 feet, and it follows the peaks and valleys along the

MAYFLY
(Order Ephemeroptera)
The translation of the mayfly's Latin name is "living a day."

crest—which is also the Virginia/West Virginia line—for about 11 miles. It then descends on the east flank and works its way up, down, and across the mountains toward the southeast.

Some stretches of the AT offer challenging climbs up steep slopes, while on other portions, hikers barely break a sweat as they follow the white-blazed trail along a ridge or plateau. These mountains are full of sandstone outcroppings with outstanding vistas, and the AT or a spur will take you to many of them. Three popular overlooks are the Rice Fields, requiring a steep climb to 3,400 feet from the southern end of Peters Mountain and a 5-mile hike; Wind Rock, an easy .75-mile loop at 4,100 feet on Potts Mountain; and Kelly Knob, a moderate, 4-mile round trip that ascends to 3,800 feet on Johns Creek Mountain.

MOUNTAIN LAKE WILDERNESS TRAILS. [Fig. 20(2)] With 25 miles of hiking trails penetrating its forests, Mountain Lake Wilderness receives its share of human visitation. Some trails are well marked and well used, while others are difficult to follow. Visitors should carry their own water, and assume that any stream or lake, no matter how remote or pristine looking, could harbor deadly bacteria or other contaminants. Hikers should be on the lookout for copperheads and rattlesnakes, both of which are very much at home in the mountains, and should prepare for rapidly changing weather at higher elevations by taking outer shells of wind-breaking clothing such as nylon or Gore-Tex.

WAR SPUR AND CHESTNUT TRAILS. [Fig. 20(4,10)] Combine these two trails for an easy, 2.5-mile loop through the awesome stand of virgin hemlock, red spruce, and balsam fir, and to War Spur Overlook for a beautiful view of the northwest slope of Johns Creek Mountain and the valley below. The trail is not blazed, but is easy to follow and may be used heavily during peak season. Blue-eyed grass (*Sisyrinchium augustifolium*), a tiny member of the iris family, blooms in early summer at the overlook.

Directions: Trailhead is 21 miles from ranger district office. Follow directions for Mountain Lake Wilderness, p. 121.

Trail: 2.5-mile loop and spur to overlook.

Elevation: 3,100 to 3,800 feet.

Degree of difficulty: Easy.

COVERED BRIDGES

Sinking Creek, in southeastern Giles County, has two covered bridges in close proximity. The most photographed is the small (55-foot), red Link's Farm Bridge [Fig. 20(13)], which is on the road to Mountain Lake. The other, just south of Link's Farm Bridge, is a 70-foot span named Sinking Creek Covered Bridge. Both were built about 1916 with modified Howe trusses.

Directions: Link's Farm Bridge: from the junction of US 460 and US 460 bypass on the west side of Blacksburg, go west 6.6 miles and turn right on VA 700. Bridge is short distance, on left.

Sinking Creek Covered Bridge: [Fig. 20(14)] from US 460 west of Blacksburg, go about 5 miles west and turn right on VA 42 at Newport. Go about 1 mile and turn left on VA 601. Bridge is on right.

NORTHERN EXTENSION OF BRUSHY MOUNTAIN, FLAT TOP MOUNTAIN, SUGAR RUN MOUNTAIN

DISMAL CREEK AND DISMAL FALLS. [Fig. 18(3)] A creek named "Dismal" is the focus of a recreation area in the national forest west of the New River in southwestern Giles County. Dismal Creek drains a basin in the southeastern slope of Flat Top Mountain, the south slope of Sugar Run Mountain, and the northwestern slope of Brushy Mountain. Before leaving Giles County, the creek tumbles over Dismal Falls, a 10-foot drop over several levels of sandstone. The erosion-resistant rock is part of a formation over 400 million years old. The creek then heads for Bland County, adding its waters to cold Kimberling Creek, fresh out of Kimberling Creek Wilderness [Fig. 18(5)] to the west. The creeks are part of the Walker Creek and New River watershed.

By itself, the waterfall would draw visitors from the heat of pavement and treeless avenues. The falls are easily accessible by car, and the cool mountain air that flows down the gorge is a welcome balm to folks from nearby Bland and Pearisburg, and to travelers on Interstate 77 with an afternoon to spare. Dismal Creek, though, has more than a pretty waterfall. There are stocked trout in the creek, a grassy camping area and wildlife pond, a campground for horseback riders, and excellent hiking opportunities, including a connection with the Appalachian Trail.

A young climax forest of hardwoods interspersed with pines covers the slopes. Three types of maples—striped, red, and sugar maples—are also found on Brushy Mountain. Growing in the Dismal Creek drainage between the falls and White Pines Horse Camp is a startling find for these parts, the Atlantic white-cedar (*Chamaecyparis thyoides*). More a tree of coastal freshwater swamps and bogs, the white-cedar has small, blueish green scales for leaves. Crush them to sniff the fragrance. Organ pipes were once made from the tree's resonant wood. Red cedar also grows throughout. The elevation at the falls is 2,300 feet, ascending to 4,000 feet on the ridges.

Directions: From Bland, in Bland County, go east on VA 42 about 13.5 miles. Go left (north) on VA 606 for 1 mile and turn right onto VA 201 just past store. Go about 1 mile to pull-off with trash receptacle marking the easy, 400-foot trail leading to the falls. Or, from Pearisburg in north-central Giles County, go south on VA 100 for 10 miles. Turn right on VA 42. After 10 miles, turn right on VA 606 and follow directions above.

Activities: Hiking, fishing, horseback riding, camping, backcountry camping, and hunting in surrounding national forest.

Facilities: 2 hiking trails, primitive campground, equestrian campground, horse trails, wildlife pond.

Dates: Open year-round.

Fees: None.

Closest town: Bland is about 16 miles southwest and Pearisburg is about 22 miles northeast.

For more information: Blacksburg Ranger District, 110 Southpark Drive, Blacksburg, VA 24060. Phone (540) 552-4641.

HIKING AT DISMAL CREEK. The well-maintained Appalachian Trail (AT), blazed with a white bar, enters Giles County near Dismal Falls. A short side trail leads north to the falls. The AT then follows the stream up the hollow, intersects with White Pine Horse Camp, and passes across the creek from Walnut Flats Campground. The AT turns north to follow the crest of Sugar Run Mountain, catches the northeast edge of Flat Top, and then heads 10 miles northeast along the top of Pearis Mountain for a meeting with the New River west of Pearisburg. The hike is mostly easy, except for the climb up Sugar Run Mountain. Scenic overlooks above the New River Valley await the hiker on the east end of Pearis Mountain.

The Ribble Trail begins farther up the road past Dismal Falls, and climbs up the hollow between Sugar Run and Flat Top mountains. This 2-mile, blue-blazed trail meets the AT at both ends, offering a 10-mile loop hike for a day's outing. Suggestion: Take the easier AT to climb the mountain and save the steeper Ribble Trail for the descent.

A guidebook is helpful for identifying the wide variety of mushrooms in the area in wet seasons. They should not be eaten, though, by anyone who is not an expert at identifying mushrooms. Even small amounts of poisonous mushrooms can be fatal, and many mushrooms are easily confused with others.

Directions: AT: access points include (1) junction of VA 42 and VA 606, (2) side trail at Dismal Falls [Fig. 18(3)], (3) White Pine Horse Camp [Fig. 18(2)], and (4) both ends of Ribble Trail [Fig. 18(9)].

RIBBLE TRAIL. Follow above directions to Dismal Falls but continue 4 miles on VA 201. Lower trailhead is at red gate where road makes right turn. Upper trailhead is farther up 201 at turnoff to Honey Springs Cabin.

Carolina Hemlock

Most hemlock in Virginia is Eastern hemlock (*Tsuga canadensis*). But a unique species, Carolina hemlock, is well suited to the rocky soil on the northwest slope of Havens WMA. The seldom-seen tree, endemic to the southern Appalachians, is at the northern extension of its small range that extends southwestward into the Carolinas, Tennessee, and northern Georgia. Subtle differences help tree enthusiasts tell the two hemlocks apart. Needles of the Carolina hemlock are spirally arranged on the branches, giving them a bottle-brush appearance, while needles of the Eastern hemlock lie flat in a single plane. Ruffed grouse eat hemlock seeds. Deer, red squirrels, and rabbits browse the twigs.

Trail: AT is a 23-mile, mountainous trek from Dismal Falls to Pearisburg, or it connects with Ribble Trail for a 10-mile loop. Ribble Trail is a 2-mile uphill path, connecting with the AT on both ends.

Elevation: AT goes from 2,100 to 3,670 feet. Ribble Trail goes from 2,560 to 3,670 feet.

Degree of difficulty: AT is easy, with moderate and steep sections. Ribble Trail is moderate with steep sections.

CAMPING AT DISMAL CREEK. Walnut Flats Campground [Fig. 18(1)] is located in a grassy area sparsely shaded by a few walnut and pine trees. Because of the lack of facilities, this primitive campground gets only light use, except during hunting season. Anyone who sits quietly near the pond here at dusk or at dawn can watch the pond life and listen to the variety of frogs.

White Pine Horse Camp [Fig. 18(2)] is small and primitive, and shaded by white pines. Orange-blazed trails for horseback riding lead out of the campground.

Directions: Follow directions above to right turn on VA 201 just past store. Go about 1.7 miles to White Pine Horse Camp on right or 2.5 miles to Walnut Flats Campground on left. AT shelter is located about 2 miles up mountain from VA 201 access at lower end of Ribble Trail.

Facilities: Walnut Flats: 6 sites with tables, grills, and lantern posts; hand-pumped well water; pit toilet. White Pine: 5 sites with grills, well water, pit toilets, loading ramp, and hitching post for horses; central corral.

Dates: Open year-round.

Fees: None.

FORT LEWIS MOUNTAIN

HAVENS WILDLIFE MANAGEMENT AREA. [Fig. 20(11)] Lightly used and steeply forested with oaks, hickories, and pines, Havens Wildlife Management Area (WMA) is just the place for those looking for a solitary outing for hiking, hunting, wildlife viewing, or just getting away from it all. The WMA is on Fort Lewis Mountain, within earshot of trucks rumbling along I-81 west of Roanoke. There are populations of deer, turkey, squirrel, and grouse on the area—even black bear—but steep and somewhat inaccessible terrain discourages all but the hardiest hunter or the most dedicated wildflower enthusiast. Several trails and gated roads that meander through the area and along the crest of Fort Lewis Mountain offer foot access, however.

Like all 29 wildlife management areas in Virginia, Havens was purchased with and is maintained through the sale of state hunting and fishing licenses. And like all wildlife management areas, the 7,190-acre Havens area is open to the public for visits at no charge. Streams on Havens are intermittent rather than permanent, so fishing is out, though several water holes for wildlife have been built. Elevations range from 1,500 feet to 3,200 feet. The area was logged prior to 1930 when the game department bought the property, and it has been slow to recover because of poor, thin soil.

The Virginia Department of Game and Inland Fisheries (VDGIF), which manages the WMA, is looking for a volunteer group interested in developing a hiking trail into the area. The trail would possibly start at the Angeline parking area and climb to connect with the Man and Horse Trail (constructed by the Civilian Conservation Corps) and the administrative access road along the ridge of Fort Lewis Mountain. Such a trail would lead through the healthy stand of Carolina hemlocks on the northwest slope. These handsome hemlocks, which grow well in rocky locations, have not been cut for decades and have grown quite tall.

Seeded power line rights-of-way and 5 acres of grassy openings are helping to improve conditions for some wildlife. The openings are planted in clover and orchard grass, specifically to attract wild turkey. The project is a joint venture of the VDGIF, the Virginia Department of Forestry, and the National Wild Turkey Federation. Both deer and turkey are using the openings. Havens is less than 45 minutes from the urban bustle of Roanoke and Salem, thus making it close and attractive to individuals and groups who like to view wildlife and wildflowers, or park the car to investigate on foot unspoiled nature in a mountain setting.

Directions: Mason Cove entrance: from I-81 west of Roanoke, take Exit 140 and go north on VA 311. After about 3 miles, turn left on VA 864. In less than 2 miles, go left on VA 622. When you see yellow hash marks on trees on left side, indicating WMA property, you can pull over anywhere, cross the creek, and walk up into the management area. Angeline Hunter Access (northwest slope): after left turn onto VA 622, drive 3 miles to small (4-car) Angeline Parking Access on left. A small footbridge spans Mason Creek. Carroll Access Road (southeast slope where gate is open only during hunting season): in downtown Salem, at junction of US 460 (Main Street)

YELLOW BIRCH
(Betula alleghaniensis)
The unique bark of the birch is thin and shreddy. This bark is flammable even when wet, so it is useful for campsites.

and VA 311, go west about .5 mile on US 460 and turn right on VA 619 (Wildwood Road). Go about 2 miles and turn right on Carroll Access Road and go about 1 mile to parking area. When gate is closed, you may pull over and walk up the road. Do not block access to gate. Several other gated roads offer walking access into the area. Consult a gazetteer or contact the VDGIF for a map.

Activities: Hunting, hiking. Target shooting and motorized vehicles are not allowed.

Facilities: Two parking areas and several foot trails. Additional parking areas are being developed along Mason Creek on VA 622.

Dates: Open year-round.

Fees: None.

Closest town: Salem is about 5 miles east.

For more information: Virginia Department of Game and Inland Fisheries, Region II Office, Route 6, Box 410, Forest, VA 24551-9806. Phone (804) 525-7522. Or, VDGIF Headquarters, 4010 West Broad Street, Richmond, VA 23230. Phone (804) 367-1000.

DIXIE CAVERNS

[Fig. 20(12)] In limestone rock at the southeastern corner of Fort Lewis Mountain is the southernmost commercial cavern in Virginia. As in many of the state's caves, saltpeter was once mined from Dixie Caverns to make gunpowder. Some also think the Shawnee Indians once obtained clay from the mines.

Most caves lead immediately down in the earth. Dixie Caverns, however, which is located on a fault line called the Salem Fault, leads up to the Cathedral Room—over 200 feet square and more than 160 feet high. Then the tour leads down to formations called Turkey Wing, Magic Mirror, Leaning Tower, Frozen Waterfall, and a 57-ton, bell-shaped formation called Wedding Bell.

The variety of formations, or speleothems, include draperies, rimstone, and flowstone, including a large and impressive flowstone speleothem called Golden Cascade. A colony of bats that inhabits the cave seems undisturbed by human intrusion, according to cave management. The guided tour takes about 45 minutes.

Directions: From I-81 in western Roanoke County, take Exit 132. Go south on US 11 a short distance to entrance on left.

Activities: Guided cave tours, camping. Fishing nearby in Roanoke River.

Facilities: Commercial cave, pottery shop, rock and mineral shop, souvenir shop. Campground with restrooms, bathhouses, hookups.

Dates: Caverns and campgrounds: open year-round. Hours are seasonal.

Fees: There is a fee for admission.

Closest town: Salem is 4 miles north.

For more information: Dixie Caverns, 5753 West Main Street, Salem, VA 24153. Phone (540) 380-2085.

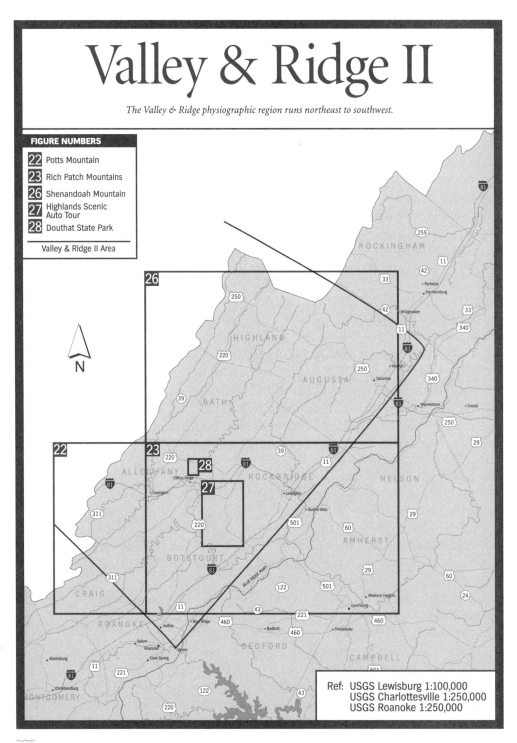

Valley & Ridge II

The Valley & Ridge physiographic region runs northeast to southwest.

FIGURE NUMBERS

22 Potts Mountain
23 Rich Patch Mountains
26 Shenandoah Mountain
27 Highlands Scenic Auto Tour
28 Douthat State Park

Valley & Ridge II Area

N

Ref: USGS Lewisburg 1:100,000
USGS Charlottesville 1:250,000
USGS Roanoke 1:250,000

Valley and Ridge II

In this book, the Valley and Ridge province is divided into three sections: Valley and Ridge I, Valley and Ridge II, and Valley and Ridge III. Valley and Ridge II includes sites ranging from wilderness areas to historic inns to outstanding state parks. The western border of this section of the Valley and Ridge province begins in Craig County and follows the West Virginia/Virginia state line until it reaches US 250 and the northern border of the Deerfield Ranger District of the George Washington National Forest. The eastern border of Valley and Ridge II begins north of Roanoke and ends north of Staunton on Interstate 81 in Augusta County. This section has some of Virginia's more popular outdoor attractions, including Douthat State Park, the James River District, and Ramsey's Draft Wilderness. (For more information on the geology of the Valley and Ridge province, see the introduction to the Valley and Ridge section, page 71.)

[*Above*: Humpback bridge on a snowy morning]

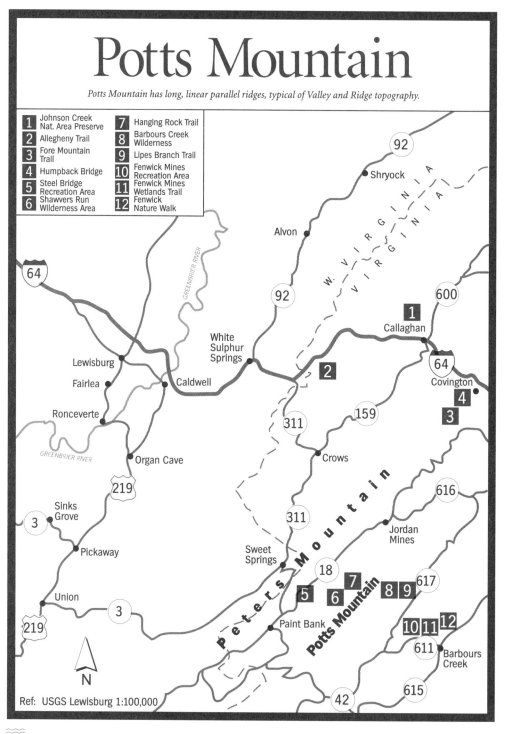

Potts Mountain

Potts Mountain has long, linear parallel ridges, typical of Valley and Ridge topography.

1 Johnson Creek Nat. Area Preserve
2 Allegheny Trail
3 Fore Mountain Trail
4 Humpback Bridge
5 Steel Bridge Recreation Area
6 Shawvers Run Wilderness Area
7 Hanging Rock Trail
8 Barbours Creek Wilderness
9 Lipes Branch Trail
10 Fenwick Mines Recreation Area
11 Fenwick Mines Wetlands Trail
12 Fenwick Nature Walk

Ref: USGS Lewisburg 1:100,000

New Castle Ranger District

[Fig. 15] The New Castle Ranger District occupies 141,879 acres of the Jefferson National Forest northwest of Roanoke and Interstate 81. At the heart of the district in Craig County is the town of New Castle, where the ranger district office is located. The district spreads across the mountainous sections of Craig County and a big bite of southwestern Botetourt County, interspersed with private lands mostly in the river drainages. On the northwestern side, the New Castle District spills over Potts Mountain into Monroe County, West Virginia.

Long, linear parallel ridges, typical of Valley and Ridge topography, include Potts Mountain, Johns Creek Mountain, Sinking Creek Mountain, North Mountain, Bald Mountain, Richpatch Mountains, Price Mountain, and Patterson Mountain. The district is bordered to the west and southwest in southwestern Craig County by the Blacksburg Ranger District along VA 636, 658, 42, 209, 651, and 620. The southeast border runs from north central Roanoke County northeast into Botetourt County along a string of connecting roads that include VA 624, 311, 698, 690, 600, 666, 684, 682, and 681, and US 220 to Eagle Rock on the James River. To the northeast is the James River District of the George Washington National Forest, separated from the Jefferson by VA 615 and 621 and by the northwest borders of Botetourt County and Alleghany County.

The New Castle District is a good choice for recreation during peak seasons. When state parks and commercial sites are busting at the seams, the campgrounds, trails, and picnic areas in these western mountains may still offer solitude. The district has two campgrounds and three picnic areas, two wilderness areas, and several networks of hiking trails. Stop by the office on the north side of New Castle for a district map and advice on trails and facilities.

For more information: New Castle Ranger District, Jefferson National Forest, VA 615, Box 246, New Castle, VA 24127. Phone (540) 864-5195.

Directions: The New Castle Ranger District office is on VA 615, 3 miles east of New Castle.

VIRGINIA SCENIC BYWAYS

The New Castle Ranger District is crisscrossed at New Castle by three scenic roads. Running northeast/southwest are VA 42 and VA 615. VA 311 heads southeast and northwest out of New Castle.

VA 42. VA 42 comes into the district from the southwest through the basin of a high valley formed by the parallel ridges of Johns Creek and Sinking Creek mountains. Along the way are nineteenth-century homes, farms with rail fences, graveyards with tombstones of Civil War veterans, and places with the curious names of Looney and The Murder Hole. Private land reaches to the ridgetop on each side of the valley, where national forest lands begin. At the northeastern end of the valley, just southwest of New Castle, the two mountains curve toward each other, nearly meeting. From the air, the highland resembles a giant index finger pointing the way to the little town.

About 7.5 miles southwest of New Castle, VA 42 crosses the Continental Divide. Waters of Sinking Creek flow southwest into the New River and eventually make it to the Gulf of Mexico. Waters of Meadow Creek flow to the northeast, tumbling over Meadow Creek Falls at the tip of the index finger. Just south of New Castle, Meadow Creek pours fresh highland water into Craig Creek and sends it on its way to the James River and the Atlantic.

VA 615. [Fig. 23] VA 615, not a straight road by most standards, nevertheless takes a much shorter route down Craig Creek Valley than does the serpentine creek itself as both creek and highway connect New Castle in Craig County to Eagle Rock in Botetourt County.

Private land also borders this road on its course down Craig Creek Valley, but side roads lead to public national forest lands. The Ferrier Trail is on Lick Mountain 9 miles southeast of New Castle. Fenwick Mines Recreation Area is on Bald Mountain, 7 miles northeast of New Castle. Craig Creek Recreation Area and a network of Patterson Mountain trails are also accessible off VA 615, 11 miles northeast of New Castle near Oriskany. At the northeast end of Craig Creek Valley is a highlight of the district—the trail up Roaring Run. Six miles northeast of New Castle is VA 606, another designated scenic road that takes off from VA 615 to the southeast. On its way to Fincastle, 606 crosses Price Mountain, intersecting the long Price Mountain Trail at the top.

VA 311. [Fig. 22] Scenic VA 311 is a popular route into the New Castle district from I-81 or from Roanoke. From Exit 140 on I-81, it's a 10-mile trip north on 311 across Catawba Mountain to the southern boundary of the district and the southern end of North Mountain. The Appalachian Trail is accessible from a parking area here.

VA 311 then turns north to follow Craig Creek to New Castle. From New Castle to the West Virginia line, the road goes through the Johns Creek valley for a few miles then snakes its way across and between a succession of ridges to the base of Peters Mountain at the West Virginia line. Along the way are placid valleys and an outstanding mountaintop view on Potts Mountain. Steel Bridge Campground is on Potts Creek (VA 18) near the northwest end of this scenic road.

NORTH MOUNTAIN TRAIL

[Fig. 20(22)] This yellow-blazed trail follows craggy peaks and swales for 13 miles along the ridge of North Mountain, opening to many panoramic views. (This is a different trail from North Mountain Trail on Great North Mountain in Augusta County.) The ridgeline is on the Craig County/Roanoke County line at the southwestern end and on the Craig County/Botetourt County line on the northeastern end. Three spurs lead down the northwest slope from the North Mountain Trail to

VA 224, branching off from the main trail at 2.4 miles (Deer Trail), 3.4 miles (Grouse Trail), and 6 miles (Turkey Trail) from the southwestern trailhead. A car waiting at the hikers' destination will keep them from having to backtrack.

The 9 miles on the southwestern end were once a part of the Appalachian Trail before the AT was rerouted. Across VA 311 from the southwestern trailhead, more trails lead to Dragon's Tooth, a fang-shaped mountain with rock outcroppings where views make the climb rewarding.

On the northeastern end, the trail connects to Price Mountain Trail, Ferrier Trail, and Lick Branch Trail. After crossing VA 606, Price Mountain Trail connects to Sulphur Ridge Trail for a 4.5-mile loop hike. Or, hikers can continue down the Price Mountain ridge to a complex of trails on Patterson Mountain in the vicinity of Craig Creek Recreation Area.

Directions: From I-81 at Roanoke, take Exit 140 and drive north on VA 311 for 9.8 miles (.2 mile past junction with VA 624) to trailhead on right.

Trail: 13-mile linear path along the rugged crest of North Mountain.

Elevation: 1,750–3,200 feet.

Degree of difficulty: Moderate, with strenuous sections.

Surface: Natural forest floor with many rocky sections.

FENWICK MINES RECREATION AREA

[Fig. 22(10)] Fenwick Mines is in Craig County, about 7 miles north of New Castle. A large open area for family or group picnics has tables and grills. Between 1892 and 1923, the Low Moor Iron Company hauled iron ore taken from nearby mines to area furnaces by railroad. Hundreds of people lived at the site and worked the nearby mines.

A mine trail leads to the remains of open pit mines and foundations of old mining structures. Two short but enjoyable trails lead out of the first parking area. Wetlands created by both beavers and humans attract a rich variety of plants and animals, making this place one of the best in the New Castle district for identifying wetland vegetation and for wildlife and birdwatching. An early-morning bird walk with binoculars is one of the best ways to appreciate the trails here.

Directions: From New Castle, drive 5 miles north on VA 615. Turn left on VA 611 and go .5 mile. Turn right on VA 685 to enter recreation area. Parking area for trails is about 1 mile, on right. For picnic area, continue .5 mile and turn right on FR 229. Picnic area is on the right. Mine trail is just past the picnic area, on left.

Activities: Hiking, picnicking, fishing, horseback riding, hunting in surrounding national forest.

Facilities: Picnic tables and shelters, restrooms, game fields, horse loading ramp. Also, picnic area, trail, and restrooms for the disabled.

Dates: Open year-round.

Fees: None.

Closest town: New Castle, 7 miles south.

For more information: New Castle Ranger District, Jefferson National Forest, VA 615, Box 246, New Castle, VA 24127. Phone (540) 864-5195.

FENWICK MINES WETLANDS TRAIL. [Fig. 22(11)] This easy path, designed especially for people with disabilities, underscores the value of wetlands for both plant and animal diversity. The trail leads first through an upland oak-hickory forest, then into a swamp (a wetland with trees), then a marsh (wetland without trees).

In the upland hardwoods at the beginning of the trail, large oaks and hickories in what is called late-order successional woodland screen out sunlight. Undergrowth is sparse. But after a bridge crossing at Mill Creek, vegetation is much smaller and thicker. Following a timber harvest here, trees are returning but are only at early successional growth stage. More sunlight filters through the smaller trees to maintain laurel and other broadleaf evergreens, which are extremely efficient light gatherers. An examination of the soil reveals high water content. It's been 70 years since the mining operation ceased, but the earthen dikes built then continue to hold water and provide habitat for a variety of moisture-loving plants and animals.

The swampy area with tree cover gives way to an open grassy marsh, where highly specialized plants withstand periodic or continuous submersion, acting as a highly efficient water filtration system. Cattails grow from the shallows. The habitat is perfect for patches of sweet pepperbush (*Clethra alnifolia*). This member of the white alder family grows 3 to 10 feet high and has upright clusters of fragrant white flowers in late summer. Narrowleaf meadowsweet (*Spiraea alba*), a shrub that may attain 6 feet, also grows in the marsh. Its steeple-shaped clusters of tiny, five-petaled white flowers bloom through the summer. The hollow stems of the plant were used by Indians for their pipes and were the inspiration for the naming of Pipestem Resort in West Virginia. Joe-pye-weed (*Eupatorium fistulosum*), American bittersweet (*Celastrus scandens*), and phlox are other varieties found here.

Newts, salamanders, snails, small fish, and insects adapted to a wet environment live in the marsh. Choruses of several varieties of frogs fill the evening with sound. Beavers and muskrats feed on the succulent plants.

RUFOUS-SIDED TOWHEE

(Pipilo erythrophthalmus)
A loud "drink-your-tea" song coming from underbrush or thicket identifies the towhee.

Wood ducks and mallards nest in the area. The familiar raspy whistle of red-winged blackbirds, the bubbly song of wood thrushes, and the calls of several varieties of warblers compete for the bird watcher's attention.

Trailheads are located on the left side of the parking area and at the picnic area.

Trail: .8-mile path through wetlands.

Elevation: 1,600 feet.

Degree of difficulty: Easy.

Surface: Crushed limestone with wood edging.

FENWICK NATURE WALK. [Fig. 22(12)] At the right side of the first parking lot is the self-guided Fenwick Nature Walk, beautifully groomed for use by those with disabilities. The short trail descends gradually along the old railroad bed, shaded by oak, cherry, birch, and hemlock. It returns along Mill Creek, carrying Bald Mountain's waters over sculpted rock ledges to Craig Creek. Shade trees and cool waters make this hike a good choice on a hot summer day.

Trail: 1-mile interpretive loop along old railroad grade and Mill Creek.

Elevation: 1,600 feet.

Degree of difficulty: Easy.

CRAIG CREEK RECREATION AREA

[Fig. 23(17)] Craig Creek Recreation Area is the New Castle Ranger District's premiere group facility. Commanding views of Craig Bluffs, warm-water fishing and canoeing, picnicking, highly diverse watchable wildlife, hiking, swimming, and group facilities are offered.

This area encompasses more than 130 acres of pastureland and woodland on a peninsula formed by Craig Creek. Acres of pastureland are available for exploration. Wildlife is abundant. Nearby is the historic iron town, Oriskany. A rail grade, now used as a road, once connected the early iron industry of Craig and Botetourt counties to the James River and the Atlantic.

Look for wildflowers of open fields such as the common evening primrose (*Oenothera biennis*), moth mullein (*Verbascum blattaria*), viper's bugloss (*Echium vulgare*), and heal-all (*Prunella vulgaris*). The transition areas between fields and woods are especially good places to find a variety of both plant and animal species.

Directions: Take VA 615 11 miles north of New Castle and go right on VA 817 in Oriskany. Go .5 mile and go right at sign into recreation area.

Activities: Primitive camping, picnicking, fishing, hiking, horseback riding, hunting in surrounding national forest.

Facilities: 7 picnic tables and grills; drinking water; vault toilets; open field for tents, RVs, and horses.

Dates: Open year-round.

Fees: None.

Closest town: Oriskany, 1 mile west. New Castle, 11 miles southwest.

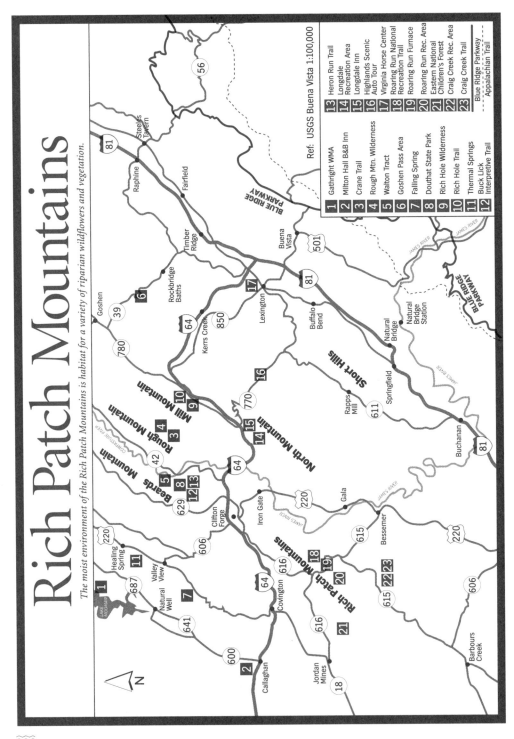

Rich Patch Mountains

The moist environment of the Rich Patch Mountains is habitat for a variety of riparian wildflowers and vegetation.

Ref: USGS Buena Vista 1:100,000

1	Gathright WMA	
2	Milton Hall B&B Inn	
3	Crane Trail	
4	Rough Mtn. Wilderness	
5	Walton Tract	
6	Goshen Pass Area	
7	Falling Spring	
8	Douthat State Park	
9	Rich Hole Wilderness	
10	Rich Hole Trail	
11	Thermal Springs	
12	Buck Lick Interpretive Trail	
13	Heron Run Trail	
14	Longdale Recreation Area	
15	Longdale Inn	
16	Highlands Scenic Auto Tour	
17	Virginia Horse Center	
18	Roaring Run National Recreation Trail	
19	Roaring Run Furnace	
20	Roaring Run Rec. Area	
21	Eastern National Children's Forest	
22	Craig Creek Rec. Area	
23	Craig Creek Trail	

For more information: New Castle Ranger District, Jefferson National Forest, VA 615, Box 246, New Castle, VA 24127. Phone (540) 864-5195.

CRAIG CREEK TRAIL. [Fig. 23(23)] At Craig Creek Recreation Area, this 2-mile loop trail leads across a low ridge forested with pines, oaks, and hickories and through open fields along Craig Creek.

Trail: 2-mile loop.

Elevation: 1,200 feet.

Degree of difficulty: Easy.

ROARING RUN RECREATION AREA

[Fig. 23(20)] At the northernmost point of the New Castle Ranger District is one of Jefferson National Forest's best-kept secrets. Roaring Run Recreation Area is located in the Rich Patch Mountains on the George Washington National Forest border south of Clifton Forge and Covington.

The area is steeped with history, both human and natural. The moist environment of the mountain gorge is habitat for a variety of riparian wildflowers and vegetation. In addition, the U.S. Forest Service has constructed attractive facilities and trails. Three interconnecting trails cover some 14 miles of scenic gorges, forested slopes, and mountain knobs with winter views.

ROARING RUN FURNACE. [Fig. 23(19)] Across the creek from the shaded picnic grounds, the remains of Roaring Run Furnace stand quiet and cool in the shadow of the Rich Patch Mountains. In the early 1800s, however, before the first artillery fire of the Civil War, the furnace glowed white hot as sandstone and quartzite containing iron ore from the mountains were fired to 2,600 degrees. Molton iron would flow from the rock into sand trenches to cool, forming ingots for the making of stoves, skillets, and other iron products for nineteenth-century Americans.

Today, trails lead hikers back into the mountain hollows and up the slopes where tram lines once shuttled back and forth to bring out the iron-laden rock. Children pick up marble-sized irregular stones and curiously examine the shiny black and green traces of slag. The colorful slag is man-made glass, a leftover or dross formed during the intense heating of sandstone and quartzite. The refuse is similar to obsidian, a volcanic glass. With its orientation toward the sun and its riparian environment, Roaring Run has the most diverse collection of wildflowers on the New Castle District—an amazing fact considering the area was environmentally terrorized by iron mining and logging. (To keep such furnaces fueled, entire mountains were stripped of their trees.)

Among the flowers to discover here are the beautiful showy orchis (*Orchis spectabilis*), the crested dwarf iris (*Iris cristata*), jack-in-the-pulpit (*Arisaema triphyllum*), bloodroot (*Sanguinaria canadensis*), black-eyed susan (*Rudbekia hirta*), trout lily (*Erythronium americanum*), and many varieties of trillium.

In spring and summer, woodland birds such as the wood thrush, ovenbird, and white-eyed vireo sing from the trees. Pine warblers, worm-eating warblers, blue-gray gnatcatchers, and white-breasted nuthatches are also present. Information boards explain the operation of the furnace, which is listed on the National Register of Historic Places.

Directions: From I-64 between Clifton Forge and Covington, take Exit 2. Go south on VA 696 for .3 mile. Turn right on VA 616 (Rich Patch Road) and drive 5.4 miles. Turn left on VA 621 (Roaring Run Road) and go 3.2 miles to recreation area entrance. From I-81, use US 220 (Exit 150 north of Roanoke) or VA 43 (Exit 167 at Buchanan) and go northwest to Eagle Rock. At Eagle Rock, take VA 615 west for 7 miles. Go right on VA 621 (Roaring Run Road) and go about 1 mile to recreation area.

Activities: Hiking, fishing for stocked trout.

Facilities: 3 trails, 15 picnic tables with grills, restrooms with pit toilets, information board. No drinking water.

Dates: Open year-round.

Fees: There is a charge for parking.

Closest town: Clifton Forge, 12 miles north.

For more information: New Castle Ranger District, Jefferson National Forest, VA 615, Box 246, New Castle, VA 24127. Phone (540) 864-5195.

ROARING RUN NATIONAL RECREATION TRAIL. [Fig. 23(18)] Roaring Run comes by its name honestly. From the 3,280-foot summit of Montgomery Knob, water comes cascading through a gap in the Rich Patch Mountains, coursing over and around boulders, shooting through flumes, hesitating only briefly in quiet pools in its eagerness to reach Craig Creek. In the most tumultuous sections, a fine mist refreshes hikers on hot summer days.

Its designation as a National Recreation Trail has engendered funding for wooden benches, boardwalks with railings over precipitous or rocky areas, and other construction that makes this short trail a pleasure to walk. However, federal budget cutting leaves in doubt maintenance and any future construction on this and the area's other two trails.

The trail culminates at a picturesque waterfall, where Roaring Run plunges 35 feet over stair-step rock ledges. Below the falls may be a lone angler, working the pools for colorful rainbow trout stocked by the state. Hemlocks that shade the trout pools along Roaring Run, sadly, are dying. The once-beautiful evergreen giants are under attack by the wooly adelgid, an exotic Asian pest. New Castle and Glenwood ranger districts have been hard hit by the predatory insect (*see* Ghost Forests, page 11).

Trail: 1.5 mile path (one-way) up gorge to falls.

Elevation: 1,160–1,520 feet.

Degree of difficulty: Easy.

Surface: Natural forest floor, wooden bridges and boardwalks, some rocky sections.

🔲 STEEL BRIDGE RECREATION AREA

[Fig. 22(5)] Steel Bridge is at the northern tip of Craig County on Potts Creek, just north of Shawvers Run Wilderness Area. Nearby Paint Bank takes its name from the red ochre that nomadic Indians once extracted from the clay soil on the banks of Potts Creek. The pigment was used to color their pottery, clothing, and other artifacts.

Among the tribes that frequented these mountains were Monacans, who came from what are now the southwest Virginia counties of Buchanan, Dickenson, and Wise. To their south were the Cherokees of North Carolina, and to the north were the fearsome Iroquois tribes of Pennsylvania and New York.

The Monacans perfected the art of hiding as the best defense from their enemies. On the thighs of young males entering manhood, the tribe tattooed its symbol of power—not a mountain lion, an eagle, or a wolf but a turtle. Now, instead of the red ochre that once lured Indians to Paint Bank, stocked trout lure modern anglers to deep pools beneath rock overhangs along the banks of Potts Creek. On hot summer days, the cold cascading water tumbling over rock ledges also invites children and adults to wade.

When the fish aren't biting, a trip to Paint Bank Trout Hatchery where the stocked trout are raised is an option. The hatchery is on VA 311, 2 miles south of Paint Bank. Shaded campsites are spread out for .5 mile at Steel Bridge, offering plenty of privacy in a beautiful setting.

MOUNTAIN LAUREL
(Kalmia latifolia)

Directions: Take VA 311 north from New Castle 16 miles to Paint Bank. Turn right on VA 18 and go 3.5 miles to campground on Potts Creek.

Activities: Camping, picnicking (at empty campsites), fishing for stocked trout, hiking, hunting in surrounding national forest.

Facilities: 20 primitive sites with tables and fireplaces, hand-pumped water, pit toilets.

Dates: Open year-round.

Fees: None.

Closest town: New Castle, 19 miles south.

For more information: New Castle Ranger District, Jefferson National Forest, VA 615, Box 246, New Castle, VA 24127. Phone (540) 864-5195. Paint Bank Trout Hatchery, Route 311, Route 1, Box 2, Paint Bank, VA 24131. Phone (540) 897-5401.

George Washington National Forest

George Washington National Forest covers a million acres.

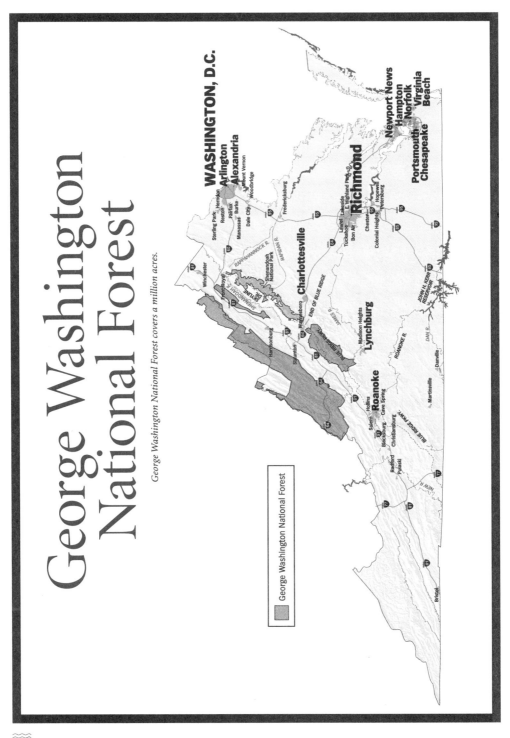

George Washington National Forest

SHAWVERS RUN WILDERNESS AREA

[Fig. 22(6)] The small Shawvers Run Wilderness Area hides its 3,467 acres in the isolated northern corner of Craig County, about 30 miles northwest of Roanoke. Its terrain is rough and mountainous. Native brook trout draw occasional fly-fishermen to the two Potts Creek tributaries here. Shawvers Run empties out the northeast end of the wilderness while Valley Branch empties out the southwest end.

Hemlock, yellow pine, and white pine provide green in the hollows throughout the year, adding their cool, dark beauty to the narrow rocky canyon through which Valley Branch is funneled. Shadbush, flowering dogwood, serviceberry, and redbud grow beneath a canopy of oaks and hickories on the slopes. Some 10 miles of old roads provide quiet approaches to the heart of this nearly unused wilderness. The roads are not maintained, so following them will mean negotiating downed trees. The Hanging Rock Trail is a popular stop for the few who go out of their way to find Shawvers Run Wilderness Area.

Directions: From New Castle, follow VA 311 for 6 miles to top of Potts Mountain. Turn right on FR 177.1, and go 3 miles to parking area on left, at wilderness border. The Hanging Rock Trail begins from this lot.

Activities: Hiking, backcountry camping, fishing for native brook trout, seasonal hunting.

Facilities: 1 short hiking trail.

Dates: Open year-round.

Fees: None.

Closest town: New Castle, 9 miles southeast.

For more information: New Castle Ranger District, Jefferson National Forest, VA 615, Box 246, New Castle, VA 24127. Phone (540) 864-5195.

HANGING ROCK TRAIL. [Fig. 22(7)] This short trail climbs then descends to Hanging Rock, a rock outcropping on the northwest ridge of Potts Mountain with outstanding views into Hanging Rock Valley. At the overlook, Shawvers Run Wilderness is northeast. The long wall-like ridge of Peters Mountain can be seen to the northwest.

Trail: 1-mile round trip to overlook and back to parking area.

Elevation: 3,650–3,800 feet.

Degree of difficulty: Easy.

Surface: Natural forest floor and rock.

BARBOURS CREEK WILDERNESS AREA

[Fig. 22(8)] The 5,700-acre Barbours Creek Wilderness covers the rugged southeastern slope of Potts Mountain in the northeastern corner of Craig County. No areas of significant human population are anywhere near this remote country. The majority of use is from anglers who cast for stocked trout in the North Fork of Barbours Creek and hikers who enjoy the peace and seclusion of the wilderness

Belted Kingfisher

A belted kingfisher (*Megaceryle alcyon*) may put on a show for people who stop to sit on a log and watch the pond. Perched on a dead limb above the water, the kingfisher plunges headlong into the water and comes up with a salamander that made the mistake of rising to the surface. The handsome, crested bird with a slate-blue back and daggerlike beak often establishes a route to travel as it feeds, perching in the same spots along the way.

interior. Barbours Creek flows beside VA 617 along the southern border of the wilderness. Forest Road 176 traces the southern boundary of the wilderness.

Red and white oaks, hickories, tulip poplars, and red maples forest the lower southeast-facing slope, while occasional stands of hemlock, rhododendron, and mountain laurel line the creeks and hide in ravines.

Chestnut oak and yellow pines favor the south and west exposures on the drier upper slope. Witch-hazel, flowering dogwood, serviceberry, and sassafras comprise some of the understory. The forest opens at the summit of Potts Mountain to reveal a 50-acre bald. During the 1930s, the summit was cleared for a fire tower which is no longer in use. Once the soil is disturbed, woody plants have a hard time regaining a foothold in the harsh environment of a mountaintop. The bald lies just outside the wilderness border on the southwestern end.

Primitive camping is available at the Pines Campground, where 17 large primitive sites offer plenty of privacy under a forested canopy. The campground serves as a base camp to horseback riders and hikers using the Lipes Branch Trail.

Directions: From New Castle, drive north on VA 615 for 2.5 miles. Turn left on VA 609 and continue for 2 miles. Turn left on VA 611 and go about 3.4 miles. Go right on VA 617 and go 5.5 miles to Lipes Branch trailhead on left, or continue short distance to Pines Campground.

Activities: Hiking, camping, horseback riding, fishing for stocked trout, seasonal hunting.

Facilities: Hiking and horse trail, primitive campground with 17 sites, pit toilets, drinking water.

Dates: Open year-round.

Fees: None.

Closest town: New Castle, 14 miles south.

For more information: New Castle Ranger District, Jefferson National Forest, VA 615, Box 246, New Castle, VA 24127. Phone (540) 864-5195.

LIPES BRANCH TRAIL. [Fig. 22(9)] This single yellow-blazed trail, which ascends Potts Mountain along Lipes Branch, provides both hikers and horseback riders access into the heart of Barbours Creek Wilderness. The first .5 mile climbs gently up the southeastern lower slope of Potts Mountain, and then it becomes steeper, using switchbacks to reach a partially cleared area at the summit with views into Alleghany County and the George Washington National Forest to the northwest.

Trail: 2.3-mile climb up Potts Mountain.

Elevation: 1,800–3,640 feet.

Degree of difficulty: Moderate, but strenuous near summit.

TINKER CREEK. Beneath busy Interstate 81 north of Roanoke and unnoticed by travelers zipping up and down the Great Valley of Virginia runs the little stream made famous by Annie Dillard's *Pilgrim at Tinker Creek* (HarperCollins, 1988).

The creek that drains the abrupt northeast-facing wall of Tinker Mountain flows south past Hollins College and Roanoke to join the Roanoke River on the south side of Vinton. South of the college, Tinker Creek is a stocked trout stream. Dillard wrote a personal narrative full of fresh insights as she explored the natural world of the stream where it flowed through her backyard.

YELLOW BUCKEYE
(Aesculus octandra)
Growing as tall as 90 feet, the yellow buckeye has 4–6 inch leaves and yellow flowers, and produces seeds protected inside smooth capsules. Buckeye seeds resemble chestnuts, but they are round while chestnuts have a pointed tip.

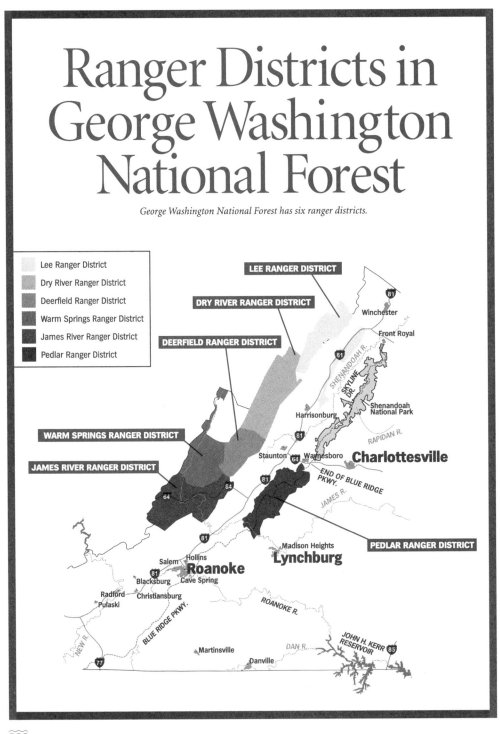

Ranger Districts in George Washington National Forest

George Washington National Forest has six ranger districts.

Lee Ranger District
Dry River Ranger District
Deerfield Ranger District
Warm Springs Ranger District
James River Ranger District
Pedlar Ranger District

LEE RANGER DISTRICT

DRY RIVER RANGER DISTRICT

DEERFIELD RANGER DISTRICT

WARM SPRINGS RANGER DISTRICT

JAMES RIVER RANGER DISTRICT

PEDLAR RANGER DISTRICT

Winchester

Front Royal

SHENANDOAH R.

SKYLINE DR.

Shenandoah National Park

Harrisonburg

RAPIDAN R.

Staunton Waynesboro **Charlottesville**

END OF BLUE RIDGE PKWY.

JAMES R.

Madison Heights

Lynchburg

Salem Hollins

Roanoke

Blacksburg Cave Spring

Radford Christiansburg

Pulaski

BLUE RIDGE PKWY.

ROANOKE R.

NEW R.

JOHN H. KERR RESERVOIR

Martinsville

DAN R.

Danville

Virginia's Western Highlands

Three mountainous counties on Virginia's western border are known as Virginia's Western Highlands. Formerly, this area was known as The Alleghany Highlands. But confusion arose. The Allegheny Mountains are a section of the Appalachian Mountains running northwest/southeast along the adjoining borders of Virginia, West Virginia, Pennsylvania, and Maryland. Did the term "Alleghany Highlands" refer to the entire Allegheny Mountain range though the spellings were different? Did it mean just Alleghany County, which has the same spelling of "Alleghany"? Or did Alleghany Highlands mean the three western counties of Bath, Highland, and Alleghany most closely associated with the Allegheny Mountains?

For marketing purposes, chambers of commerce and tourist bureaus needed to come to an agreement. They chose "Virginia's Western Highlands" for the three-county area and abandoned the word "Alleghany" and its confusing spellings. Use of the word still lingers. For no matter how it's spelled—even "Alliganey" can be found on old scouting maps—the Algonquin Indian word for "endless" inspires wanderlust.

On the west side of Alleghany, Bath, and Highland counties, Allegheny Mountain rises steeply to more than 4,000 feet to meet the West Virginia line at the crest. The ridgeline becomes higher on its northward run, reaching 4,100 in the remote Laurel Fork area northwest of Monterey.

On the eastern side of this formidable ridge are hundreds of thousands of acres of mountains and river valleys open to the public. Two ranger districts of the George Washington National Forest [Fig. 25]—the James River and Warm Springs districts—brim with campgrounds, hiking trails, picnic areas, and more. Lake Moomaw, which spreads across the Alleghany/Bath border, offers water sports, fishing, and recreation. The Gathright Wildlife Management Area adjoining the recreation areas of Lake Moomaw provides inroads to deer, turkey, and ruffed grouse habitat. Virginia Power provides a recreation area and fishing on Back Creek below its pump storage reservoir in northwestern Bath County. Laurel Fork Special Management Area invites quiet study.

Douthat State Park [Fig. 28] and Rough Mountain Wilderness [Fig. 23(4)] in southeastern Bath County offer yet more choices. One can hike, swim, paddle a canoe, and camp in the park where there are restaurants, running water, shelter, and human companionship. There's also the solitude of undisturbed backcountry wilderness.

Headwaters for the historic James River lie in the Highlands in the cold-water trout fisheries of the Jackson River, Bullpasture River, and Back Creek and in the warmer Cowpasture River. Scenic drives, bed and breakfast inns, quaint villages, mountain crafts, and a plush resort town add to the list of things to see and do in the Highlands. Interstate 64, VA 39, and US 250 lead through mountain gaps to run east-west through the Highlands. VA 42 and US 220 access these counties from the north and south.

For more information: Alleghany Highlands Chamber of Commerce, 241 West Main Street, Covington, VA 24426 (main office), or 501 East Ridgeway Street, Suite C, Clifton Forge, VA 24422. Covington office, phone (540) 962-2178. Clifton Forge office, phone (540) 862-2178.

JOHNSON CREEK NATURAL AREA PRESERVE

[Fig. 22(1)] On a steep, shale cliff between Covington and the West Virginia line, Johnson Creek Natural Area Preserve protects one of Virginia's finest examples of shale barren habitats. Here, on steep precipices that rise some 300 feet above Johnson Creek, gnarled and stunted pines, cedars, and oaks struggle to survive in a harsh environment. More than a dozen endemic species—plants that occur only on shale barrens—cling to life on the unstable slopes. At least eight plants that are rare in Virginia have adapted to the shallow, nutrient-poor soil. An example is white-haired leatherflower (*Clematis viorna*), which takes its name from white, feathery seed tips.

Shale barrens are found mainly in the Valley and Ridge province of western Virginia, eastern West Virginia, and southern Pennsylvania. The rare community is characterized by steep eroding slopes with thin soils and surface temperatures that may reach 150 degrees in summer. The barrens usually face south and often occur where a bend in a river has eroded banks.

Shale barrens lie in what is called a rain shadow. Most of the East's precipitation is delivered by clouds formed over the Gulf of Mexico and blown inland from the southwest. When these clouds reach the Appalachians, they are forced upward and most of their moisture is released quickly. By the time clouds make it up and over the mountains, they have less moisture left for slopes on the east side—slopes in the rain shadow. These slopes, including shale barrens, receive significantly less precipitation because they must rely on rain from Atlantic hurricanes and northeasters powerful enough to cross the Blue Ridge.

Umbrella Magnolia

Taking its name from its whorled leaves which resemble an umbrella, this small tree is fairly common at low altitudes. It frequents protected ravines where the soil is moist and displays showy white flowers in the spring. *Magnolia tripetala* is fragrant from a distance, but up close, the blossoms have a disagreeable odor.

Many of the plants that adapt to these desertlike conditions are plants you might find in a rock garden such as stonecrop (*Sedum sarmentosa*) and other sedums, alumroot or palace purple (*Heuchera americana*), and moss phlox (*Phlox subulata*). On the bluffs, stiff reindeer lichen covers almost every inch of ground not taken up by a twisted pine, cedar, rotting adelgid, or hollow stump. These plants have mechanisms to endure the heat, sun, and poor soil. Some have thick, waxy leaves to prevent water loss. Others have hairy stems and leaves to shade the plant from the intense sun. Deep extensive root systems on many plants help claim a purchase in the loose shale.

The preserve was acquired by The Nature Conservancy on behalf of the Commonwealth of Virginia as a Partners in Conservation Project. Johnson Creek was dedicated as a Virginia Natural Area Preserve in 1990 to be managed by the Department of Conservation and Recreation. The pine-covered bluffs are visible from VA 661 about 3 miles northwest of the Alleghany County town of Callaghan. The preserve is operated as a satellite of Douthat State Park. Until public access is developed, anyone interested in learning more about it should contact the park superintendent. At the top of the bluffs, the shale ground between the towering rock cliffs gradually becomes steeper as it slopes toward the valley below, making it dangerous for hikers. A person could begin to slide and not be able to stop.

AMERICAN BEECH
(Fagus grandifolia)
This beech is identified by thin gray bark and papery leaves that may stay on all winter to twist and rustle in the wind.

Virginia probably contains more shale barrens than Pennsylvania, Maryland, and West Virginia combined. Above Potts Creek south of Covington (also in Alleghany County) is another example of this habitat. The 9-acre Potts Creek Shale Barren was acquired by The Nature Conservancy in 1986. Three rare species endemic to this south-facing slope are chestnut lipfern (*Cheilanthes castanea*), Kate's mountain clover (*Triflium virginicum*), and Virginia nailwort (*Paronychia virginica*). Visitation is also restricted here because of the difficult terrain and fragile plant community.

For more information: Department of Conservation and Recreation, Division of Natural Heritage, 1500 East Main Street, Suite 312, Richmond, VA 23219. Phone (804) 786-7951. For access information, contact Park Superintendent, Douthat State Park, Route 1, Box 212, Millboro, VA 24460. Phone (540) 862-8100.

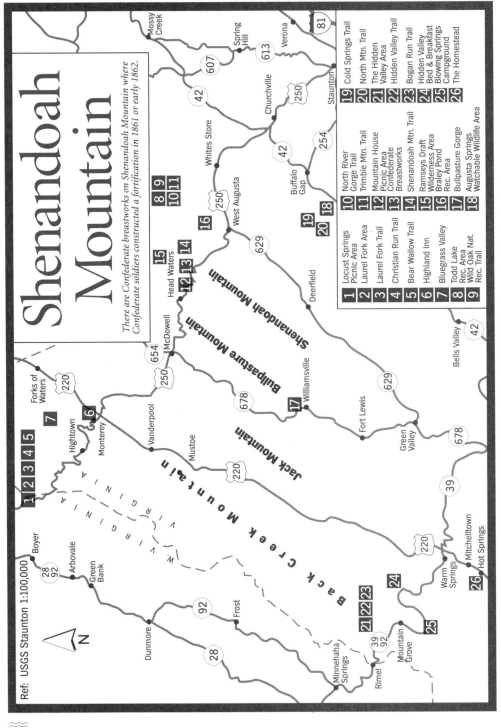

Shenandoah Mountain

There are Confederate breastworks on Shenandoah Mountain where Confederate soldiers constructed a fortification in 1861 or early 1862.

Ref: USGS Staunton 1:100,000

1	Locust Springs Picnic Area
2	Laurel Fork Area
3	Laurel Fork Trail
4	Christian Run Trail
5	Bear Wallow Trail
6	Highland Inn
7	Bluegrass Valley
8	Todd Lake Rec. Area
9	Wild Oak Nat. Rec. Trail
10	North River Gorge Trail
11	Trimble Mtn. Trail
12	Mountain House Picnic Area
13	Confederate Breastworks
14	Shenandoah Mtn. Trail
15	Ramseys Draft Wilderness Area
16	Braley Pond Rec. Area
17	Bullpasture Gorge
18	Augusta Springs Watchable Wildlife Area
19	Cold Springs Trail
20	North Mtn. Trail
21	The Hidden Valley Area
22	Hidden Valley Trail
23	Bogan Run Trail
24	Hidden Valley Bed & Breakfast
25	Blowing Springs Campground
26	The Homestead

HISTORIC INNS OF THE WESTERN HIGHLANDS

HIGHLAND INN. [Fig. 26(6)] With its country charm and Victorian architecture, the Highland Inn on Main Street in Monterey has gained a place on the National Register of Historic Places. While in Monterey, visit the nearby Maple Museum's exhibits on the making of maple syrup. The museum is on VA 220 south of downtown.

For more information: Highland Inn, Monterey, VA 24465. Phone (540) 468-2143. Maple Museum, phone (540) 468-2550.

THE HOMESTEAD. [Fig. 26(28)] For more than 200 years, visitors have sought out The Homestead at Hot Springs for recreation. Built in 1766, the inn served first as a refuge for those who sought the healing powers of the area's warm springs bubbling from the ground. Several presidents have stayed at The Homestead. The Japanese Embassy staff in Washington, D.C., was interned in these grand quarters during World War II. This National Historic Landmark is located on US 220 between Covington and Warm Springs. Golf courses, tennis courts, riding trails, sporting clays, ski slopes, and four-star dining have been added to the warm baths in more modern times.

For more information: The Homestead, PO Box 2000, Hot Springs, VA 24445. Phone (540) 839-1766 or (800) 838-1766.

LONGDALE INN. [Fig. 23(15)] Formerly the home of ironmaster William Firmstone, the Longdale Inn is located at the heart of the Longdale Furnace Historic District west of Lexington. It makes a comfortable base of operations for exploring the mountains, trails, streams, and backroads here. The exterior of the 1873 Victorian structure, built when Ulysses S. Grant was president, is painted dusty rose. Inside, original brass carbide chandeliers hang from 11-foot canvas ceilings trimmed in laurel leaf, and floor-to-ceiling windows offer mountain views.

Directions: From I-64 east of Clifton Forge, take Exit 35 and go west .5 mile on VA 269. Inn is on left.

For more information: Longdale Inn, 6209 Longdale Furnace Road, Clifton Forge, VA 24422. Phone (540) 862-0892 or (800) 862-0386 (for reservations).

MILTON HALL BED AND BREAKFAST INN. [Fig. 23(2)] Constructed in 1874, this National Historic Landmark was built on the national forest border south of Lake Moomaw. The English country manor has many gables, buttressed porch towers, and Gothic trimmings.

Directions: From I-64 west of Covington, take Exit 10 and follow VA 159 south to Marathon Gas Station. Turn right on VA 600, following signs to Gathright Dam and Lake Moomaw. Take the first right onto Indian Draft Road (still VA 600), going under I-64. After underpass, take immediate left on FR 201. Large brick manor house is on hill on the right.

For more information: Milton Hall Bed and Breakfast Inn, 207 Thorny Lane, Covington, VA 24426. Phone (540) 965-0196.

HIDDEN VALLEY BED AND BREAKFAST. [Fig. 26(24)] If this pre–Civil War plantation house on the Jackson River looks vaguely familiar, it might be because it's the site of the 1992 filming of *Sommersby*, with Richard Gere and Jodie Foster. Using bricks made of mud from the banks of the Jackson River, slaves built the mansion in 1748 for Jacob Warwick. The Warwick mansion, or "Warwickton" as it was called, is listed in the National Register of Historic Homes and has been converted to a bed and breakfast in recent years. An interpretive center in the summer kitchen is open weekends. The inn is located on national forest land on the Jackson River, west of Warm Springs in Bath County.

Directions: Go west from Warm Springs on VA 39 for 3 miles. Turn right onto VA 621 and go 1 mile north. Go left on FR 241 and continue 2 miles to Hidden Valley.

For more information: Phone (540) 839-3178.

HUMPBACK BRIDGE

[Fig. 22(4)] Located west of Covington in Alleghany County, Humpback Bridge is the nation's only surviving curved-span covered bridge. Yet three such bridges, bowed upward in the center, are thought to have been within a mile of each other in this area. The 100-foot span was constructed in 1857 as part of the Kanawha Turnpike in an attempt to link easterners with the Mississippi River Valley. In 1929 when a new bridge was built nearby, the bridge was abandoned and left to slowly decay. In 1954, Covington businessmen and women found the funds necessary to restore it. A 5-acre wayside was set aside where visitors can enjoy picnic lunches and imagine the clip-clop of horses' hooves echoing from the bridge.

Directions: From I-64 west of Covington, take Exit 10 and go east on US 60 .5 mile. Wayside is on the right. Or take US 60 west from Covington. Wayside is about 3.5 miles west of point where US 60 crosses river on west side of Covington.

Activities: Picnicking.

Facilities: Picnic tables.

Dates: Open year-round.

Fees: None.

Closest town: Covington, about 3.5 miles.

For more information: Alleghany Highlands Chamber of Commerce, 241 West Main Street, Covington, VA 24426. Phone (540) 962-2178.

VIRGINIA HORSE CENTER

[Fig. 23(17)] Equestrian events such as rodeos, sales, competitions, and shows are held year-round in the indoor coliseum and outdoor rings of the Virginia Horse Center. The center is located just north of Lexington off VA 39 at the intersection of I-64 and I-81.

For more information: Virginia Horse Center, PO Box 1051, Lexington, VA 24450. Phone (540) 962-9622.

FALLING SPRING

[Fig. 23(7)] Falling Spring is a rarity—an incredibly beautiful waterfall that requires very little effort to view. The falls are at a pullover on US 220 about 7 miles north of Covington. Here, 7,000 gallons of water a minute plunge over a sheer, 200-foot bluff to the rocks below. A fine mist hangs in the air providing moisture for such plants as jack-in-the-pulpit, touch-me-not, and a variety of ferns.

Thomas Jefferson once admired the scene and called Falling Spring "the only remarkable cascade in this country." (In fairness to other falls, he probably intended "country" to mean "area.") The major source of the cascade is a warm spring that rises to the surface about 1 mile north of the

Falling Spring was a favorite of Thomas Jefferson, who called it "the only remarkable cascade" in this part of Virginia.

falls. The water rises along a fault line through Falling Spring Valley's underground honeycomb of limestone caves, picking up minerals from the rock.

White calcite crystals form on the edges of fallen leaves and twigs along the stream. Look for examples of this phenomenon on the east side of the highway, just above the falls. The calcite—the same material in stalactites hanging from cave ceilings—is evidence of water that is super-carbonated, or filled with minerals such as calcite and dolomite. The warm water runs under the road near the pullover and then over the erosion-resistant Tuscarora sandstone cliff and drains the area between Warm Springs Mountain and Little Mountain. Falling Spring is the name not only of the falls and the valley it drains but also of the creek that carries the water and the community where the water enters the Jackson River.

THERMAL SPRINGS

[Fig. 23(11)] Normally, water bubbling from underground springs is cold. But in areas where the earth's crust is faulted and folded, cracks allow water from much deeper to rise to the surface. At these deeper levels, basement rock under tremendous pressure is hot. If water rises quickly enough, it may reach the surface before it cools.

Many hot springs, or thermal springs as they are also called, contain minerals that people drink or bathe in for their supposed curative powers. Bath County takes its name from its many such springs. A look at a map shows a 16-mile-long line of thermal springs concentrated along US 220. About 7 miles north of Covington, US 220 enters Falling Spring Valley. From south to north, the highway passes Falling Spring, Healing Springs, Hot Springs, and Warm Springs. A fracture in the underlying rock in the valley center reaches down to deep limestone rock of the early Paleozoic Era—rock that is 500 million years old or older. The springs that are forced to the surface here are much warmer than those in the sides of the valley where the fractures do not go nearly as deep.

The Homestead [Fig. 26(26)] at Hot Springs operates an indoor pool and two restored eighteenth- and nineteenth-century bathhouses (separate facilities for men and women) fed by thermal springs. The octagonal wooden bathhouses are located beside the road at Warm Springs. The men's opened in 1761 and the women's in 1836. Steam rises from the warm water where the stream flows beside the parking area on US 220. The temperature in the rock pools is a balmy 98.6 degrees.

JAMES RIVER RANGER DISTRICT

[Fig. 25] The 164,260 acres of the James River District spread across all of Alleghany County and take in the upper James River in northern Botetourt County. The district is the southernmost of the George Washington National Forest. To the west, Alleghany Mountain separates the district from West Virginia and the Monongahela National Forest. Interstate 64 passes east/west through the center of the district. The highway connects the western mountains with Interstate 81, running north/south in the Shenandoah Valley.

Generally, private lands lie in the lush valleys along the major creeks and rivers, while the mountains are the public's to explore and enjoy. Public recreation areas are clustered at the southern end of Lake Moomaw (the northern end is in the Warm Springs District) and in the Longdale Furnace area on the east side of Alleghany County. The district's Low Moor Shooting Range, between Clifton Forge and Covington, is open year-round. Shooting lanes of various lengths provide a chance to sight in a gun or practice target shooting. The district office in Covington can provide not only a district map and brochures on the most popular trails but also a sheet on any other trail of interest to a hiker.

Directions: Office is located in Covington. Take Exit 16 from I-64 and go west on US 220 for .1 mile to office, on right. For shooting range, take Exit 21 off I-64 and go south on VA 616 for 1.6 miles. Range is on the left. Other sites are described below.

For more information: James River Ranger District, 810-A Madison Avenue, Covington, VA 24425. Phone (540) 962-2214.

HIKING THE JAMES RIVER DISTRICT. Hiking opportunities on 80 miles of trails are almost limitless. Brochures at the ranger district office give detailed mile markers of the more popular trails.

ALLEGHENY TRAIL. [Fig. 22(2)] Twelve miles of the Allegheny Trail pass through the James River district. This strenuous long-distance trail follows the Eastern Continental Divide in the rugged Allegheny Mountains of West Virginia and Virginia. When completed, the yellow-blazed footpath will extend 330 miles from Preston County, West Virginia, near the Pennsylvania border, to the Appalachian Trail in Monroe County, West Virginia. The trailhead is 12 miles west of Covington at Exit 1 off I-64.

Trail: 15.5-mile completed section of 330-mile ridgetop trail under construction.
Elevation: 2,625–3,400 feet.
Degree of difficulty: Moderate, with strenuous sections.
Surface and Blaze: Natural forest floor with grassy and rocky sections. Yellow blaze.

FORE MOUNTAIN TRAIL. [Fig. 22(3)] The 14.8-mile Fore Mountain Trail is one of the best-known trails, and it gets heavy use from hikers, Douthat Lake campers, horseback riders, and ATVs. The blue-blazed path travels through upland hardwoods and pines typical of high- elevation forests of the Alleghany Mountains and opens to expansive views. Look for a variation on woodland wildflowers and wildlife at several grassy areas and at the Smith Creek crossing. Smith Creek is stocked with brook trout.

The strenuous trail begins at Dolly Anne Work Center just off US 60 east of Covington. The end is near Douthat State Park where it becomes the Middle Mountain Trail and continues north another 5.5 miles to FR 125. Good areas for primitive camping are at mile 8.5. Parking is available at mile 10.2, where the trail crosses VA 606. A side trail, the scenic 9-mile Dry Run Trail, intersects Fore Mountain Trail at mile 6.1 then heads back to Covington. The Dry Run Trail (also blue-blazed) passes near Big Knob, the highest point in Alleghany County (4,072 feet). The trailhead is at

LEAST SHREW
(*Cryptotis parva*)
This mammal is also known as the "bee" shrew because it sometimes nests in beehives and feeds on bees and their larvae.

the end of Cyprus Street in Covington.

Trail: 14.8-mile linear path along Fore Mountain ridge, descending to Smith Creek and climbing Middle Mountain.

Elevation: 1,200 to 3,000 feet.

Degree of difficulty: Moderate to strenuous.

Surface: Natural forest floor with grassy and rocky sections.

EASTERN NATIONAL CHILDREN'S FOREST. [Fig. 23(21)] The Eastern National Children's Forest is a unique site in the southern portion of the James River District. In 1971 a wildfire destroyed trees on 1,176 acres on Potts Mountain, about 22 miles south of Covington. On April 28, 1972, on the 150th anniversary of Arbor Day, more than 1,000 children from Virginia, West Virginia, Maryland, and Pennsylvania planted shortleaf pine trees on the charred site. The planting was one of three National Children's Forests originally established in the United States.

HIGHBUSH BLUEBERRY
(Vaccinium corymbosum)

The names of the children participating in the forest restoration are stored in a time capsule to be opened in the year 2072. Near the time capsule is a monument to the children. The stone monument is at the trailhead for a paved .25-mile loop trail (handicapped accessible) which offers a glimpse of the trees, wildflowers, and animals now living in the young forest. Many different plants have developed in the understory including grapevine, black gum, various oaks, and greenbrier.

The Forest Service is considering construction of two additional loop trails—a 1.5-mile loop and a 3.5-mile loop—starting and ending on the existing trail.

Directions: From Covington go south on VA 18 for 8 miles. Turn left on VA 613 and drive 3 miles to end of road. Turn right on FR 351 and go .8 mile to parking area on right. To the northwest of the parking area, across Potts Valley, is an impressive view of Peters Mountain. Trailhead is on left behind monument.

Activities: Hiking.

Facilities: Hiking trail.
Dates: Open year-round.
Fees: None.
Closest town: Covington, 8 miles north.
Trail: .25-mile handicapped-accessible loop.
Elevation: 1,860 feet.
Degree of difficulty: Easy.
Surface: Paved.
For more information: James River Ranger District, George Washington National Forest, 810-A Madison Ave., Covington, VA 24425. Phone (540) 962-2214.

Ovenbird

The secretive, ground-nesting ovenbird (*Seiurus aurocapillus*) is much easier seen than heard. This thrushlike wood warbler takes its name from its oven or dome-shaped nest. The side-entrance nest is well hidden on the leafy forest floor, but it is vulnerable nevertheless to predatory skunks and opossums. The ovenbird likes open, mature forests.

LONGDALE RECREATION AREA.

[Fig. 23(14)] Longdale Recreation Area is a day-use area in the James River District, east of Clifton Forge. A small lake for swimming and access to several hiking trails that lead to spectacular views are highlights. Longdale was constructed by the Civilian Conservation Corps in the late 1930s and was called Green Pastures. The hand-built dam, bathhouse, picnic shelter, and two restrooms are original buildings.

Green Pastures was one of very few such areas built for African Americans who were prevented from using forest facilities during the days of segregation. It was heavily used. In 1963 it was opened to all races and the name was changed to Longdale.

Trails here include Anthony's Knob Trail, Blue Suck Run Trail, YACCer's Run Trail, and North Mountain Trail. Rock cliffs and ridgetops are visible from several areas, and thickets of rhododendron bloom in May. The James River District office can supply trail maps. Some trails are in poor condition and have faded or nonexistent blazes.

Directions: From I-64 east of Clifton Forge, take Exit 35. Drive west on VA 850 about 2 miles to entrance, on left.
Activities: Picnicking, swimming, hiking.
Facilities: Picnic shelter with 6 tables, fireplace, and 2 grills (nonreservable) plus 25 more tables and grills. Also, 2-acre swimming lake, restrooms, bathhouse with cold-water showers, hiking trails.
Dates: Memorial Day–Labor Day.
Fees: A fee is charged per car.
Closest town: Clifton Forge, 9 miles west.
For more information: James River Ranger District, George Washington National Forest, 810 A Madison Avenue, Covington, VA 24426. Phone (540) 962-2214.

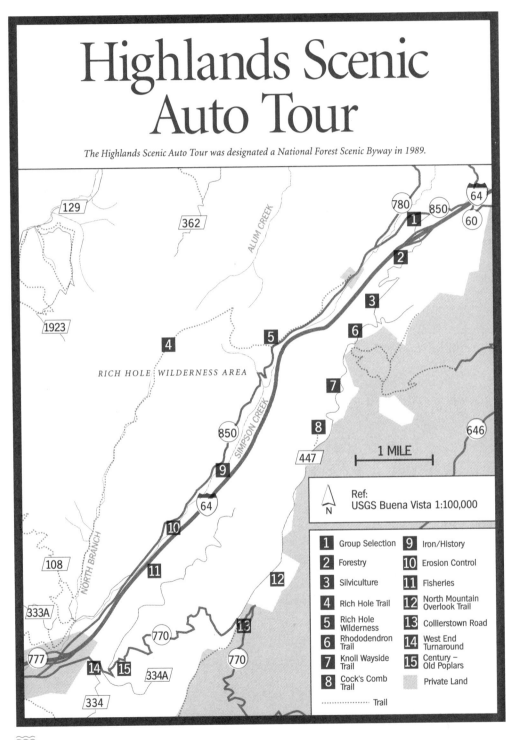

Highlands Scenic Auto Tour

The Highlands Scenic Auto Tour was designated a National Forest Scenic Byway in 1989.

Ref:
USGS Buena Vista 1:100,000

1 MILE

RICH HOLE WILDERNESS AREA

1	Group Selection	9	Iron/History
2	Forestry	10	Erosion Control
3	Silviculture	11	Fisheries
4	Rich Hole Trail	12	North Mountain Overlook Trail
5	Rich Hole Wilderness	13	Collierstown Road
6	Rhododendron Trail	14	West End Turnaround
7	Knoll Wayside Trail	15	Century – Old Poplars
8	Cock's Comb Trail		Private Land

·············· Trail

HIGHLANDS SCENIC AUTO TOUR. [Fig. 27, Fig. 23(16)] The James River District's auto tour was designated a National Forest Scenic Byway in 1989. It deserves the recognition. The Highlands Scenic Auto Tour is a 19-mile loop between Clifton Forge in Alleghany County and Interstate 64 at Lexington. The drive combines a mix of mining and logging history, fantastic views, craggy cock's comb rock formations, century-old poplars, hiking opportunities, and a ride along a wilderness border.

Just south of the tour route, on the western side of VA 269, stand the 100-foot brick smokestacks and remains of one of the first iron blast furnace operations in the South. Iron forged here was used in making the Confederacy's *Merrimac* (or *CSS Virginia*), America's first ironclad ship. Stops on the tour relate to this furnace.

Although known for its remoteness, the tour is half on one side of Interstate 64 and half on the other. But visitors forget the interstate immediately as the road climbs North Mountain. In fact, this area is a fine place to see wildlife, including white-tailed deer, wild turkey, ruffed grouse, and occasionally bobcats. In September and October, look for migrating hawks and other birds of prey above the open bluffs on North Mountain. If time allows for just part of the drive, the most scenic route is on the southeastern side of I-64 on North Mountain. This road is known locally as Top Drive. The view to the east from the sheer cliffs at the top is unmatched. Stunted shadbush (serviceberry) trees cling to ledges on the precipitous bluffs. In April, their white blooms against the valley floor far below are photographic material. Brochures available at the district office (and sometimes at the information boards at each end of the tour) provide important information on the views and the area's history.

Mile 2.4: Rhododendron Trail. [Fig. 27(6)] This short walk is handicapped accessible. The rhododendrons here are about 100 years old. The twisted, hard wood has withstood untold ice storms and gale-force winds. The trail leads to an overlook with a view of the Rich Hole Wilderness.

Mile 4.2: Cock's Comb. [Fig. 27(8)] The ragged rock formation above a moderately steep but short (.25-mile) trail here resembles a cock's comb. The rock is composed of erosion-resistant sandstone that was originally deposited at the bottom of an ancient ocean. The horizontal layers were turned vertically and pushed up from the valley floor by pressure from shifting continental plates.

Mile 5.8: North Mountain Overlook Trail. [Fig. 27(12)] An easy path leads to views from rocky bluffs of Lake Robertson and the valley of Buffalo Creek. To the northeast are two rounded knobs called Big House Mountain and Little House Mountain. To the southeast, the Short Hills range rises abruptly from the valley floor. The Blue Ridge Mountains are in the distance.

Mile 6.7: Collierstown Road. [Fig. 27(13)] Go right. This road and hand-laid rock retaining walls remain much as they looked in 1826 when they were constructed. The road provided access for a pig iron furnace and iron mines in the valley below and subsequently was used by farmers to take produce to market.

Mile 9.5: Century-old poplars.

Mile 9.9: West Entrance Turnaround and Information Board. Depressions in the earth are remnants of charcoal hearths. If you had stood here 100 years ago, the hills would have been devoid of large trees, and charcoal hearths would be burning. The trees were cut to fuel the pig iron furnaces.

Mile 16.1: Rich Hole Wilderness. [Fig. 27(5)] The wilderness borders the road on the northeast side.

Directions: From I-64 west of Lexington, take Exit 43. Go south short distance on VA 780. Turn left on FR 447 (Top Drive) to begin 19-mile loop tour. Follow FR 447 for 7 miles to junction at top of North Mountain with VA 770, then descend on VA 770 to VA 850 at west end. Then follow VA 850 east to starting point.

Activities: Scenic driving, hiking, mountain biking, horseback riding, fishing, seasonal hunting.

Facilities: Information board at each end.

Closest town: Lexington, about 12 miles east.

For more information: James River Ranger District, George Washington National Forest, 810 A Madison Avenue, Covington, VA 24426. Phone (540) 962-2214.

RICH HOLE WILDERNESS. [Fig. 27(5), Fig. 23(9)] This 6,450-acre wilderness is located about 15 miles west of Lexington in the James River District of the George Washington National Forest, tucked in the northeastern spur of Alleghany County and western Rockbridge County. The shape of Rich Hole is a long northwest/southeast-oriented rectangle, protecting the watersheds of Alum Creek on the northern end and the North Branch of Simpsons Creek on the southern end. The Bath County line marks the western boundary. US 60/VA 850 and Interstate 64 roughly parallel the eastern boundary.

Established by Congress in 1988, the wilderness is home to a diverse array of flora and fauna, including stands of old-growth hardwoods in fertile, northeast-facing coves in the headwaters of Alum Creek. In fact, Rich Hole takes its name from the rich soils in these coves or "holes" on Brushy Mountain. Cove hardwoods here include northern red oak, basswood, tulip poplar, sugar maple, green ash, and cucumbertree. The trees are widely spaced, reaching heights of 130 feet or more, with carpets of ferns and mosses in the dark forest below. The parklike appearance in the open understory is typical of mature cove forests. In the colorful understory of the rich coves, where the canopy has not shaded them out, are redbud, flowering dogwood, and blueberry and evergreen heath thickets of rhododendron, fetterbush, and mountain laurel. In a cove forest, bird species are as diverse as species of trees and shrubs. The large, colorful pileated woodpecker may fly from tree to tree ahead of hikers or sound its raucous cackle from somewhere just out of sight. Darting about in the understory, small birds such as the golden-crowned kinglet and various warblers may be spotted. Salamanders and small, ground-dwelling mammals such as the white-footed mouse dwell in the mosses and ferns of the forest floor.

White-tailed deer, ruffed grouse, and wild turkey are more likely to be spotted outside of old-growth areas of the forest where trees are smaller and undergrowth thicker—in other words, where there is food and cover. Most of the dry slopes of Brushy and Mill mountains are covered with mixed hardwoods such as chestnut oak, American beech, and hickory and evergreens that include pitch pine, Virginia pine, and white pine. Tenacious table mountain pines grow on exposed ridges. The trees are in various stages of succession as the forest recovers from previous logging. Signs of earlier iron mining remain throughout (*see* Highland Scenic Auto Tour, page 161).

Hikers on the Rich Hole Trail pass near the old-growth hardwoods in the Alum Creek drainage and also by a huge black cherry and a stand of large Eastern hemlocks in the North Fork drainage. The White Rock Trail, which forms the southern boundary of the wilderness, has very large oaks.

Directions: The wilderness is located on the northwest side of I-64 between Exit 43 in Rockbridge County and Exit 35 in Alleghany County.

Activities: Hiking, backcountry camping, seasonal hunting, native trout fishing.

Facilities: None.

Closest town: Clifton Forge, about 9 miles west.

For more information: James River Ranger District, George Washington National Forest, 810 A Madison Avenue, Covington, VA 24426. Phone (540) 962-2214.

RICH HOLE TRAIL. [Fig. 27(4), Fig. 23(10)] This is the only maintained trail within the wilderness. From the southern trailhead, the path makes a gradual climb up the North Branch of Simpsons Creek to the crest of Brushy Mountain then makes a right turn in the area of the old-growth forest and steeply descends the mountain's eastern slope to the upper trailhead. An old pair of nonslippery shoes will help the hiker make the many crossings of North Branch. Along the trail, the forest opens to impressive views at rocky ledges.

Another possibility is a shorter but steep trek from the northern trailhead up Brushy Mountain to the old-growth forest and back. The old-growth hardwoods are about a mile from the northern trailhead. They are on the north end of the trail near the summit where a ridge separates the two watersheds.

Directions: Upper trailhead: From westbound I-64, in the northeastern corner of Alleghany County, take Exit 43 and go right at stop sign. After .3 mile, go left on VA 850. Drive 2.6 miles to trailhead parking area on right. From eastbound I-64, take Exit 43 and turn left at stop sign. Then follow above directions. Lower trailhead: From I-64, take Exit 35. Turn east on VA 850 and drive 1.3 miles, past small bridge. Turn left on FR 108. Go 1.3 miles to parking area on left. Trailhead is a 1.3-mile hike (or drive if gate is open) from this parking area.

Trail: 6-mile gradual climb from lower trailhead, ending in steep descent to upper trailhead.

Elevation: 1,500 to 3,500 feet.

Degree of difficulty: Moderate.

Surface: Natural forest floor with rocky sections and many stream crossings.

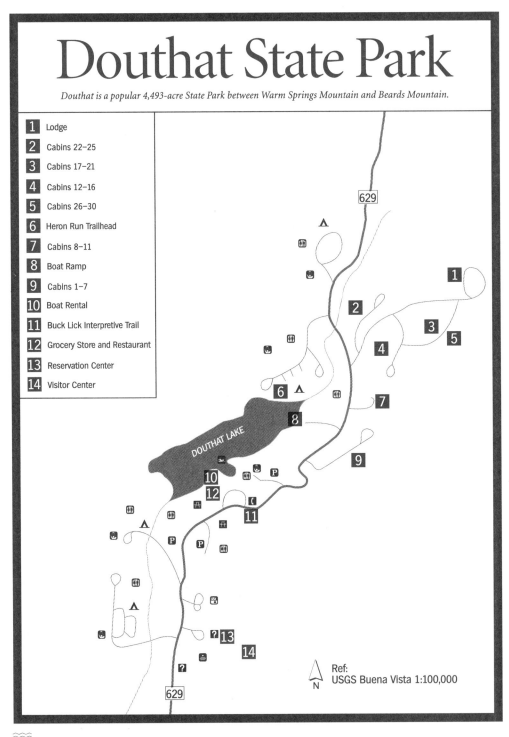

Douthat State Park

Douthat is a popular 4,493-acre State Park between Warm Springs Mountain and Beards Mountain.

1 Lodge
2 Cabins 22–25
3 Cabins 17–21
4 Cabins 12–16
5 Cabins 26–30
6 Heron Run Trailhead
7 Cabins 8–11
8 Boat Ramp
9 Cabins 1–7
10 Boat Rental
11 Buck Lick Interpretive Trail
12 Grocery Store and Restaurant
13 Reservation Center
14 Visitor Center

629

DOUTHAT LAKE

Ref:
USGS Buena Vista 1:100,000

629

🦫 DOUTHAT STATE PARK

[Fig. 23(8), Fig. 28, Fig. 21(28)] The 4,493 acres of Douthat State Park lie between Warm Springs Mountain and Beards Mountain in southern Bath County. The cold mountain waters of Wilson Creek flow into little, 50-acre Douthat Lake, the park's focal point. Wilson then heads south to join the Jackson River at Clifton Forge. The park is known for its spectacular mountain scenery, trout fishing, swimming beach, many wooded hiking trails, attractive campgrounds, and rustic but comfortable cabins. It's also ideally situated for exploration in the surrounding Warm Springs and James River ranger districts of the George Washington National Forest.

One of Virginia's original six state parks, Douthat still benefits from the meticulous construction of the Civilian Conservation Corps (CCC). The CCC was established by President Franklin D. Roosevelt in 1933 to provide Depression-era men with work. At Douthat, an estimated 600 men cleared trails and built a dam and spillway, log cabins, guest lodges, a restaurant, an information center, a swimming beach, and picnic areas.

The work has held up over the years—so well, in fact, that on Douthat's fiftieth anniversary in 1986, the park was recognized as a Registered Historic Landmark. Look for such adornments as hand-carved wooden doorknobs and hinges and hand-wrought iron door and shutter latches. Where tributary streams go beneath the road, often hidden from view, are expertly crafted culverts with stone archways.

Diners in the Lake View Restaurant [Fig. 28(12)] overlooking the 50-acre lake can admire the work of the CCC as they down a slice of homemade apple pie.

Besides the Buck Lick Interpretive Trail [Fig. 28(11), Fig. 23(12)] on dry land, Douthat has a watery self-guided trail by paddleboat around Douthat Lake. Visitors can rent a boat at the boat concession near the beach and spend a leisurely morning or afternoon discovering the lake's beaver activity, cattails, dragonflies, fish, and bird life. The park has a camp store adjoining the restaurant. Nearby Clifton Forge has laundromats, grocery stores, and pharmacies.

Directions: Located on the Bath County/Alleghany County border, north of Clifton Forge. To get there, take Exit 27 from Interstate 64 on the east side of Clifton Forge, and go north 7 miles on VA 629 (along Wilson Creek) to park.

Activities: Camping, hiking, mountain biking, trout fishing, boating (electric motors only), swimming, interpretive programs.

Facilities: Restaurant, gift shop, camp store, amphitheater, visitor center, 40 miles of hiking trails (biking allowed on most), nature trail, 50-acre lake with swimming beach, boat ramp and boat storage, and rental of rowboats, canoes, waterbikes, and paddleboats. Picnic areas and shelters have drinking water, grills, and modern restrooms. Accommodations include 3 campgrounds with 88 sites and central bathhouses (water and electric hookups in 2 campgrounds); 15 group campsites; 30 fully supplied, climate-controlled rental cabins and 2 rental lodges, all with fireplaces and electric appliances.

Dates: Day-use, year-round. Camping and cabins, Mar. 1–Dec. 1 (may vary). Boat launch and boat storage available year-round.

Fees: A fee is charged for day-use admission for swimming, campsites, and cabins, and at Creasy Lodge and Douthat Lodge.

Closest town: Clifton Forge, 7 miles south.

For more information: Douthat State Park, Route 1, Box 212, Millboro, VA 24460. Phone (540) 862-8100. For reservations, call (800) 933-PARK.

FLORA AND FAUNA AT DOUTHAT. Trilliums, which may be found throughout the woods at Douthat in the spring, are particularly abundant in Campground A. Look for the bright pink petals of low-growing gaywings or fringed polygala (*Polygala paucifolia*) in the cabin area in May and June. The flower belongs to the milkwort family of plants which, according to folklore, will increase milk production when fed to cows or nursing mothers.

Both pink lady slipper (*Cypripedium acaule*) and yellow lady slipper (*Cypripedium calceolus*) grow at Douthat. The pink variety prefers dry woods. The yellow favors limestone wetlands and rich woods. It is more rare than the pink in Virginia. Neither should be picked.

Other woodland flowers here include bloodroot (*Sanguinaria canadensis*), crested dwarf iris (*Iris cristata*), mayapple (*Podophyllum peltatum*), and rue anemone (*Anemonella thalictroides*). Large flame azalea (*Rhododendron calendulaceum*) bloom in the boat launch area. In late summer or early fall, park visitors can sample the delicious fleshy fruit of the little pawpaw tree behind Creasy Lodge. They can, that is, if raccoons, opossums, squirrels, and black bears don't beat them to it.

Flowering dogwood, mountain laurel, autumn olive, rhododendrons, and American barberry add color and interest to the understory. Barberry (*Barberis canadensis*) is a low shrub that has thorns at the base of the leaves. Its beautiful red fruits are sought throughout the fall and winter by many birds including ruffed grouse and bobwhite. Running cedar and Christmas ferns carpet the forest floor with green even in the dead of winter.

FLAME AZALEA
(Rhododendron calendulaceum)

Wild turkey are common at Douthat. The gobbling of the males on the mountainsides echoes across the lake in early spring. Occasionally, the "perk-perk" of the females can be heard. White-tailed deer and gray foxes and other woodland animals come to drink from the lake at dusk. Beaver and muskrat leave a V trail as they cross the open water. Canada geese with goslings and wood ducks with ducklings poke about the lake edges in spring. From a favorite perch on a dead limb, the handsome kingfisher studies the water. If a minnow swims too close to the surface, the kingfisher will plunge headlong into the lake to catch it. Red-tailed hawks and even an occasional bald eagle circle the air above the lake.

CAMPING AND LODGING AT DOUTHAT STATE PARK. To camp near the lake, ask for the Campground A. Boat mooring is available here also. Wilson Creek, which flows through the campground, will attract curious children and adults to look for salamanders, minnows, and streamside wildflowers. A fly-fisherman may wade the shallows searching for trout. If mayflies or caddisflies are hatching, he'll be casting a few feathers carefully tied to a hook to resemble the latest hatch. Campground C has several sites with more privacy. Campsites tend to be small and have picnic tables, grills, and lantern posts. Hardwoods and pines provide shade.

Whip-poor-will

On spring nights, the rhythmic, wild whistle of the whip-poor-will (*Caprimulgus vociferus*) echoes across Douthat Lake. This strictly nocturnal member of the nightjar family stakes out a route. Beginning at the same time each evening and again before dawn, it calls for a few minutes from each spot along the route. Up close, a tiny "cluck" is audible just before the whistle. Dusty roadsides are a favorite location, and the whip-poor-will's eyes reflect red in car headlights.

The rustic Douthat State Park cabins are well spaced among big shade trees. Nothing noisier than the hollow scraping of an oar against a canoe down at the lake disturbs the tranquility of a fall morning spent rocking and reading. The cabins have newly installed air conditioning and heating, but a glowing fire in the fireplace may be all the heat necessary in spring and fall.

HIKING AND BIKING AT DOUTHAT STATE PARK. The 6-foot-wide trails built by the CCC remain today to invite hikers and bikers to enjoy the lake path, find Stony Run and Blue Suck falls, or climb the difficult path to Tuscarora Overlook. Lengths of the 24 trails vary from a mere .3 mile to 4.5 miles, but an infinite number of connections in the 40 miles of trails at Douthat make much longer hikes possible. Douthat has more trail mileage than any other state park in Virginia. Also, several paths lead to longer trails in the surrounding George Washington National Forest.

Stick to more level trails around the lake for the easier hikes. Trails up Middle Mountain to the west and Beards Mountain to the east offer strenuous climbs. Many hikers take cameras along for the stunning mountain and lake photo opportunities. From Beards Mountain, one can see the Cowpasture River to the east and Rough Mountain Wilderness beyond.

Douthat has 12 suck licks which are small springs formed when salty sulphur water drains from underground rock. Deer and other wildlife are drawn to these springs to lick the salty water for sodium. The Buck Lick Interpretive Trail, Blue Suck

Falls, and Claylick Draft (on Beards Mountain) take their names from these springs. None of the suck licks are accessible by trail at this time. Douthat's trails are blazed and easy to follow. The park office has detailed trail maps. With the extensive networking of trails here, it's easy to become interested in the scenery and miss a connection. Bikers should ask which of the trails they are permitted to use and what safety requirements are.

BUCK LICK INTERPRETIVE TRAIL. [Fig. 28(11), Fig. 23(8)] Pick up a $.50 booklet at the park office to explain the 17 learning stations on this easy, red-blazed loop. The trailhead is in the parking area near the entrance to the lakeside concession area. Allow about 50 minutes to enjoy the features and wildflowers along the trail. Included in the tour are such plants and animals as white pine, white and black oak, sassafras, American chestnut, rhododendron, lichens, squirrel, raccoon, white-tailed deer, and bobwhite quail.

Of course, interpretive trail markers cannot designate the many interesting insects, amphibians, ferns, wildflowers, and the like. For instance, the dogtooth violet (*Erythronium americanum*) grows on the Buck Lick trail. This member of the lily family has mottled green leaves with brown spots that give its presence away before the yellowish blossoms appear in early spring.

Trail: .3-mile interpretive loop near lake.

Elevation: 1,450 feet.

Degree of difficulty: Easy.

HERON RUN TRAIL. [Fig. 28(6), Fig. 23(13)] This easy, blue-blazed trail is one of the most popular at the park for its lakeside scenery. In fall, red maples, yellow poplars, and evergreens reflect their colors in Douthat Lake. The trailhead is in the lakeside loop of Campground A.

Trail: .8-mile trail (1.6-mile round trip) on west side of lake.

Elevation: 1,450 feet.

Degree of difficulty: Easy.

FISHING AT DOUTHAT AND LITTLE WILSON CREEK. [Fig. 28] Douthat is one of just three fee-fishing areas in Virginia. Twice a week, from April through October, the Virginia Department of Game and Inland Fisheries stocks catchable-size rainbow, brown, and brook trout in Douthat Lake and a 4-mile section of Wilson Creek. The fee-fishing area extends above and below the lake to the national forest boundary. Anglers must have a Virginia fishing license and must pay a daily fee. A trout stamp is not necessary during the fee-fishing season but is required during the rest of trout season.

Douthat is an ideal place for children to learn to catch trout. Regulations have been modified to allow children 12 and under to fish without a daily permit if they are accompanied by an adult with a permit. The combined creel of adult and child may not exceed six trout. A small-children-only section has been set aside on Wilson Creek just below the dam. Good bass fishing and fair fishing for bluegill and catfish also keep anglers busy on the lake. Chain pickerel fishing is excellent, especially in October. The small lake is a place for anglers who like to cast from boats or shoreline without the wake and noise of gas-powered boats, which are not permitted.

Daily permits, trout stamps, and fishing licenses are available at the park boat dock or camp store.

Dates: May vary annually. Trout season open year-round. Fee fishing, Douthat Lake and Wilson Creek above lake, first Sat. in Apr.–Oct. 31.

Fees: A fee is charged for fishing.

For more information: Contact park or call (804) 525-FISH.

WARM SPRINGS RANGER DISTRICT

[Fig. 25] The huge Warm Springs Ranger District (171,526 acres) occupies most of Bath County except the northeastern tip. The district also includes the western side of Highland County. For its entire 50-mile length, the district borders West Virginia's Monongahela National Forest. Several trails provide a backcountry connection between the two states.

Beautiful mountain scenery adds to the pleasure of fishing, wading, or swimming in Warm Springs District waters. Miles of hiking trails provide choices from easy riverside walks to remote backcountry climbs up steep mountainsides. Bolar Mountain and Bolar Flat recreation areas on the northwest side of deep Lake Moomaw are managed by the Warm Springs Ranger District (*see* Lake Moomaw, page 173). Hidden Valley and Blowing Springs recreation areas provide bases for investigating the cold trout waters of the Jackson River and Back Creek and their watersheds. The Walton Tract provides access to the warm waters of the Cowpasture.

Horseback riders have several options. The district office recommends the remote Laurel Fork area of Highland County (*see* page 182) for more experienced riders. Riders can choose from many trails and gated roads at the Hidden Valley area. The Lime Kiln and Hickman Draft/Beards Mountain areas get significant amounts of horse use. Maps and directions are available at the district office.

Directions: Office is located south of Hot Springs in south central Bath County. From junction of VA 220 and VA 39 just east of Warm Springs, go south on VA 220 about 5 miles to office, on left.

For more information: Warm Springs Ranger District, George Washington National Forest, Route 2, Box 30, Hot Springs, VA 24445. Phone (540) 839-2521.

THE COWPASTURE RIVER AND THE WALTON TRACT

[Fig. 23(5)] Anglers can try for smallmouth bass, rock bass, muskies, redbreast sunfish, and stocked muskies among the smooth, tawny-colored rocks of the shallow, crystal-clear Cowpasture River. The river flows through the east side of the Warm Springs District southward into the James River District. It joins the colder Jackson at Iron Gate, southeast of Clifton Forge, to form the James River. Just a short stretch of about 6 miles between US 60 and the confluence with the Jackson is legally navigable. But farther north (upriver) are two U.S. Forest Service public bank accesses. One is on VA 614 at the junction with VA 678 near Williamsville in northern Bath County. Another is a 3-mile section of the river where it flows through the Walton Tract of the James River District northeast of Clifton Forge. Canoe put-in and take-out points are provided. A swinging bridge across the river leads to the Beard's Mountain Trail and ultimately to Douthat State Park.

The Cowpasture and its tributary, the Bullpasture River, take their names not from domestic cattle but from the elk that once roamed western Virginia. (There's also a Calfpasture River across Shenandoah Mountain to the east.) The mountains and valleys were lush hunting grounds for Indians, especially the Shawnee. Researchers think the roaming elk herds were probably kept in balance until settlers arrived and the Indians acquired firearms. So clear is the water of the Cowpasture that a bluegill or watersnake casts a shadow against the smooth rock bottom even in deep pools. The river's clarity makes it a pleasure to wade, swim, fish, or just to watch aquatic life.

The water boatman, a bug with legs that work like oars, is a tiny predator on the water surface. Dragonflies and damselflies light briefly on reeds. A quiet approach is necessary to get close enough to identify them. These members of the family Odonata can be told apart by the position of their wings. The dragonfly resembles a little biplane with its two pair of wings held horizontally straight out from its body. The smaller, more fragile-looking damselfly holds its wings pressed together lying parallel to its back. Wood ducks and mallards are summer residents along the river. In the

River Otter

Historically, the northern river otter was one of the most widespread mammals west of the Blue Ridge Mountains and was once found over most of North America. The otter's torpedo-shaped body and tail that accounts for a full third of its body weight make it perfectly adapted to its aquatic habitat. But stream pollution, loss of habitat, and hunting and trapping pressure took their toll, and the river otter (*Lutra canadensis*) nearly disappeared from the landscape. Along with the beaver, the otter is slowly making a comeback in marshy areas of the Tidewater and Piedmont in Virginia. Now the state is attempting to reestablish populations in the mountains where otters have been absent since the turn of the century. State research biologists purchased 17 otter from Louisiana, equipped some of them with radio collars, and turned them loose in the Cowpasture River. The first stocking was in the spring of 1989. The otters took to their new habitat immediately and spread into adjacent watersheds. Although humans were the cause of their disappearance, humans may also enable the otters' return.

RIVER OTTER
(Lutra canadensis)
Sociable animals, river otters wrestle, play tag, and roll around riverbanks and in water. Their streamlined bodies, webbed toes, and eyes and ears that can be closed underwater make them well suited for life in and around water.

neighboring fields, the nasal "p-e-e-n-t" of American woodcocks in their courtship flights can be heard. Bobwhite quail, though declining throughout Virginia, still call. Wild turkey and ruffed grouse are common woodland birds.

More information and maps are available from the James River and Warm Springs ranger districts of the George Washington National Forest.

Directions: For the Walton Tract, from I-64 east of Clifton Forge, take Exit 27 and go north on VA 42 about 11 miles. Turn left on VA 626 and follow signs about 1 mile to river.

ROUGH MOUNTAIN WILDERNESS

[Fig. 23(19)] Rough Mountain is an aptly named wilderness of 9,300 rugged acres about 7 miles northeast of Clifton Forge in Bath County. It encompasses all but the northeastern end of Rough Mountain. VA 42 borders Rough Mountain on the northwest side. Pads Creek and the CSX Railroad are on the southeast border. To the southeast are Mill and Brushy mountains and Rich Hole Wilderness, separated from Rough Mountain by a tract of George Washington National Forest.

The steep terrain of Rough Mountain is covered mostly with an oak-hickory forest typical of dry Appalachian slopes. Elevations range from 1,150 feet on the Cowpasture River on the western side to 2,840 feet on Griffith Knob.

Directions: For overland (trail-less) access to northern end and ridgetop hike, from I-64, take Exit 29 and go north on VA 42 about 15 miles. Go right on FR 462 and drive .2 mile to gate. Park off the road and hike past gate about .75 mile to road's end. The ridgetop is another .25-mile uphill trek through the woods. Bushwhack south along the rough, rocky ridgetop for about 1.5 miles to a sign denoting the wilderness boundary. Griffith Knob is on the southern end—a 10.5-mile (one-way) up-and-down hike from trailhead across rocks, through thickets, and across grassy summits. A compass, topo map, and plenty of water are necessities. Pack enough water for the equally difficult return trip.

For eastern access and Crane Trail go southeast from Millboro on VA 633 for about 4 miles. Turn right on FR 129 and drive 5 miles along the South Fork of Pads Creek to small parking area near tracks of Chesapeake & Ohio Railroad. Hike north along old road beside tracks for about a mile to reach trailhead, which is across Pads Creek on left. Railroad itself is posted private property.

Activities: Hiking (strenuous), backcountry camping, seasonal hunting.

Facilities: None.

Dates: Open year-round.

Fees: None.

Closest town: Clifton Forge, about 7 miles southwest.

For more information: Warm Springs Ranger District, George Washington National Forest, Route 2, Box 30, Hot Springs, VA 24445. Phone (540) 839-2521.

CRANE TRAIL. [Fig. 23(3)] This unblazed path begins a mile north of parking area on east side and leads west across Chesapeake & Ohio Railroad and Pads Creek, a tributary of the Cowpasture River. It then steeply ascends Rough Mountain 1.6 miles to ridgetop suitable for camping (no water or other facilities). The trail leads down the other side of Rough Mountain about 1.4 miles toward VA 42. Posted signs mark the wilderness boundary and beginning of private property. Hikers without permission should turn back here. The trail terminates at a small parking area on private property along VA 42.

For those who like solitude and the challenge of wilderness travel, a 4.5-mile (one-way) bushwhack south along the ridgetop from the Crane Trail leads to Griffith

Knob with its beautiful views. No water is available, so hikers should carry enough for the return trip.

Trail: 3-mile (one-way) steep climb over Rough Mountain from east and back, plus 1-mile hike between parking area and trailhead.

Elevation: 1,360 to 2,530 feet.

Degree of difficulty: Moderate, with difficult sections.

TURKEY VULTURE
(Cathartes aura)
The vulture's wings form a "V" when gliding.

Surface: Natural forest floor, with grassy sections and rocky sections.

LAKE MOOMAW AND GATHRIGHT WILDLIFE MANAGEMENT AREA

LAKE MOOMAW. [Fig. 23(1)] Lake Moomaw is 12 miles long and covers 2,350 acres on the Bath County/Alleghany County border. Created with the construction of the 257-foot-tall Gathright Dam in 1981 for flood control, the lake has an average depth of 80 feet. Unlike many large bodies of water, gasoline-powered boats have not taken over this out-of-the-way lake. Canoes and kayaks have 43 miles of shoreline to range with no fear of bothering private property owners. The lake is surrounded by more than a million acres of George Washington National Forest and the 13,428-acre Gathright Wildlife Management Area (WMA).

Moomaw is home to 25 species of fish. Smallmouth bass are dominant at the lower end of the lake and in the headwaters. Three- and 4-pounders are common in the spring. Look for largemouth bass up to 5 and 6 pounds and catfish in the range of 10 to 16 pounds. Crappie fishing is outstanding. Sizzling in frying pans over evening campfires will be tasty crappie of 1.5 pounds or more. Anglers without boats fish around dock pilings for nice bluegill. Also, the state-record yellow perch (2 pounds, 3 ounces) came from Moomaw in 1995.

Stocked brown trout are growing to 2 or 3 pounds. The best time to catch them is from January to June before water levels are drawn down and temperatures increase. Neither a trout license nor a National Forest Stamp is required, but a Virginia fishing license is required. Trailered boats must be launched at ramps at Fortney Branch (southern tip), Bolar Flat (northwest side), or Coles Point (near dam). Hand-carry boats can be put in at McClintic Point on the northwest side near the upper end and at Midway Point between Bolar Flat and McClintic Point.

The attractive recreation areas north of the dam are managed by Warm Springs Ranger District. These include Bolar Mountain, Bolar Flat, and Greenwood Point. The James River Ranger District manages the southern end where popular Coles Point and Morris Hill recreation areas attract crowds on summer weekends. Arrive early in peak season to secure a campsite. The U.S. Army Corps of Engineers operates a visitor center at the dam.

Spectacular displays of wildflowers are scattered along the roadside and fields on the back entrance to Lake Moomaw along the Richardson Gorge Road (VA 603). Trillium, wild ginger (*Asarum canadense*), and columbine (*Aquilegia canadensis*) are among the many varieties. Land on both sides of this road is private.

GATHRIGHT WILDLIFE MANAGEMENT AREA. [Fig. 23(1)] Gathright Wildlife Management Area's (WMA) 13,428 acres are divided into two tracts by Lake Moomaw. The largest tract is on the western side of the lake, and it lies on the eastern slope of Allegheny Mountain and the southern end of Bolar Mountain. Five parking areas on VA 600 along Mill Creek provide access to gated roads which are opened for hunting seasons. The other tract is on Coles Mountain on the eastern side of the lake.

Stands of oak-hickory and mixed oaks are the major forest types. In fertile hollows, tulip poplar grows. The area is managed by the Virginia Department of Game and Inland Fisheries for forest wildlife such as wild turkey, white-tailed deer, ruffed grouse, and gray squirrel. Management practices include small clear-cuttings, plantings of grass and clover for wildlife openings, and tree thinning to enhance production of hard mast such as acorns, an important source of food for game animals.

The combined resources of lake, national forest, and WMA attract a variety of animals that need large tracts of undeveloped land. An example is the endangered bald eagle, a species uncommon to the mountains of Virginia. Eagle perches have been built in secluded areas to encourage eagles to use the lake area. The management agencies have also built at least five waterfowl islands below the McClintic Bridge. Ducks and geese are now using these islands for nesting. Natural islands within the lake are also managed for waterfowl nesting and feeding areas. Canada geese in particular have benefitted from these sites.

Directions: Lake Moomaw is in the southwestern corner of Bath County.

Gathright WMA and Bolar Flat, Bolar Mountain, and Greenwood Point recreation areas: From junction of VA 39 and VA 220 just east of Warm Springs, go west 11.3 miles on VA 39 and turn left on VA 600. After 2.5 miles, WMA begins (look for yellow WMA signs and parking areas on right side for next 5 miles). At 7.5 miles road forks. Right fork leads to Bolar Mountain camping and picnicking and left fork

(VA 603) leads to Bolar Flat boat launch and picnic area. Greenwood Point is a primitive campground that can be reached by boat or by hiking the 3.3-mile Greenwood Point Trail from Bolar Mountain.

Gathright Dam and Coles Mountain Recreation Area: From VA 220 at Hot Springs, go west 2.7 miles on VA 615. Turn left (south) on VA 605 and go 3 miles. After crossing the dam, take entrance road, FR 601.

Morris Hill Recreation Area and Fortney Branch (boat launch): Take Exit 16 from I-64 at Covington and take US 220 north 4 miles. Turn left on VA 687 and go north 3 miles. Turn left on VA 641 and go west 1 mile. Turn right on VA 666 and go north 5 miles. For Morris Hill, from VA 666 turn right on VA 605 and go 2 miles to entrance road, FR 603, on left. For Fortney Branch, turn left on VA 605 and follow signs 1 mile to launch.

Activities: Lake Moomaw: Camping, picnicking, boating, fishing, water skiing, swimming, hiking. National Forest and Gathright WMA: Hiking, seasonal hunting, backcountry camping.

Facilities: Bolar Mountain: 3 campgrounds with 90 sites, 60 picnic sites, picnic shelter, flush toilets, hot showers, electric hookups, trailer dump station, beach with bathhouse, volleyball and play area, docks, amphitheater. **Bolar Flat:** 50 picnic sites, picnic shelter, 4-lane boat ramp, dock, flush toilets, marina, camp store, fishing pier with access for the handicapped, swimming beach, hiking trails, drinking water, restrooms. **Coles Mountain Recreation Area:** Swimming beach, bathhouse, hot showers, flush toilets, 80 picnic sites, shelters, boat launch, dock, fishing pier with access for the handicapped. **Morris Hill Recreation Area:** Campground has 55 sites with grills and picnic tables. Hot showers, flush toilets, trailer dump station, lake access trails. Nearby picnic area has tables, shelters, toilet facilities, hiking trails. **Fortney Branch:** 4-lane boat launch, dock, drinking water, toilet facilities, lake trails, and fishing access. Gathright WMA: 5 parking areas along VA 600 and inroads open seasonally.

Dates: Camping, May 1–Nov. 1. Marina gas sales and boat rental, summer. Boat launching, fishing, hiking, 24 hours a day, year-round.

Gathright WMA: Open year-round to foot travel and backcountry camping. Gated roads are open during hunting seasons.

Fees: Lake Moomaw: A fee is charged for admission and campsites. Gathright WMA: None.

Closest town: Warm Springs, 14 miles east of western section of Gathright WMA, 7 miles east of eastern section of Gathright WMA, and 19 miles from Bolar Mountain Recreation Area. Hot Springs, 9 miles northeast of Gathright Dam.

For more information: James River Ranger District, George Washington National Forest, 810 A Madison Avenue, Covington, VA 24426. Phone (540) 962-2214.

Warm Springs Ranger District, George Washington National Forest, Route 2, Box 30, Hot Springs, VA 24445. Phone (540) 839-2521.

For reservations at Coles Point, phone (800) 280-CAMP.

Gathright WMA, Virginia Department of Game and Inland Fisheries, Region IV Office, PO Box 996, Verona, VA 24482. Phone (540) 248-9360.

THE LOWER JACKSON RIVER

In years past, the 19-mile stretch of the Jackson River between Gathright Dam on Lake Moomaw and Covington has provided high-quality trout fishing on a large river. However, disputes between property owners and fishermen make floating this section a dicey business. A recent decision by the Virginia Supreme Court upheld an old law on the books giving certain landowners along the Jackson the right to prohibit fishing through their property. In these areas, boaters can float through but not fish. Five public access sites have been developed where bank fishing is permitted, however. Otherwise, landowners' permission should be obtained. The first public access site, managed by the U.S. Army Corps of Engineers, is just below the dam spillway off VA 605. The second is Johnson Springs off VA 687. The third, Falling Spring, is off VA 721. The fourth is Indian Draft located off VA 687. The fifth is Petticoat Junction also located off VA 687.

For more information: Virginia Division of Game and Inland Fisheries, Verona Regional Office, PO Box 996, Verona, VA 24482. Phone (540) 248-9360.

THE HIDDEN VALLEY AREA

[Fig. 26(21)] Hidden Valley, rich in history and pastoral charm, lies at the upper reaches of the Jackson River about 6 miles west of Warm Springs. This Bath County treasure is worth the trouble to find. The blue-green Jackson is famous among fly-fishermen for its stocked and native trout. Twenty miles of trails vary from easy footpaths that follow the river to strenuous climbs over Back Creek Mountain. Wildflowers typical of streamsides, fields, rock ledges, and forests find suitable habitat in Hidden Valley. Wildlife clearings attract white-tailed deer in early evenings. Bald eagles occasionally scavenge the riverbanks.

AMERICAN TOAD (Bufo americanus) Despite popular myth, toads do not cause warts.

Reservations are required to enter the grounds of historic Warwick Mansion, but you can see it from the river. Hidden Valley Campground, with its large, sparsely forested sites, is a favorite for fly-fishermen interested in the Jackson which flows beside the campground.

Blowing Springs Campground [Fig. 26(25), Fig. 29] is located on VA 39 where O'Rourke Draft flows into Back Creek, another stocked trout stream. Hunters, fishermen, and those looking for private sites away from crowds enjoy this spot. The campground takes its name from nearby springs which emit strong gusts of cool air. The air comes from pockets and chambers that have developed in porous underground rocks.

At the northern end of Hidden Valley is Poor Farm, one of the most popular fishing, hunting, and primitive camping spots in the Warm Springs District.

Bluebells

In early spring, bluebells (*Mertensia virginica*) grow in profusion under sycamores and apple trees along the first stretch of the Hidden Valley Trail on the Jackson River, especially before the wide field on the right gives way to woods. The trumpet-shaped flowers, common in flood plains, are well adapted to the moist soil under the canopy of hemlock and sycamores.

Where it flows through here, the Jackson River is regularly stocked with trout. Plenty of trails at both areas lead along the rivers and streams, up into gorges, over mountains and through fields and pastures in both areas. The well-packed and maintained trails are perfect for mountain biking, too. You won't find a better combination of good riding conditions, scenery, variety of topography, and lack of traffic than on the network of hiking trails and backroads here.

Directions: For Hidden Valley, go west from Warm Springs on VA 39 for 3 miles. Turn right onto VA 621 and go 1 mile north. Go left on FR 241 and continue 1.5 miles to primitive campground or 2 miles to Hidden Valley parking area in front of Warwick Mansion. For Blowing Springs, go west from Warm Springs on VA 39 for 9 miles to campground on left. For Poor Farm, from Warm Springs, go north on US 220 about 9.5 miles. Turn left on VA 623 and drive about 2 miles to area.

Activities: Primitive camping, trout fishing, hiking, mountain biking, hunting.

Facilities: Campgrounds have drinking water, toilet facilities, and trailer dump station. Hidden Valley has 30 primitive campsites, each with picnic table, lantern post, and grill. Blowing Springs has 23 sites with picnic tables and grills and 6 picnic sites. Both have stocked trout stream and hiking/biking trails. Poor Farm has stocked trout area of Jackson River.

Dates: Mar. 15–Jan.1.

Fees: A fee is charged for use of the campgrounds.

Closest town: Warm Springs, 6 miles southeast of Hidden Valley, 9 miles east of Blowing Springs, and 11 miles south of Poor Farm.

For more information: Warm Springs Ranger District, George Washington National Forest, Route 2, Box 30, Hot Springs, VA 24445. Phone (540) 839-2521.

HIDDEN VALLEY TRAIL. [Fig. 26(22)] This streamside path follows the Jackson River 3.95 miles upriver. The first part of the trail is along the edge of a wide field with Cobbler Mountain in the background. Then the path leads into the woods where cool air from the Jackson feels refreshing on a hot summer day. A field guide will come in handy to help identify the many spring, summer, and fall wildflowers.

In late summer, look for the occasional yellow-fringed orchid (*Habenaria ciliaris*) in the open woods. This very showy orchid is leafy with a terminal cluster of yellow-orange blossoms with fringed petals. Other flowers along the trail include the cardinal flower (*Lobelia cardinalis*), round-lobed hepatica (*Hepatica americana*), spring beauty (*Claytonia virginica*), and several varieties of trillium.

In one section of the trail, jutting rock ledges provide a contrasting backdrop to soft hemlocks. Sheltered woodlands where hemlocks grow usually have rhododendron and mountain laurel, and this river valley is no exception. The trail is the main link to an extensive network of hikes on Back Creek Mountain, Little Mountain, Cobbler Mountain, Warwick Mountain, Rocky Ridge, and Berry Knob. Look for well-marked trailheads at the Hidden Valley campground and across the Jackson River from Warwick Mansion.

Before the Hidden Valley Trail reaches the swinging bridge, a 1.2-mile trail to the right follows Muddy Run up a scenic gorge. At the bridge the 1.4-mile Jackson River Gorge Trail connects to the Hidden Valley Trail for a loop hike. At mile 1.7, a swinging bridge will take you across the river. Past the bridge, the trail is less heavily used. Special-regulation trout fishing is in effect on the Jackson River from the bridge for 3 miles upriver to the last ford on FR 481D. Artificial lures and single-hooks must be used. The creel limit is two fish of 16 inches or more per day. This section is stocked regularly several times a year with catchable-sized trout, and good populations are always present. Because the special-regulation section is accessible only by foot travel, anglers can expect solitude and good fishing.

HIDDEN VALLEY TRAIL. 3.95-mile linear path north along the Jackson River, providing connections to Bogan Run, Jackson River Gorge, Muddy Run, and, at its northern end, FR 241.

Elevation: 1,950 feet.

Degree of difficulty: Easy.

BOGAN RUN TRAIL. [Fig. 26(23)] For a real workout, take this link from the Hidden Valley Trail northwest across Back Creek Mountain. You'll pass Warwick Mansion, and then you'll enter a canopy of scarlet and chestnut oak as you climb 1,460 feet to cross Back Creek Mountain.

The trail ends on the west side near VA 600 on posted, private land. The Forest Service hopes to reroute the trail ending to allow vehicle access from VA 600. For now, however, hikers must backtrack to the starting point.

Trail: 5.5-mile climb (one-way) up Back Creek Mountain.

Elevation: 1,950 to 3,411 feet.

Degree of difficulty: Moderate, with steep sections.

BULLPASTURE GORGE & HIGHLAND WILDLIFE MANAGEMENT AREA

[Fig. 26(17)] The Bullpasture River is best known by anglers for its stocked trout. But the river and its environs delight everyone who drives the 12 scenic miles of VA 678 south of McDowell. In October, when trout stocking begins, a fly-fisherman or woman wading among the boulders and dancing waves is the perfect subject for a photograph. Red and yellow foliage of maples and poplars stand out on the mountainside in the background. The hemlock-lined banks are dark in the foreground. On the next cast, there's a distinct possibility a 4-pound rainbow just might add a bowed rod to the picture.

Several pullovers along the edge of the Highland Wildlife Management Area (WMA) provide access to fishermen, wildflower enthusiasts, birders, and photographers. The WMA borders the river in the area of the gorge and just upriver from the gorge. The upriver portion is where most of the fishing, camping, and picnicking takes place. The public land here is one of three tracts that make up the 14,283 acres of the Highland Wildlife Management Area. This one is on Bullpasture Mountain which butts up against the northern end of Tower Hill Mountain to try to subdue the Bullpasture River as it passes between.

A second tract is on Jack Mountain southwest of McDowell. A small third tract is on Little Doe Hill about 2 miles west of McDowell and bordering the north side of US 250. The Jack Mountain tract has an 80-acre opening of bluegrass sod that was formerly used as summer pasture. This opening and several small wildlife clearings make good places to find wildlife, wildflowers, and butterflies. Vegetation at the edges of the clearings is especially attractive to animals. Bullpasture Mountain is best known for its deer and turkey populations. The more rugged Jack Mountain is known for its deer, turkey, and bear. Fair numbers of ruffed grouse, squirrels, and rabbits also live in these forests.

At the picnic area near Bullpasture Gorge, a swinging bridge spans the Bullpasture River. The woodlands on the other side are an ideal place to find wildflowers. Growing in the rich, sandy soil are red trillium (*Trillium erectum*), bluebell (*Mertensia virginica*), common blue violet (*Viola papilionacea*), and crested dwarf iris (*Iris cristata*), to mention a few.

Directions: Bullpasture Mountain and Bullpasture Gorge: From US 250 at McDowell, in Highland County, go south on VA 678 about 12 miles to Bullpasture Gorge and southern end of Highland WMA. Parking and picnic area is next to road, on left.

JACK MOUNTAIN. [Fig. 26] From McDowell, go west on US 250 about 1.75 miles. Go left (south) on VA 615 and drive about 2 miles to area. Go right on Cobbs Hill Road or left on Buck Hill Road into Highland WMA. Buck Hill Road is gated except during hunting seasons.

Activities: Fishing for stocked trout, hiking, seasonal hunting, swimming, snorkeling.

Facilities: Stocked trout waters, 20 miles of mountain roads including seeded roads for wildlife, foot trails, picnic tables, toilets, cable suspension footbridge.

Dates: Open year-round to foot travel. Gated roads on Highland WMA may be open to vehicular travel during hunting seasons.

Fees: None.

Closest town: Williamsville, at southeastern end of gorge. McDowell, about 12 miles north of Bullpasture Gorge.

BLUEGRASS VALLEY

[Fig. 26(7)] The people of Highland County say proudly that they have more sheep than people. Bluegrass Valley is a good place to make their case. "Valley" is a relative term. In Highland County, no place is low. At the center of the 18-mile-long Bluegrass Valley floor at High Town, where US 250 intersects VA 640, the elevation is over 3,000 feet. Snowy Mountain, to the northeast, rises to 4,500 feet.

Highland, named for its mountains, has the highest mean elevation of any county in the state. In fact, according to the Virginia Department of Game and Inland Fisheries, the county is generally regarded as having the highest average elevation of any county east of the Mississippi. No wonder it's sometimes called Little Switzerland. A 50-mile east-west drive on US 250 is all that separates Bluegrass Valley from the Shenandoah Valley town of Staunton and Interstate 81. Fifty miles would be nothing on the arrow-straight interstate running north/south through the Shenandoah Valley. But five mountain ranges lie between the Shenandoah Valley and this remote outpost that's just a short hike from the state of West Virginia. First, heading west from Staunton, there's Great North Mountain. Then Shenandoah Mountain. Then Bullpasture and Jack mountains and finally the gap between Back Creek and Monterey mountains. That's a lot of hairpin turns and two-lane road between the two towns. But the isolation of Bluegrass Valley is what makes it special.

Golden-crowned Kinglet

Old conifers are a good place to listen for the cascading chatter of the golden-crowned kinglet (*Regulus satrapa*). The tiny bird may ignore the presence of visitors as it deftly extracts insects from tree bark. Binoculars will help bird watchers identify the male by its orange- and yellow-striped crown. The females and young males lack the orange stripe.

This serene land between Back Creek and Lantz mountains seems a holdover from another time. Life is measured not so much with clocks and schedules but as a span between the planting of grain to the first rain. Time flows gently from one season to the next, measured as a color change from summer's lush greens to the bronze, crimson, and gold of fall to the browns and grays of winter.

VA 640, the single highway running through the narrow valley, is often devoid of a single car. Rising away from the road are highland pastures, climbing up the mountains on either side. In summer, sheep graze the steep hillsides above bottomlands of lush grain fields that move with the breeze. The low drone of bees in honeysuckle may be the only sound.

Golden-winged warblers have been spotted at beaver ponds located at the US 250 crossing of Back Creek just west of Hightown. Cedar waxwings, chestnut-sided warblers, and dark-eyed juncos are common summer breeders. In winter, a golden eagle may be spotted perched in a craggy tree. Twenty feet beneath the snag that holds the eagle is the object of interest—a healthy rainbow trout made sluggish by the cold.

GOLDEN-CROWNED KINGLET
(Regulus satrapa)
A restless, flitting movement and a high, thin "ssst" identify the kinglet.

Bluegrass Valley is a wintering ground for the eagles, and local residents have become familiar with their presence. Rough-legged hawks are also winter residents.

The junction of US 250 and VA 640 at Hightown marks the separation between two watersheds. A turn onto VA 640 south follows tumbling Back Creek in the headwaters of the Jackson River. The Jackson will head for the James River and pass the state capital at Richmond on its way to the Chesapeake Bay.

Keeping VA 640 company to the north is a small stream with a responsible-sounding name—South Branch of the Potomac. The waters, which are stocked trout waters, are heading for the nation's capital at Washington, D.C., and then into the Chesapeake Bay. The land along the highway is private land. Wherever there are signs on trees indicating stocked waters, though, anglers may fish without landowner permission. In addition to a state fishing license, a trout license is needed October 1 through June 15 when stockings take place, but the trout license is not required during the rest of the year. Creel limit is six trout of 7 or more inches in length, although these regulations may vary from year to year.

Directions: From Staunton, take US 250 west for 50 miles to Hightown. Turn right or left on VA 640.

Activities: Scenic drive, fishing for stocked trout.

Closest town: Monterey, 6 miles east.

For more information: Alleghany Highlands Chamber of Commerce, 241 West Main Street, Covington, VA 24426. Phone (540) 962-2178. For trout fishing, Virginia Department of Game and Inland Fisheries, Verona Field Office, PO Box 996, Verona, VA 24482. Phone (540) 248-9360; daily stocking information (804) 525-FISH.

🟦 LAUREL FORK AREA

[Fig. 26(2)] On a map, Virginia's western border resembles a torn piece of paper. One of those ragged edges is where the northern tip of Highland County reaches into West Virginia's Plateau country and borrows a slice of northern boreal forest. The forest gives Virginia 25 species of plants and animals found nowhere else in the state.

The area is called Laurel Fork, named after the high-altitude native trout stream flowing through the middle. Waters from this wild, remote mountain plateau will eventually join the Potomac River to flow past the Lincoln Memorial and the Washington Monument at the nation's capital and then into the Chesapeake Bay.

The Nature Conservancy manages a 324-acre preserve at Laurel Fork. Most of this northern tip of Highland County, however, is part of the 10,000-acre Laurel Fork Special Management Area of the George Washington National Forest. The word "special" fits in more ways than one.

Laurel Fork—where plants and animals are more typical of coniferous forests far to the north—is the best example of the northern boreal forest complex in Virginia. Residents include such animals as the snowshoe hare, red squirrel, fisher, and red-breasted nuthatch. Here, the federally endangered northern flying squirrel builds dens in old woodpecker holes. Young squirrels must practice jumping and gliding from one tree limb to another to get the hang of it. As dusk turns to dark, the tiny novices may appear side-by-side on a limb outside a tree hole to begin practice.

Fishers are usually found in New England and Canada. This relative of martens and wolverines is one of the few animals that has figured out how to make a meal out of a porcupine. At Laurel Fork, however, the fisher feeds on small mammals, carrion, birds, fern tips, and fruits. Its fur is a beautiful dark brown to black with white on the tips, giving it a frosted appearance. The red-breasted nuthatch creeps head downward on tree trunks just as its larger cousin, the white-breasted nuthatch, does. This coniferous-forest dweller smears the opening of its nesting cavity with pitch. It can't help getting into the gooey mess itself, giving it an unkempt look. Birds to look for also include the black-throated green warbler, golden-crowned kinglet, and northern junco. Other species protected at the Special Management Area include the Cheat Mountain salamander, southern water shrew, and a plant called the hairy woodmint.

Beavers—another common component of boreal forests—are capable of dramatically altering the landscape. True to form, the large rodents have dropped large trees in the drainages, creating shallow ponds and meadows that attract mink, muskrat, waterfowl, frogs, and salamanders. Moisture-loving grasses, wildflowers, and shrubs that spring from these beaver-created wetlands add an interesting mix to Laurel Fork. Beaver activity is mostly west of the Laurel Fork stream.

The unusual forest is a result of a complex combination of influences, including Laurel Fork's altitudes that vary from 2,600 to 4,100 feet. Elevation alone, however, is not enough. Another important factor is the area's position on what is called the

Appalachian extension of the northern boreal forest—a connection to the great boreal forests across Canada, northern Europe, and Asia. The fingerlike extension reaches from northern North America down a narrow corridor of the Appalachians through Pennsylvania, West Virginia, and as far south as northern Georgia.

SOUTHERN FLYING SQUIRREL
(Glaucomys volans)
This squirrel doesn't fly but glides.

Boreal forests typically support a few dominant species. Across northern North America, entire sections of boreal forests may be comprised solely of balsam fir and white spruce. Along the Appalachian extension, though, red spruce grows in place of white spruce and Fraser fir replaces balsam fir. Firs and spruces may be told apart in a variety of ways. The needles on fir trees are flat while spruce needles are round. Also, the cones of fir trees stand up from the branches while the cones of spruce hang down. As boreal forests mature and the canopy grows denser, increasing darkness shades out the understory and leaves low-spreading shrubs or just mosses and ferns to carpet the floor. Decomposing needles form a soft mat underlain by highly acidic soil called gray spodosol. Boggy areas are common.

According to the U.S. Forest Service, Laurel Fork's trees were almost completely logged out before the land was purchased in 1922. Prior to logging, the forest was comprised of 40 percent spruce, 20 percent hemlock, and the remainder a mix of beech, birch, maple, oak, and cherry.

Although the percentage of evergreens is not as great as it was before logging, Laurel Fork still sustains a significant boreal forest but with a greater mix of northern hardwoods than it had in the original old-growth forest. Locust Springs Picnic Area [Fig. 26(1)] offers tables, an Adirondack shelter, water, and toilet facilities. Two hiking trails—Buck Run Trail and Locust Spring Run—lead southeast down drainages to the Laurel Fork Trail.

Directions: From Staunton, take US 250 west through Monterey to West Virginia. Go right (north) on WV 28 and drive about 6 miles. Turn right on FR 106 and follow signs to Locust Springs Picnic Area.

Activities: Hiking, fishing for native trout, backcountry camping, seasonal hunting, horseback riding.

Facilities: Picnic area, picnic shelter (where camping is allowed), hand-operated water pump, fire rings, vault toilet, 28 miles of hiking trails.

Dates: National Forest Special Management Area is open year-round. The Nature Conservancy's preserve is closed except for guided field trips.

Fees: None.

Closest town: Thornwood, West Virginia, about 7 miles southwest of picnic area.

For more information: Laurel Fork Special Management Area: Warm Springs Ranger District, George Washington National Forest, Route 2, Box 30, Hot Springs, VA 24445. Phone (540) 839-2521. Laurel Fork Preserve: The Nature Conservancy's Virginia Field Office, phone (804) 295-6106.

HIKING AT LAUREL FORK. Many of the 28 miles of beautiful hiking trails in the area make use of the old tram roads that were used to carry the trees out of the forest. Despite the steep terrain of the area, the railroad grades provide easy walking trails. The Laurel Fork Trail [Fig. 26(3)] is the main artery of the trail system. It follows the meandering path of Laurel Fork southwest to northeast through the area, and other trails branch off from it. Abundant pockets of rhododendron bloom along the trail in June. Fly-fishermen pursue the secretive native brook trout that hide in quiet pools of Laurel Fork. During periods of high water, Laurel Fork may be impossible to cross.

Other interesting trails include Buck Run, a 2.9-mile path from Locust Springs Picnic Area to the Laurel Fork Trail. Along the way are beaver ponds and fern, spruce, and cranberry bogs. Christian Run Trail [Fig. 26(4)] is a short, 1.5-mile (one-way) visit to old fields from pioneer homestead days. Bear Wallow Trail [Fig. 26(5)] is a 2.7-mile (one-way) trek to more beaver ponds and to openings with outstanding views.

All trails are blazed with blue paint. Maps of the trail system are available from the Warm Springs Ranger District office.

Laurel Fork Trail: 6-mile path (one-way) along Laurel Fork.

Elevation: 3,280 to 3,540 feet.

Degree of difficulty: Easy.

Surface and blaze: Old tram-line bed and stream crossings. Blue blaze.

AMERICAN MOUNTAIN-ASH
(Sorbus americana)
Found along swamp borders as well as on mountainsides, the mountain-ash produces clusters of orange-red fruit for birds and rodents.

GOSHEN PASS AREA

[Fig. 23(6)] In northern Rockbridge County, an easy hop from Interstate 64 is Goshen Pass and the Goshen–Little North Mountain Wildlife Management Area. Goshen Pass is a narrow sliver of gorge carved through the southern end of Little North Mountain by the Maury River. It assumes various personalities depending on the season. On summer afternoons, the laughter of children mingles with the shouts of college students from nearby Lexington's Virginia Military Institute or Washington & Lee University. In one way or another, everyone—including adults at picnic tables along the river's edge—is savoring a small spot of isolated beauty in northeastern Rockbridge County. The children splash and play in pools beneath apartment-size boulders. The college students squirt down long, slippery river boulders using inner tubes and belly slides. Everybody, including a fly-fisherman casting for stocked trout, stops to admire the skill of a kayaker shooting the rapids.

Goshen Pass, between Lexington and the town of Goshen, is only 100 yards wide in places and a short 7 miles long. The Maury River follows VA 39 through the popular gorge with its steep forested slopes and exposed cliffs and its several pull-offs for photography or fishing. This is a busy place on summer weekends.

Then in fall, when swimmers and picnickers are gone, orange-clad hunters spread out across adjoining Goshen–Little North Mountain Wildlife Management Area. The 33,697-acre wildlife management area, purchased through funds from hunting and fishing license sales, is managed by the state Department of Game and Inland Fisheries for deer, turkey, grouse, and squirrels. An occasional black bear also wanders through this largest wildlife management area in the state.

Goshen Pass and the rugged, beautiful Maury River divide the public lands of Goshen–Little North Mountain Wildlife Management Area into two large parcels. The parcels offer hunters, hikers, and mountain bikers a network of trails and roads leading to all parts of the wildlife management area. The area is maintained in a primitive state. There are no campgrounds or other facilities. Gated wildlife management area roads are open to foot travel year-round. Some are open to vehicular travel during hunting seasons.

Directions: From Goshen in northwestern Rockbridge County, go east on VA 39 about 2 miles. Pullovers beside river are along the next 7-mile stretch. Parking area and swinging bridge are about halfway along this stretch.

Activities: Fishing, tubing, kayaking, canoeing, hiking, picnicking, seasonal hunting, backcountry camping, scenic drive.

Facilities: Riverside parking, hiking trails, swinging bridge, stocked trout river, scattered picnic tables and grills at pull-outs along river.

Closest town: Goshen is about 2 miles northwest of upper end of Goshen Pass. Lexington and I-64 are 12 miles southeast of lower end of Goshen Pass.

For more information: Virginia Department of Game and Inland Fisheries, Region IV Office, PO Box 996, Verona, VA 24482. Phone (540) 248-9360.

The Shenandoah Mountains

Two ranger districts of the George Washington National Forest [Fig. 25]—
Deerfield Ranger District and Dry River Ranger District—lie end-to-end in the
Shenandoah Mountains west of Staunton and Harrisonburg.

Long Shenandoah Mountain which dominates the scene has its beginnings in
northeastern Bath County at Green Valley. The ridge runs northeastward along the
western borders first of Augusta County then of Rockingham County. The two
ranger districts take in Shenandoah Mountain and most of the mountainous area to
the east, ending at the western edge of the Shenandoah Valley.

DEERFIELD RANGER DISTRICT

The Deerfield Ranger District of the George Washington National Forest spreads
across 164,183 acres of western Augusta County, eastern Highland County, and
northeastern Bath County. The Cowpasture River defines the western boundary.
Scenic highways (US 39 on the south and US 42 on the east) roughly define two
sides. US 250, which connects the city of Staunton in Augusta County to the town of
Monterey in Highland County, runs along the border for about 3 miles on the
northeastern edge. Then the boundary veers northwest of US 250 taking in the
headwaters of the Calfpasture and Cowpasture rivers. The line goes across the top of
Hankey Mountain and around the north side of Ramseys Draft Wilderness connecting with the southern corner of Pendleton County, West Virginia.

American Redstart

The American redstart (*Setophaga
ruticilla*) is one of the most abundant
forest birds. Its success can be tied directly
to its favorite habitat—second-growth
forests—the kind that covers most of
North America. This wood warbler
requires large tracts of unfragmented
woodlands, so the Deerfield Ranger
District is just about perfect. With his
black body, orange markings, and white
belly, the mature male is easiest to spot.
However, he remains a duller olive brown
with yellow markings—like the female—
for the first year.

The national forest lies mostly in
three large tracts around a Y-shaped
valley of private land. Great North
Mountain and Crawford Mountain lie
end-to-end to make up one tract on the
eastern side. The southern end of long
Shenandoah Mountain forms a second
tract on the district's western side. At the
top of the Y is Walker Mountain, the
third tract, which rises from the valley
floor southwest of the village of Deerfield, separating Deerfield Valley along
VA 629 from pretty Marble Valley along
VA 600.

VA 629 runs the entire length of
pastoral Deerfield Valley, passing by
farms outlined by long white fences, past
churches, swinging bridges, country
stores, old log cabins, forested hollows,

Bloodroot is one of the first wildflowers to bloom in the spring. Its common name refers to the bright orange-red juice found in its stems and roots which was used by Indians as a paint and a dye. The flower contains an alkaloid that has antiseptic and anticancer properties.

rocky creeks, and mountain backdrops—a road as appealing and full of charm as many with official scenic status. The placid Calfpasture River flows first through Deerfield Valley, between West Augusta and Deerfield, then veers south into equally bucolic and lovely Marble Valley along VA 600. Where it passes close to the highway, the river adds beauty to the landscape but its waters are considered nonnavigable, which puts it off limits for recreation.

Mountain slopes in the Deerfield District are forested with typical eastern deciduous hardwoods interspersed with pines. Hardwoods include such trees as chestnut oak, northern red oak, white oak, shagbark and pignut hickories, red maple, tulip poplar, and American beech. A sequence of blooms comes in spring from understory trees and shrubs: first from shadbush then Eastern redbud, flowering dogwood, mountain laurel, deerberry, and blueberry. Hemlocks, sycamores, and thickets of mountain laurel and rhododendron line the ravines.

The creamy white blossoms of bloodroot (*Sanguinaria canadensis*) sprout almost magically from the leaf litter of forested slopes in spring. Occasional sprinklings of large-flowered trillium (*Trillium grandiflorum*), painted trillium (*Trillium undulatum*), or the foul-smelling purple trillium (*Trillium erectum*) add their colors of white, pink, and magenta. In late summer, roadsides are dotted with blue from chicory (*Chichorium intybus*), yellow from black-eyed susan (*Rudbeckia hirta*), white from Queen Anne's lace (*Daucus carota*), and even occasional patches of red raspberries warmed by the sun.

Two recreation areas—Mountain House and Braley Pond—offer fishing, hiking, and picnicking. Although there are no developed campgrounds, the district is highly prized by seekers of solitude for its 124 miles of hiking trails. Backpackers, mountain bikers, anglers, hunters, and horseback riders take advantage of national forest policy of allowing backcountry camping anywhere. A third recreation area—Confederate Breastworks—attracts those interested in Civil War history.

Directions: District office is located on VA 254, 1 mile west of Staunton.

Activities: Hiking, fishing, picnicking, seasonal hunting, horseback riding, mountain biking, backcountry camping.

Facilities: Picnic area, historic area, 124 miles of trails, rifle range.

Closest town: Staunton, 9 miles west from eastern edge of district.

For more information: Deerfield Ranger District, George Washington National Forest, Route 6, Box 419, Staunton, VA 24401. Phone (540) 885-8028.

AUGUSTA SPRINGS WATCHABLE WILDLIFE AREA. [Fig. 26(18)] This 50-acre tract on the eastern end of Great North Mountain is a department superstore to wildlife. It has marshes, open grassy fields, and an oak-hickory upland forest.

The open fields attract such species as meadowlark, bluebird, goldfinch, bobwhite quail, red fox, rabbit, vole, and mice. White-tailed deer, gray fox, bobcat, and woodcock are just a few examples of animals that benefit from a combination of woods and fields.

Marshes are typically rich with life. There are varieties of dragonflies, damselflies, crane flies, salamanders, turtles, snails, and nematodes. Canada geese feed in both the marsh and the field. The yellow-striped heads of baby wood ducks peek from the holes of large nest boxes. The marsh can be a noisy place in spring and summer with spring peeper frogs, cricket frogs, and pickerel frogs clamoring for attention from the opposite sex.

The Augusta Springs area is attractive to humans as well. A half mile of boardwalks make it easier to get close to wetland critters that usually must be viewed from long distances. Among the watched wildlife are beaver, muskrat, water snakes, red-winged blackbirds, great blue herons, green herons, great egrets, and spring and fall migrating waterfowl. The area is managed as part of the National Watchable Wildlife Program. Federal and state agencies, conservation organizations, and private businesses cooperate to enhance wildlife habitat and build public viewing stations.

Directions: From Staunton, go west on VA 254 for 9 miles. Continue straight on VA 42 at Buffalo Gap and drive 8.5 miles. Look for the brown sign with binoculars symbol that marks Watchable Wildlife Areas.

Activities: Wildlife and birdwatching, wildflower identification, photography, nature study.

Facilities: Handicapped-accessible interpretive nature trail, boardwalks, restrooms. Wildlife viewing blinds in planning stage.

Dates: Open year-round.

Fees: None.

For more information: Deerfield Ranger District, George Washington National Forest, Route 6, Box 419, Staunton, VA 24401. Phone (540) 885-8028.

Closest town: Craigsville, 4 miles southwest.

BRALEY POND RECREATION AREA. [Fig. 26(16)] Situated at the north end of scenic Deerfield Valley, Braley Pond Recreation Area is an ideal spot for picnicking, fishing, and hiking. The 4.5-acre pond was constructed by the U.S. Forest Service for flood control. Artificial reefs and other fish structures have been added. Keeper-sized rainbow trout are stocked, and largemouth bass, bluegill, and channel catfish have been introduced. Bank fishing is possible all the way around, and hand-carried boats without motors are allowed.

The picnic area is set in a stand of white pines. Surrounding the recreation area are remote, undeveloped mountain lands offering good hiking, hunting, camping, and photo opportunities. Primitive camping is also allowed among the trees of the recreation area.

Directions: From the junction of VA 275 and US 250 west of Staunton, drive about 15 miles west on US 250. Turn right on VA 715 and take the next left onto FR 348.1. Follow signs about .5 mile to parking lot.

Activities: Fishing, picnicking, hiking, mountain biking, horseback riding, seasonal hunting in surrounding national forest.

Facilities: 5-acre fishing pond, 10 picnic tables and grills, toilets.

Dates: Open year-round.

Fees: None.

Closest town: Staunton, 16 miles east.

For more information: Deerfield Ranger District, George Washington National Forest, Route 6, Box 419, Staunton, VA 24401. Phone (540) 885-8028.

MOUNTAIN HOUSE PICNIC AREA AND CONFEDERATE BREASTWORKS. [Fig. 26(12,13)] Mountain House is a day-use picnic area near the site of a former wayside on the old Parkersburg Pike (now US 250) across a series of mountain ranges to Parkersburg, West Virginia. A tollhouse constructed here before the Civil War became a popular rest stop in the late 1800s. Ramseys Draft Wilderness Area trailhead is located on the access road behind the picnic area.

The Confederate Breastworks are on Shenandoah Mountain about 2 miles west of Mountain House Recreation Area. Here, Confederate

WILD TURKEY
(Meleagris gallopavo)
Turkeys can fly well for short distances but prefer to run.

soldiers constructed a long trenchlike fortification in 1861 or early 1862 to protect the valley from invasion by Union forces from the west. Troops that built the fortifications were probably members of the 12th Georgia Infantry Regiment serving under General Edward "Allegany" Johnson. After a breach in the fortifications, General Johnson pulled back. With the arrival of General Stonewall Jackson, Union troops were rebuffed at the Battle of McDowell (May 8, 1962) and driven back into the Jackson River Valley toward West Virginia.

A short loop trail follows the remnants of the breastworks, and the trailhead for the northern 7.1-mile section of the Shenandoah Mountain Trail is here. The panoramic view of the Cowpasture River Valley to the west is, by itself, worth the stop.

Directions: From junction of VA 275 and US 250 west of Staunton, drive about 20 miles west on US 250 to Mountain House Recreation Area, at junction with FR 68, on right. Mountain House is about 5 miles past turnoff to Braley Pond. The parking area for Confederate Breastworks is about 2 miles farther on right side of US 250 at top of Shenandoah Mountain.

Activities: Picnicking, hiking, fishing in Ramsey's Draft (check Virginia Department of Game and Inland Fisheries for latest regulations).

Facilities: Mountain House has 10 picnic tables with grills, toilets, and trailhead for Ramseys Draft. No drinking water. Confederate Breastworks historic site has loop trail and toilets.

Dates: Open year-round.

Fees: None.

Closest town: Staunton, approximately 22 miles east.

For more information: Deerfield Ranger District, George Washington National Forest, Route 6, Box 419, Staunton, VA 24401. Phone (540) 885-8028.

HIKING THE DEERFIELD DISTRICT. An extensive trail system totaling 124 miles makes hiking a highlight of the district. Some trails are long, running along mountain ridges, giving backpackers a challenge and rewarding them with outstanding views. The terrain is rough and mountainous, but, for the most part, trails are wide, well signed, and well groomed. The notable exceptions are the Ramseys Draft Wilderness trails, purposely left in a more natural state.

Wanderers on district

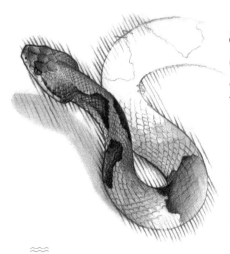

COPPERHEAD (Agkistrodon contortrix) The copperhead is a pit viper with a sensory pit between its eyes that detects prey.

trails see or find signs of white-tailed deer, black bear, wild turkey, ruffed grouse, bobcats, mink, and gray squirrel. Bird watchers on a spring morning are treated to the songs of migrating warblers and indigo buntings. On summer nights, bone-tired hikers slip into their sleeping bags on Shenandoah Mountain to be lulled to sleep by the hoot of a great horned owl or haunting call of a whip-poor-will.

In fall, hikers along ridgetop trails walk a carpet of fallen red, yellow, and gold leaves beneath red maples, tulip poplars, and white and red oaks. Above them, hawks and other birds of prey ride the updrafts along the ridges heading south ahead of winter. A light January snowfall requires a traveler to engage his four-wheel drive to cross Great North Mountain on US 250 on his way to frozen Braley Pond where his footprints will be the only sign of a human.

SHENANDOAH MOUNTAIN TRAIL. [Fig. 26(14)] This 30.7-mile path, blazed with yellow diamonds, follows the ups and downs along the crest of Shenandoah Mountain for the entire length of the district. It features excellent views of Deerfield Valley to the east and Cowpasture River Valley to the west. In the fall, the foliage of red maples, birches, locusts, chestnut oaks, scarlet oaks, and tulip poplars is brilliant against evergreen hemlocks, pines, rhododendron, and mountain laurel.

The long, linear Shenandoah Mountain Trail connects with several old roads and other trails to provide shorter loop hikes. Skillful grading of the trail on the mountain's rough terrain can be credited to the men of the Civilian Conservation Corps (CCC) who built it in the 1930s. Because of the trail's gradual changes in altitude, cross-country skiers and mountain bikers also use it. However, where the 7.1-mile section north of US 250 meanders into and out of Ramseys Draft Wilderness, biking and skiing may be difficult. In keeping with the intent of the wilderness, trail maintenance is limited to what is necessary for safe passage. Parts of the Shenandoah Mountain Trail are designated as especially suitable to horse travel. The district office can provide a brochure.

Directions: From junction of VA 275 and US 250 west of Staunton, drive about 22 miles west on US 250 to Confederate Breastworks parking area on top of Shenandoah Mountain. From here a 7.1-mile section leads north and a 23.6-mile section leads south.

Trail: 30.7-mile linear path along crest of Shenandoah Mountain.

Elevation: 3,000–3,600 feet.

Degree of difficulty: Moderate, with strenuous sections.

Surface and blaze: Natural forest floor with rocky sections. Blazed with yellow diamonds.

NORTH MOUNTAIN TRAIL. [Fig. 26(20)] Solitude and spectacular views are the rewards for taking this 14.5-mile path along the ridge of Great North Mountain. Though steep in places, the trail is suitable for day hiking, backpacking, and horseback riding. It passes just below the 4,458-foot peak of Elliott Knob, one of the highest points of the George Washington National Forest and the site of an old fire tower. (Another unrelated North Mountain Trail is in the New Castle Ranger District.) Where the North Mountain Trail terminatess on the northern end, the 8-mile Crawford Mountain Trail begins.

The altitude at Elliott Knob is sufficient for trees more typical of northern forests such as red spruce, yellow birch, and sugar maple. However, many other complex factors such as soil composition, weather, slope orientation, and distance from other pockets of high-altitude trees also influence which trees take hold in a particular area. With the exception of a few scattered examples of northern species near the summit, Elliott Knob is not a holdout for alpine flora and fauna in the way that the Laurel Fork area is in northwest Highland County, farther west.

Near Elliott Knob, the 2.2-mile Cold Springs Trail [Fig. 26(19)] descends steeply down the western slope of North Mountain Trail to the Cold Springs Road (FR 77). This was the route to the fire tower which was in use in the 1950s. Rock ledges provide views of Deerfield Valley.

Directions: For northern trailhead, take VA 254 from Staunton west to Buffalo Gap. Go south on VA 42 for .7 mile. Turn right by a white church onto VA 688, and go about 2 miles to trailhead on top of North Mountain. For southern trailhead, from Craigsville, in southwestern Augusta County, go south on VA 42 for 2 miles. Turn right on VA 687 and go 3 miles to top of mountain. For Cold Springs trailhead, from US 250 at West Augusta, go south on VA 629 for 3 miles. Turn left on VA 688 and drive about 2 miles. Go right on FR 77 and drive 3.3 miles to trailhead parking.

Trail: 14.5-mile linear path along ridge of North Mountain.

Elevation: 1,600 to 4,458 feet.

Degree of difficulty: Moderate, with strenuous sections.

Surface: Natural forest floor with rocky sections.

RAMSEYS DRAFT WILDERNESS AREA

[Fig. 26(15)] The 6,519 rugged, steep acres of Ramseys Draft Wilderness lie on the southeastern slope of Shenandoah Mountain and on the north side of US 250 about 20 miles northwest of Staunton. The word "draft" is an old mountain word for "creek." Ramseys Draft, in the headwaters of the Calfpasture River, flows through the middle of the wilderness. The creek begins in the northeastern end of the wilderness as a right and left fork on either side of Hardscrabble Knob which, at 4,280 feet, is the area's highest point. The branches merge and flow southwestward through the wilderness to exit at the southern end.

About 29 miles of trails allow access around and into this wilderness. However, heavy rains from hurricanes Camille in 1969 and Agnes in 1972 and major flooding in 1985 changed the course of streams and caused severe washouts on some trails, most notably on Ramsey's Draft Trail, which is the main artery through the wilderness. An impressive mature forest—a magnet to nature lovers—lies at the heart of this wilderness. According to the U.S. Forest Service, the virgin stream-bottom stand of cove hardwoods, white pine, and hemlock is more than 300 years old—one of only a handful of virgin tracts of its size in the East. Most trees in this tract, located between the right and left forks of Ramseys Draft, are original growth.

The journey is not easy across rough wilderness terrain to reach the big evergreens and hardwoods, but getting there is half the fun. Those who make the trek are invariably stunned when they arrive to stand beneath forest giants that were already a century old when the country declared its independence. There's a desire just to touch the massive trunk of a hemlock that is more than 300 years old. Hikers stand in amazement as they look up at the towering canopy of white oaks and tulip poplars which may climb to heights of 120 feet or more.

The exhilarating scene is tempered by sadness, though. The giant hemlocks are obviously diseased, slowly succumbing to the persistent attack of the forest pest called the wooly adelgid (*see* Ghost Forests, page 11). With no remedy in sight, the aged evergreens will one day be gone, allowing sunlight through the canopy to begin anew the succession of understory plants that culminates in old-growth forest.

RAMSEYS DRAFT TRAIL. [Fig. 26(15)] This 7-mile trail (14-mile round trip) leads up Ramseys Draft through a mature forest managed essentially as wilderness since 1935. To the northwest is the ridgeline of Shenandoah Mountain, and to the southeast is Bald Ridge. At about 4 miles into the wilderness, the creek splits into a left and right fork at the base of Hardscrabble Knob. The large stand of virgin forest begins here and follows the left fork away from the trail. The trail accompanies the right fork around the east side of Hardscrabble Knob, and then it climbs to the 4,282-foot summit from the back side. Circuit

GALAX

(Galax rotundifolia)
Also called "coltsfoot," galax is widespread in the mountains. It is evergreen but may turn purple or bronze in winter, and it is often used as a holiday decoration.

hikes are possible with trail connections at the northern end of the wilderness.

A major flood in 1985 changed the course of Ramseys Draft in places and washed out much of an old road that once served as the Ramseys Draft Trail. Even before that time, hikers had to make 13 stream crossings. With its wilderness designation, the Draft is being left in its disheveled state. The trail is sometimes hard to follow even with orange blazes.

Just hiking the 4 miles up the draft to the old-growth forest—an 8-mile round trip—can easily take a day's time. Despite the arduous hike, Ramsey's Draft Trail is so heavily used that rangers are concerned it may lose its wilderness character. Hikers should tread lightly, stay on paths, and be careful not to harm vegetation. Other wilderness areas may offer more solitude. Because of numerous stream crossings, the hike should not be attempted in periods of high water. The debris-strewn path slows hiking and can sap the strength of the unfit.

Six other trails provide access to Ramseys Draft. These include Shenandoah Mountain Trail (north and south ends), Bald Ridge Trail, Sinclair Hollow Trail, and

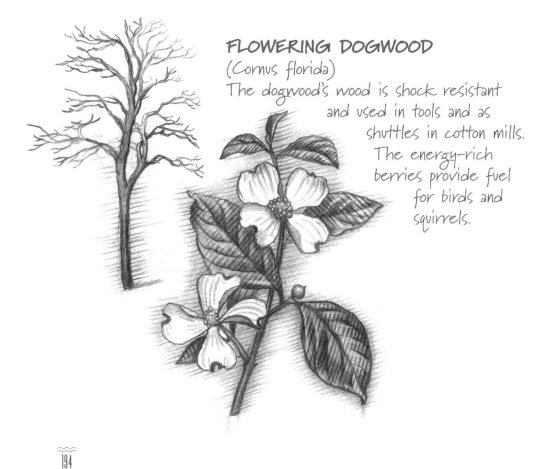

FLOWERING DOGWOOD
(Cornus florida)
The dogwood's wood is shock resistant and used in tools and as shuttles in cotton mills. The energy-rich berries provide fuel for birds and squirrels.

Wild Oak Trail (two sections). A map of the wilderness and its trails is available from the district office in Staunton.

Directions: From the junction of VA 275 and US 250 west of Staunton, drive about 20 miles west on US 250 to Mountain House Picnic Area on right. Turn right into Mountain House picnic area and go .1 mile to trailhead parking.

Trail: 7-mile (one-way) rough trail with numerous stream crossings up Ramseys Draft, then along right fork of creek to summit of Hardscrabble Knob. Old-growth forest begins after 4 miles where Ramseys Draft splits into left and right fork. The largest trees are along left fork.

Elevation: 2,200–4,482 feet.

Degree of difficulty: Moderate, with difficult sections and a strenuous climb at the far end beyond old-growth forest.

Surface: Natural forest floor, old roadbed, downed trees, stream crossings.

The Appalachian Cove Forest

Cove forest (such as the stand of virgin trees at Ramseys Draft Wilderness Area) is the name for a type of forest community unique to the Appalachians. American basswood is an indicator tree. Other canopy trees of cove forests may include tulip poplar, sugar maple, red maple, yellow birch, beech, white ash, bigleaf magnolia, Allegheny chinquapin, bitternut hickory, and Eastern hemlock. Farther south, Carolina silverbell is an important indicator tree for cove forests.

A colorful understory is characteristic of cove forests and may include such trees as Eastern redbud, sourwood, Fraser magnolia, witch-hazel, and flowering dogwood. However, the dark, dense canopy at Ramseys Draft has shaded out most undergrowth. Before cove forests mature into old-growth stands where the thick canopy shades out the undergrowth, everything appears abundant—trees, shrubs, wildflowers, birds, even salamanders. Birds tend to sort themselves out in tall forests. Some hunt the canopy, some the middle, and some the undergrowth. In cove forests, the American redstart and various flycatchers share the canopy. Also, the Blackburnian warbler may challenge the limits of hearing with its high, thin call from above.

Where there is laurel and azalea, listen for the buzzy sound of the worm-eating warbler. The yellow-breasted chat prefers tangled growth and dense brush for nesting. Its unusual combination of chirps and whistles is sometimes delivered from a perch high above its low but well-hidden nest. Wildflowers indicative of cove forests include wood anemone, mayapple, red trillium, white trillium, wild ginger, Canada violet, large-leaved white violet, and hepatica.

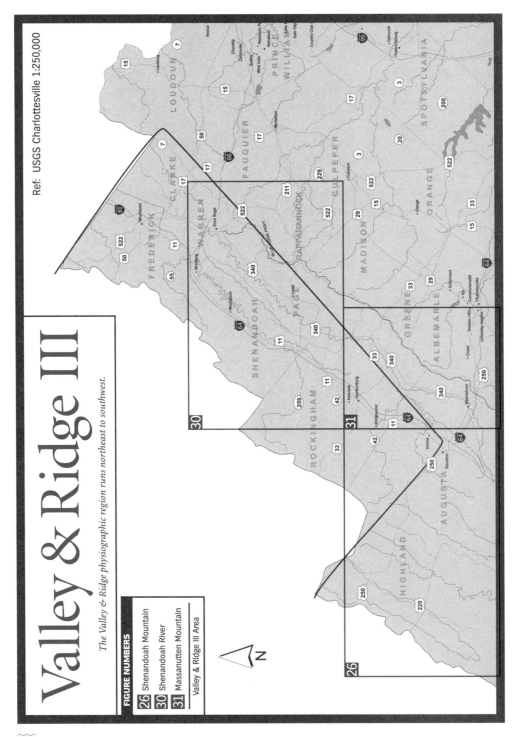

Ref: USGS Charlottesville 1:250,000

Valley & Ridge III

The Valley & Ridge physiographic region runs northeast to southwest.

FIGURE NUMBERS

26 Shenandoah Mountain
30 Shenandoah River
31 Massanutten Mountain

Valley & Ridge III Area

N

Valley and Ridge III

T his book divides the Valley and Ridge province into three sections: Valley and Ridge I, Valley and Ridge II, and Valley and Ridge III. The final section and northernmost section of the Valley and Ridge province, Valley and Ridge III, consists of two ranger districts of the George Washington National Forest, the sites of the famous Shendandoah Valley, and the Shenandoah River. Beginning with the Dry River district in the Shenandoah Mountains, this section extends roughly from Staunton to Winchester, bordered on the east by the mountains of the Blue Ridge and on the west by the West Virginia state line. The area includes the counties of Augusta, Rockingham, Page, Shenandoah, Warren, Frederick, and Clarke. The Shenandoah Valley entry overlaps the previous section, Valley and Ridge II, south to Natural Bridge. (For more information on the geology of the Valley and Ridge province, see the beginning of the Valley and Ridge section, page 71.)

[*Above*: Fly-fishing on the Jackson River]

The Dry River Ranger District

[Fig. 25] With 227,000 acres, Dry River is the largest ranger district of the George Washington National Forest. Forming a long northeast/southwest-trending rectangle, the district lies in the Shenandoah Mountains west of Harrisonburg, taking in the northern tip of Augusta County and western side of Rockingham County. It also spills over Shenandoah Mountain into West Virginia to the base of the mountain. Running along the district's western side in Pendleton County, West Virginia, is a tributary of the Potomac with the lanky name of South Fork of the South Branch of the Potomac River.

Much of the activity on the Dry River Ranger District centers around small lakes and along the main river drainages, especially in the southeastern corner. Draining the eastern slope of Shenandoah Mountain are three rivers—the North River (southern end of district), the Dry River (central part), and the North Fork of the Shenandoah River (northern end). Several small, man-made lakes have been created on these rivers. Three campgrounds and four picnic areas are positioned to take advantage of the scenery, good fishing, and recreation connected with the rivers and lakes in the Virginia portion of the Dry River District. The rest of this expansive tract is left to those who enjoy following backroads and trails. Backcountry camping is permitted anywhere within the national forest unless posted.

Camping and picnicking are available at North River, Hone Quarry, and Todd Lake recreation areas. Picnic tables are also located at Shenandoah Mountain (on FR 85 near Reddish Knob) and at Blue Hole Picnic Area (on North Fork of the Shenandoah at the northern end of the district).

Above North River Campground is Elkhorn Lake, a 54-acre reservoir with a threefold purpose—to provide flood control, a water supply for the city of Staunton, and recreation. Its reputation as a fishery for largemouth bass and stocked rainbow trout makes it a popular destination for anglers. Channel catfish, bluegill, and green sunfish also swim beneath the deep green surface. Elkhorn has three handicapped-accessible fishing platforms and a dirt ramp for small boats (no gasoline motors). Other stocked lakes in the district include Hearthstone Lake off FR 101 west of Stokesville, Hone Quarry on FR 62 off VA 257 west of Dayton, and Briery Branch Lake on VA 924 off VA 257 west of Dayton.

TODD LAKE RECREATION AREA

[Fig. 26(8)] Todd Lake is snugged into the secluded Trimble Mountains southwest of Bridgewater. The 20-acre recreation area has a sandy beach on a 7.5-acre lake, camping, hiking, and picnicking. The lake is open for swimming, boating (no motors), and fishing. Campsites and picnic grounds have tables, grills, restrooms, flush toilets, warm showers, and a waste disposal unit. Hiking trails include the 1-mile Todd Lake Trail and the 4-mile Trimble Mountain Trail.

DRY RIVER AND SWITZER LAKE. Dry River, from which the district takes its name, is not really dry. During the doldrums of summer, though, it disappears from view beneath the rocky rubble of the bed. Sometimes only pools are left here and there to indicate the river is not dead but in hiding. Water flows beneath the porous surface, connecting the pools.

Dry River runs southeastward through the heart of the Dry River District along US 33. In a 14-mile stretch of river above Rawley Springs, on the eastern edge of the district, the Virginia Department of Game and Inland Fisheries stocks trout in spring when water levels are high enough. Game department signs along the road lead anglers to the stocked section. The river drainage is on the eastern slope of Shenandoah Mountain. A dam on the Skidmore Fork of the river, high in the Shenandoah Mountains near the West Virginia line, forms deep Switzer Lake. (Don't be confused by another stream called Skidmore Fork in the North River drainage to the south.)

Switzer Lake's water is clear and cold enough year-round to support what is called a "put-and-grow" population of brook trout. The game department stocks fingerling brookies which grow to catchable size in a few years. Tiger and brown trout have also been stocked in the past. Anglers who don't mind the lack of facilities have caught brook trout up to 3 pounds and tigers and brown trout up to 4 pounds.

Ruffed Grouse

The Dry River Ranger District has a sizeable population of grouse (*Bonasa umbellus*). Early settlers found the birds abundant and easy to kill. In fact, grouse were sometimes called "fool hens." Pioneers claimed they could walk up to roosting birds and pop them with a stick, but pioneer stories and folklore occasionally get misshapen from too much handling. Just consider Daniel Boone and the bear, or Paul Bunyan and Babe The Blue Ox. Few people would refer to a grouse as a fool hen now. All animals and birds learn caution if they're hunted over several generations. The most likely way to see a grouse today is in a blur of wings and tail feathers as the bird flushes at your feet and rockets away through the understory. Of course a grouse will crash dive through a plate-glass window from time to time. But that's because it has filled its crop with the fermented berries of autumn.

The lake also supports warm-water species such as nice-sized largemouth bass and crappie. When the bass and crappie aren't biting, there are small but abundant bluegill and pumpkinseed and hybrid sunfish, rock bass, and bullhead catfish.

Access is by trails along the west bank and by a primitive boat launch (no gasoline motors—this lake provides Harrisonburg's drinking water). Also, a road leads to the upper end of the lake. Early in the morning or at dusk, a quiet wildlife watcher can sometimes see deer, gray foxes, raccoons, and other animals come to water's edge to drink. Belted kingfishers (*Ceryle alycon*) plunge headlong into the lake for salamanders or minnows that rise to the surface. The lake is accessible by FR 227 off US 33 west of Harrisonburg, near the West Virginia state line.

Directions: The district office is located at 112 North River Road off US 42 in Bridgewater.

Elkhorn Lake, Todd Lake Campground, and North River Campground: From the junction of VA 275 and US 250 west of Staunton, drive about 15 miles west on US 250. Turn right on VA 715 and drive about 4.5 miles (road becomes FR 96) to FR 95. For Todd Lake Campground, go left on FR 95 and drive about 2 miles. Go right on FR 95A and continue about 3 miles to campground. For Elkhorn Lake and North River Campground, from FR 96 go right on FR 95. Follow signs to Elkhorn Lake or, for the campground, continue about 2.5 miles to intersection with FR 95B, go right and follow signs.

Hone Quarry Campground: Take VA 257 west of Dayton about 10 miles. Go right on VA 62 and follow signs.

Activities: Camping, fishing, picnicking, hiking, mountain biking, horseback riding, seasonal hunting, wildlife observation, wildflower identification, photography.

Facilities: Todd Lake: 20 large campsites, picnic tables, grills, restrooms, flush toilets, warm showers, waste disposal unit. North River Campground: 10 small, shaded sites, picnic tables, grills, pit toilets, hand-pumped water. Hone Quarry: 10 large sites in hemlock grove, picnic tables, grills, pit toilets, hand-pumped water, waste disposal unit.

Dates: (These may vary from year to year.) Todd Lake Recreation Area: May 15– Dec. 8 (water cut off after Oct. 30). North River Recreation Area: Mar. 1–Dec. 8. Hone Quarry: year-round.

Fees: There is a charge for camping and day use at Todd Lake. There is a charge at North River and Hone Quarry for campsites and for seasonal passes (including other national forest recreation areas).

For more information: Dry River Ranger District, 112 N. River Road, Bridgewater, VA 22812.

HIKING THE DRY RIVER DISTRICT

A total of 163 miles of mountainous trails gives plenty of options to casual hikers, serious backpackers, mountain bikers, horseback riders, bird watchers, and hunters. Backcountry camping is permitted in the national forest unless posted otherwise.

WILD OAK NATIONAL RECREATION TRAIL. [Fig. 26(9)] Three trails— Chestnut Ridge Trail, Hankey Mountain Trail, and North River Trail—are combined to form this 26-mile loop along ridgetops around the North River headwaters. The white-blazed circuit hike was designated a National Recreation Trail in 1979. Each of the three sections has steep sections that make a challenging though scenic day-hiking opportunity. A multiple-day backpacking trip is made possible by completing the loop.

The well-maintained Wild Oak Trail also connects with several other trails, which include the Bear Draft Trail (2 miles), White Oak Draft Trail (2.8 miles), Dowells Draft Trail (4 miles), Bald Ridge Trail (8.3 miles), Tearjacket Trail (1.3 miles), and Grooms Ridge Trail (4 miles; all trail distances are one-way). A topo map or a district map, available from the ranger district office, and a compass will help with routing decisions. Hikers can combine nature study with their trek by carrying a notebook and identifying the 40 species of trees and 50 species of wildflowers listed on the route. The Wild Oak Trail gets its name from the variety of oaks along the way, which include scarlet oak (*Quercus coccinea*), black oak (*Quercus velutina*), northern red oak (*Quercus borealis*), blackjack oak (*Quercus marilandica*), white oak (*Quercus alba*), chestnut oak (*Quercus montana*), and post oak (*Quercus stellata*). In the understory are blueberries, deerberry, azalea, mountain laurel, witch-hazel, and dogwood.

Birds a hiker might hear or see include American redstart (*Setophaga ruticilla*), white-eyed vireo (*Vireo griseus*), wood thrush (*Hylocichla mustelina*), ovenbird (*Seiurus aurocapillus*), tufted titmouse (*Parus bicolor*), white-breasted nuthatch (*Sitta carolinensis carolinensis*), Carolina chickadee (*Penthestes carolinensis carolinensis*), brown creeper (*Certhia familiaris americana*), ruffed grouse (*Bonasa umbellus*), wild turkey (*Meleagris gallopavo*), and a variety of woodpeckers, owls, sparrows, and warblers.

Those hiking during hunting seasons, especially during the two-week deer season each November, should wear blaze orange and expect plenty of company on the trail. This area is prime hunting territory.

Directions: Follow directions toward Todd Lake (*see* Dry River and Switzer Lake, page 199). After left turn onto FR 95, trailhead parking is .2 mile, on right.

Trail: 26-mile loop following ridgetops and circling headwaters of the North River.

Elevation: 1,600 feet at North River Gap to 4,351 feet on Little Bald Knob.

Degree of difficulty: Moderate, with some very steep sections.

Surface: Natural forest floor with rocky sections.

NORTH RIVER GORGE TRAIL. [Fig. 26(10)] This beautiful 4.2-mile footpath leads through hardwood forest along a particularly scenic stretch of the North River. The North River forms from runoff from the 4,000-foot summit of Shenandoah Mountain several miles to the west. The river gathers strength as it is funneled through a gorge between Trimble Mountain and Lookout Mountain.

The trail has gentle grades, but it requires hikers to ford the North River nine times. During periods of high water or freezing weather, the stream crossings may be treacherous or impossible. Spring and summer streamside wildflowers include jack-in-the-pulpit or Indian turnip (*Arisaema triphyllum*), partridgeberry (*Mitchella repens*), jewelweed (*Impatiens capensis*), cardinal flower (*Lobelia cardinalis*), and trillium. A shrubby understory of black willows, hazel alders, rhododendron, wild hydrangea, and arrowwood thrive in the damp mist. Trail maps are available from the district office in Bridgewater.

Directions: For downriver trailhead, follow directions for Todd Lake (*see* Dry River and Switzer Lake, page 199) to turn onto FR 95. After making the left turn, go about 1.2 miles to gated road on south side of road. Upriver trailhead is at North River Campground (*see* Dry River and Switzer Lake, page 199).

Trail: 4.2-mile path from FR 95 to North River Campground.

Elevation: 1,400 to 1,600 feet.

Degree of difficulty: Easy, except when high water or icy conditions cause stream crossings to become treacherous.

Surface: Natural forest floor with rocky sections, 9 stream crossings, and at south end, suspension bridge.

TRIMBLE MOUNTAIN TRAIL. [Fig. 26(11)] This is a 4-mile loop with excellent views of Reddish Knob and Shenandoah Mountain to the west and North River Gorge to the east. The yellow-blazed trail begins near the entrance to Todd Lake Campground, and its gentle grades follow a deer path along the ridge of Trimble Mountain. Bordering the trail are thickets of mountain laurel with strong, twisted wood. The evergreen shrubs have shiny leaves and produce profuse white or pale pink blooms in early June. Several varieties of moss and fragile lichens also grow along the path.

Eroding rock from the Paleozoic Era may expose fossils of plants from an ancient sea. The rock comes from the Pennsylvanian Period of some 300 million years ago, when algae were plentiful and ferns grew from seedlike bodies. The first reptiles were evolving, but dinosaurs would not develop for another 75 million years. At about the halfway point, a stand of dead trees is a reminder of the devastation that ice storms can cause. These trees were damaged by a heavy icing on Easter, 1978.

Wildlife in the area includes the white-tailed deer, wild turkey, ruffed grouse, raccoon, and gray fox. The gray fox, unlike its cousin the red fox, occasionally climbs trees and prefers open forests to fields. It rarely invades a chicken house, relying instead on its expertise at mousing. Woodpeckers such as the downy woodpecker, redheaded woodpecker, and yellow-bellied sapsucker are common along sections of the trail.

Directions: Trailhead is on south side of FR 95 about .25 mile east of Todd Lake entrance. Follow trail signs to dam and turn right before crossing dam. The Todd Lake Trail is an easy 1-mile path over the dam and around the lake.

Trail: 4-mile loop from Todd Lake Campground to Trimble Mountain.

Elevation: 2,000 feet to 2,476 feet.

Degree of difficulty: Easy to moderate.

Surface and blaze: Natural forest floor, grassy areas and rocky sections. Yellow blaze.

Lee Ranger District

[Fig. 25] The Lee Ranger District, the northernmost district of the George Washington National Forest, is divided into two tracts with the Shenandoah Valley and the towns of New Market and Woodstock between them. Remnants from the colonial era, the Civil War, and the CCC construction following the Great Depression open windows to the area's rich history. Several recreation areas offer base camps for learning the history and exploring nearly 300 miles of trails that lead into 189,082 acres of national forest. Residents of Washington, D.C., who are just a couple of hours away from the district, are frequent visitors.

A large, scenic portion of the western tract is in West Virginia, extending almost to WV 259. The western part of Shenandoah County, including North Mountain, Little Sluice Mountain, Little North Mountain, and Paddy Mountain, comprises most of the Virginia part of the western Lee District.

Tucked into the beautiful mountains and streams of Hardy County, West Virginia, is newly renovated Trout Pond Recreation Area, with opportunities for camping, fishing, boating, swimming, and hiking. The area has 17-acre, 45-foot-deep Rockcliff Lake with stocked trout, a swimming beach, and space for canoes and small boats. Trout Pond, the 2-acre, 35-foot-deep natural lake that gives the recreation area its name, is an interesting phenomenon in a landscape riddled with sinkholes and depressions.

The popular eastern tract of the Lee District occupies the slopes of 50-mile-long Massanutten Mountain which rises from the northern Shenandoah Valley north of Harrisonburg and east of Interstate 81. VA 211 runs east-west across the mountain, connecting the towns of New Market on I-81 and Luray on US 340. Elevations on the mountain range from 800 feet to 3,300 feet. Predominate rock formations consist of easily eroded Martinsburg shale and limestone often capped with more resilient Massanutten sandstone. The Massanutten Visitor Information Center [Fig. 30(10)] is on VA 211 where the road crosses Massanutten Mountain.

The serpentine North Fork and the South Fork of the Shenandoah River border Massanutten Mountain on the west and the east, respectively, adding excellent smallmouth bass fishing and peaceful canoe float trips to the district's attractions. Also, in the heart of Massanutten Mountain, north of the visitor center, is a bowl of private land called Fort Valley. VA 678 runs north-south through this quiet valley of farms and forests where mountains keep modern civilization at bay. Look for signs along Passage Creek denoting stocked trout waters.

Elizabeth Furnace and Camp Roosevelt offer mountain recreation in the eastern Lee District, while High Cliff Canoe Camp provides a pleasant stopover for boaters on the South Fork of the Shenandoah River. Backcountry camping is permitted anywhere on national forest lands, except where posted. Both the western and eastern tracts of the Lee District have a nearby resort. To the west is Bryce Resort, offering

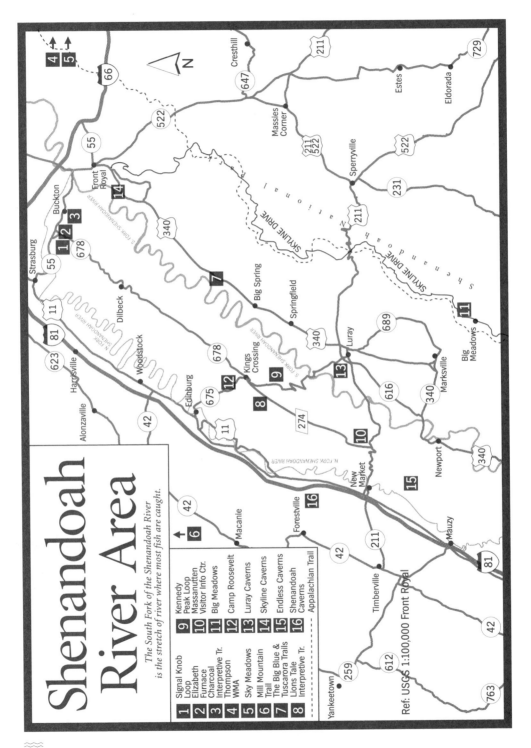

Shenandoah River Area

The South Fork of the Shenandoah River is the stretch of river where most fish are caught.

1	Signal Knob	**9**	Kennedy Peak Loop
2	Elizabeth Furnace	**10**	Massanutten Visitor Info Ctr.
3	Charcoal Interpretive Tr.	**11**	Big Meadows
4	Thompson WMA	**12**	Camp Roosevelt
5	Sky Meadows	**13**	Luray Caverns
6	Mill Mountain Trail	**14**	Skyline Caverns
7	The Big Blue & Tuscarora Trails	**15**	Endless Caverns
8	Lions Tale Interpretive Tr.	**16**	Shenandoah Caverns
		- - -	Appalachian Trail

Ref: USGS 1:100,000 Front Royal

snow skiing, grass skiing, golf, tennis, horseback riding, and swimming. It's located at Bayse on the eastern slope of Great North Mountain west of Mount Jackson. To the east is Massanutten, on the southern end of Massanutten Mountain, offering day and night skiing and snowboarding. Guided horseback trips and cabin rentals are available from Fort Valley Stable.

Two ATV (all-terrain vehicle) trails—Peters Mill Run and Taskers Gap—are located southeast of Edinburg, near the ranger district office. All trails except interpretive trails are open to mountain bikers and equestrians, though rocky terrain and steep inclines make some trails too difficult.

The mountains yield a wealth of wildflowers. Common plants to look for in the woods, at the edge of the woods, and along streams include bloodroot (*Sanguinaria canadensis*), large-flowered trillium (*Trillium grandiflorum*), spotted touch-me-not (*Impatiens capensis*), common blue violet (*Viola papilionacea*), spiderwort (*Tradescantia virginiana*), wild columbine (*Aquilegia canadensis*), and wood vetch (*Vicia caroliniana*), one of our few native vetches. Along the roads and fields are sprinklings of blues, yellows, and mauves—blues from chicory (*Chicorium intybus*) and bachelor's button (*Centaurea cyanus*); yellows from black-eyed susan (*Rudbeckia hirta*), common mullein (*Verbascum blattaria*), and tickseed sunflower (*Bidens aristosa*); and mauves from spotted joe-pye-weed (*Eupatorium maculatum*) and wild bergamot (*Monarda fistulosa*).

Wildlife of the Lee Ranger District includes the black bear, white-tailed deer, red and gray fox, bobcat, gray squirrel, ruffed grouse, and wild turkey. Several species of owls, including screech, barred, barn, and great horned, will add their mysterious hoots to a quiet summer night. The tiny saw-whet owl—no taller than a pencil—is an occasional winter visitor. Though rarely spotted during the daytime, this nocturnal owl is easy to approach. Birds typical of Appalachian woodlands, such as vireos, thrushes, tanagers, warblers, nuthatches, flycatchers, and sparrows make birdwatching rewarding. In September and October, birds of prey can be spotted soaring along the ridgelines.

Directions: District office is located at junction of I-81 (Exit 279) and VA 265 at Edinburg in Shenandoah County. From I-81, take Exit 279 and go east .2 mile. Turn left on Windsor Knit Road and drive .2 mile. Go left on Molineu Road to parking lot.

Massanutten Resort: From US 33 at Elkton, drive 6 miles west to VA 644 and entrance on right. From I-81 at Harrisonburg, take Exit 247. Drive 10 miles east on US 33 to VA 644 and entrance on left.

Activities: Camping, hiking, mountain biking, horseback riding, ATV riding, fishing, swimming and canoe camping on Shenandoah River, seasonal hunting, cross-country skiing, scenic drives. Downhill skiing, snowboarding, swimming, tennis, and golf at nearby resorts.

Facilities: Nearly 300 miles of trails for hiking (including 6 interpretive trails), biking, and horseback riding, and 2 ATV trails. Campgrounds, picnic areas, car- and boat-accessible campgrounds, visitor center, stocked trout streams, navigable river, scenic roads, nearby resorts.

For more information: Lee Ranger District, 109 Molineu Road, Edinburg, VA 22824. Phone (540) 984-4101. Bryce Resort, PO Box 3, Bayse, VA 22810. Phone (800) 821-1444 or (540) 856-2121. Massanutten Resort, PO Box 1227, Harrisonburg, VA 22801. Phone (800) 207-MASS or (540) 289-9441. Fort Valley Stable, 299 South Fort Valley Road, Fort Valley, VA 22652. Phone (540) 933-6633.

Closest town: Edinburg is .5 mile east of district office.

THE MASSANUTTEN VISITOR INFORMATION CENTER

[Fig. 30(10)] Located at the southern end of Massanutten Mountain on US 211, the center is a good place to begin exploring the eastern Lee District. From mid-April through mid-November, staff is available to answer questions and provide information on forest activities and recreation opportunities. The center stocks a complete line of environmental education books, field guides, fishing and hiking publications, and numerous maps of the district and the entire George Washington and Jefferson National Forests.

Trailheads for two interpretive trails—Discovery Way Trail and Wildflower Trail—are at the visitor center. The self-guided Discovery Way Trail begins just south of the parking lot. This .2-mile paved path is handicapped accessible. Discoveries the hiker makes include a rock with living skin, an Indian toothbrush, and tea trees.

The .5-mile Wildflower Trail begins on the east side of the parking lot and connects the visitor center with the New Market Gap picnic area and with the 24.5-mile Massanutten Mountain Trail. The path retraces Confederate General Stonewall Jackson's footsteps during his famous Shenandoah Valley campaign of the Civil War.

From mid- to late May, pink lady slippers put on a showy display under the tree canopy along the trail and at the picnic area. Even botanists are often stumped in figuring the complex factors that allow a plant to thrive in one place and not another. John Coleman, district ranger, speculates that something as simple as a subtle increase in light when deadwood was cleared resulted in perfect conditions for the lady slippers. Visitors are asked to leave these endangered flowers for others to enjoy.

North of the visitor center on FR 274 are two more interpretive trails—the paved .3-mile Massanutten Storybook Trail (handicapped accessible) and the Lion's Tale Trail (soon to be handicapped accessible). The Storybook Trail is 1.5 miles north of the visitor center and the Lion's Tale Trail is 8 miles north, just south of Camp Roosevelt.

Directions: From I-81, take Exit 264. Travel east on VA 211 to New Market and continue 3 miles to visitor center.

Activities: Nearby hiking, mountain biking, horseback riding, picnicking.

Facilities: Information station, restrooms, drinking water. Hiking trails and picnic tables with grills nearby.

Dates: Open daily mid-Apr.–mid-Nov.

Fees: Trail brochures are free. There is a charge for books and maps.

For more information: Massanutten Visitor Center, 3220 Lee Highway, New Market, VA 22844. Phone (540) 740-8310.

Closest town: The town of New Market is 3 miles west.

CAMP ROOSEVELT

[Fig. 30(12)] "The Army With Shovels," as the Civilian Conservation Corps (CCC) came to be known, began its work by establishing Camp Roosevelt in 1933. President Franklin D. Roosevelt, who mobilized this vast supply of willing manpower in March of 1933 during the Great Depression, was on hand for the dedication of this first of 1,500 camps across the United States.

Located on VA 675, 9 miles north of the Massanutten Visitor Information Center, the site that once served as a base of operations for the first CCC men now provides campers, picnickers, and hikers a base for exploring Massanutten Mountain and Fort Valley. Some of the original construction remains. The CCC worked to control floods and erosion, planted trees, fought forest fires, and built roads, trails, bridges, and recreation areas. The Lion's Tale National Recreation Trail [Fig. 30(8)] is about 1 mile south of the recreation area on FR 274.

Directions: From Edinburg, go southeast on VA 675 for 9 miles. From the Massanutten Visitor Information Center, go north on FR 274 for 9 miles, then .1 mile east on VA 675.

Activities: Hiking, camping, picnicking, mountain biking, horseback riding, cross-country skiing.

Facilities: 10 campsites with tables and grills, 15 picnic sites, flush toilets, drinking water, small playfield, disposal station.

Dates: Open early May–late Oct. (may vary).

Fees: There is a charge for campsites.

For more information: Lee Ranger District, 109 Molineu Road, Edinburg, VA 22824. Phone (540) 984-4101.

Closest town: Edinburg is 9 miles northwest.

Peregrine Falcon

The endangered peregrine falcon (*Falco perigrinus*) disappeared from the Virginia mountains a generation ago. In a cooperative program to reestablish this marvelous predator, state and federal biologists raised and released 60 young peregrines in their native haunts of mountain cliffs surrounding the Shenandoah Valley. The sleek birds of prey are now regularly seen in Shenandoah, Page, Rockingham, Augusta, and Amherst counties in Virginia and in Hardy and Pendleton counties in West Virginia. Peregrines are masters of speed. While diving for prey, they've been clocked at speeds in excess of 200 miles per hour, making them the world's fastest animal.

ELIZABETH FURNACE

[Fig. 30(2)] At the northern end of Massanutten Mountain is Elizabeth Furnace, where iron ore was melted down more than 150 years ago. A 30-unit family campground and 54-site picnic area with two shelters are located here. Several trails, including the Pig Iron Interpretive Trail, radiate from the area. This easy .25-mile loop passes the remains of Elizabeth Furnace and describes the pig iron industry of the nineteenth century. Passage Creek, which flows through the area, is stocked with trout by the Virginia Department of Game and Inland Fisheries.

Directions: From VA 55 at Waterlick (east of Strasburg), drive south on VA 678 for 4 miles to picnic area.

Activities: Camping, picnicking, hiking, fishing for stocked trout, mountain biking, horseback riding, cross-country skiing, wildflower identification, wildlife watching, group camping by reservation.

Facilities: 30 campsites with tables and grills, 54 picnic sites and 2 shelters, drinking water, toilet facilities, warm showers. Group campground (reservation only).

Dates: Open year-round.

Fees: There is a charge for campsites.

For more information: Lee Ranger District, 109 Molineu Road, Edinburg, VA 22824. Phone (540) 984-4101, for information and group reservations.

Closest town: Waterlick is 4 miles north.

HIKING THE LEE RANGER DISTRICT

[Fig. 30] With 75 blazed trails covering nearly 300 miles, the Lee Ranger District is a natural for hikers, bikers, cross-country skiers, and equestrians. The hikes range from short, easy interpretive trails to long treks over rough terrain more suitable for backpackers. The western portion of the district gets lighter use than the eastern portion.

LION'S TALE INTERPRETIVE TRAIL. [Fig. 30(8)] This .5-mile rope-guided loop has a surface of crushed limestone. This trail is handicapped accessible.

Directions: From Massanutten Visitor Center, drive 8 miles north on FR 274 to trailhead on left.

Trail: .5-mile, rope-guided loop hike for the visually impaired.

Elevation: 1,600 feet.

Degree of difficulty: Easy.

Surface: Crushed limestone.

CHARCOAL INTERPRETIVE TRAIL. [Fig. 30(3)] Beginning at the Elizabeth Furnace Picnic Area, this easy, .5-mile trail describes the charcoal industry, an outgrowth of the pig iron industry. The Pig Iron Trail adjoins Charcoal Interpretive Trail at .25 mile.

Trail: .5-mile, self-guided interpretive trail.

Elevation: 900 feet.

Degree of difficulty: Easy.

SIGNAL KNOB LOOP. [Fig. 30(1)] This strenuous 10.2-mile hike combines four trails to make a loop, leading to an important Union and Confederate outpost during the Civil War. Overlooks into both the Shenandoah Valley and Fort Valley demonstrate the importance of Fort Valley as a place to protect and hide troops during the Civil War. Hikers can enjoy the pinks and whites of azalea, mountain laurel, and dogwood in spring. Blueberries ripen along the footpath in late summer. The four trails are Signal Knob (yellow blaze), Massanutten Mountain West (orange blaze), Bear Wallow (blue blaze), and Bear Wallow Spur (white). The trailhead is at the Bear Wallow/Signal Knob parking lot on VA 678 about 1 mile north of the Elizabeth Furnace picnic area.

Trail: 10.2-mile steep loop composed of 4 trails.

Elevation: 900 feet–3,000 feet.

Degree of difficulty: Moderate, with steep climb.

Surface and blaze: Natural forest floor with rocky sections. Signal Knob: yellow blaze. Massanutten Mountain West: orange blaze. Bear Wallow: blue blaze. Bear Wallow Spur: white blaze.

KENNEDY PEAK LOOP. [Fig. 30(9)] This moderately strenuous 5.4-mile loop climbs to an observation tower with beautiful views of Page Valley to the east of Massanutten Mountain. Begin the hike at Edith Gap, heading north on the Massanutten Mountain East Trail (orange blaze). At 2.4 miles, take the white-blazed spur .3 mile to the observation tower.

Directions: From Camp Roosevelt, take VA 675 east to Edith Gap at top of Massanutten Mountain.

Trail: 5.4-mile loop to Kennedy Peak and back to Edith Gap.

Elevation: 1,849–2,560 feet.

Degree of difficulty: Moderate, with steep climb.

Surface and blaze: Natural forest floor with rocky sections. Orange and white blaze.

MILL MOUNTAIN TRAIL TO BIG SCHLOSS. [Fig. 30(6)] Wolf Gap, a primitive campground with 10 heavily wooded sites, can be used as a base for this popular hike in the western portion of the Lee Ranger District. The reward for the moderate 2-mile (one-way) climb along the ridge of Mill Mountain is Big Schloss, a picturesque area of huge rocks with panoramic views into Trout Run Valley in West Virginia and views of Little Schloss Mountain and Great North Mountain in Virginia. The free campground at Wolf Gap is open all year and used only lightly. Tables, pit toilets, and a hand water pump are provided.

Directions: From Edinburg, drive 11 miles west on VA 675 to Wolf Gap campground. Orange-blazed Mill Mountain trailhead is near campsite number 9. Hike about 2 miles to join white-blazed Big Schloss Trail and climb .33 mile to rock formation. Return on the same trail.

Trail: 4.5-mile round trip from Wolf Gap campground to Big Schloss.

Elevation: 2,400–2,964 feet.

Degree of difficulty: Moderate.

Surface and blaze: Natural forest floor with considerable rocky sections. Orange and white blaze.

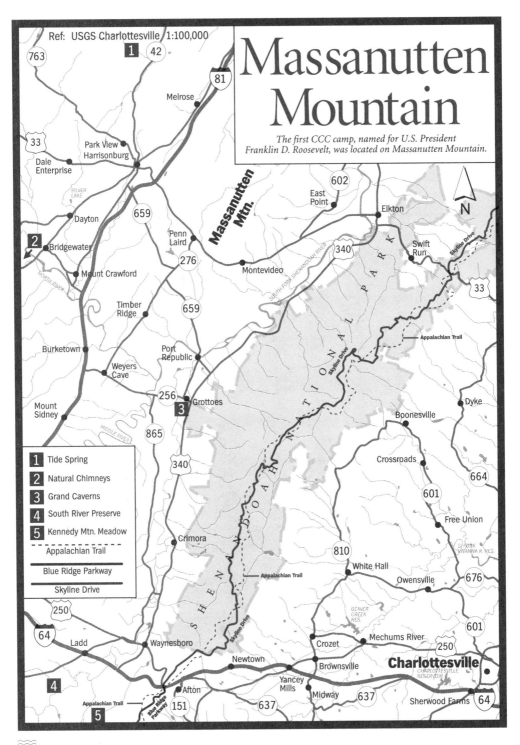

Ref: USGS Charlottesville 1:100,000

Massanutten Mountain

The first CCC camp, named for U.S. President Franklin D. Roosevelt, was located on Massanutten Mountain.

763 · 1 · 42 · 81

Melrose

33 · Park View · Harrisonburg

Dale Enterprise

SILVER LAKE

602

East Point

Elkton

Dayton · 659

2 · Bridgewater

Penn Laird

276

Swift Run

340

Skyline Drive

Mount Crawford

NORTH RIVER

Montevideo

SOUTH FORK SHENANDOAH RIVER

33

Massanutten Mtn.

Timber Ridge · 659

Burketown

Weyers Cave

Port Republic

Appalachian Trail

Mount Sidney

MIDDLE RIVER

256

3 · Grottoes

865

Dyke

Boonesville

Crossroads

664

340

601

Free Union

N. FORK RIVANNA R. RES.

1 Tide Spring
2 Natural Chimneys
3 Grand Caverns
4 South River Preserve
5 Kennedy Mtn. Meadow
- - - Appalachian Trail
—— Blue Ridge Parkway
—— Skyline Drive

Crimora

810

White Hall

Owensville · 676

250

64 · Ladd

Waynesboro

Newtown

BEAVER CREEK RES.

Crozet

Mechums River

250

601

Brownsville

Charlottesville

CHARLOTTESVILLE RESERVOIR

4

Afton

Appalachian Trail

Blue Ridge Parkway

5 · 151

637

Yancey Mills

Midway · 637

Sherwood Farms · 64

SHENANDOAH NATIONAL PARK

Skyline Drive

Appalachian Trail

N

Shenandoah Valley

The Shenandoah Valley of Virginia—famous in song and rich in history—is a lush green tapestry some 200 miles long and 25 to 40 miles wide.

From the air or from one of the mountain peaks on either side of the valley, the several streams and rivers twisting down from the ridges and across the valley have the appearance of a shimmering network of intricate and beautiful threads.

Legend has it that Shenandoah is an Indian word meaning "daughter of the stars." Another possibility is a translation of the Iroquois *Skahentowane*, meaning "great meadow" or "big flat place."

Still another Indian word, *Schinhandowi*, translates to "river through the spruces." Whatever the origin of the valley's name, its gentle beauty has no doubt impressed humans since the days the Shenandoah was a vast prairie.

When natural wildfires did not occur, Native Americans set fires up and down the valley each year to keep brush and trees from encroaching on their hunting grounds. The valley grasses and abundant water attracted large animals—elk, woods bison, deer—that the Indians followed and hunted.

In fact, an old buffalo trail ran the length of the Great Valley, as the Shenandoah is sometimes called. Shawnee, Monacan, and Cherokee tribes followed the buffalo. The rudimentary road was then widened by the wagon trains of settlers from the East headed west and south. US 11 was built to follow closely the old wagon trail, and today busy I-81 runs parallel to the trail and to the Valley Pike, as US 11 came to be known.

The Shenandoah Valley begins in the north near Winchester. Its southern boundary is sometimes described as "just south of Lexington." According to the state's tourism map, the Shenandoah Valley continues all the way south to Roanoke and Salem and is overlapped by the Roanoke Valley.

The Shenandoah Valley is clearly defined, however, to the east and west. The ragged peaks of the Allegheny Mountain range lie to the west. Forty miles to the east are the rounded peaks of the old, eroded Blue Ridge range. Both mountain ranges are visible on a drive through the Shenandoah Valley or on a float down one of its rivers.

The Shenandoah Valley was known as the Breadbasket of the Confederacy during the Civil War. As a result, General Sheridan's Union troops destroyed homes, barns, livestock, corn cribs, and crops on the valley's largest farms. Scores of bloody battles were fought up and down the length of this fertile land.

Many of the valley's typically small towns had been ravaged by war's end. The Valley of Virginia is known for its apple orchards, college towns, great rivers for floating and fishing, limestone caves, ski and golf resorts, Civil War battlefields, and panoramic views of some of the oldest mountains in the world.

LIMESTONE ARCHES, TOWERS, & CAVES OF THE SHENANDOAH VALLEY

THE CHEMISTRY. A particular chemistry is necessary to form limestone caves, natural bridges, and rock towers. The first requirement is weakly acidic groundwater. The second is rock soft enough for the water to erode. In the Shenandoah Valley and in fact, in the entire Valley and Ridge province, rainwater or stream water percolates through limestone soils deposited millions of years ago by decaying plants and animals. The decay produces carbon dioxide. Groundwater mixes with the carbon dioxide to form a weak acid called carbonic acid, or H_2CO_3.

Though weak, the acidity is enough to gradually erode underlying limestone and dolomite rock as groundwater seeps through cracks and fissures. Over time, cracks are enlarged, and underground chambers form. These connect with other widening openings until entire networks lace the underground. Rock that is more impenetrable, or harder to dissolve, may remain in magnificent towers or spans across openings gouged by the acid water.

Over thousands of years, a stream may sink a hundred or more feet underground as it erodes downward. In some cases, the entire process stays underground. In other cases, the stream carves out amphitheaters or tunnels above ground.

Three such examples of exposed formations in southwestern and western Virginia are Natural Tunnel in Scott County, Natural Bridge in Rockbridge County, and Natural Chimneys in Augusta County. When visiting these formations, look for the stream that is now flowing 100 feet or more below its former course. (*See* Natural Bridge, page 271; Natural Chimneys, page 214; Natural Tunnel State Park, page 83.)

WILD AND COMMERCIAL CAVES AND CAVERNS OF THE SHENANDOAH VALLEY. The work of underground acid water has resulted in approximately 3,000 known caves in Virginia, ranging in size from cramped crawlways to magnificent chambers large enough to dance the Virginia reel in. Most of the caves lie in the honeycomb of soluble carbonate rock (limestone and dolomite) of the Valley and Ridge province.

After chambers or caverns are opened underground, the slow dripping of water laden with calcium carbonate or calcium sulfate produces the sometimes-grand and delicate cave decorations, or speleothems, such as stalactites and stalagmites. When water leaves the soil above and enters the air of a cave, the excessive calcium carbonate load it has picked up in the soil precipitates out as calcite, the main ingredient of limestone, and the building of fragile formations begins. The process, in human terms, is imperceptible. One inch of growth may take 7,000 years.

Imagine the discoverers of these stunning calcite structures which had lain beneath the earth's surface for millions of years and grown to enormous proportions. Perhaps it was a torchlight which first illuminated rows of giant columns resembling a pipe organ. Hanging from cave ceilings were bursts of white spikes suggesting orchids or stars. Pools reflected shimmering limestone cascades and draperies.

A handful of commercial caves offer guided tours through some of the finest achievements of this dripping of water. Seven commercial caverns lie along Interstate 81 in the Great Valley of Virginia. All but two (Natural Bridge Caverns and Dixie Caverns) are clustered around Massanutten Mountain in the northern Shenandoah Valley. On the east side of the Massanutten range are Grand Caverns (Grottoes) [Fig. 31(3)], Luray Caverns (Luray) [Fig. 30(13)], and Skyline Caverns (Front Royal) [Fig. 30(14)]. Luray Cavern is the largest in the eastern United States. On the west side are Endless Caverns (southwest of New Market) [Fig. 30(15)] and Shenandoah Caverns (northwest of New Market) [Fig. 30(16)]. The Massanutten Caverns at Keezletown are no longer open. Admission fees vary and all except Grand Caverns are open year-round.

The remainder of the estimated 3,000 caves in Virginia are mostly wild caves, lacking artificial lighting, paved walkways, and admission fees. Many still have unexplored tunnels and chambers. As 95 percent of the caves are on private property, caving groups have sprung up to obtain permission to safely explore and protect wild caves.

One area popular with spelunkers is in the Burnsville area of northern Bath County, northeast of Falling Spring Valley. Trila Roberts, owner of Robert's Grocery in Burnsville, can direct you to one of several undeveloped large caverns and sunken caves that is safe to explore on your own. Landowners' permission is required for any caves on private property.

The nonprofit National Speleological Society has several chapters, or grottoes, spread across the state that welcome new members. These groups sponsor trips, offer training, teach and practice cave conservation, and generally provide a safe framework for studying caves. Highland Adventures, a Highland County outfitter, also conducts cave tours throughout western Virginia.

CAVE LIFE. An interesting variety of critters has adapted to cave life. Perhaps the best-known example of an animal that uses caves is the bat. Eight species of these much-maligned mammals are found in Virginia caves. Three of these—the Indiana bat (*Myotis sodalis*), gray bat (*Myotis*

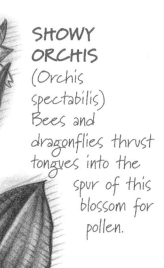

SHOWY ORCHIS (Orchis spectabilis) Bees and dragonflies thrust tongues into the spur of this blossom for pollen.

grisescens), and Virginia big-eared bat (*Plecotus townsendii virginianus*)—are on the federal endangered species list. The guano, or droppings, of bats and the decaying bodies of dead bats are important as nutrients to other cave life.

Less well known is an assortment of millipedes, crustaceans, spiders, crickets, and salamanders that have adapted to caves. Some of these tiny creatures are troglobitic—that is, they are totally adapted and never leave the cave. Such animals are generally unpigmented and eyeless since color and eyes are of no use in the total darkness of caves.

For more information: National Speleological Society, 2813 Cave Avenue, Huntsville, AL 35810-4413. Phone (205) 852-1300. Web site: nss@caves.org. Highland Adventures (tours of wild caves, rock climbing, mountain bike rental, and excursions), PO Box 151, Monterey, VA 24465. Phone (540) 468-2772. Virginia Division of Mineral Resources, Box 3667, Charlottesville, VA 22903. Phone (540) 293-5121. Robert's Grocery, Burnsville, VA 24487. Phone (540) 925-2215.

Phone numbers for commercial caverns are Luray, (540) 743-6551; Skyline, (800) 296-4545; Endless, (800) 544-CAVE; and Shenandoah, (540) 477-3115. Others are described elsewhere in book.

NATURAL CHIMNEYS

[Fig. 31(2)] At Mount Solon, southwest of the Shenandoah Valley town of Harrisonburg, are seven limestone towers that rise from 65 feet to 120 feet above a level, grassy floodplain. The North River, patient architect of the impressive towers, flows unobtrusively by on its way to the Shenandoah.

Once privately owned, Natural Chimneys is now managed by the Upper Regional Valley Park Authority. The 134-acre park has a campground open year-round (limited services during winter), a 3-mile interpretive trail that explains the towers, picnic shelters, and a pool. Birders have identified 125 species of birds here.

Inspired by the castlelike appearance of the towers, organizers staged an unusual jousting event at Natural Chimneys in 1821. Contestants riding swift horses at full gallop attempted not to unseat one another but to spear a series of tiny hanging rings. The event was so popular, it continues to this day, held annually on the third Saturday of August. It is billed as the longest continuously running sporting event in America.

Directions: From I-81, take Exit 240 and drive 3.5 miles west on VA 257 to Bridgewater. Turn left on VA 42 and drive 3.8 miles. Turn right on VA 747 and drive 3.5 miles to Mount Solon. Turn right on VA 731 and drive .6 mile to park entrance.

Activities: Hiking, biking, camping, picnicking, swimming, birdwatching.

Facilities: Self-guided trail, 136-site campground with hookups, picnic shelter, pool, camp store, hot showers, restrooms, laundry facilities, 2 playgrounds.

Dates: Chimneys, open daily, year-round. Camping, open year-round (limited facilities Dec. 1–Mar. 1).

Fees: There is a charge per car or per person for groups for day use. Residents of Staunton, Harrisonburg, Augusta County, and Rockingham County, free.

For more information: Natural Chimneys Regional Park, Upper Valley Regional Park Authority, PO Box 478, Grottoes, VA 24441. Phone (540) 350-2510 or (540) 249-5729.

GRAND CAVERNS

[Fig. 31(3)] On a hillside southwest of the little town of Grottoes are three entrances to an underground system called Grand Caverns. An unknown person first stumbled upon one of the entrances in the 1780s. The single entrance in use today was discovered in 1804 by a 17-year-old boy, Bernard Weyer, searching for his raccoon trap. The cavern was once called Weyers Cave, and a nearby town still has that name.

CATAWBA RHODODENDRON
(Rhododendron catawbiense)
This shrub forms dense thickets on mountain slopes.

Thomas Jefferson once visited the caverns, General Stonewall Jackson quartered his troops there during the Civil War, and many early-nineteenth-century dances were held in the cave's 5,000-square-foot Grand Ballroom.

Grand Caverns, known for its spacious rooms, also has Cathedral Hall—one of the largest rooms of any cavern in the East. Massive columns, beautiful draperies of rippling flowstone, and rare shield formations line the 280-foot-long, 70-foot-high room. To let the natural beauty of the formations show, minimal use is made of colored lights in the caverns. The park is managed by the Upper Valley Regional Park Authority.

Directions: From I-81, take Exit 235 and go east 6 miles on VA 256 to Grottoes. Turn right on VA 825 and look for park entrance on right.

Activities: Cavern tour, hiking, biking, picnicking, swimming, miniature golf, tennis.

Facilities: Hiking and biking trails, picnic shelters, swimming pool, miniature golf, tennis courts, gift shop.

Dates: Open Apr.–Oct. and weekends in Mar. Groups only Nov.–Feb. (reservations required).

Fees: There is a charge for admission.

For more information: Grand Caverns, Upper Valley Regional Park Authority, PO Box 478, Grottoes, VA 24441. Phone (540) 249-5705 or (540) 249-5729.

TIDE SPRING

[Fig. 31(1)] In the 1920s, families would pack a picnic basket on Sunday afternoons and head for a scenic overlook or an idyllic millpond. Around Harrisonburg, one of the favorite destinations was a stretch of rolling farm pastureland near the community of Cherry Grove in Rockingham County.

The attraction was neither overlook nor millpond, but a hole in the ground. At one moment, water would pour out of the hole, sometimes at a rate of 1,000 gallons a minute. Then the water would shut off abruptly, like a faucet. No one knew why.

The place was called Tide Spring for its resemblance to ocean tides. In 1936 the ebbing and flowing water caught the attention of the state geologist, who apparently had more humor than explanations. He wrote the phenomenon off as "uncanny," calling it perhaps the work of "mischievous elves" residing in underground caverns.

According to current thinking, Thomas Jefferson, who wrote about the spring in 1787, may have been much closer to the scientific explanation. Jefferson speculated that Tide Spring was a "syphon fountain."

Scientists and geologists today say that Tide Spring is a reservoir in the porous limestone and dolomite rock typical of the region. It belongs to a type of spring with a variety of names—ebb and flow spring, periodic stream, temperamental spring, and breathing spring. Only a few exist in the world, and Tide Spring is one of the most unusual.

The complex dynamics involve a syphoning action with a self-cycling timer. As the reservoir beneath the surface fills with groundwater, water is forced to the surface where it overflows and runs to a nearby stream.

When the rising column becomes higher than the source end, pressure changes cause the flow not only to shut off but also to flow backward to regain equilibrium. The action is turbulent and noisy and so interesting to watch that the landowner allows school groups to visit his farm.

BANDED
SCULPIN
(Cottus
carolinae)
A bottom-
dweller, the
sculpin walks
using leglike
fins.

Shenandoah Valley Ponds and Wetlands

Most of the fertile limestone soil and relatively flat terrain of the Shenandoah Valley has been plowed by farmers or used by industry over the years. However, an occasional isolated pond, sinkhole, wet or dry prairie, or marsh escapes disturbance. Perhaps a patch of private land is too difficult or boggy to farm or a railroad track separates a sinkhole from the industry that owns the property.

SOUTH RIVER PRESERVE

[Fig. 31(4)] A plant employee with a side interest in botany takes a lunch break and steps across the railroad track into another world. He or she begins to find plants rare but native to Virginia—queen-of-the-prairie, rattlesnake master, buckbean, four-flowered loosestrife.

Just such a scenario occurred in Augusta County, resulting in the establishment of The Nature Conservancy's first preserve in the Shenandoah Valley. The wetland, now called the South River Preserve, is a 14-acre natural area bordering the Alcoa Building Products manufacturing plant at Stuarts Draft.

This spring-fed wet prairie was typical Shenandoah Valley habitat before European settlers arrived, but it is now one of the last such wetlands remaining in Virginia. In the Shenandoah Valley before 1800, woods bison and elk roamed grassy prairies in the Shenandoah Valley similar to those of the Midwest.

Settlers and Indians armed with rifles killed off the large grazers, however. With the coming of agriculture and the suppression of both man-made and natural wildfires that renewed the prairies, the former grasslands became largely a topic for evening porch conversation among old people. In fact, a former owner ditched this Stuarts Draft wetland in an attempt to farm it, but a persistent underground spring stymied the effort.

The rich variety of native plants and associated habitat attracts woodcocks, red-winged blackbirds, mallards, Canada geese, goldfinches, meadowlarks, bobwhites, and common snipe. King rails can sometimes be heard calling at dusk. The spotted turtle, rare in the valley, is also a resident of the preserve. Beavers, which are making a comeback in many parts of Virginia, have moved in, creating dams and ponds on the property.

SILVER LAKE

[Fig. 31] This 10-acre spring-fed lake is well known by area bird watchers for its waterfowl. The City of Harrisonburg lake lies just north of Dayton. Overshadowing Silver Lake is Mole Hill, the eroded remains of a volcano.

The volcano was active 50 million years ago, in the Eocene Epoch of the Cenozoic Era. Shallow seas covered large areas of the continent then, and horses, monkeys, and whales were evolving.

Like an oasis among subdivisions and cultivated fields, the shallow lake attracts migrating waterfowl, warblers, terns, and egrets in spring. Among the ducks reported by local bird watchers are blue-winged and green-winged teal, redhead, greater and lesser scaups, American black duck, bufflehead, hooded merganser and others. Caspian, forster's, and black terns; and great and common egrets have been sighted.

Resident birds include several species of swallows, Canada geese, belted kingfishers, and American woodcocks.

Directions: From VA 42 at Dayton, turn north onto VA 732. Go .2 mile and turn right onto VA 701. Lake is about .5 mile ahead, on left.

Activities: Year-round fishing for stocked trout.

Facilities: None.

Dates: Open year-round.

Fees: None.

Closest town: Dayton is .5 mile south.

For more information: Virginia Department of Game and Inland Fisheries, Region IV, PO Box 996, Verona, VA 24482. Phone (540) 248-9360.

KENNEDY MOUNTAIN MEADOW

[Fig. 31(5)] Another tiny preserve called Kennedy Mountain Meadow protects a rare community related to a complex of sinkhole ponds. Near Sherando, just a few miles southeast of the South River Preserve, is a seasonally flooded, natural meadow with a 1.5-acre pond on the property of a hunt club. Kennedy Mountain Meadow is at the edge of Big Levels in the Pedlar Ranger District of the George Washington National Forest.

The porous bedrock and soil hold water in spring and fall but dry up the rest of the year. In Virginia, this type of sinkhole pond is found only in Augusta and Rockingham counties.

Two native plants that have adapted to the unusual conditions are Virginia sneezeweed (*Helenium virginicum*) and black-fruited spikerush (*Eleocharis melanocarpa*).

The Nature Conservancy has a land-management agreement with the owner to protect the preserve. Because of the fragile nature of the environment, it is not open to the public.

Virginia Sneezeweed

The globally endangered Virginia sneezeweed (*Helenium virginicum*), known to exist in just two Virginia counties, thrives in the dolomite soil of Kennedy Mountain Meadow. Blooms with numerous yellow petals appear in late summer. The rare, herbaceous member of the sunflower family gets its name sneezeweed honestly. Allergy sufferers may be glad the plant is not as common as ragweed and plantain.

Shenandoah River

[Fig. 29(30), Fig. 30] The Shenandoah River is as beautiful as its name. A broad, shallow river that threads its way through the rich, scenic farmland of the Shenandoah Valley of Virginia, the Shenandoah River and its two major tributaries, the North Fork and South Fork, glide by apple orchards, hay fields, rail fences, and dark forests. As paddlers navigate the gentle meanders of the mature river, they are treated to the changing scenery of the Blue Ridge Mountains to the east, the limestone and sandstone cliffs of Massanutten Mountain in the center of the Shenandoah Valley, and the Allegheny Mountains to the west. The river system flows northeasterly from its headwaters in Augusta and Rockingham counties until it merges with the larger Potomac River at Harpers Ferry, West Virginia.

Canoes, kayaks, or car-top boats such as john boats are ideal for exploring the Shenandoah system. Because of numerous shallows, ledges, and rapids—not to mention several old dams and low-water bridges that require portaging—motorized craft are uncommon on the river. Local people, however, have devised an ingenious method of attaching pitchforks to the props on boat motors, thus allowing the lower unit of the motor to kick up and out of harm's way when shallow water is encountered.

The North Fork of the Shenandoah River begins in the mountains of northern Rockingham County near the community of Fulks Run. It is a small river with clear water, pleasant scenery, and lots of wildlife—deer, wild turkey, beaver, raccoons, muskrats, Canada geese, and great blue herons—along its banks. Because it is narrow and shallow with only mild whitewater, the North Fork may require walking down the middle of the river and dragging a boat or canoe during dry summer months.

After flowing through a gap in Little North Mountain, the North Fork enters the Shenandoah Valley at Cootes Store west of Broadway. The North Fork of the Shenandoah River then slides along the western edge of Massanutten Mountain, which rises like a loaf of bread in the middle of the Shenandoah Valley floor. The river takes a turn around the north end of 50-mile-long Massanutten Mountain then heads east for some 4 miles to its juncture with the larger South Fork of the Shenandoah River at Front Royal. The two forks—the North Fork and South Fork—of the Shenandoah then become the main stem, or the Shenandoah River proper.

Actually, when most people refer to the Shenandoah River, they're including both the South Fork of the Shenandoah as well as the main stem. The South Fork—a broad, lengthy, and serpentine river—is the stretch where most fish are caught. It is also where several outfitters have established liveries that rent canoes and tubes for floating.

The South Fork of the Shenandoah forms at the community of Port Republic in the southwestern tip of Rockingham County. Trip planning is easy because, in addition to the services of outfitters, the Virginia Department of Game and Inland Fisheries has built public access points the entire length of the South Fork as well as on the main stem. The U.S. Forest Service has also built canoe launches on some of its lands bordering the South Fork. If you enter the river at Port Republic, check out the state highway markers on US 340 which runs parallel to the Shenandoah. A major Civil War battle was fought at Port Republic, where the cool South River out of Waynesboro and Grottoes combines with the warmer waters of the Middle River and North River that wind lazily across the valley floor from the western mountains.

Here the good fishing and floating begins. These features, along with accessibility, camping opportunities, outfitters, and beauty, make the Shenandoah a popular river— sometimes too popular. The South Fork below Luray can get crowded on summer weekends as scores of rental canoes paddled by city-weary visitors from Washington, D.C., bump and splash their way downriver. The moderately clear South Fork meanders northeasterly through Page Valley, which is part of the Shenandoah Valley, between Massanutten Mountain on the west side and the Blue Ridge range to the east.

A cautionary note: PCBs released by a Front Royal manufacturer in the main stem of the Shenandoah make eating fish from that section risky. The South Fork of the Shenandoah retains mercury leaked from an upriver Waynesboro plant. A public health advisory on this section suggests that small children and pregnant women avoid eating fish from the South Fork. Anglers interested in additional details regarding the health advisories should contact the Virginia Department of Health at (804) 786-1763.

FISHING THE SHENANDOAH

[Fig. 31] The South Fork is renowned for its smallmouth bass fishing. Smallmouth are abundant throughout the Shenandoah system, but the South Fork is most easily accessible and may well have the best fishery. The Virginia Department of Game and Inland Fisheries maintains many public access sites for boats and canoes. The sites are evenly spread throughout the South Fork's course. Several access sites also allow boaters to enter the river from national forest land on the west side of the river between Luray and Front Royal.

Don't expect big bass. The average smallmouth in the Shenandoah measures less than 14 inches. For the best sport, try light spinning tackle or fly-fishing gear. Small crayfish imitations are popular lures on the river. So are minnow-type lures such as Rapalas and Rebels. A slot limit applies. All bass in the slot between 11 and 14 inches—the best size for reproduction—must be returned to the river. Bass below and above the slot limit are legal to keep. Panfishing is excellent throughout. A few walleye may be found in the lower reaches of the South Fork from Newport Dam downstream. Channel catfish are also plentiful. The North Fork is smaller than the South Fork and has fewer developed public access points, so entry to the river is limited. The main stem of the Shenandoah River, like its North Fork and South Fork tributaries, is an excellent river for smallmouth bass, rock bass, redbreast sunfish, and channel catfish.

Public access points to the main Shenandoah are maintained at Front Royal (the beginning of the main stem) at Riverton and Morgan's Ford, at the VA 17/VA 50 bridge at Berry's Ferry, and at the VA 7 bridge at Castleman's Ferry.

FLOATING THE SOUTH FORK

[Fig. 31] For a leisurely day of sight-seeing and fishing, take one of the many float trips available on the Shenandoah. The state Department of Game and Inland Fisheries operates several free ramps and access points strategically placed along the river so that floaters can choose between day trips of 4 to 18 miles.

For a free color brochure and map, with good fishing spots highlighted and danger areas pinpointed, ask the Virginia game department for a copy of Shenandoah River Float Trips. Call (540) 248-9360 or write Department of Game and Inland Fisheries, 4010 West Broad Street, Richmond, VA 23230.

A busy canoe livery that can put you on the river for a few hours or a few days is Shenandoah River Outfitters, 6502 South Page Valley Road, Luray, VA 22835. Phone (540) 743-4159. Rates include all gear, canoes, and shuttle service. Trips of varying lengths can be arranged, with overnight camping and hot meals included.

On the Lee Ranger District of the George Washington National Forest is High Cliff Canoe Camp, with free primitive campsites accessible only by river or by hiking in. The campground is on the west side of the river below Goods Mill. In fact, the entire stretch on river left between Goods Mill at VA 684 and Burners Ford at VA 664 is national forest, so camping is permitted. The few private homes within the national forest should be avoided, and campers should carry all trash away.

Also, the new Andy Guest/Shenandoah River State Park is being developed for day use about 1.5 miles downriver of the Bentonville low-water bridge on VA 613. Yellow park-boundary signs are on trees on river right just before a couple of canoe take-out points.

Picnic tables are available, and an access road is planned for completion sometime in 1998. The staff of Sky Meadows State Park at Delaplane is managing the park at present.

Cucumbertree

This hardiest member of the magnolia family is widespread and favors rich, moist soils of protected valleys and streambanks. The greenish-yellow flowers may not appear until the tree is 25 or 30 years old. The tree takes its name from its small, leathery, cucumber-shaped fruits. Birds and rodents eat the bright seeds. *Magnolia acuminata* grows 45 to 90 feet tall, reaching its greatest size in the southern Appalachians.

For more information: Lee Ranger District, George Washington National Forest, 109 Molineu Road, Route 4, Box 515, Edinburg, VA 22824. Phone (540) 984-4101. Virginia Department of Game and Inland Fisheries, 4010 West Broad Street, Richmond, VA 23230. Phone (804) 248-9360. For information on Andy Guest/Shenandoah River State Park, contact Sky Meadows State Park, 1012 Edmonds Lane, Delaplane, VA 20144. Phone (540) 592-3556.

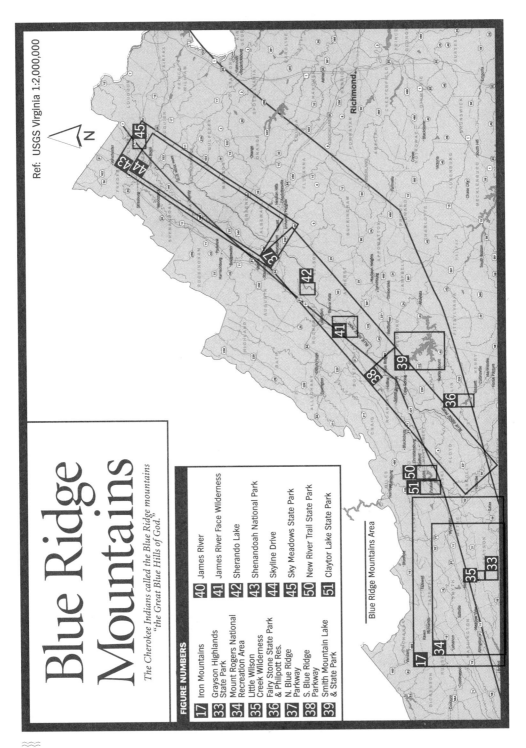

Ref: USGS Virginia 1:2,000,000

N

Blue Ridge Mountains

The Cherokee Indians called the Blue Ridge mountains "the Great Blue Hills of God."

FIGURE NUMBERS

17	Iron Mountains	40	James River
33	Grayson Highlands State Park	41	James River Face Wilderness
34	Mount Rogers National Recreation Area	42	Sherando Lake
35	Little Wilson Creek Wilderness	43	Shenandoah National Park
36	Fairy Stone State Park & Philpott Res.	44	Skyline Drive
37	N. Blue Ridge Parkway	45	Sky Meadows State Park
38	S. Blue Ridge Parkway	50	New River Trail State Park
39	Smith Mountain Lake & State Park	51	Claytor Lake State Park

Blue Ridge Mountains Area

The Blue Ridge

For residents along the old "Valley Pike " (US 11), sunrise over the gentle Blue Ridge and a cup of coffee are a comfortable way to start a day. The mountains are always there—appearing uncomplicated, solid, enduring. Solid and enduring, yes. For the Blue Ridge are not only the highest but are among the oldest mountains of the Appalachians and of the nation. The range is made up largely of billion-year-old metamorphic and igneous bedrock thrust upward with the rest of the Appalachians about 250 to 300 million years ago.

But uncomplicated? The mountains do appear deceptively simple, often wrapped in the soft blue haze that suggested their name. Beginning with the name, however, this range is anything *but* simple. First, there's a distinction between the terms Blue Ridge *province* and Blue Ridge *escarpment*. The rounded, weathered Blue Ridge province—the defining eastern boundary of the Appalachians—extends from

[*Above:* St. Mary's Falls in the Pedlar Ranger District]

northern Georgia 615 miles northeast to southern Pennsylvania. The range separates the Great Valley of Virginia on the west from the Piedmont on the east. The Blue Ridge province keeps travelers along Interstate 81 company for the highway's entire 323-mile run through the state, though the Massanutten Mountains block the view for 50 miles.

The city of Roanoke—where the Roanoke River cuts through the mountains—is the dividing line between two different configurations of the Blue Ridge province. The ridge that runs northeast from Roanoke is rarely more than 14 miles wide, rising sharply from the valley floor, with smaller associated ridges extending from the main one. Southeast of Roanoke the mountains broaden into a plateau, punctuated with clusters of mountain peaks. The plateau widens to more than 50 miles across at the North Carolina border and 70 miles across farther south.

In Virginia, the plateau is called the Blue Ridge Highlands. The mountain ranges along the western portion of the plateau (along the North Carolina/Tennessee border) are known collectively as the Unaka Mountains. An escarpment along the eastern edge of the plateau plus the narrow ridge of the Blue Ridge that runs north from Roanoke to southern Pennsylvania makes up the Blue Ridge front or escarpment, or simply the Blue Ridge.

Travelers can ride the crest of the Blue Ridge on the Skyline Drive (north of Waynesboro) and the Blue Ridge Parkway (south of Waynesboro), with grand views of the Piedmont to the east and the mountains and valleys to the west. The ridge they ride and the mountains of the Blue Ridge province to the west—though still impressive—are now rounded, weathered. Geologists use the term "subdued" for these worn-down remnants of ancient mountains. Crags, cliffs, and talus slopes are rare. Instead of peaks, the mountains generally have rounded summits, which slope gradually away to steep sides and ravines.

Birth of the Blue Ridge

Forces that formed the ancient rocks of the Blue Ridge are only partially understood, for the events were many and complex. Of course, the fact that the occurrences took place millions, even billions of years ago further clouds the picture. Geologists believe the Grenville Orogeny—a collision of earth's sliding plates—formed the basement rock of the Blue Ridge, forcing up the first Appalachians that wore down before the present-day mountains formed. That event happened more than 1 billion years ago. As the continents broke apart about 750 million years ago, a sustained period of volcanic action followed. Evidence of viscous lava flows can still be found at Mount Rogers in the southwestern Blue Ridge Highlands.

A final orogeny—again a collision caused by continental drift—ended a mere 250 million years ago. The basement rocks were once again forced up and over adjacent younger layers of rock to the west. If layers of younger sedimentary rock such as limestone were on top, they completely eroded away to expose the ancient bedrock once again. Because of the east-to-west direction of the thrust, younger rocks in Shenandoah National Park are exposed to the west, and older Precambrian granites to the east. The metamorphic and igneous rocks—gneisses, schists, quartzites, greenstones, and granites—were formed by intense pressure and heat, and left few fossils.

Pedlar Ranger District of the George Washington National Forest holds many natural treasures.

Water Gaps and Wind Gaps

The Roanoke and two rivers to the north—the James and the Potomac—still follow their ancestral course, predating the Blue Ridge. These three rivers carved gorges, or water gaps, through the uplifting Blue Ridge, keeping pace with the forces creating the mountains.

In other cases, wind gaps are left where a river used to flow through the rising mountains, but did not keep up with the mountain's growth. Streams draining the Shenandoah Valley left evidence of several attempts to make an eastward escape before being diverted north to the Potomac. The valley was on a much higher plain, and the mountains were possibly little more than knobs showing above the horizon. But the streams easily wore down the highly erodible limestone and gradually wore down tougher sandstone as the valley formed, but the resistant granite and gneiss bedrock of the Blue Ridge on the eastern edge was a formidable barrier.

As individual streams were diverted north, they joined the Shenandoah River. Examples of the wind gaps they left behind are Goose Creek at Manassas Gap (where I-66 crosses the Blue Ridge east of Front Royal), Gap Run at Ashby Gap (10 miles north, at the US 17 crossing in Clarke County), and Beaverdam Creek at Snickers Gap (9 miles farther north at the VA 7 crossing).

The South River at Waynesboro once flowed east through Rockfish Gap into what is now the Rockfish River in Nelson County. It, too, was finally "captured" by the Shenandoah and diverted to the Potomac.

Altitude Means Diversity

Altitudes in the narrow Blue Ridge province north of Roanoke rarely reach heights above 3,000 to 3,500 feet. Exceptions are The Priest in Nelson County, Mount Pleasant in Amherst County, and, on the Page/Madison county line, Hawksbill and Stony Man mountains. All are above 4,000 feet.

In the Iron Mountains of the Blue Ridge Highlands to the south, however, are Virginia's highest mountains. Mount Rogers is 5,729 feet and Whitetop Mountain is 5,540 feet. This collection of summits in the southeastern corner of the Blue Ridge Highlands are the remnants of the volcanism of 750 million years ago. The mountains and associated alpine forest communities are a centerpiece of Mount Rogers National Recreation Area.

Extremes in elevation, among other factors, result in great variety of forest communities. Forest types range from southern hardwoods such as sycamore, persimmon, American beech, and pawpaw at lower elevations to a few patches of spruce-fir forests on high summits. Between are typical oak-hickory forests, cove forests of white basswood, tulip poplar, and Eastern hemlock, and, on upper and north-facing slopes, tracts of northern hardwoods such as yellow birch, sugar maple, and American mountain-ash. Dominant trees, however, account for just 100 of the 1,600 species of higher-order plants identified in just the northern section of the Blue Ridge.

The diverse and complex communities of dominant trees and other species—shrubs, flowers, ferns, aquatic life, wildlife, insects—associated with the various types of forests are discussed in the introduction and as they relate to each site.

Virginia's Blue Ridge Highlands

The highlands, unlike most of the more sharply defined Blue Ridge province north of Roanoke, were broad enough for entire communities to settle. Examples are the towns of Troutdale and Independence in Grayson County, Fancy Gap in Carroll County, Meadows of Dan in Patrick County, and Floyd in Floyd County. The descendants of tough German and Scots-Irish settlers who scratched out an existence on thin mountain soil still hold to many customs and traditions of their ancestors.

During the hard work day, they would compose songs in their minds while planting cabbage, digging potatoes, tending cattle, or hanging leaves of Burley tobacco in their barns. Before television, families and neighbors would gather on front porches in the cool of the evening to make music and tell tales. On Saturday nights, they celebrated the week's work not as couch potatoes, but with exuberance. They'd break out the banjo and fiddle. The entire community would gather at a local barn to clap their hands, stomp their feet, and swing that gal.

Today, traditional mountain music—and the weekly barn dances—are more than passing fancies. The driving rhythm and energetic dances are in the blood. In the town of Floyd (on US 221 in Floyd County), for example, the rollicking music of the Friday Nite Jamboree still rings down the mountain hollows. On the third Saturday of each month, the people of Galax, on the Carroll/Grayson county line, celebrate with their own Mountain Music Jamboree. Galax is also home to the world-re-nowned Old Fiddlers Convention each August. Many communities celebrate apple-butter making, maple-sugar time, storytelling, mountain crafts, squaredancing, and harvest time (*see* Appendix C).

The Glades and Big Spring Bog

[Fig. 17(15)] In Grayson County, on the plateau between the Blue Ridge escarp-ment and the Iron Mountains to the northwest, is an area of wetlands known as The Glades. Big Spring Bog Natural Area Preserve is one of these wetlands. The preserve was acquired by The Nature Conservancy, transferred to the Virginia Department of Conservation and Recreation, and dedicated in 1990. The preserve encompasses 50 acres of land approximately 7 miles south of Galax, just north of the Virginia/North Carolina line.

Soil in the area is saturated with magnesium, creating a harsh environment that keeps out invading trees and shrubs and stunts the growth of common plants. With

the lack of competition from the usual domi-nant plants, rare species are surprisingly abundant. Eleven globally rare plants, includ-ing largeleaf grass-of-Parnassus, Gray's lily, and shortleaf sneezeweed, thrive at Big Spring Bog.

The bog turtle (*Clemmys muhlenbergii*) is a rare, small freshwater turtle found in Virginia only on the southern Blue Ridge Plateau. Its habitat is upland freshwater wetlands in open fields, meadows, marshes with slow-moving streams, ditches, and boggy areas. Because of the fragile nature of the wetland, access is allowed for research and educational purposes only.

BOG TURTLE
(Clemmys muhlenbergi)
This turtle is only 4 inches long.

For more information: Virginia Department of Conservation and Recreation, Division of Natural Heritage, 1500 East Main Street, Suite 312, Richmond, VA 23219. Phone (804) 786-7951.

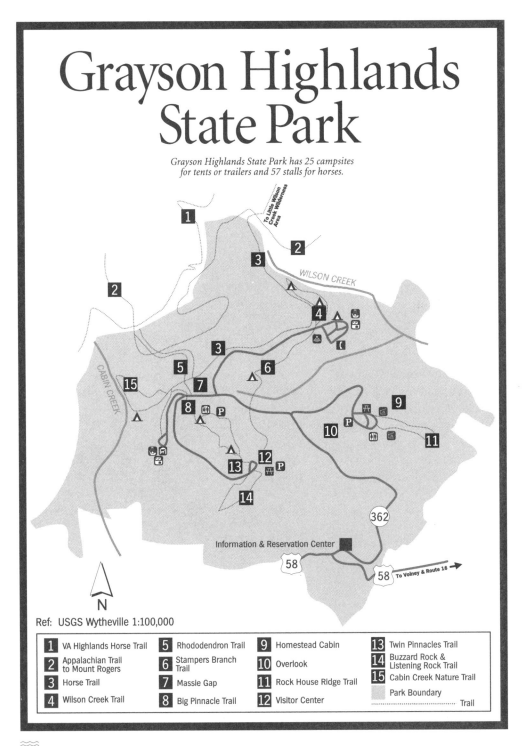

Grayson Highlands State Park

Grayson Highlands State Park has 25 campsites for tents or trailers and 57 stalls for horses.

Ref: USGS Wytheville 1:100,000

N

1	VA Highlands Horse Trail	**5**	Rhododendron Trail	**9**	Homestead Cabin	**13** Twin Pinnacles Trail
2	Appalachian Trail to Mount Rogers	**6**	Stampers Branch Trail	**10**	Overlook	**14** Buzzard Rock & Listening Rock Trail
3	Horse Trail	**7**	Massie Gap	**11**	Rock House Ridge Trail	**15** Cabin Creek Nature Trail
4	Wilson Creek Trail	**8**	Big Pinnacle Trail	**12**	Visitor Center	Park Boundary
						Trail

Grayson Highlands State Park

[Fig. 32(33), Fig. 33, Fig. 34(17)] Many people discover Grayson Highlands State Park by accident. After all, it's a back door to neighboring Mount Rogers National Recreation Area (NRA) and provides one of the easiest access points for a hike to Virginia's highest peak in the NRA to the north.

The road into Grayson takes hikers to a parking lot at Massie Gap that's 4,200 feet above sea level—a good running start at the 5,729-foot peak of Mount Rogers. But this windswept, often fog-shrouded piece of the Blue Ridge Highlands is far more than just an entrance to the federal recreation area.

The 4,935-acre Grayson Highlands State Park showcases the natural beauty of waterfalls, spruce-fir forests, igneous rock outcroppings, native trout streams, rugged mountains, and high alpine meadows with panoramic vistas of valleys below. A community of hardy wildflowers, shrubs, insects, birds, amphibians, and mammals that can withstand the harsh conditions of the open highlands have adapted to life in the alpine meadows.

As beautiful as the highlands of Grayson are, the landscape's original beauty has been altered. At one time, every fourth tree in the mountains was a chestnut, but blight killed all the massive chestnut trees in the early 1900s. After the blight, the mighty trees' naked and deathly gray skeletons stood 120 feet high, anchored by a trunk 10 feet in diameter, until loggers hauled out every available tree for its valuable, decay-resistant wood. About the same time, logging and fires decimated the virgin stands of other forest species. They, too, had been untouched by ax or saw and were of impressive size and variety.

It took only 12 years for the logging companies to clear the highest elevations of magnificent virgin red spruce, hemlock, and Fraser fir. At Massie Gap [Fig. 33(7)] in Grayson Highlands State Park, 1 acre of giant red spruce trees produced an impressive yield of 100,000 board feet of lumber—enough to build 30 average-size houses.

Foresters say that trees in the Grayson Highlands area today may be no more than one-third the size of those in the original virgin forests. But trees (with the exception of American chestnuts, still beset by blight) renew themselves. They come back in time. After decades of protection, the forests of Grayson Highlands are striking in both size and diversity. If not disturbed, eventually the park will support another tall evergreen forest. However, the severe climate, strong winds, and loss of soil following logging operations make for a slow recovery.

Because of extreme changes in elevation (from 3,698 feet at the park entrance to 5,089 feet at the feet of Little Pinnacle), the predominant forests in Grayson Highlands State Park change from northern hardwood (including yellow birch, sugar maple, American mountain-ash, American beech, and northern red oak) to spruce and fir. From a distance, Mount Rogers stands out not just for its height but also because it has a dark cap. The color is traceable to the dark green of the spruce-fir

Rhyolite

Mountaintops with rhyolite mantles of light grey or, more commonly, pinkish to reddish brown are a common sight in Arizona. But this tough volcanic rock is rare in the East. During its formation, vapors were trapped in the viscous rhyolite, creating frothy areas that gradually pit and erode to form weird and grotesque shapes. The rhyolite on Haw Orchard Mountain is bluish gray to purple. The rock was prized by various Indian tribes as a raw material for tools because of its property of making a very sharp edge when flaked.

forest, a northern forest community that grows only at high elevations this far south. Mount Rogers and neighboring Whitetop Mountain are visible from several park trails. Whitetop is so named because, even after valley snows melt, the 5,540-foot-tall bald peak is still visibly white. On a clear day, the Blue Ridge Parkway, a federal mountain highway, is visible some 70 miles to the south. The parkway follows the backbone of the Blue Ridge range through Virginia and North Carolina (*see* Blue Ridge Parkway, page 253).

Grayson Highlands State Park is the only park in Virginia to provide a special area for visitors to bring and stable their own horses. The area is also popular with winter campers, cross-country skiers, trout anglers, deer and turkey hunters, and scientists who come to examine the unusual high-mountain bogs of Grayson.

The picnic area is next to a rebuilt homestead site, complete with two log cabins, a springhouse, and a cane mill. Like other mountains in the Blue Ridge range, the peaks of Grayson Highlands are rounded, not sharp—the result of eons of wear by wind, rain, and melting snow. The high peaks in this area, however, are composed of rhyolite, a volcanic rock almost as hard as granite. That is why they eroded slower than surrounding mountains and why they remain today the highest cluster of peaks in Virginia.

Directions: Park is located in western Grayson County, a few miles from North Carolina border. From I-81 at Abingdon, take Exit 19. Go east on US 58 about 32 miles to park entrance. Or from I-81 at Marion, take Exit 45. Go south on VA 16 about 21 miles to Volney. Then follow US 58 about 8 miles west to park entrance.

Activities: Camping, hiking (including guided hikes), horseback riding, mountain biking, interpretive programs, seasonal hunting and fishing.

Facilities: Fishing, 9 hiking trails, 4 mountain biking trails, interpretive trail, visitor center, craft shop, camp store, amphitheater. Picnic area with drinking water, grills, restrooms, reservable shelters. Camping: 73 sites, 40 with electric and water hookups, and two bathhouses. For horses and riders: 2 miles of bridle paths, 67 horse stalls (38 covered), 24 campsites, bathhouse and hot showers, dump station.

Dates: Open daily for day use year-round. Trails close at sundown. Stable and campground open Mar.–Nov. Visitor center, interpretive programs, camp store open generally Memorial Day–Labor Day.

Fees: There is a charge for parking, camping, and stables.

Closest town: Volney is 8 miles east. Damascus is 22 miles west.

For more information: Grayson Highlands State Park, 829 Grayson Highland Lane, Mouth of Wilson, VA 24363. Phone (540) 579-7092. Information brochures: phone (800) 786-1712.

MASSIE GAP

[Fig. 33(7)] Logs from the dense forest of virgin spruce and fir trees that once covered Massie Gap were cut and transported by railroad north over Pine Mountain to a sawmill at Fairwood. The old railroad grade now provides parts of several hiking trails including the Rhododendron Trail and the Cabin Creek Trail.

After the trees were removed, sunlight bathed a forest floor that had existed in darkness. Layers of organic material became tinder-dry. When lightning or sparks from the log trains ignited the material, it would smolder for weeks, killing off vegetation and seeds that might survive a quicker fire. With no vegetation to hold it, rich soil that had built up over the eons eroded away. After complete devastation, hardy plants such as fireweed (*Epilobium augustifolium*) and fire cherry or pin cherry (*Prunus pensylvanica*) took hold. As new soil built up gradually, grasses were able to survive and provide pasture for cattle. Scattered red spruces have also returned.

Open balds such as this one—and the one atop the peak of Whitetop visible to the west—remain for a number of reasons. First, soil buildup is painstakingly slow. Second, occasional fires—and the grazing ponies at Massie Gap—keep the balds open. And third, wind, cold temperatures, and shrouds of acid-laced fog make the summits the last places to recover from deforestation.

Arrowheads and pieces of stone tools left by Indian tribes have been discovered at Massie Gap. Native Americans perhaps used the area for seasonal hunting grounds. Besides the abundant wildlife were such bonuses as spring water and the igneous rock rhyolite, a material that holds a sharp edge and makes superior tools and weapons.

The parking lot at Massie Gap is the starting point for many hikes. Trails that begin here

CARDINAL FLOWER
(*Lobelia cardinalis*)
A favorite stop for hummingbirds, this flower grows up to 5 feet tall.

include Big Pinnacle [Fig. 33(8)], Cabin Creek [Fig. 33(15)], and Rhododendron [Fig. 33(5)]. The blue-blazed Rhododendron Trail provides connections with the Virginia Highlands Horse Trail [Fig. 33(1)], the Appalachian Trail, and Mount Rogers National Recreation Area to the north.

THE TRAILS OF GRAYSON HIGHLANDS

The nine trails of Grayson Highlands lead to such features as overlooks, water-falls, mountain meadows, and log cabins. Life of early settlers and high-altitude flora and fauna are two themes. The trails are easy to moderate in difficulty. None is more than 2 miles in length. Small shelters provide protection from sudden storms.

Lower trails such as Wilson Creek and Rock House Ridge are good alternatives when fog rolls in to obscure upper trails. Woodland wildflowers such as pink lady slipper (*Cypripedium acaule*), native lily-of-the-valley (*Convallaria montana*), jack-in-the-pulpit (*Arisaema triphyllum*), painted trillium (*Trillium undulatum*), and umbrella plant (*Peltiphyllum*) grow along the trails. These flowers remain because hikers have practiced restraint and left them for others to enjoy.

More than 2 miles of orange-blazed horse trails wander through the park. An excellent base camp for equestrians on the Virginia Highlands Horse Trail is available at Grayson, with a stable and adjacent campground on Haw Orchard Mountain.

Mountain biking is allowed in the Wilson Creek drainage in the northeastern and eastern sections of the park. Bikers may use the horse trail from Massie Gap to the campground, the Seed Orchard Road, the old Upchurch Road, and the Service Road. Surfaces are gravel and/or dirt with many rocky sections and stream crossings. Helmets are recommended because of the rocky terrain. Trail maps for hikers, horseback riders, and mountain bikers are available.

RHODODENDRON TRAIL. [Fig. 33(5)] This 2.5-mile hike connects Massie Gap with the white-blazed Appalachian Trail to the north. Many hikers use the Rhododendron Trail to make a 4.3-mile (one-way) trek to Mount Rogers, Virginia's highest point.

The trail first leads across a field and then follows an old wagon road across a hillside where wild ponies graze. At the top of the hill on the right is the head of Sullivan Swamp. The water table is just below the surface of this boggy depression. An

GARTER SNAKE
(Thamnophis sirtalis)
Garter snakes have three stripes, one on back and one on each side. They're often found near water.

insulating covering of moss keeps the water and air cool.

The moss-covered bogs such as Sullivan Swamp are called muskegs, a plant community usually associated with Canada and Alaska. Such bogs still harbor boreal plants and animals from the last Ice Age, 10,000 years ago. Most northern species died off or migrated north with the retreating ice. Only a few Appalachian peaks and bogs are high enough to sustain them. Fraser fir, red spruce, and big-toothed aspen are three boreal trees that grow in Sullivan Swamp. Painted trillium (*Trillium undulatum*) is another bog-loving plant that thrives in the moisture of the swamp. A V-shaped splash of pink at the base of a wavy white leaf is an identifying mark. Trillium, which are members of the lily family, have three petals, three sepals, and leaves in whorls of three.

On the way to the Appalachian Trail connection, the path crosses three rugged, rocky outcrops of Wilburn Ridge. The ridge was named for Wilburn Waters, a famous bear hunter and wolf trapper of the 1800s. The high, windy slopes give visitors the feeling of being on top of the world. Since there's no view from tree-covered Mount Rogers, photographers can get their fill of outstanding vistas and alpine landscapes here on Wilburn Ridge. Wildflowers add a changing mosaic of color spring through fall. Orange hawkweed (*Hieracium aurantiacum*), for example, sends up its single dandelionlike flower among the rocks. The plant's name comes from an old belief that hawks ate the orange flowerheads to aid vision.

At the AT connection is Rhododendron Gap, where hikers pass through the dense thickets of Catawba rhododendron or mountain rosebay (*Rhododendron catawbiense*) that give the trail its name. The evergreen shrub is called purple laurel by mountain folk.

From Rhododendron Gap, it's an easy 2-mile hike to the rounded summit of Mount Rogers. Although the trees block the view from Virginia's highest peak, they are interesting because they comprise the best spruce-fir forest in Virginia.

Trail: 3-mile, blue-blazed trail from Massie Gap across rocky ridge, providing connection to AT and to Mount Rogers.

Elevation: 4,600 feet at Massie Gap to 5,526 feet at Wilburn Ridge.

Degree of difficulty: Moderate.

Surface and blaze: Grassy and rocky. Blue blaze.

COMMON FOXGLOVE (Digitalis purpurea) This is the source of digitalis, a drug used to treat heart disease.

TWIN PINNACLES AND BIG PINNACLE TRAILS. [Fig. 33(8, 13)] Twin Pinnacles Trail is an easy, 1.6-mile loop on Haw Orchard Mountain connecting the park's two highest peaks—Little Pinnacle (5,089 feet) and Big Pinnacle (5,068 feet). The loop that connects the pinnacles is accessible from an easy trail behind the visitor center (closed in winter) or by Big Pinnacle Trail.

Big Pinnacle Trail is a short but steep .4-mile climb from Massie Gap parking lot. At the intersection with Twin Pinnacles Trail, go right to climb to Big Pinnacle (steep only at the base) or left to Little Pinnacle. Many hikers make return trips to the peaks to experience the 360-degree view of surrounding mountains in different seasons and in different weather conditions. Strong updrafts on Haw Orchard Mountain are the norm, especially on Big Pinnacle. On clear days, the two highest points in Virginia are visible to the northwest—Mount Rogers (5,729 feet) and Whitetop (5,520 feet).

The Big Pinnacle Trail ascends through heath thickets of mountain laurel, rosebay rhododedron, flame azalea, huckleberry, and minniebush into the northern hardwood forest of Haw Orchard. Minniebush (*Menziesia pilosa*) is a low Appalachian shrub with small, bell-shaped flowers. In early summer, their white-to-purplish color combines with the whites, pinks, reds, and red-oranges of the other heaths in a brilliant display. Bloom times on the peaks may be as much as a month behind those in the valley. Witch-hazel, which also grows among the boulders along the Twin Pinnacles Trail, has spidery yellow blossoms in late fall. A forked stick from the witch-hazel tree is used to locate underground water in a technique called "witching."

Trails: Big Pinnacle Trail is a .4-mile climb on Haw Orchard Mountain from Massie Gap to Twin Pinnacles Trail. Twin Pinnacles is a 1.6-mile loop connecting Big Pinnacle and Little Pinnacle.

Elevation: 4,680 at Massie Gap to 5,089 feet on Little Pinnacle.

Degree of difficulty: Easy, with short, steep section at top of Big Pinnacle Trail.

Surface and blaze: Grassy and rocky sections. Big Pinnacle: Yellow blaze. Twin Pinnacles: Red blaze.

WILSON CREEK TRAIL. [Fig. 33(4)] The 1.8-mile, white-blazed Wilson Creek Trail begins across the road from the log cabin just before the entrance to the campground. In summer, the woods along the steep path to Big Wilson Creek are carpeted with ferns. Fraser magnolia and striped maples are in the understory as the path descends to the stream. The striped maple is a small northern tree. Its green bark has vertical white stripes.

Yellow birch and rosebay rhododendron shade the rushing stream where boulders form pools and hide brook and rainbow trout. These trout were stocked during the Depression era and adapted well to cold Big Wilson Creek. In mid- to late July, the rhododendron's white blossoms begin dropping into the swirling waters and plunging over the 25-foot waterfall along the trail.

The dark, tea-colored water of the creek is caused by tannin which leaches from plants in a bog in the creek's headwaters. Big Wilson drains Pine Mountain in Mount Rogers National Recreation Area. Along the trail, the creek separates Grayson Highlands State Park and the Little Wilson Creek Wilderness.

Trail: 1.8-mile loop from parking lot near campground.

Elevation: 4,275 feet to 4,100 feet.

Degree of difficulty: Moderate.

Surface and blaze: Natural forest floor, with rocky sections. White blaze.

ROCK HOUSE RIDGE TRAIL. [Fig. 33(1)] Rock House Ridge and Trail are named for a huge boulder at the trailhead. The underside of the boulder slants to provide a picnic shelter. The many Indian artifacts discovered here indicate the rock has provided shelter for many humans over the years. The Cherokee were probably one of the tribes that frequented the area.

Near the trailhead are two rebuilt log cabins, a springhouse, and a cane mill illustrating the harsh life of early settlers. At the mill, sorghum was ground to make molasses. The trail passes through a thick canopy of rosebay rhododendron, then through mountain laurel and chestnut oak, then sugar maple, then large white oaks, and finally to an open field of blackberries and wildflowers above Mill Creek.

The trailhead is across the road from the second parking lot in the picnic area.

Trail: 1.2-mile loop to meadow above Mill Creek.

Elevation: 3,930 to 3,850 feet.

Degree of difficulty: Easy to moderate.

Surface and blaze: Natural forest floor. Blue blaze.

CABIN CREEK NATURE TRAIL. [Fig. 33(15)] This easy 1.9-mile loop down to Cabin Creek from the Massie Gap parking area has two waterfalls at its bottom. One of the falls is a split stream that tumbles 25 feet over the rocks into a clear, dark pool.

Big-toothed aspens (*Populus grandidentata*), rare this far south, grow along the trail. The triangular leaves have large teeth and are green above, silvery below. As with quaking aspen, the long petioles or leaf stems cause the leaves to tremble and rattle in the slightest breeze. From the fast-growing network of aspen roots, "clone" stems emerge to form new trees. Some clones in Minnesota contain nearly 50,000 trees. One is estimated to be 8,000 years old—possibly one of the oldest organisms on earth.

Trail: 1.9-mile loop from Massie Gap parking area to Cabin Creek and waterfalls.

Elevation: 4,600 feet at Massie Gap to 4,400 feet.

Degree of difficulty: Easy.

Surface and blaze: Natural forest floor. Orange blaze.

BIRDFOOT VIOLET
(Viola pedata)
This violet is identified by its bird's-foot shaped leaves.

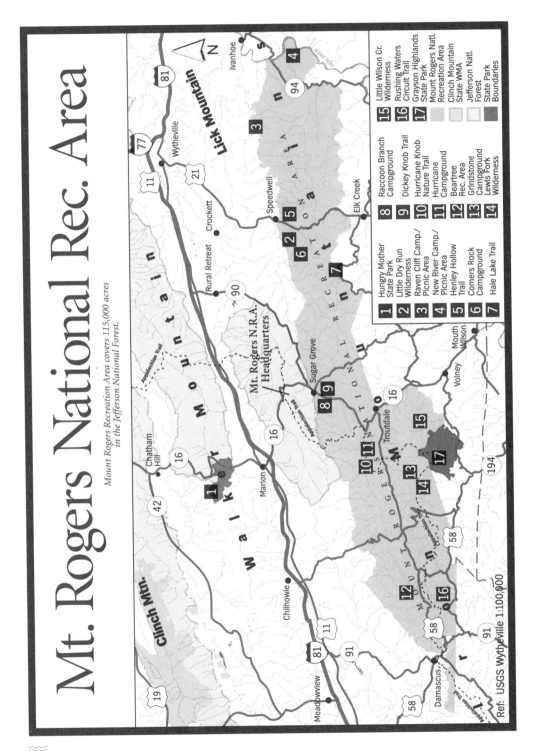

Mt. Rogers National Rec. Area

Mount Rogers Recreation Area covers 115,000 acres in the Jefferson National Forest.

1 Hungry Mother State Park	**8** Raccoon Branch Campground	**15** Little Wilson Cr. Wilderness
2 Little Dry Run Wilderness	**9** Dickey Knob Trail	**16** Rushing Waters Circuit Trail
3 Raven Cliff Camp./ Picnic Area	**10** Hurricane Knob Nature Trail	**17** Grayson Highlands State Park
4 New River Camp./ Picnic Area	**11** Hurricane Campground	Mount Rogers Natl. Recreation Area
5 Henley Hollow Trail	**12** Beartree Rec. Area	Clinch Mountain State WMA
6 Comers Rock Campground	**13** Grindstone Campground	Jefferson Natl. Forest
7 Hale Lake Trail	**14** Lewis Fork Wilderness	State Park Boundaries

Ref: USGS Wytheville 1:100,000

Mount Rogers National Recreation Area

[Fig. 34)] High, wild, and lovely, Mount Rogers National Recreation Area (NRA) is unique in Virginia. Often called the "rooftop of Virginia," all of the state above 5,000 feet in elevation is in this area where the three counties of Grayson, Washington, and Smyth meet. As a result, this is a land of contrast and surprise unlike anything else in the state. Visitors compare it to a Canadian-type climate with its spruce-fir remnant forest. Others imagine a chunk of Montana Big Sky country transported to the Blue Ridge Mountain range when they experience the recreation area's high, timbered ridges that suddenly open to grassy alpine meadows in the thin, crisp air.

On a summer day it is possible to leave the humid lowlands in shorts and shirt and need jeans and jacket by the time the drive to the mile-high county is complete. In winter, it is equally possible to begin the trip from the valleys with windshield wipers working and need snow gaiters on the crest. Elevations, after all, range from 2,000 feet at Damascus and the New River to 5,729 feet on Mount Rogers, the highest point in Virginia.

At 150,000 acres, Mount Rogers National Recreation Area—a part of the Jefferson National Forest—is one of the largest public recreation areas in the East. The area was established in 1966 to take pressure off Shenandoah National Park to the north and Great Smoky Mountains National Park to the south, and it is located within a day's drive of almost one-third of the population of the United States. One of the attractions to the federal recreation area is its variety of forest communities. Mount Rogers National Recreation Area runs 60 miles from Damascus, near the North Carolina line, to the New River's passage through the Blue Ridge on the Wythe/Carroll county line. As valleys and remote coves climb to cool, moist mountain peaks, habitat for plants and animals varies widely.

The rocky, treeless meadows at the top—kept open and brush-free by controlled burning and by grazing cattle and feral ponies—contrast with the forested areas of northern hardwoods, red spruce, and Fraser fir. Emerging from deep woods to alpine meadows that allow panoramic, long-range views of 50 miles or more is a rare experience in the southern Appalachian range. Black bears, hunted almost to extinction in the area, are being restocked by the Virginia Department of Game and Inland Fisheries. Deer hunting is popular in fall and winter. Some of the state's most impressive bucks are taken in the high country. Hunters also walk the mountains to look for grouse and ever-increasing flocks of wild turkeys.

Nearly 160 different species of birds have been identified in the area. Certain species of endangered or threatened salamanders, such as the golden pygmy salamander (*Desmognathus wrighti*), have carved an isolated niche for themselves in the NRA.

More than 300 miles of trails lace Mount Rogers National Recreation Area. There are also two small lakes, more than 100 miles of tumbling trout streams (both stocked and native), a 66-mile horse trail, three federal wilderness areas, seven car campgrounds, and Virginia's highest automobile road which permits nonwalkers to savor the spectacular views from Whitetop Mountain.

At 5,540 feet, Whitetop is the second highest mountain in Virginia. ("Whitetop" is sometimes spelled as one word, as in U.S. Forest Service publications, or two words, as on state highway maps.) Since the forested summit of Mount Rogers has no view, the exposed bald on Whitetop—the northernmost bald in the southern Appalachians—is a popular place. On a clear day, the view from Whitetop includes not only the rounded and ancient mountains of the Blue Ridge range but also distant peaks progressively fading to lighter blues in the bordering states of North Carolina and Tennessee.

A well-stocked visitor center [Fig. 34] with exhibits and helpful staff is located at the entrance to the NRA on VA 16, about 7 miles south of Marion in east-central Smyth County. Also, information, brochures, and maps are available at two more U.S. Forest Service facilities—one located in a red caboose at the west end of Damascus in southeastern Washington County (junction of AT and Virginia Creeper Trail) and another at the old Green Cove Depot along the Virginia Creeper Trail. Green Cove is on VA 600 off US 58, about 15 miles east of Damascus.

Competing interests for use of the Mount Rogers area have caused emotions to boil in recent years. Groups with an interest in widened roads to accommodate large trucks, to provide more access for a particular sport (all-terrain-vehicles, for example), or to allow residential and commercial development are at loggerheads with conservationists, environmentalists, and other recreationalists who favor keeping things as they are. For the moment, a push to widen US 58 at the southwestern end to four lanes has been quashed.

Directions: The vast Mount Rogers NRA is freely accessible from all sides. US 58 runs east from Damascus through the southern end. From I-81, Exit 45, at Marion in central Smyth County, VA 16 leads south across the NRA, passing a beautiful, well-stocked information center after 7 miles. A 15-mile drive south of Wytheville on US 21, through Speedwell leads into the eastern portion of the recreation area. VA 94 provides access to the eastern end, which is bordered by the New River and New River Trail State Park. Other information stations are at Damascus and Green Cove on the southwestern end.

Activities: Scenic drives, camping, hiking, mountain biking, horseback riding, cross-country skiing, picnicking, swimming, trout fishing, seasonal hunting, interpretive programs.

Facilities: Visitor center, 7 campgrounds with no hookups (3 with showers and restrooms, 4 with water and pit toilets), picnic tables and group shelters, small lake with swimming beach, long and short hiking trails, long horse trail and horse campgrounds, interpretive trails, 3 wilderness areas, native and stocked trout streams, scenic byway.

Dates: The NRA is open year-round. Visitor center is open daily.

Fees: There is a charge at the developed campgrounds.

Closest town: Marion, in central Smyth County, is 7 miles north of the visitor center. Damascus, in southeastern Washington County, is at the southwestern tip of the NRA.

For more information: Mount Rogers National Recreation Area, Route 1, Box 303, Marion, VA 24354. Phone (800) 628-7202 or (540) 783-5196.

DAMASCUS

[Fig. 34] The little town of Damascus, about 25 miles east of Bristol, has embraced its wealth of important trails with fervor. Damascus is located at the southwest edge of the highlands on the Tennessee border. The Appalachian Trail, which runs from Georgia to Maine, comes into the state from the south and runs down the town's Main Street before climbing into the Mount Rogers National Recreation Area. Here, in what is called "the friendliest town on the trail," AT hikers are invited to rest up before continuing their journey.

Damascus is also a stopover between the Great Valley of Virginia and the Blue Ridge Mountains for hikers heading east or west along the Virginia Creeper Trail. The Transcontinental Bicycle Route, which crosses the country from Oregon to Virginia, winds its way through Damascus on VA 58 and VA 91. The town honors trail users with a week-long festival on the city streets each spring (*see* Appendix C).

MOUNT ROGERS SCENIC BYWAY

[Fig. 34] In 1988, the U.S. Forest Service designated two connected stretches of highway as the Mount Rogers Scenic Byway. One section of the byway is US 58 between Damascus (southeastern Washington County) and Volney (southwestern Grayson County). The other is VA 603 between Troutdale (northwestern Grayson County) and Konnarock (southeastern Washington County). The two stretches form a Y and total 45.7 miles. By adding a 7-mile stretch of VA 16 connecting the top of the Y between Volney and Troutdale, a loop can be made, totaling 52.7 miles, beginning at Damascus, passing through Konnarock, and looping back to Konnarock.

Starting the journey from Damascus, drive east on US 58 for 32.5 miles to Volney. US 58 is the major access road for Grayson Highlands State Park and is the easiest way to access the high country of Mount Rogers NRA. Because of its curves and winding character, it's not suitable for vehicles longer than 35 feet. Check the odometer or set the car's trip meter to keep track of distances.

Damascus is interesting as a town that caters to hikers on the Appalachian Trail and the Virginia Creeper Trail which pass through it. Visitors pass Virginia Creeper trailheads at mile .9 (rustic railroad trestle) and mile 3.1 (Straight Branch). Beartree Campground is at mile 6.8. At mile 7 is lovely Whitetop Laurel Gorge, where a trail leads to a wildlife watching area.

At mile 16.5, US 58 passes the southwestern slopes of Whitetop Mountain, the second highest peak in Virginia (5,540 feet), and at mile 17.4, the byway passes a junction with VA 600. Check the odometer if you take a side trip so you can refigure the mileage when you return to the scenic byway. VA 600 goes north to Whitetop Mountain and Elk Garden Gap (4,420 feet) where you can park and take the AT east (round trip of 9 miles) to the top of Mount Rogers.

Between the scenic byway on US 58 and Elk Garden Gap, VA 89 goes left off the west side of VA 600. It then climbs about 3 miles nearly to the summit of Whitetop, making it the highest automobile road in the state. Returning to US 58 to continue the scenic drive, go east for 1.5 miles and cross Helton Creek (mile 18.9 of the byway), a clear mountain stream where native trout fishing is allowed. At mile 21.3 is Mount Rogers School. Typical of schools earlier in the century, it's one of the few remaining that teaches grades K through 12 in one building. It has the smallest high school enrollment in Virginia.

The byway passes the entrance to Grayson Highlands State Park at mile 24.9 before reaching Volney at mile 32.5. Drive 7 miles north to Troutdale and head west on VA 603 for the second stretch. At 1.9 miles is Fox Creek Falls with several small cascades and excellent trout fishing. Children (and adults) may enjoy searching among the rocks of Fox Creek for salamanders, crayfish, bugs, and other stream life.

At mile 2.2, the byway enters Fairwood Valley with its pastures, apple trees, and abundance of wildflowers. Many hiking and riding trails cross this area. At mile 2.8 is a horse livery with seasonal rentals for rides into the high country.

The Appalachian Trail crosses at mile 4.1. Grindstone Campground (and Whispering Waters Nature Trail) is at mile 6.1. A spur to the popular Mount Rogers Trail up Elk Ridge leads southeast out of the campground. At mile 12.3 is Konnarock. Like Troutdale, the quiet village was once a busy logging town. At mile 13.2, VA 603 joins US 58 to finish the trip.

RECREATION AND PICNIC AREAS IN MOUNT ROGERS
BEARTREE RECREATION AREA. [Fig. 34(12)]

Directions: Located about 7 miles east of Damascus off VA 58. Go north on FR 837 for 1.5 miles to group campground or 3.8 miles to family campground.

Facilities: 80 campsites, flush toilets, warm showers, dump station, children's playground, 14-acre stocked fishing lake (no gasoline motors, licenses required), swimming beach, bathhouse, hiking trails, mountain biking trails. Group campsites and picnic shelter (reservations required).

Dates: Open mid-Mar.–Dec. 1. Interpretive programs on summer weekends Memorial Day–Labor Day.

Fees: This is a fee area.

For more information: For reservations phone (800) 280-CAMP.

COMERS ROCK CAMPGROUND/PICNIC AREA. [Fig. 34(6)]

Directions: Located on FR 57, which connects to US 21 about 5 miles south of Speedwell. From US 21, go 3.5 miles west on FR 57.

Facilities: 10 campsites on ridge, several picnic sites, small group picnic shelter made of stone during CCC days, drinking water, vault toilets. Iron Mountain Trail runs through campground. Other trails give access to Little Dry Run Wilderness. Observation platform atop Comers Rock about .5 mile to west. 5-acre Hale Lake, stocked with trout in season, is 2 miles west.

Fees: There is a fee for camping or picnicking.

Dates: Open year-round.

GRINDSTONE CAMPGROUND. [Fig. 34(13)]

Directions: Located on VA 603, about halfway between Troutdale and Konnarock.

Facilities: 100 campsites, flush toilets, warm showers, drinking water, dump station, children's playground.

Dates: Open May–Nov. Interpretive programs on summer weekends Memorial Day–Labor Day.

For more information: Reserve some sites by calling (800) 280-CAMP. The rest are first come, first served.

HURRICANE CAMPGROUND. [Fig. 34(11)]

Directions: Located 2 miles off VA 16, about halfway between Sugar Grove and Troutdale. Go west on VA 640 for 2 miles. Turn left on FR 84 and go .5 mile. Gravel road is too steep for some large vehicles.

Facilities: 29 campsites spread beneath trees along creek, flush toilets, warm showers, drinking water, large grassy field for games, excellent trout fishing in Hurricane and Comers creeks in spring and early summer.

Dates: Open Mar.–Oct.

Fees: This is a fee area.

NEW RIVER CAMPGROUND/PICNIC AREA. [Fig. 34(4)]

Directions: Located off VA 602 near Byllesby Dam, within a few hundred feet of New River and New River Trail State Park. From Ivanhoe, take VA 94 about 5.5 miles and look for Byllesby Dam sign and VA 602 on left.

Facilities: 16 campsites, picnic tables, picnic shelter, drinking water, vault toilets. More solitude than better-known areas of Mount Rogers NRA. River access for hikers, bikers, canoeists, inner-tubers.

Fees: This is a fee area.

RACCOON BRANCH CAMPGROUND. [Fig. 34(8)]

Directions: Located beside VA 16 about 2.3 miles south of Sugar Grove (11 miles south of I-81 at Marion).

Facilities: 20 paved campsites, flush toilets in summer (no showers), vault toilets in winter, drinking water, hiking, mountain biking, fishing. Virginia Highlands Horse Trail passes nearby. Dickey's Knob offers beautiful views of Rye Valley and Sugar Grove.

Fees: This is a fee area.

RAVEN CLIFF CAMPGROUND/PICNIC AREA.[Fig. 34(3)]

Directions: Located just off VA 619, 2 miles east of Cripple Creek community and 6 miles east of Speedwell and US 21.

Facilities: 20 campsites and walk-in tent sites beside Cripple Creek. Picnic sites, group picnic shelter for 75 people (by reservation). Large grassy area for games, magnificent cliffs, historic iron furnace, excellent fishing for trout and smallmouth bass.

Dates: Open year-round.

Fees: This is a fee area.

THE TRAILS OF MOUNT ROGERS NRA

[Fig. 34] Avid hikers would be hard put to find a better place to hike than Mount Rogers National Recreation Area. Only Shenandoah National Park in Virginia's northern Blue Ridge can compare. Over 350 miles of trails offer endless options for exploring the various forest communities of the NRA. Four fascinating long trails, each with its own character, and a network of shorter trails blanket the area.

Long trails include a 64-mile stretch of the Georgia-to-Maine Appalachian Trail (AT), 17 miles of the Virginia Creeper Trail, the 50-mile Iron Mountain Trail, and the 66-mile Virginia Highlands Horse Trail. The Virginia Creeper Trail is a 33.4-mile gradual ascent along an old railroad grade between Abingdon and the North Carolina line east of Damascus and Green Cove. Several connections with the AT make a variety of loop hikes possible. (*See* Virginia Creeper Trail, page 307, and Appalachian Trail, page 303.)

The orange diamond-blazed Virginia Highlands Horse Trail extends from Elk Garden east to VA 94 near the New River. Equestrians are also allowed to use all but a few of the other Mount Rogers trails (which are clearly signed). Other prominent trails for horses are Iron Mountain, New River, and Virginia Creeper. The major exception is the AT, which is reserved for hikers.

High elevations, heavy snows, and gentle grades on some trails make Mount Rogers NRA one of the state's best destinations for cross-country skiers. While there are no designated snow trails, many miles of primitive roads and hiking trails provide excellent opportunities to enjoy the quiet of a winter snowfall.

Mountain bikers flock to Mount Rogers for the variety of terrain. The Virginia Creeper Trail, with its long, gentle downhill grade between Whitetop Station and Damascus, is many a

BLACK BEAR
(Ursus americanus)
This bear can grow to 400 pounds.

biker's idea of heaven. Rental bikes are available from local outfitters (*see* Appendix D). NRA staff can help visitors plan their hikes according to individual preferences and abilities. Trails lead through high mountain meadows, into boreal forests reminiscent of Canada, through canopies of rhododendron, along rushing streams, and to overlooks with grand views. There are a variety of publications available to help identify flora and fauna of the fields and forests.

Crowded conditions during peak seasons may occur at Beartree Recreation Area and on the Virginia Creeper Trail, the AT, the Mount Rogers Trail, and Wilburn Ridge. Trails are generally well maintained and blazed. Some may be harder to follow than others. A detailed topo map and compass are always a good idea. Another option for exploring the high country is a covered wagon ride into the crest zone. Mount Rogers High Country Outdoor Center at Troutdale can arrange day trips, overnight covered wagon treks, and overnight horse trips with pack mules. For more information call (540) 677-3900.

Here's a sampling of trails in the Mount Rogers NRA (wilderness trails in next section), from west to east. For those in campgrounds, see section on recreation areas for directions.

American Woodcock

The woodcock (*Scolopax minor*), like the camel, seems to have been designed by a committee. The nearly neckless and tailless bird appears off-balance with its extremely long, straight bill. The upper mandible of the beak is flexible at the tip—a useful tool for grasping earthworms beneath the soil without opening the beak. The well-camouflaged "timberdoodle" is so invisible in the ground leaf litter that it sometimes doesn't fly until almost underfoot. Then it bursts from the ground and zigzags away in a whistling of wings.

The courtship flight of the male often takes place at dusk over a field with nearby woods. The male spirals high into the air then plummets toward the ground with a chittering call. Both male and female fly above the field making their "peeent" call. The American woodcock is in trouble throughout its range due to loss of habitat. In Virginia, a 2.5 percent annual decline has led to reductions in hunting season.

RUSHING WATERS CIRCUIT TRAIL. [Fig. 34(16)] This 15.75-mile loop combines portions of the Virginia Creeper, AT, and trails on Iron Mountain. The trail begins along the tumbling, clear waters of Whitetop-Laurel Creek and climbs to the crest of Iron Mountain for panoramic views of Whitetop Mountain and Mount Rogers. Foot travel only on AT; hikers, horseback riders, and mountain bikers allowed on Virginia Creeper and Iron Mountain trails.

To start, as you face the trail from the parking lot, turn left and hike toward Damascus on the Virginia Creeper (downstream). At mile 4.2, turn right onto blue-blazed trail to reach the AT. At mile 4.3, turn left on AT. Cross US 58 at mile 6.3 and at mile 6.4, turn right onto Feathercamp Trail and follow blue blazes. At mile 8.6, turn right on Iron Mountain Trail (yellow blazes). Sandy Flats Shelter is at mile 8.9. At mile 10.7 (Shaw Gap), turn right on Beartree Gap Trail. Bear right at mile 10.8 and continue down Beartree Gap Trail. Cross Beartree Campground Road at mile 13.2. Turn right at mile 13.5 and cross Beartree Lake Dam. Turn right just past dam, and at mile 13.7, cross US 58. At mile 13.9, turn left on AT and return to parking area.

Directions: From Damascus, take US 58 east 10 miles. Turn right on VA 728 and follow to Creek Junction Parking Lot. Note: VA 728 is narrow, steep, and possibly too difficult for larger vehicles.

Trail: 15.75-mile loop ascending Iron Mountain.

Elevation: 2,300 feet to 3,800 feet on Iron Mountain Trail west of Shaw Gap.

Degree of difficulty: Moderate, with strenuous section.

Surface and blaze: Natural forest floor. AT, white blaze; Iron Mountain Trail, yellow blaze; Feathercamp and Beartree Gap trails, blue blaze.

HURRICANE KNOB NATURE TRAIL. [Fig. 34(10)] This scenic loop to Hurricane Knob begins near campsite #5 at Hurricane Campground. It runs along Hurricane Creek, a stocked trout stream, for about .5 mile, crossing two wooden bridges. After leaving the creek, the trail ascends to Hurricane Knob and into a beautiful forested area before returning back down to the campground.

Trail: 1.14-mile loop to Hurricane Knob.

Elevation: 2,800 feet to 3,200 feet.

Degree of difficulty: Easy to moderate.

DICKEY KNOB TRAIL. [Fig. 34(9)] Dickey Knob Trail is at Raccoon Branch Campground in the central section of Iron Mountain off VA 16. The trailhead is near campsite #4 at the confluence of Dickey Creek (a stocked trout stream) and Raccoon Branch. Go right for the Dickey Knob Trail after crossing bridge (or left for 6.6-mile round trip on Raccoon Branch Trail). Several wooden footbridges provide creek crossings on this 4.8-mile (round-trip) climb up a narrow path to a spectacular cliff view of Rye Valley, Sugar Grove, and beyond. The trail is not blazed but is easy to follow. Mountain bikes are allowed.

Trail: 4.8-mile (round-trip) climb up Dickey Knob.

Elevation: 2,880 feet to 3,649 feet.

Degree of difficulty: Moderate to difficult.

HALE LAKE TRAIL. [Fig. 34(7)] This short loop trail (.58 mile) skirts around picturesque Hale Lake. Located just inside Grayson County at the corners of Smyth and Wythe counties, the lake is a popular fishing spot toward the eastern end of Iron Mountain. The easy, lightly used trail goes in and out of the woods offering several good views. It's unblazed but easy to follow. Only foot travel is allowed.

Directions: From Speedwell in southwestern Wythe County, go 4 miles south on US 21. Turn right on FR 57 (can be muddy at times), drive 6 miles, and follow signs. Lake is on right.

Trail: .58-mile loop around Hale Lake.
Elevation: 3,300 feet to 3,350 feet.
Degree of difficulty: Easy.

HENLEY HOLLOW TRAIL. [Fig. 34(3)] This lightly used trail just east of Dry Run Wilderness and US 21 combines solitude with beautiful scenery. The 3.16-mile path follows a creek up into Henley Hollow, passing several small waterfalls. It emerges at a gap at FR 787 on Horse Heaven Mountain. Foot, bicycle, and horse travel allowed.

Directions: From Speedwell, in southwestern Wythe County, go 2 miles south on US 21. Trailhead is at parking area on left (east side).
Trail: 3.16 mile (one-way) climb up Henley Hollow.
Elevation: 2,485 feet to 3,800 feet.
Degree of difficulty: Moderate.

LEWIS FORK WILDERNESS

[Fig. 34(14)] With Virginia's highest mountain at its heart, 5,730-acre Lewis Fork Wilderness is visited by multitudes of outdoor lovers who want to experience the alpine altitude, smell the fragrant spruce-fir forest, or spend a night under the boughs of these ragged-looking evergreens. Lewis Fork Wilderness straddles the Smyth/Grayson county line northwest of Grayson Highlands State Park. Elevations range from 3,280 feet to 5,729 feet atop Mount Rogers.

The wilderness contains or is intersected by several important trails—the Appalachian Trail (AT), the Virginia Highlands Horse Trail, the Mount Rogers Trail, and the Mount Rogers Spur Trail. Several hikes to the summit of Mount Rogers are possible, with all trails connecting to the AT and then the Spur Trail. These trails provide access to the wilderness at three places: from VA 600 at Elk Garden Gap on the western border (AT and Horse Trail), from the state park (AT and Horse Trail), and from VA 603 on the northern border (AT and Mount Rogers Trail).

Expect to have company on these trails during summer and fall. Several less-traveled paths (but not to the summit) are available for those who desire the solitude normally associated with wilderness. One of these is the 3-mile (one-way) blue-blazed Grassy Branch Trail. This shady, easy hike uses the contours of the northwest flank of Mount Rogers. It connects VA 603 south of Grindstone Campground with VA 600 north of Elk Garden Gap. There are several stream crossings.

Two more lightly used trails are the 3.1-mile (one-way) Helton Creek Trail and the 2.5-mile (one-way) Sugar Maple Trail on the south side of the wilderness. The moderately difficult blue-blazed Sugar Maple Trail, which passes through pastures, wet forests, and meadows, can be combined with the more difficult but picturesque Helton Creek Trail for a circuit. For those who enjoy wildflowers, these trails are a good place to carry a guidebook. The trailhead is on County Road 783, off US 58, 19 miles east of Damascus.

FOREST COMMUNITIES OF LEWIS FORK. The sheer variety of forest communities in Lewis Fork fascinates nature lovers. In addition to the oaks and hickories that dominate most eastern deciduous woodlands, there are several other forest types. The rich, moist soil of deep coves supports dark forests of hemlock, rhododendron, red and sugar maples, white basswood, tulip poplar, and beech. On the upper slopes are northern hardwoods such as yellow birch, sugar maple, northern red oak, American beech, and striped maple. The brilliant fall color of Mount Rogers's western slopes comes from an abundance of red and sugar maples.

When first-time visitors see the alpine meadows of Wilburn Ridge between the wilderness and Grayson (*see* Grayson Highlands State Park, page 229), it makes a lasting impression. And those who make it to the summit never forget the boreal forest of red spruce, Fraser fir, and yellow birch with its rare community of northern wildlife, birds, and plants.

For more on the habitat associated with boreal forests, see Laurel Fork (page 182). For more on Appalachian cove forests, see Little Dry Run Wilderness of Mount Rogers (page 247); Ramseys Draft Wilderness (page 192); and Rich Hole Wilderness, (page 162).

MOUNT ROGERS TRAIL. [Fig. 34] The Mount Rogers National Recreation Trail is a scenic hike from Fairwood Valley up the northern slope of Mount Rogers. Combined with the Appalachian Trail and a spur trail, the 6.2-mile one-way hike to the summit of Mount Rogers makes a nice overnight trip.

The trail first ascends Mount Rogers and runs southwest along Elk Ridge. After 4 miles, the Mount Rogers Trail crosses the AT and dead-ends on the Virginia Highlands Horse Trail on the northwestern side of the Mount Rogers peak.

To reach the peak, turn left (southeast) on the white-blazed AT. (To the right, the AT descends about 2 miles to a parking lot at Elk Garden Gap on VA 200.) After turning left, follow the AT for 1.7 miles as it circles the summit on the southern side. Then go left on the Mount Rogers Spur Trail to the 5,729-foot peak. (For a shorter climb to the summit, start from the VA 600 parking area at Elk Garden Gap and follow the AT about 4 miles east, then .5 mile to the summit on the Spur Trail.)

The trailhead is .4 mile east of Grindstone Campground on VA 603 (6 miles west of Troutdale). The trail can also be accessed by a spur from the campground. Although the trail leads immediately into wilderness, don't be surprised to find other hikers along this popular path. Climbing the state's tallest mountain has a certain allure.

Trail: 4-mile (one-way) climb up Elk Ridge to the AT on the northwest flank of Mount Rogers. Combines with 1.7-mile section of AT and .5-mile spur to peak for 6.2-mile (one-way) hike.

Elevation: 3,720 feet to 5,120 feet at AT connection (or 5,729 feet at summit).

Degree of difficulty: Moderate to difficult.

Surface and blaze: Natural forest floor. Blue blaze. (AT is white blazed.)

▦ LITTLE DRY RUN WILDERNESS

[Fig. 34(2)] Little Dry Run Wilderness is a small, 2,858-acre tract of the Iron Mountains located on the lightly used east end of Mount Rogers NRA. It's in the southwestern corner of Wythe County, with US 21 defining its eastern boundary.

Elevations range from 2,440 feet along Little Dry Run at the northeast boundary to 3,614 feet near the center. The area has a number of small ridges with oak-hickory forests, as well as drainages with Appalachian cove hardwoods such as white basswood, tulip poplar, sugar maple, white ash, and Eastern hemlock. This area of the Iron Mountains is one of the rare places where round-leaf birch (*Betula uber*) is found. Nesting birds such as the wood thrush, summer tanager, red-eyed vireo, and ovenbird seek out the dense cover of understory trees such as Eastern redbud, Fraser magnolia, witch-hazel, and mountain maple.

In early spring, look for the low-growing, delicate wood anemone (*Anemone quinquefolia*) in the coves. The slender stalks of the little plants tremble in the wind, explaining why they are sometimes called wind flowers. Other wildflowers typical of Appalachian cove forests include mayapple (*Podophyllum peltatum*), large-flowered trillium (*Trillium grandiflorum*), red trillium (*Trillium erectum*), foamflower (*Tiarella cordifolia*), solomon's seal (*Polygonatum*), and false solomon's seal (*Smilacina racemosa*). Wildlife is diverse and abundant, and Little Dry Run is a native trout stream. The Little Dry Run Trail is the single path leading into the wilderness. The 3.9-mile path (one-way) connects Comers Rock Campground (on FR 57, 2 miles west of US 21) with US 21 on the east (trailhead on US 21 is 2 miles south of Speedwell). By starting at the campground, you'll be hiking downhill instead of climbing.

After leaving the campground, the trail crosses the Virginia Highlands Horse Trail which skirts the entire western and southern boundary. After the crossing, it heads down Little Dry Run and is sometimes hard to follow. If you stay on the creek, however, you'll come back onto the trail.

DWARF GINSENG
(*Panax trifolius*)
Believed by some to be an aphrodisiac, ginseng has been overcollected.

Little Wilson Creek Wilderness

The many trails of Little Wilson Creek Wilderness are well marked and maintained.

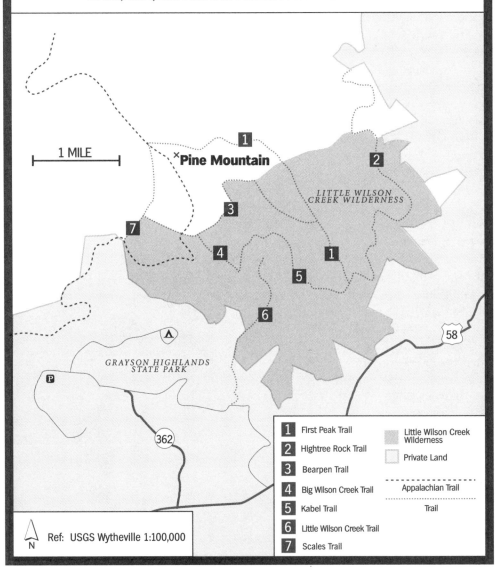

1 MILE

×**Pine Mountain**

LITTLE WILSON CREEK WILDERNESS

1

2

3

7

4

1

5

6

58

GRAYSON HIGHLANDS STATE PARK

362

1	First Peak Trail		Little Wilson Creek Wilderness
2	Hightree Rock Trail		Private Land
3	Bearpen Trail		
4	Big Wilson Creek Trail		Appalachian Trail
5	Kabel Trail		Trail
6	Little Wilson Creek Trail		
7	Scales Trail		

Ref: USGS Wytheville 1:100,000

N

Little Wilson Creek Wilderness

[Fig. 34(15), Fig. 35] In the western end of Grayson County, snugged up against the northeastern border of Grayson Highlands State Park, is Little Wilson Creek Wilderness. Wilson Creek defines the border between the park and the 3,900-acre wilderness.

The first two of three peaks with numbers for names (First Peak, Second Peak, and Third Peak) at the eastern edge of Pine Mountain are at the heart of the wilderness. The highest point of the wilderness is the 4,857-foot summit of Second Peak. Little Wilson Creek, which gave the wilderness area its name, drains the western slopes of all three peaks.

Unlike some wilderness trails, the many trails of Little Wilson Creek are well marked and well maintained. Besides part of the AT, which makes a sweep through the northwest corner, the First Peak Trail [Fig. 35(1)] and Bearpen Trail [Fig. 35(7)] are most heavily used. Solitude is easier to find on Little Wilson Creek [Fig. 35(6)], Kabel [Fig. 35(5)], and Hightree Rock [Fig. 35(2)] trails.

Besides the typical oak-hickory forest, look for Fraser magnolia and yellow birch in moist areas and a spruce-fir forest at higher elevations. Trail features include a grassy bald and an open, rocky meadow (Bearpen Trail), the clear, cold waters of Little Wilson Creek (Little Wilson Creek Trail), and outstanding views (First Peak, Kabel, Big Wilson Creek, and Hightree Rock trails).

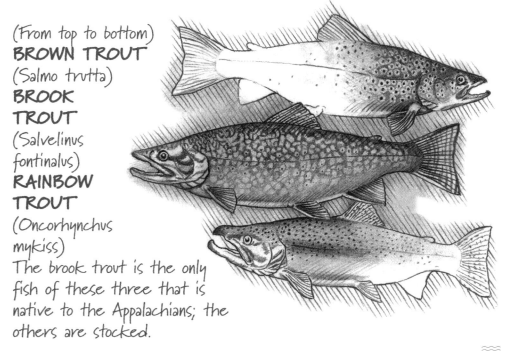

(From top to bottom)
BROWN TROUT
(Salmo trutta)
BROOK TROUT
(Salvelinus fontinalus)
RAINBOW TROUT
(Oncorhynchus mykiss)
The brook trout is the only fish of these three that is native to the Appalachians; the others are stocked.

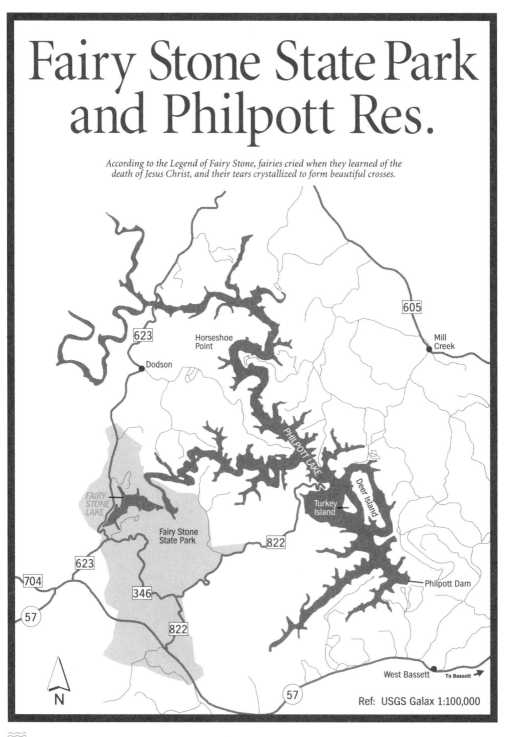

Fairy Stone State Park and Philpott Res.

According to the Legend of Fairy Stone, fairies cried when they learned of the death of Jesus Christ, and their tears crystallized to form beautiful crosses.

605

623

Horseshoe Point

Mill Creek

Dodson

PHILPOTT LAKE

FAIRY STONE LAKE

Turkey Island

Deer Island

Fairy Stone State Park

822

623

704

346

57

822

Philpott Dam

West Bassett   To Bassett

57

Ref: USGS Galax 1:100,000

N

Fairy Stone State Park

[Fig. 36] There's a bit of magic in Fairy Stone State Park. The 4,670-acre park is one of only three known areas in the world where brown staurolite crystals were compressed under great natural heat and pressure to form shapes that suggest Maltese, Roman, or St. Andrew's crosses. The other two locations are Switzerland and the nearby mountains of North Carolina.

The "fairy stones," as they were called by Blue Ridge mountain people, were considered good-luck pieces and were worn or carried to ward off illness, accidents, and denizens of the nether world. Early Scots-Irish settlers also brought to Virginia the concept of trolls, spirits, and fairies. A mountain myth suggests that the brown, cross-shaped stones were fairy tears shed at the time of Christ's death and the tears turned to crystal when they fell to the ground. The manner in which the crosses were formed is better understood now. As the earth's crust heated, folded, and cooled during the formation of the Appalachian Mountain range, iron aluminum silicate—the basic ingredient of fairy stone crosses—crystallized into six-sided shapes. The staurolite crystals, like quartz and diamonds, are harder than surrounding materials. The crystals therefore erode slower and come to the earth's surface, retaining their original shape, as softer surrounding material washes away.

The fairy stone crosses are still sold today in the park and at nearby stores and service stations. Visitors can also search for their own fairy stones in the park along walking trails and old creek beds after hard rains have scoured away loose soil. Fairy Stone State Park lies in the gentle foothills of the Blue Ridge in Henry and Patrick counties. It opened in 1936 and was one of Virginia's original six state parks built by the Civilian Conservation Corps. The 168-acre Fairy Stone Lake is the park's centerpiece. Visitors can fish for bass, sunfish, channel catfish, and crappie. Game department samplings have turned up good numbers of largemouth bass in the lake, including some 8-pounders.

Directions: From Martinsville, take VA 57 west about 17 miles and go right on VA 346 about 1 mile to park.

Activities: Camping, hiking, mountain biking, picnicking, swimming, boating (electric motors only), fishing, interpretive programs.

Facilities: Cabins, 14 miles of trails, lake, rowboat and paddleboat rental, swimming beach, picnic area and shelter, amphitheater, visitor center, 51 campsites with hookups, bathhouse.

Dates: Hiking, biking, and boating permitted year-round. Campgrounds and cabins available spring–fall. Swimming and visitor center open Memorial Day–Labor Day.

Fees: There is a fee for day use, camping, cabins, and rental boats.

Closest town: Martinsville is 17 miles east.

For more information: Fairy Stone State Park, Route 2, Box 723, Stuart, VA 24171. Phone (540) 930-2424.

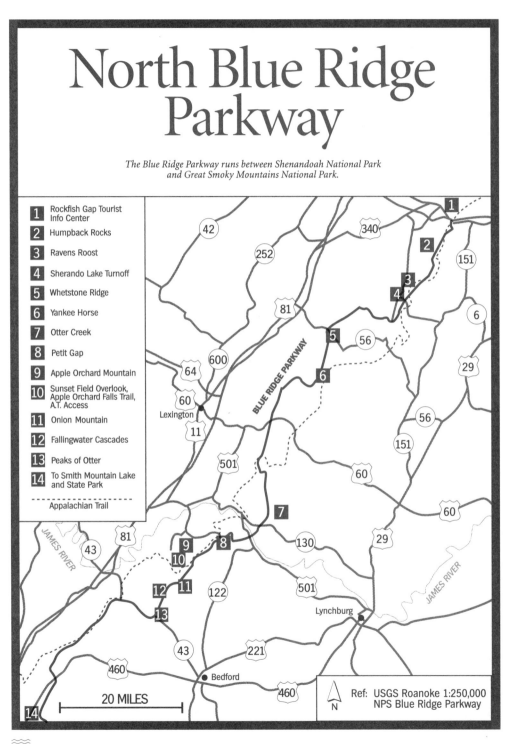

North Blue Ridge Parkway

The Blue Ridge Parkway runs between Shenandoah National Park and Great Smoky Mountains National Park.

1 Rockfish Gap Tourist Info Center
2 Humpback Rocks
3 Ravens Roost
4 Sherando Lake Turnoff
5 Whetstone Ridge
6 Yankee Horse
7 Otter Creek
8 Petit Gap
9 Apple Orchard Mountain
10 Sunset Field Overlook, Apple Orchard Falls Trail, A.T. Access
11 Onion Mountain
12 Fallingwater Cascades
13 Peaks of Otter
14 To Smith Mountain Lake and State Park
------ Appalachian Trail

Ref: USGS Roanoke 1:250,000
NPS Blue Ridge Parkway

20 MILES

Blue Ridge Parkway

[Fig. 37, Fig. 38] The road-among-the-clouds meanders 469 scenic miles without a stop sign or billboard, following the sinewy crest of the Blue Ridge from the Shenandoah National Park in Virginia to Great Smoky Mountains National Park on the North Carolina/Tennessee state line. On its northern end, at Rockfish Gap near Waynesboro, it connects with the Skyline Drive. Skyline Drive continues north along the crest of the Blue Ridge another 105 miles, finally coming down from the heights at Front Royal in northern Virginia. The low point on the Parkway is 649 feet elevation on the James River. The highest point is at Richland Balsam in North Carolina at 6,053 feet.

In Virginia, the Parkway climbs to 3,950 feet at mile 76.5 on Apple Orchard Mountain. (This point is just south of where Rockbridge, Botetourt, and Bedford counties meet.) Although more than 2,100 feet lower than North Carolina's Parkway heights, the altitude and exposure are severe enough to stunt the wind-sculpted red oaks on the ridgeline.

Virginia Senator Harry F. Byrd was largely responsible for getting a bill through Congress authorizing Depression-era funding for the Blue Ridge Parkway. His idea was to extend Virginia's Skyline Drive southward from Waynesboro and connect Shenandoah National Park to the Great Smoky Mountains National Park.

North Carolina lobbied successfully to keep the southern portion of the highway in North Carolina rather than routing it into neighboring Tennessee. Governors of states north of Virginia were approached about extending the drive northward through their states, but they were not interested. President Franklin D. Roosevelt signed the bill on June 22, 1936, and construction of the mountaintop highway got underway.

Looking at the meandering highway that follows the contour of the ridges, it's difficult to imagine the hardships faced to construct it. Steep terrain, mountainsides eroded by overuse, granite and gneiss bedrock, and extreme winter weather on the ridges presented tremendous obstacles. Skilled Italian and Spanish stonemasons were hired to build sturdy walls and bridges still in place today. The highway was finished 51 years later when the final section was completed September 11, 1987, near Grandfather Mountain, North Carolina.

The Parkway is numbered with concrete mileposts the entire length, beginning with milepost 0 at Rockfish Gap. The highway leaves Virginia at the North Carolina state boundary at mile 216.9. The speed limit on the Parkway is 45 miles per hour and is strictly enforced. Roadside parking is permitted wherever there is room to pull 6 to 12 feet off the pavement.

Visitor centers, gasoline, food, lodging, picnicking, hiking, and fishing are available along the highway. Campgrounds, picnic areas, and lodges are open May 1 through October with limited facilities available in winter. Sections of the Parkway are often closed by snow and ice.

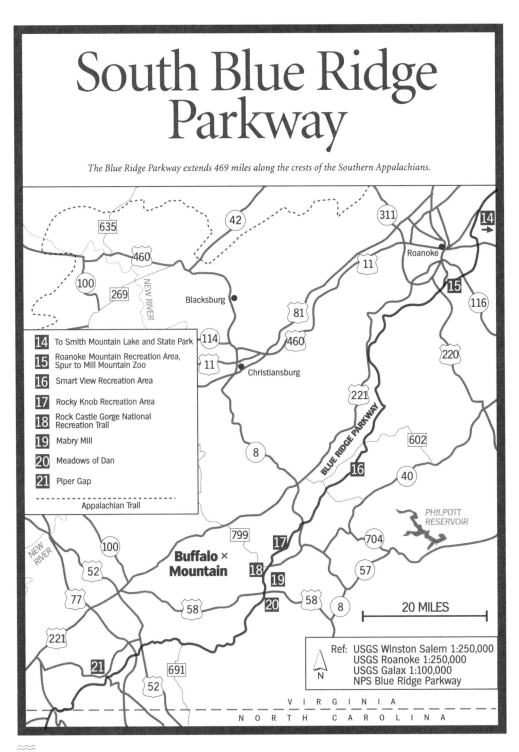

South Blue Ridge Parkway

The Blue Ridge Parkway extends 469 miles along the crests of the Southern Appalachians.

635
42
311
14
→
460
Roanoke
11
100
15
269
NEW RIVER
116
Blacksburg
81
114
460
220
11
Christiansburg
221

14 To Smith Mountain Lake and State Park
15 Roanoke Mountain Recreation Area, Spur to Mill Mountain Zoo
16 Smart View Recreation Area
17 Rocky Knob Recreation Area
18 Rock Castle Gorge National Recreation Trail
19 Mabry Mill
20 Meadows of Dan
21 Piper Gap
- - - - - - - - Appalachian Trail

8
602
BLUE RIDGE PARKWAY
16
40

PHILPOTT RESERVOIR

799
17
704
100
NEW RIVER
Buffalo ×
52
Mountain
18
57
19
77
58
20
58
8
20 MILES
221

Ref: USGS Winston Salem 1:250,000
USGS Roanoke 1:250,000
USGS Galax 1:100,000
NPS Blue Ridge Parkway
21
691
N
52

V I R G I N I A
N O R T H   C A R O L I N A

The National Park Service, which administers a narrow corridor of land that contains the Blue Ridge Parkway, leases farmland along the road in many places to private individuals. National forest lands lie outside this corridor for some 100 miles between the Parkway's northern terminus at Rockfish Gap to just north of Roanoke.

North of the James, the Pedlar Ranger District of the George Washington National Forest, interspersed with private tracts, keeps the Parkway company. South of the James, it's the Glenwood Ranger District of the Jefferson National Forest. Many side trips to waterfalls, interpretive hikes, lakes, campgrounds, and picnic areas are available for travelers. (*See* Pedlar Ranger District, page 275, and Glenwood Ranger District, page 265.)

Those who drive the Parkway are treated to natural beauty composed of mountain pastures and farms, old barns, chestnut rail fences, and fields of cabbage and corn, less intruded upon by commercialization than other parkways and interstates.

But recently, the view from the Parkway has been deteriorating. Modern building materials such as vinyl and aluminum are not always as pleasing to the eye as the silos, wooden barns, and shake shingles of yesteryear. Rotting rail fences are slowly giving way to barbed wire with yellow connectors. With no cable to bring television to the mountaintop, satellite dishes spring up like weeds. Instead of being stored in rustic barns, hay bales are covered with black plastic—described by one observer as looking like giant dinosaur eggs. It's no different from changes happening elsewhere, but some feel the Parkway needs a helping hand to preserve the rustic, somnolent beauty that still brings visitors in droves.

So Parkway administrators are working with coalitions of interested citizens to protect and restore the appearance. Solutions lie in such tactics as giving tax credits to farmers who lease land along the Parkway for adhering to visual guidelines, lobbying for a share of federal funds to maintain old stone walls, and finding groups to adopt rail fences or wooden barns.

One such group is Friends of the Blue Ridge Parkway, a nonprofit, volunteer organization dedicated to preserving and protecting the highway as a national

RACCOON
(*Procyon lotor*)
The raccoon often appears to wash its food, resulting in its Latin name, "lotor," meaning "a washer."

treasure. Programs focus on conservation, preservation, education, and advocacy.

In an effort to curb encroaching development, the newly organized Blue Ridge Parkway Foundation encourages people to leave money in their wills to buy land and conservation easements along the Parkway.

Also, polluted air from modern industry has gradually compromised visibility along the Parkway and the Skyline Drive. Crystal-clear days when the Alleghenies to the west are starkly outlined are now the exception instead of the rule.

Despite the gradual changes, the highway along the Blue Ridge remains a destination for travelers in Virginia and North Carolina. Spring displays of rhododendron, mountain laurel, and azalea are stunning against the hazy backdrop of blue and green peaks and valleys.

In fall, when the air is perhaps clearest, motorists flock to the Blue Ridge to see foliage that is brilliant against the blue October sky over the mountains. Dogwood, sourwood, sugar maple, and tupelo (black gum) turn deep red. Tulip poplars and hickories become bright yellow. Oaks add refinement with their more subtle bronzes, crimsons, rusts, and golds.

Along the roadsides are a variety of wildflowers and flowering trees and shrubs. Many travelers time their visits to coincide with the showiest display of all—the rhododendron bloom in June. But from the earliest spring bloomers such as shadbush (serviceberry) and redbud in April, through the dogwood, azalea, and mountain laurel bloom, there's plenty of color to make a drive or hike worthwhile.

Wildflowers such as Queen Anne's lace (*Daucus carota*), joe-pye-weed (*Eupatorium purpureum*), black cohosh (*Cimicifuga racemosa*), and goldenrod (*Solidago*) are obvious from a car window. But, as with wildflowers everywhere, some Parkway wildflowers grow close to the ground and are unremarkable until viewed up close. Their colorful common names provide helpful tips in committing them to memory.

In spring, colonies of trout lily (*Erythronium americanum*) produce single yellow flowers between two basal leaves with brown spots, similar to the markings on brown and brook trout. The flower's other name, dogtooth violet, refers to the fanglike shape of the underground bulb. Another low-grower is coltsfoot (*Tusilago farfara*). It has a yellow dandelionlike flower, but the hoofprint-shaped leaf which suggests its name is very unlike a dandelion. The scaly stem resembles that of Indian pipe (*Monotropa uniflora*). Pussytoes (*Antennaria plantaginfolia*), a cluster of small fuzzy white flowers resembling a cat's paw, are also found here.

Wildlife is abundant on the Parkway, but not as visible as along the Skyline Drive. Because the Drive passes through the Shenandoah National Park where no hunting is allowed, deer, wild turkey, and even the occasional black bear, bobcat, and fox are less shy. Groundhogs sit erect along the roadsides and chipmunks entertain campers as they scurry back and forth from burrows under logs or roots.

Hawk Migration
and the Blue Ridge Parkway

From early September through November, hawks and other birds of prey from the northern section of the United States begin a migration to the southern latitudes for winter—to Mexico, Central America, and South America.

The birds use the mountain ridges that make up the Appalachian range for their avian highway. This highway includes the Blue Ridge and, to a smaller extent, the Allegheny Mountains of Virginia to the west.

The mountain updrafts permit the soaring hawks to travel long distances with little effort. The late naturalist Edwin Way Teale once rented a plane to fly with the migrating hawks. He was astonished to find that the birds use the updrafts so efficiently that they occasionally travel hundreds of miles without a single wing beat.

"Hawk" migration is a bit of a misnomer. Eagles, kestrels, vultures, ospreys, and peregrine falcons also join the exodus, but the bulk of the migration is made up of buteos (broad-winged, red-tailed, and red-shouldered hawks) and the more slender, agile accipiters such as Cooper's and sharp-shinned hawks.

How many migrators come pouring down the crest of Virginia's mountains each fall? No one is sure, but the numbers are staggering. Virginia has about 10 established hawk lookouts where volunteers sit all day and attempt to count the birds going by in September and October. Most lookouts are in the mountains where ridges run northeast to southwest, the direction the birds are headed.

One day in 1985, a motherlode of hawks came by Rockfish Gap at milepost 0 on the Blue Ridge Parkway. Watchers estimated that 10,000 broad-winged hawks passed by the mountain gap that memorable September 15. At another favorite spot—Linden Fire Tower in northern Virginia—birders counted more than 17,000 broad-wings on a single day during the third week of September.

Visitors can hawk-watch from almost any overlook along the two mountain highways—the Skyline Drive and the Blue Ridge Parkway—that follow the spine of the Blue Ridge range. A certain amount of luck is involved in choosing a day when hundreds of birds pass by.

Hawks often travel in "kettles," or spiraling columns of birds, that tower so high the birds may appear little more than windblown specks. Seven-power binoculars will aid in identification. The best time to spot hawks is 10 a.m. to noon and 2 p.m. to 4 p.m.—after the sun warms the air currents, with a respite in the middle of the day. The week of September 15 is normally the peak of the migration, with the week of October 1 offering the most variety. A volunteer organization called the Hawk Migration Association of North America keeps records on migrations and publishes a newsletter.

Directions: The Blue Ridge Parkway comes into Virginia from North Carolina in Grayson County, a 7-mile drive south from Galax on VA 89. To access northern end of Blue Ridge Parkway (also southern end of Skyline Drive), drive 4 miles east from Waynesboro in Augusta County on US 250 to top of Afton Mountain, turn right after you go under interstate bridge, and follow signs.

Activities: Scenic drive, hiking, biking, picnicking, camping, fishing, interpretive programs, cross-country skiing, mountain climbing, and hanggliding.

Facilities: In Virginia, 4 campgrounds, 1 lodge, housekeeping cabins, 1 gas station, 4 visitor centers, 4 restaurants, 6 picnic areas, along with numerous tables at overlooks, 3 self-guided trails plus other hiking trails, fishing lakes, and streams. *See* Mileposts, page 259.

Dates: Parkway is open year-round, unless snow and ice force winter closings. Peaks of Otter Lodge is open year-round. Rocky Knob cabins are open June–Labor Day. Services and facilities elsewhere are open May 1–Oct. 31.

Fees: There is no charge for scenic drives. There is a charge for camping and lodging.

Closest town: Waynesboro, in Augusta County, is 3 miles west of northern end of Parkway. Roanoke, the largest city on the Parkway, is 2 miles west of Parkway near Milepost 222 via US 220. Galax, on border of Carroll and Grayson counties, is 7 miles north of Parkway's entrance into North Carolina. Access also available from many towns along the Parkway.

For more information: Peaks of Otter Lodge, PO Box 489, Bedford, VA 24523. Phone (800) 542-5927 or (540) 586-1081. Rocky Knob Cabins, National Park Concessions, Inc., Meadows of Dan, VA 24120. Phone (540) 593-3503. Parkway Headquarters, 400 BBT Building, Asheville, NC 28801. Phone (704) 271-4779. (*See* Appendix B for events and organizations related to the Blue Ridge Parkway.)

HIKING, BIKING, AND FISHING THE BLUE RIDGE PARKWAY

Forty-five hiking trails lead from the Parkway to interesting rock formations, waterfalls, fishing lakes, rhododendron thickets, and meadows of wildflowers. Some of these are covered in more detail in Mileposts (p. 259) or with descriptions of the Pedlar (p. 275) and Glenwood (p. 265) ranger districts of the national forest. The Appalachian Trail roughly parallels the Parkway from mile 0 at Rockfish Gap to mile 103 north of Roanoke, although the trail and road are miles apart for much of that stretch. The AT crosses the Parkway at mile 51.5, mile 74.9, mile 76.3, mile 90.9, and mile 97. AT access is also available as it runs near the Parkway at mile 71, mile 74.7, mile 78.4, and mile 80.5 (shelter available). At mile 103, the AT takes off across the Great Valley of Virginia for the western Virginia mountains, leaving the Parkway for the remainder of the highway's southern stretch in Virginia. (For more on the AT, see page 303.)

Bicyclists are allowed to use both the Blue Ridge Parkway and the Skyline Drive, but bicycling is discouraged on the Skyline Drive. The Parkway administration has

The stunning view from Ravens Roost at mile 10.7 on the Blue Ridge Parkway is unforgettable.

safety recommendations, a list of elevation changes on specific portions of highway, and overnight planning tips for bicyclists. Sudden changes in weather should be expected in all seasons. Elevations that range from 600 feet to 6,000 feet can be challenging, but gentle grades are the rule, and the effort is rewarded by picturesque travel across two states.

A state fishing license is required to fish streams and lakes along the Parkway. Creel limits and regulations, which vary from year to year, are available from the Virginia Department of Game and Inland Fisheries.

IMPORTANT BLUE RIDGE PARKWAY MILEPOSTS
Mile 0: Rockfish Gap. [Fig. 37(1)] Tourist Information Center, behind gas station, US 250 and I-64.

Mile 5.8: Humpback Rocks. [Fig. 37(2)] Small visitor center and self-guided trail through authentic mountain farmstead, moved from another site. Hiking trail from parking area (at mile 6.1) leads .75 mile to The Rocks, a humped outcropping visible for miles from the Shenandoah Valley below.

Mile 10.7: Ravens Roost. [Fig. 37(3)] Mountain climbers and hanggliders practice their skills from the rocky outcrops at the parking lot. Views of Torry Ridge and Shenandoah Valley to west.

Mile 16: Sherando Lake turnoff. [Fig. 37(4)] Visitor center operated by Nelson County Tourism. Recreation area in George Washington National Forest (*see* Pedlar Ranger District, page 275) is 4.5 miles from Parkway via VA 814.

Mile 29: Whetstone Ridge. [Fig. 37(5)] Named for a sharpening stone used by mountain people and created from fine-grained sandstone found in the ridge. Restaurant.

Mile 34.4: Yankee Horse. [Fig. 37(6)] According to stories, a Union soldier's horse fell here during the Civil War and had to be shot. See reconstructed spur of old logging railroad by taking a short walk to Wiggam Falls.

Mile 58 to 63.6: Otter Creek. [Fig. 37(7)] Runs 10 miles down the Blue Ridge to James River. Campground, restaurant, gas (mile 60.8), interpretive programs. Otter Lake (mile 63.1) offers fishing, trail. Exhibit shelter (mile 63.6) interprets James River and Kanawha Canal. There is a footbridge across James to restored canal lock and a self-guided trail from shelter along river bluff.

Mile 71: Petit Gap. [Fig. 37(8)] Derived from early settler named "Poteet." Road to west (FR 35) leads 7 miles to Cave Mountain Lake Recreation Area. Glenwood Ranger District. Swimming, picnicking, camping.

Mile 76.5: Apple Orchard Mountain. [Fig. 37(9)] Parkway climbs to 3,950 feet, its highest altitude in Virginia. Pines such as table mountain pine, pitch pine, and Virginia pine and northern tree species such as yellow birch, northern red oak, red spruce, and American mountain-ash face a harsh existence on the exposed summit.

The shrubby mountain ash (*Sorbus americana*) has a rounded crown and feathery, pinnately compound leaves. The flat-topped clusters of white flowers produce distinctive, bright, red-orange berries by August. Squirrels, ruffed grouse, and songbirds find them more palatable than do humans. Along the ridge, note the unusual abundance of persimmon trees (*Diospyros virginiana*), a southern species

RED-EYE VIREO
(*Vireo olivaceus*)
This vireo is identified by its white stripe above red eyes and by its persistent singing.

usually associated with rich bottomlands. If the fruits are absent, the persimmon can be identified by its charcoal-colored bark, broken into small squarish blocks. Shining a light into a persimmon tree at night may reveal the reflected eyes of most any nocturnal critter. As the fleshy fruits of persimmons ripen in fall, raccoons, opossums, deer, wild turkeys, songbirds—almost all animals—find them irresistible. People also

PITCH PINE
(Pinus rigida)

enjoy the pale orange-colored fruits when they are soft and fully ripe. However, persimmons still a bit green have an astringence that is memorable. The season's first frost is usually a signal to give them a cautious try.

Mile 78.4: Sunset Field Overlook, Apple Orchard Falls Trail, AT access. [Fig. 37(10)] Take 1.2-mile (one-way) trek to spectacular falls that drops 200 feet in series of cascades. At 1.1 miles, the trail passes a huge overhanging rock on the right—a good shelter in a storm. At 1.2 miles, add a steep extra .2 mile to view the falls from below. Turn back here or continue trail down mountain. Trail enters headwaters of North Creek, following old woods road downstream. Streamside wildflowers are abundant. At 3.4 miles is FR 59 and lower trailhead parking (*see* Glenwood Ranger District, page 265).

Directions: For lower trailhead, at Exit 168 on I-81, about 2 miles north of Buchanan, go 3 miles southeast on VA 614. Turn left on FR 59 and go 4.5 miles to trailhead.

Trail: 1.2-mile (one-way) hike to falls or 3.4 miles (one-way) to bottom. AT crossing is at .2 mile.

Elevation: 1,500 feet to 3,500 feet.

Degree of difficulty: Moderate, with strenuous section from falls to bottom.

Surface and blaze: Natural forest floor. Blue blaze.

Mile 79.7: Onion Mountain. [Fig. 37(11)] Short loop trail through rhododendron and mountain laurel thickets.

Mile 83.4: Fallingwater Cascades. [Fig. 37(12)] Visible along a steep 1.6-mile loop trail shaded by rhododendron and hemlock. Glenwood Ranger District.

Mile 84 to 87: Peaks of Otter. [Fig. 37(19)] Historic destination point for many travelers. Lodge and restaurant (mile 85.6), visitor center with exhibits (mile 86). Gasoline, campgrounds, picnic area, shuttle bus, and steep trail to scenic summit of Sharp Top (3,875 feet). Sharp Top and Flat Top (elevation, 4,001 feet) are Peaks of Otter, forming headwaters of Otter River. Fallingwater Cascades Trail and Flat Top Trail combine to make National Recreation Trail that includes a cascading mountain creek, rocky outcrops with top-of-the-world views. Shuttle (fee) to Sharp Top for those who don't want to make the short, steep climb.

Mile 112.2: Smith Mountain Lake and State Park. [Fig. 39, Fig. 37(14), Fig.

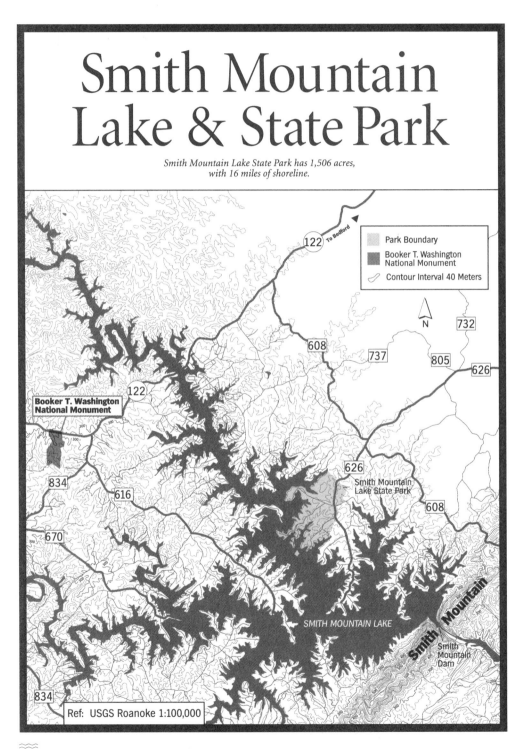

Smith Mountain Lake & State Park

*Smith Mountain Lake State Park has 1,506 acres,
with 16 miles of shoreline.*

122 To Bedford

Park Boundary

Booker T. Washington
National Monument

Contour Interval 40 Meters

N

732

608

737

805

626

122

Booker T. Washington
National Monument

834

616

626

Smith Mountain
Lake State Park

608

670

834

SMITH MOUNTAIN LAKE

Smith Mountain

Smith
Mountain
Dam

Ref: USGS Roanoke 1:100,000

38(14)] VA 24 leads east to sprawling Smith Mountain Lake in the foothills of the Blue Ridge. To create this second-largest body of fresh water in Virginia (Buggs Island Lake is the largest), the Roanoke River was dammed in 1960 as a power source, backing up 20,000 acres of water. The state stocks muskie, walleye, and striped bass.

In addition to several private facilities around the lake, including campgrounds, restaurants, and marinas, Smith Mountain Lake State Park occupies 16 miles of shoreline on the north side. Facilities at the park include miles of hiking trails, 500-foot swimming beach, boat ramp, campground, and interpretive programs. Park interpreters teach wilderness skills, conduct twilight programs, and guide canoe trips on the lake. Call (540) 297-6066 for a brochure. To get to the park, go east 18 miles on VA 24, then south on VA 735, VA 732, and VA 626.

Mile 120.3: Roanoke Mountain Recreation Area. [Fig. 38(15)] Outstanding views from 4-mile side trip on Roanoke Mountain. Popular launch site for hang-gliders. Camping, hiking, interpretive programs.

Mile 120.4: Spur to Mill Mountain Zoo. [Fig. 38(15)] Follow signs for 3-mile side trip to small zoo with 45 species of exotic and native animals on 10-acre site. Unadvertised highlight is a garden of propagated wildflowers established by local horticultural society.

Mile 154.5: Smart View Recreation Area. [Fig. 38(16)] Picnicking, hiking. Along Smart View Trail are redbud, sassafras, pink and flame azaleas, columbine, yellow stargrass, fire pink, beard tongue, deptford pink.

Mile 167 to 174: Rocky Knob Recreation Area. [Fig. 38(17)] Rocky Knob (elevation 3,572 feet) rises from the plateau like the crest of a wave. Visitor center, spacious campground, interpretive programs, Rock Castle Gorge National Recreation Trail and other trails, picnic area, housekeeping cabins.

Note grove of Chinese chestnuts in campground, planted in 1952 in attempt to find species to replace American chestnut, wiped out by blight. However, the Chinese variety does not grow tall enough for timber production and does not produce as many chestnuts as the American variety.

ROCK CASTLE GORGE NATIONAL RECREATION TRAIL. [Fig. 38(18)] The Rock Castle Gorge Trail, valued for its scenery, waterfalls, old homesites, and fishing, was designated a National Recreation Trail in 1982. The strenuous hike is a 10.6-mile loop combining scenic Blue Ridge Parkway overlooks and a climb up Rocky Knob with a trip into Rock Castle Gorge. At Rocky Knob is a log shelter constructed by the Civilian Conservation Corps in the 1930s. In the gorge, anglers wade Rock Castle Creek to try for native brook trout (single hooks, artificial lures only). Tall poplars shade a primitive campground on the creek. The name "Rock Castle" comes from quartzite crystals found in the hollows. The crystals have a six-sided shape resembling castle towers. Trailheads are at several overlooks between mile 167 and 174.

BUFFALO MOUNTAIN. [Fig. 38] From The Saddle, a swale between peaks of Rocky Knob, the humped form of Buffalo Mountain can be seen rising from the plateau to the southwest. Buffalo Mountain, recently acquired by the state as a Natural Area Preserve, is one of the most significant natural areas in Virginia.

The combination of high elevation (3,971 feet), wind-exposed openings at the summit, and magnesium-rich soils make Buffalo Mountain unique. Subalpine vegetation such as three-toothed cinquefoil and Rocky Mountain woodsia grow on the windy, treeless summit.

The south face of the mountain contains grassy, prairielike openings with mid-western grasses and wildflowers such as big bluestem and blazing star. Wet seeps along the base of the mountain support globally rare grasses and wildflowers such as bog bluegrass and large-leaved grass-of-parnassus. The Buffalo is the only known location in the world for a mealybug called *Puto kosztarabi*. The new preserve is not yet open for public visitation.

For more information: Virginia Department of Conservation and Recreation, Division of Natural Heritage, 1500 E. Main Street, Suite 312, Richmond, VA 23219. Phone (804) 786-7951.

Mile 176.1: Mabry Mill. [Fig. 38(19)] One of the most photographed mills in the world, Mabry was operated by E. B. Mabry from 1910 to 1935. A trail leads to the gristmill, sawmill, and blacksmith shop. Old-time skills are demonstrated in summer. A restaurant and gift shop are located here.

Mile 177.7: Meadows of Dan. [Fig. 38(20)] Mountain community with restaurants, crafts, gift shops, homemade goods. Stocked and native trout fishing in scenic headwaters of Dan River and around Pinnacles of Dan to the southeast.

For more information: Virginia Department of Game and Inland Fisheries, Region II, 910 Thomas Jefferson Road, Forest, VA 24551-9223. Phone (804) 525-7522.

Mile 206.1: Piper Gap. [Fig. 38(21)] Crooked Creek Wildlife Management Area—a fee fishing area where just about anyone can catch trout—is about 5 miles west on VA 620. From mid-March through Labor Day, Crooked Creek is stocked with scrappy, flashing trout every night except Sunday. Three miles of the stream are stocked by the state fish and game department and 3 miles are left as native brook trout waters. A well-stocked concession stand sells licenses, permits, and snacks.

Mile 216.9: North Carolina/Virginia state line.

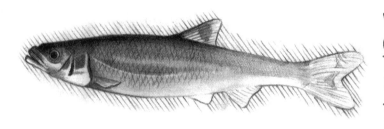

WARPAINT SHINER

(Luxilus coccogenis)
Deriving its name from its bright red cheeks, this shiner grows to 5 inches long.

Glenwood Ranger District

The Glenwood Ranger District, the northernmost district of the Jefferson National Forest, is in the mountains of the Blue Ridge northeast of Roanoke and just east and south of the James River in Botetourt and Rockbridge counties. Interstate 81 and the towns of Troutville, Buchanan, and Glasgow are on the western side.

The major tract of the district's 74,128 mountainous acres lies between the James River on the west and the crest of the Blue Ridge Mountains on the east. On the northern end, the James turns east and cuts through the Blue Ridge to enter the Piedmont. Just north of the river is the Pedlar Ranger District, the southernmost district of the George Washington National Forest. A 53-mile stretch of the 2,150-mile Appalachian Trail (AT) and 40 miles of the Blue Ridge Parkway run southwest/northeast through the district.

For 13 miles on the southern end, the Glenwood becomes a narrow band bordering the Blue Ridge Parkway. Another small tract lies on North Mountain to the west, across the Great Valley of Virginia where Alleghany, Botetourt, and Rockbridge counties meet. This little piece of the Glenwood abuts the James River District's eastern border.

Two wilderness areas—James River Face [Fig. 40(10), Fig. 41] and Thunder Ridge [Fig. 40(11), Fig. 41]—protect 11,500 acres of some of the most rugged, wild, and botanically diverse mountains in the state.

Cave Mountain Lake Recreation Area [Fig. 40(12)], a hub of activity on the Glenwood, is located near the northeastern end of the district at one of very few places that's not steep. North Creek Campground [Fig. 40(13)], in the heart of the district east of Buchanan, is the perfect base camp for trout anglers, hikers, wildlife watchers, and naturalists. Backcountry camping is permitted anywhere in the national forest except where posted. Commercial campgrounds are also in the area.

The district is known by area anglers for both its warm-water and cold-water fishing, by hikers and equestrians for its challenging trails, and by paddlers in the James River Gorge for the spectacular scenery of James River Face Wilderness.

The Glenwood Information Center is located in Natural Bridge [Fig. 40(8)] near the intersection of US 11 and VA 130. The district office is about 1.5 miles south of Natural Bridge on VA 130.

For more information: Glenwood Ranger District, PO Box 10, Natural Bridge Station, VA 24579. Phone (540) 291-2189.

FLORA AND FAUNA OF THE GLENWOOD DISTRICT

White-tailed deer and wild turkeys are abundant, as are smaller animals such as squirrels, rabbits, raccoons, foxes, opossums, and chipmunks. Black bears, normally solitary creatures, are spotted from time to time in a patch of blueberrries. In summer, during the breeding season of bears, a male may follow a female along a

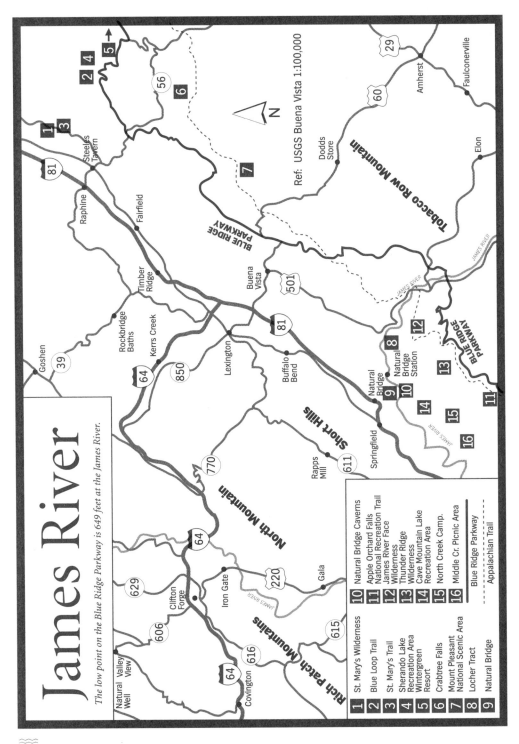

James River

The low point on the Blue Ridge Parkway is 649 feet at the James River.

Ref: USGS Buena Vista 1:100,000

1	St. Mary's Wilderness	10	Natural Bridge Caverns
2	Blue Loop Trail	11	Apple Orchard Falls National Recreation Trail
3	St. Mary's Trail	12	James River Face Wilderness
4	Sherando Lake Recreation Area	13	Thunder Ridge Wilderness
5	Wintergreen Resort	14	Cave Mountain Lake Recreation Area
6	Crabtree Falls	15	North Creek Camp.
7	Mount Pleasant National Scenic Area	16	Middle Cr. Picnic Area
8	Locher Tract		Blue Ridge Parkway
9	Natural Bridge		Appalachian Trail

slope as they methodically lift rocks in an endless search for grubs, ants, or sala-manders. Bears will even endure hornet stings to get at the larvae in a nest.

A rich variety of plant and animal communities accompanies the various habitats of the district. In thickets at the edge of Cave Mountain Lake you may hear the slow "kaup-kaup-kaup" of the elusive yellow-billed cuckoo. The jay-sized "rain crow" often calls before an approaching storm.

Along streamsides and along the James River are spring peeper frogs, cricket frogs, salamanders, turtles, and water snakes. Honeysuckle, blackberries, multiflora rose, jewelweed, and New Jersey tea (*Ceanothus americanus*) thrive along streams, road-sides, and the edges of woods. Fast-growing pokeweed (*Phytolacca americana*) rises to heights of 10 feet seemingly overnight, giving credence to the phrase "growing like a weed."

Large hemlocks, tulip poplars, and white basswood grow in protected coves above an understory of rhododendron, red maple, greenbrier, grape, poison ivy, and a rich variety of other plants. Such areas attract hooded warblers, Carolina chickadees, Carolina wrens, and wood thrushes, to name a few.

On the dry slopes, under a canopy of hickories, white and red oaks, and pines is an understory of red maples, witch-hazel, black gum, flowering dogwood, highbush blueberry, deerberry, and mountain laurel. Emerging through the leaf litter in spring and summer are such wildflowers as wood lily (*Lilium philadelphicum*), bloodroot (*Sanguinaria canadensis*), large-flowering trillium (*Trillium grandiflora*), and pale, saprophytic Indian pipe (*Monotropa uniflora*). Indian pipe is white because it does not produce chlorophyll. For nourishment it depends instead on mycorrhiza—an association between a fungus and its roots. Tiny evergreen plants such as pipsissewa (*Chimaphila maculata*), spotted wintergreen (*Chimaphila umbellata*), and galax (*Galax rotundifolia*) add their flowers to the mix.

Galax can be identified by its shiny, dark, evergreen, heart-shaped leaves growing just above the ground. In early summer, a long stalk with milk-white flowers rises above the leaves.

On the high ridges are red and white oak, chestnut oak, pitch pine, and trees of northern forests such as yellow birch, table mountain pine, northern red oak, and even a few red spruce. In many areas of the Glenwood District, the southern pine beetle is devastating stands of southern varieties of pine. When populations are high enough, even Eastern white pines are affected. Some of these white pines grow along North Creek—an important trout fishery. An appreciable increase in sunlight through a destroyed canopy could make the water too warm for trout. Entire plant and animal communities become dependent on both the shade and nutrients in the soil beneath a stand of pines.

The hemlock wooly adelgid is infesting hemlocks in sheltered ravines. Hemlocks also provide shade for mountain trout streams and associated plants, insects, birds, and wildlife.

RECREATION AREAS OF GLENWOOD RANGER DISTRICT

Recreation on the Glenwood District is based at four areas—Cave Mountain Lake Recreation Area, Middle Creek Picnic Area, North Creek Campground, and Hopper Creek Group Campground. The Locher Tract, a grassy area on the James River, provides an overnight camping spot for those floating the James River or a base camp for exploring the James River Face Wilderness. All areas are in the wide portion of the Glenwood Ranger District bordered by the James River between Buchanan and Glasgow. The Hopper Creek group facility, open year-round, offers a private area in the northern end of the district for groups of up to 50 people. Reservations are required.

CAVE MOUNTAIN LAKE RECREATION AREA. [Fig. 40(12)] Scenic Cave Mountain Lake is the centerpiece of this recreation area—easily the most popular spot on the district. A swimming beach, bathhouse, and hookups for the campsites add to its appeal as a family campground. Adjacent to the beach is a large grassy field for sunning and games. Reservations are required for a group picnic area and log picnic shelter.

The Wildcat Mountain Trail, a 4-mile loop over rough terrain, was developed primarily for use by campers. Heading south from the campground, it climbs from 1,200 feet at the campground to 2,700 feet on Wildcat Mountain.

Directions: Located in the southern tip of Rockbridge County, 8 miles south of Natural Bridge. From Natural Bridge, go 3.2 miles east on VA 130. Turn right on VA 759 and go 3.2 miles. Turn right on VA 781 and go 1.6 miles to entrance.

Activities: Camping, hiking, picnicking, seasonal hunting in surrounding national forest, interpretive programs, swimming.

Facilities: 42 campsites (electrical and water hookups, tables, lantern posts), flush toilets, handicapped-accessible bathhouse with warm showers, trailer waste disposal

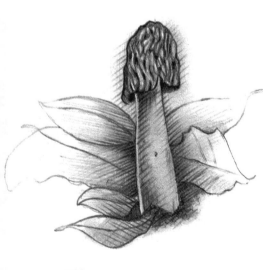

EARLY MOREL

(Verpa bohemica)
Growing up to 4 inches tall, this morel is identified by a yellow-brown, bell-shaped cap atop a hollow, light-colored stem. It grows in wet areas.

station, 300-foot swimming beach, group picnic area and shelter (reservations required), hiking trails.

Dates: Open May 1–first week in Nov. Swimming beach open during summer.

Fees: There is a charge for day use, camping, group picnic area.

Closest town: Natural Bridge is 8 miles north.

For more information: Glenwood Ranger District, PO Box 10, Natural Bridge Station, VA 24579. Phone (540) 291-2189.

MIDDLE CREEK PICNIC AREA. [Fig. 40(14)] This attractive creekside picnic area near Buchanan provides shade for family outings and proximity to stocked trout waters for anglers. The Appalachian Trail comes through the area.

Directions: From I-81, Exit 168, about 2 miles north of Buchanan, go 4.7 miles east on VA 614. Turn left on VA 618 to picnic area. The area is also accessible from Powell Gap on the Blue Ridge Parkway, near milepost 91, via VA 618. The road follows McFalls Creek (wild trout fishery) down McFalls Ridge. At the confluence of McFalls Creek and Jennings Creek, go left on VA 614. Picnic area is on the right.

Activities: Picnicking, fishing, hiking, seasonal hunting.

Facilities: 10 picnic sites, drinking water, vault toilets, trout stream.

Dates: Open year-round.

Fees: None.

Closest town: Buchanan is 6.7 miles west.

For more information: Glenwood Ranger District, PO Box 10, Natural Bridge Station, VA 24579. Phone (540) 291-2189.

NORTH CREEK CAMPGROUND. [Fig. 40(13)] This more primitive area is in an area of the national forest where conservation and appreciation of natural habitat take precedence over timber production. North Creek, a cold-water trout stream, drains a scenic deep hollow below 200-foot Apple Orchard Falls. The giant snail-eating ground beetle (*Scaphinotis webbi*) and oak fern (*Gymnocarpium dropteris*) are among rare species in 1,825 acres under protection. Despite its primitive nature, the campground is popular and can be full during peak season. Arrive early to assure yourself a site.

Directions: From I-81, about 2 miles north of Buchanan, take Exit 168 and drive 3 miles southeast on VA 614. Turn left on FR 59 and go 2.4 miles to campground. (For lower terminus of Apple Creek Falls and Cornelius trails, go 2 miles farther.)

Activities: Primitive camping, hiking, fishing for native and stocked trout, seasonal hunting.

Facilities: 16 primitive campsites, drinking water, vault toilets, hiking trails, stocked and native trout stream.

Dates: Open year-round.

Fees: There is a charge for camping.

Closest town: Buchanan is 7.4 miles west.

LOCHER TRACT. [Fig. 40(7)] The Locher Tract is a primitive picnic area (no tables or running water) consisting of an open grassy field on the James River. A .7-mile nature trail runs along the river, through the woods, and around a beaver pond. Wildlife openings, nesting boxes, grazing areas, and wetlands attract a variety of songbirds, waterfowl, wading birds, amphibians, frogs, and salamanders. Wildflower species are also diverse. Bring insect repellent in warm weather. In addition to the nature trail, the trailhead for the 4.1-mile Balcony Falls Trail is here.

Directions: From Natural Bridge on US 11 (off I-81, Exit 175 or 180), follow VA 130 south for 3.2 miles. Turn right on VA 759 and drive .9 mile. Turn left on VA 782. Where the paved road makes a sharp right turn, just past James River Recreation Area, keep straight on gravel road. Go about .7 mile on VA 782 and FR 3093 to Locher Tract and Balcony Falls trailhead.

Activities: Fishing, primitive camping, picnicking, hiking.

Facilities: Hiking trails.

Dates: Open year-round.

Fees: None.

Closest town: Natural Bridge is about 6 miles west.

For more information: Glenwood Ranger District, PO Box 10, Natural Bridge Station, VA 24579. Phone (540) 291-2189.

THE TRAILS OF GLENWOOD RANGER DISTRICT

Besides the 53-mile section of Appalachian Trail (AT) running the length of the district, hiking trails lace the area and some are open to equestrians. The 65-mile Glenwood Horse Trail, completed in the early 1990s, provides outstanding riding on terrain varying from gravel roads to difficult single-track trails through mountainous terrain. Area clubs and individuals help take care of the trail. In fact, despite the rough terrain of the Glenwood, most trails are surprisingly well kept, well signed, and easy to follow. That's a good thing because these paths lead to beautiful waterfalls, wild trout streams, unusual topography, and spectacular scenery. With the exception of the AT, trails are only lightly used.

APPLE ORCHARD FALLS NATIONAL RECREATION TRAIL. [Fig. 40(6)] This strenuous 3.4-mile (one-way) hike to a spectacular 200-foot cascade can be combined with the 2.9-mile Cornelius Creek Trail for a challenging loop. See section on Blue Ridge Parkway, Mile 78.4, for description from upper trailhead and directions to lower trailhead.

Apple Orchard Mountain and the hollows along North Creek, as with many cool, moist places in the Appalachians, are the preferred habitat of ginseng (*Panax quinquefolium*), a perennial herb. This once-common plant suffers from overcollecting. It has long been used as a mild stimulant and aphrodisiac in the Far East. In an attempt to take pressure off the threatened native plant, commercial growing of ginseng is not considered a violation of the Endangered Plant and Insect Species Act. The white to greenish white flower is surrounded by a whorl of three to five compound leaves.

FISHING THE GLENWOOD DISTRICT

Excellent fishing for smallmouth bass, sunfish, catfish, and muskie is available on the historic James River on the district's border. An especially scenic stretch is where the James cuts a deep gorge through the mountains of the Blue Ridge on the district's northern end (*see* James River, page 324).

Fishing for native and other wild trout is normally reserved for the young and fit who are able to climb into remote hollows to find these cold-water fish. However, in the Glenwood District, state and forest service roads run not only along the stocked trout streams but also along some wild trout waters, making them far more accessible than most trout streams. Sections of North Creek, Middle Creek, and Jennings Creek (marked with white game department signs) are stocked with rainbow, brown, and brook trout. Trout less than 7 inches must be released. No more than six fish may be creeled per day.

The upper section of North Creek (above the first bridge upstream of the North Creek Campground) is designated for special regulations. These special regulations require the use of single-hook artificial lures and the release of all trout of less than 9 inches. The lower portion remains put-and-take fishing for stocked trout. Creel and size limits may vary from season to season. The Glenwood District office or the Virginia Department of Game and Inland Fisheries can provide current regulations.

For more information: For current creel limits, seasons, and license requirements in Rockbridge County waters, contact the Virginia Department of Game and Inland Fisheries (VDGIF), Region IV Office, PO Box 996, Verona, VA 24482. Phone (540) 248-9360. For waters in Botetourt County, contact VDGIF Region II Office, Route 6, Box 410, Forest, VA 24551. Phone (804) 525-7522.

NATURAL BRIDGE AND NATURAL BRIDGE CAVERNS

[[Fig. 40(8), Fig. 23] Natural Bridge in Rockbridge County is one of the Seven Natural Wonders of the World. The 215-foot-high rock span above a narrow gorge lies not near but under the old Valley Pike, US 11. Cedar Creek, which helped sculpt the limestone rock, flows beneath it.

The Monacan Indians marveled at the size of the ancient arch and worshiped it as The Bridge of God. George Washington surveyed it (his initials are still visible on the rock wall), and Thomas Jefferson once owned it. During the Revolutionary War, the bridge was used as a shot tower. Balls of molten lead were dropped from the top, cooled as they fell, and formed round shot.

The bridge is now privately owned but open for public viewing daily. After dark, a sound and light show called *The Drama of Creation* explains how the 215-foot arch came into being. A hike beyond the bridge leads to lace waterfalls. Trees typical of limestone soils, such as northern white cedar and arborvitae, grow along the path. The shaded gorge offers refuge for northern tree species such as hemlock, beech, and yellow birch.

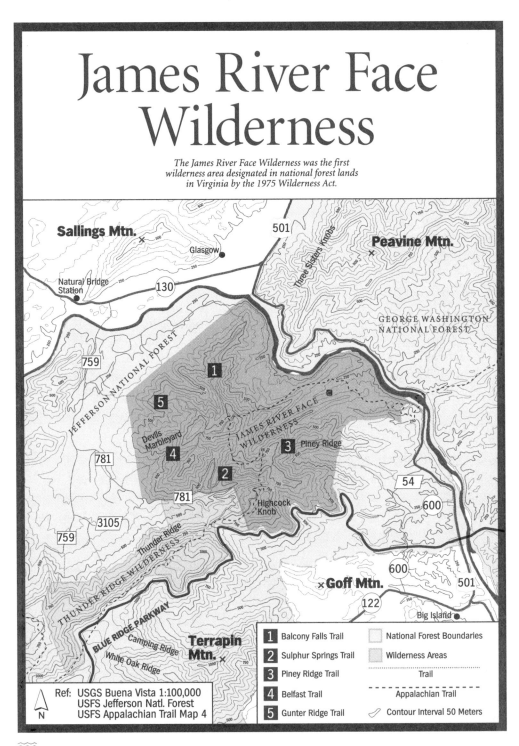

James River Face Wilderness

The James River Face Wilderness was the first
wilderness area designated in national forest lands
in Virginia by the 1975 Wilderness Act.

Sallings Mtn.

Glasgow

501

Peavine Mtn.

Three Sisters Knobs

Natural Bridge
Station

130

GEORGE WASHINGTON
NATIONAL FOREST

759

JEFFERSON NATIONAL FOREST

1

5

Devils
Marbleyard

4

3 Piney Ridge

JAMES RIVER FACE
WILDERNESS

781

2

54

781

Highcock
Knob

600

3105

759

Thunder Ridge

600

THUNDER RIDGE WILDERNESS

Goff Mtn.

501

122

Big Island

BLUE RIDGE PARKWAY

Camping Ridge

White Oak Ridge

Terrapin
Mtn.

1	Balcony Falls Trail		National Forest Boundaries
2	Sulphur Springs Trail		Wilderness Areas
3	Piney Ridge Trail		Trail
4	Belfast Trail		Appalachian Trail
5	Gunter Ridge Trail		Contour Interval 50 Meters

N
Ref: USGS Buena Vista 1:100,000
USFS Jefferson Natl. Forest
USFS Appalachian Trail Map 4

The same chemistry that formed the bridge also created Natural Bridge Caverns. Tours are conducted daily into the labyrinth of underground streams, waterfalls, and catacombs 347 feet below the surface. A wax museum and gift shop with country crafts and homemade candies are nearby.

Directions: From I-81 in Rockbridge County, take Exit 175 and go north on US 11, or Exit 180 and go south on US 11. Follow signs. (US 11 goes over Natural Bridge.)

Activities: Tour to Natural Bridge and into caverns, hiking.

Facilities: Walkways, restaurant, hotel, restrooms, gift shop, wax museum.

Dates: Open summer and winter. Hours are seasonal.

Fees: There is a charge for the bridge tour and caverns or wax museum. Package prices and group rates are available.

For more information: Natural Bridge, PO Box 57, Natural Bridge, VA 24578. Phone (800) 533-1410 or (540) 291-2121.

Closest town: Lexington is 10 miles north.

JAMES RIVER FACE WILDERNESS

[Fig. 40(10), Fig. 41] The James River Face Wilderness was the first designated wilderness on national forests in Virginia after the 1975 Wilderness Act. It's also one of the largest wilderness areas in the state. The 8,903-acre area, dissected by the Rockbridge County and Bedford County line, is at the northern end of the Glenwood Ranger District, bounded to the north by the James River Gorge. Elevations range from 650 feet at the James River to 3,073 feet at Highcock Knob. (The Appalachian Trail crosses this peak in the southeastern part of the wilderness.)

The area has an unusually large diversity of vegetation, especially in the James River Gorge. Carolina hemlock (*Tsuga caroliniana*) is at the northern extent of its range here. Paper birch (*Betula papyrifera*)—the tree with the distinctive white papery bark and black markings characteristic of New England forests—is at the southern extent of its range.

There are six maintained trails, including the Appalachian Trail, within the wilderness. Because of the steep terrain, trails tend to be difficult, with switchbacks. The Belfast Trail, a 2.8-mile (one-way) trail in the western portion of James River Face, has an interesting feature. At about 1.5 miles, the trail leads to the Devils Marbleyard, a large scenic outcrop of huge loose boulders, where views of Arnold Valley and the Thunder Ridge Wilderness are impressive.

For more information: Glenwood Ranger District, PO Box 10, Natural Bridge Station, VA 24579. Phone (540) 291-2189.

BALCONY FALLS TRAIL. [Fig. 41(1), Fig. 40(7)] This 4.1-mile path begins at the Locher Tract on the James River. It follows an old woods road about 1.2 miles. It then climbs, with switchbacks, through frequent changes in forest types from pines to mixed hardwoods. At 2.3 miles, it enters James River Face Wilderness and ascends to top-of-the-world views on a ridge. Far below are the town of Glasgow and the James River Gorge, where kayakers and canoeists brave the rapids of Balcony Falls. For trailhead, follow directions to Locher Tract (page 269). On the ridgetop, the trail connects to the Appalachian Trail, and to Sulphur Spring, Gunter Ridge, Belfast, and Piney Ridge trails for plenty of circuit options. *Note: Horses are permitted on this trail and on connecting Sulphur Spring and Piney Ridge trails.*

Trail: 4.1-mile (one-way) climb, with switchbacks, from Locher Tract into James River Face Wilderness to scenic views and connections with other trails.

Elevation: 800 feet to 2,250 feet.

Degree of difficulty: Difficult.

THUNDER RIDGE WILDERNESS

[Fig. 40(11), Fig. 41] The small, 2,344-acre Thunder Ridge Wilderness lies high on the northeastern slope of the Blue Ridge, its eastern side accessible by the bordering Blue Ridge Parkway. To the north, separated by a narrow corridor of nonwilderness where a forest service road runs down the mountain, is James River Face Wilderness. The road is FR 35, connecting the Blue Ridge Parkway, milepost 71, at Petit Gap (spelled "Petites Gap" and "Petite Gap" on various maps) with recreation areas in Arnold Valley on the district's northern end.

Elevations on Thunder Ridge range from 1,320 feet at the northwestern corner to 4,200 feet on Apple Orchard Mountain. The Appalachian Trail runs the ridgeline, cutting through the southern edge of the wilderness and coming in again at the northern section. A portion of the 65-mile Glenwood Horse Trail goes through the wilderness beside FR 35. Other access is limited because of the steep, rugged terrain, and blow-downs caused by ice storms and winds.

For more information: Pedlar and Glenwood Ranger District, PO Box 10, Natural Bridge Station, VA 24579. Phone (540) 291-2189.

HIGHBUSH BLACKBERRY
(Rubus allepheniensis)
This bramble produces a delectable fruit that is popular food for wildlife.

Pedlar Ranger District

[Fig. 25] The Pedlar Ranger District of the George Washington National Forest gives the public access to 144,906 acres of the Blue Ridge mountains. It lies on both sides of the Blue Ridge Parkway between Waynesboro and the James River. National forest lands run east and west to the bottom of the main ridge. The district office is at Buena Vista in Rockbridge County. Under consideration is a proposal to close the Buena Vista office and use the Glenwood District Office at Natural Bridge.

Attractions on the district in the northwest corner include Sherando Lake Recreation Area, a favorite family refuge from summer heat, and the St. Mary's Wilderness, featuring a hike up a scenic gorge. On the east side of the Blue Ridge in Nelson County is Crabtree Falls, where hikers face a challenging climb along a scenic, five-tiered waterfall. Mount Pleasant National Scenic Area in northern Amherst County has more hikes and outstanding views.

The Blue Ridge Parkway comes into the Pedlar Ranger District from the north at about mile 2 and leaves it at about mile 64. Fifty-eight miles of the Maine-to-Georgia Appalachian Trail also run through the Pedlar District. The trail passes just below the district's highest point at the 4,072-foot summit of Rocky Mountain in northern Amherst County.

FISHING THE PEDLAR DISTRICT

The Pedlar Ranger District has several options for anglers. Two lakes are available at Sherando Lake Recreation Area (*see* p. 277). Mill Creek and Coles Run reservoirs—Augusta County water-supply lakes—opened to anglers in 1990. They are managed as put-and-grow lakes and were stocked with brook trout beginning in 1989. Historically, 13-inch wild brookies have come out of these waters. The stocked fish are now 8 to 14 inches. There are no facilities, and access is about a .5-mile walk to Coles Run and a 1.5-mile walk to Mills Creek. The Pedlar River is a seasonally stocked trout stream featuring numerous small falls and deep pools.

Directions: Trails to both the Mills Creek and Coles Run reservoirs lead south off the Coal Road (FR 42), south of Sherando in southeastern Augusta County. The Coal Road runs along the northern and western base of a flat-topped mountain called Big Levels. For both trails, from Sherando, go north on VA 664 for 1.7 miles and turn left on FR 42. For the Mills Creek trailhead, go about 1 mile west on FR 42 and park at anglers parking lot, on left. An information board with fishing regulations and map is beside the trailhead. Above the reservoir, Mills Creek is a native trout stream. For Coles Run Trail, go about 4 miles west from VA 664 to gated road on left.

For the Pedlar River, go east from Buena Vista into Amherst County on US 60. After US 60 goes under the Blue Ridge Parkway on top of the mountain, continue east for about 3 miles. To follow upper Pedlar, go north on VA 605. For lower Pedlar, go south along FR 39 and take side roads along right side to access river.

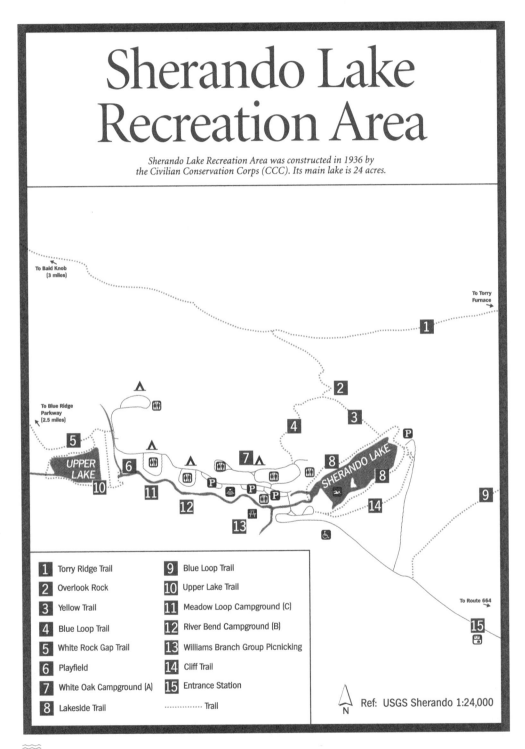

Sherando Lake Recreation Area

Sherando Lake Recreation Area was constructed in 1936 by the Civilian Conservation Corps (CCC). Its main lake is 24 acres.

To Bald Knob
(3 miles)

To Torry
Furnace

To Blue Ridge
Parkway
(2.5 miles)

UPPER
LAKE

SHERANDO LAKE

To Route 664

1	Torry Ridge Trail	9	Blue Loop Trail
2	Overlook Rock	10	Upper Lake Trail
3	Yellow Trail	11	Meadow Loop Campground (C)
4	Blue Loop Trail	12	River Bend Campground (B)
5	White Rock Gap Trail	13	Williams Branch Group Picnicking
6	Playfield	14	Cliff Trail
7	White Oak Campground (A)	15	Entrance Station
8	Lakeside Trail	··········	Trail

N

Ref: USGS Sherando 1:24,000

For more information: For current creel limits, seasons, and license requirements, contact the Virginia Department of Game and Inland Fisheries, Region IV Office, PO Box 996, Verona, VA 24482. Phone (540) 248-9360.

SHERANDO LAKE RECREATION AREA

[Fig. 42] Sherando Lake has been popular with residents of eastern Augusta County since its construction by the Civilian Conservation Corps (CCC) in 1936. The beautiful, 24-acre main lake is set in a mountain hollow on the east flank of steep Torry Ridge, less than 5 miles from the Blue Ridge Parkway. The lake has a swimming area with a sand beach and a bathhouse with warm showers. The large, sturdy buildings are consistent with durable CCC construction. Those who prefer shade to the sunny beach can spread blankets on the spacious lawn beneath giant oak trees.

Picnickers also have shade at widely spaced lakeside tables beneath a canopy of deciduous trees. While the hamburgers are frying on the grill, families can hike the Lakeside Trail, which makes an easy 1-mile loop around the lake. Someone's got to go find Dad, who's found a spot between some alders where he can cast to largemouth bass, bluegill, redear sunfish, or stocked trout.

An upper lake (7 acres) was constructed in 1958 for flood control. Anglers who desire a more remote experience prefer this lake, which also has an encircling trail for bank fishing. No trout license is required from June 16 through September 31, when general statewide fishing regulations apply. From October 1 through June 15, a trout license is required. A National Forest Stamp is required all year and so is a Virginia fishing license. Visitors who come to the recreation area during the fall hunting season should wear blaze orange on the trails. The surrounding national forest is heavily hunted, especially during the two-week deer season in November.

Directions: From I-64 south of Waynesboro, in eastern Augusta County, take Exit 96 (Sherando Lake Exit) and go 2 miles south on VA 624 to Lyndhurst. Bear left onto VA 664 and continue 8 miles to Sherando Lake entrance, on right.

Activities: Hiking, swimming, fishing, boating on lower lake (no motors), picnicking, interpretive programs.

Facilities: Visitor center with maps and interpretive materials, 2 lakes, swimming beach, bathhouse, showers, wading area, 3 campground loops with total of 65 sites, group camping area for 125 people (by reservation only), hiking trails, picnic tables, trailer dump station, drinking water.

Dates: Gates open daily, year-round. Swimming and picnic areas close at dark. Camping permitted Apr. 1–Oct. 31. Camping in organization area Nov. 1–end of hunting season (no water).

Fees: There is a charge for camping and day use.

Closest town: Stuarts Draft is 10 miles west. Waynesboro is 14 miles north.

For more information: Glenwood and Pedlar Ranger District, PO Box 10, Natural Bridge, VA 24579. Phone (540) 291-2188.

HIKING AT SHERANDO LAKE RECREATION AREA

In addition to easy trails around both the upper and lower lake, Sherando Lake Recreation Area offers several other paths with more strenuous climbs up the surrounding mountains. The .75-mile Cliff Trail (unblazed) on the eastern side of the main lake can be combined with the lakeside trail for a loop hike with excellent views. The 2.5-mile orange-blazed White Rock Gap Trail follows Back Creek upstream from the upper lake, past an old homesite, and out on the Blue Ridge Parkway, milepost 18.5. Defoliated and dying hardwoods along the trail are evidence of gypsy moth damage. Hemlocks also show the effects of a pest with no known natural enemies, the hemlock wooly adelgid.

BLUE LOOP TRAIL. [Fig. 40(2), Fig. 42(4)] Beginning near site #6 in Campground A, the Blue Loop Trail climbs .9 mile to the top of Torry Ridge on the northwestern side of the main lake where it joins the Torry Ridge Trail. After a 1-mile walk northeastward along Torry Ridge, with views of Sherando Lake below, the Blue Loop Trail branches to the south and descends to the entrance road on the east side of the recreation area.

Trail: 3-mile trail ascending and descending Torry Ridge, forming a loop when combined with entrance road.

Elevation: 1,850 feet to 2,550 feet.

Degree of difficulty: Moderate, with strenuous climb.

Surface and blaze: Natural forest floor. Blue blaze (also a yellow blaze on Torry Ridge portion).

ST. MARY'S WILDERNESS

[Fig. 40(15)] St. Mary's Wilderness—even the name sounds like a sonnet on a breeze. A tinkling of water over moss-covered rocks. A play of light and shadows on crystal-clear pools. St. Mary's Wilderness has all these and more. In fact, this 10,090-acre wilderness would do better with a less lyrical name. The fragile beauty hinted at in the name draws so many hikers, campers, and partiers that the wilderness has been "loved to death," as one ranger put it. The well-traveled footpath up lovely St. Mary's gorge and the accompanying trail of human detritus has somewhat marred the wilderness ambiance St. Mary's once had.

The St. Mary's River empties a steep, narrow gorge on the southwest side of Big Levels in the southern tip of Augusta County. St. Mary's Falls, a double waterfall over big rock boulders about 2 miles up the gorge, is the destination for many hikers. A refreshing pool collects water at the bottom of the falls. Just about every level spot along the way has remnants of campfires.

Humans are not alone in leaving tracks in the gorge. In fact, torrential downpours from Hurricane Camille in 1969 and Hurricane Agnes in 1972 wiped out an old logging road up the gorge, divided and changed the lower course of the stream, heaped debris into great piles across what road remained, and helped a group of citizens obtain wilderness designation for St. Mary's in 1984. Of course, had the area not been mined and logged in the early 1900s, the trees and soil may have been better able to withstand the powerful floodwaters. Acid rain has been blamed for decimating the native trout fishery here, but some brookies remain to give catch-and-release fly-fishermen a thrill. Only single barbless hooks may be used.

Nature lovers and trout anglers who seek solitude should look elsewhere or visit the area during off-seasons. However, St. Mary's does have a lot to offer. Its reputation as a first-class mountain gorge along the pretty St. Mary's River is well deserved.

About 17 miles of trails are in the area. Exploring some of the lesser-used trails turns up more waterfalls and rock cliffs and remnants of former manganese mining, including a settling pond, an old railroad grade, and several concrete footings of a former mining camp. A topo map and a compass are always a good idea when hiking such wilderness areas. Conscientious hikers and anglers help not only by packing out their own candy wrappers and aluminum cans but also by picking up trash left by others.

FLORA AND FAUNA OF ST. MARY'S

Several springs and freshets entering St. Mary's along the trail are good places to look for moisture-loving wildflowers. These include spotted touch-me-not or jewelweed (*Impatiens capensis*), jack-in-the-pulpit (*Arisaema triphyllum*), and the tiny, four-petaled white blossoms of cut-leaved toothwort (*Dentaria laciniata*). Mayapple or mandrake (*Podophyllum peltatum*) and hay-scented ferns carpet the forest floor in places. The dramatic red spikes of the cardinal flower (*Lobelia cardinalis*) are occasionally found. Where sunlight bathes the streambanks, thickets of blackberry, purple-flowered raspberry, multiflora rose, and honeysuckle thrive.

Tulip poplars, hemlocks, and oaks make up much of the canopy along the stream. Oaks and hickories typical of eastern deciduous forests dominate the slopes, while a few stunted table mountain pines can be found mixed in with chestnut oaks, hickories, and pin oaks in the harsher environment of the exposed ridgetops.

In midsummer, black bears are attracted to sun-ripened highbush blueberries (*Vaccinium corymbosum*) and cranberries (*Vaccinium macrocarpon*) at Green Pond. Green Pond, fed only by precipitation, is on the spreading, relatively flat top of a mountainous area known as Big Levels. A layer of peat forms an impenetrable basin that holds the water. The pond usually dries up in summer.

Signs of bear activity include scrape marks in rotting logs where bears have searched for ants and shredded bark and vertical tooth marks on pine trees where bears have slurped up pine resin. A bear also will pick a prominent tree along a trail and stand on its hind legs while rubbing itself against the tree, occasionally biting and scratching the tree. These "bear trees" serve to notify other bears of territorial claims. Bears sometimes get in the habit of walking in each other's footprints to and from feeding areas such as the blueberry patches at Green Pond. Gradually, a zigzag trail of paw indentations develops. If the bears abandon the trail, seeds pressed into the paw prints will sprout and form a zigzag trail of grass clumps.

Ruffed grouse, woodcocks, wild turkeys, white-tailed deer, gray squirrels, gray foxes, skunks, and chipmunks are also in the area. The unbroken woods are a haven for species such as the yellow-eyed vireo, ovenbird, wood thrush, pileated woodpecker, scarlet tanager, worm-eating warbler, and hooded warbler.

Directions: Lower trailhead: From I-81, take Exit 205 south of Staunton and go 1.5 miles east on VA 606 to Steeles Tavern. Go left on US 11 for 100 yards. Turn right on VA 56 and go 1.2 miles. Turn left on VA 608 and go 4.8 miles. Go right on FR 41 and drive 1.5 miles to parking area. Upper trailhead: From Blue Ridge Parkway

The Nelson County Flood of 1969

History may remember Hurricane Camille as the monster storm that wreaked havoc among the Gulf states. If Virginia is not included in the public memory, that's because lines of communication—telephones, highways, mail service—were down in rural Nelson County, Virginia. By the time news crews found out what the dying remnants of Camille had done to this sparsely populated county on the east side of the Blue Ridge, the nation's attention was diverted elsewhere. Even the nearby communities of Waynesboro and Charlottesville, beset with their own flooding, took awhile to learn of the devastation.

When Camille arrived, a large tropical air mass was already in place over Nelson County, dumping torrential rains. Soil on the steep mountain slopes was supersaturated. Then, on the night of August 19, 1969, rainfall to challenge existing world records for 24 hour periods fell overnight. Amounts in excess of 25 inches—and possibly as high as 37 inches in one area—were recorded. Whole sections of mountainsides, including trees and soil right down to bedrock, slid off into the narrow hollows, damming the streams. Water and debris built up tremendous pressure behind these false dams, finally breaking loose in raging torrents, taking entire settlements out with them.

People fleeing their homes remember the strobe-light effect of constant lightning which they used to find their way through the night woods to high ground or to a neighbor's house. They describe the experience as similar to walking beneath a waterfall. A baby being carried in her father's arms had to be turned over to keep from drowning. In the hellish night, one family that had built several homes along tiny Davis Creek lost 21 members to a surging wall of water—parents, aunts, uncles, children, even babies. The county itself lost 120 people—more than 1 percent of its population. Some bodies were never recovered. Some bodies that were recovered were never identified.

The mountainsides still bear the scars. From US 29 running north/south through the county, patches of bedrock not yet covered by vegetation on the steep slopes are grim reminders of that August night. And the people—who still look nervously out their windows when it rains—bear their own deep wounds.

milepost 22.2 (Bald Mountain overlook), take FR 162 (gate may be closed) 3.8 miles south to Green Pond. The road is best suited to vehicles with a high clearance.

Activities: Hiking, primitive camping, seasonal hunting.

Facilities: None.

Dates: Open daily, year-round.

Fees: None.

Closest town: Steeles Tavern is 7.5 miles southwest of lower trailhead.

For more information: Pedlar Ranger District, 2424 Magnolia Avenue, Buena Vista, VA 24416. Phone (540) 261-6105.

ST. MARY'S TRAIL. [Fig. 40(16)] This is the main trail of the wilderness. The unblazed path leads up a scenic narrowing gorge toward St. Mary's Falls. After a stream crossing, which can be treacherous in freezing weather, and .5-mile short of St. Mary's Falls, the trail forks. St. Mary's Trail makes a right turn to head south up Mine Bank Mountain to a boggy area called Green Pond, located just outside the wilderness. St. Mary's Falls Trail, however, continues along the main stream and dead-ends at a double waterfall at the base of steep rock cliffs.

Trail: 6.9-mile (one-way) climb up scenic gorge to mountaintop pond. .5-mile spur leads to St. Mary's Falls for 2-mile (one-way) hike.

Elevation: 1,700 feet to 3,200 feet.

Degree of difficulty: Moderate to falls (on .5-mile spur off St. Mary's Trail), with stream crossing that can be difficult in wet seasons or in icy conditions. Upper portion of St. Mary's Trail has difficult steep ascent to Green Pond.

Surface: Natural forest floor, rocky sections, stream crossing.

CRABTREE FALLS

[Fig. 40(3)] In a mountain gorge in western Nelson County is Crabtree Falls, consisting of five tiers of major falls and several smaller ones. Crabtree Falls plummets 1,200 feet down the northern flank of a 4,063-foot-high mountain called The Priest. The icy waters of the falls are in the headwaters of the Tye River, which gained notoriety in the devastating flooding rains of Hurricane Camille in 1969. The Tye River nearly moved the little community of Massies Mill on VA 56 off the map.

The falls have their own reputation for taking lives with no help from the Tye. Over the years, 22 people have fallen to their death. Many of the accidents occurred when people at the top tried to get a closer look by walking out onto the rocks. These rocks are covered with a clear, algaelike material which makes footing very treacherous. The U.S. Forest Service has installed handrails, steps, observation platforms, walls, and warning signs to make the falls accessible and safe. With signs and railings now in place, such accidents can be avoided by staying on the trail.

Despite the remote location high in the Blue Ridge, the falls are sought after for their scenery by hikers and photographers. The footpath to the falls leads from the lower parking lot across a beautiful arched wooden bridge that spans the South Fork of the Tye River. Then the trail winds through hemlocks and past an old family graveyard. It's an easy 10-minute walk to the first of five major cascades.

From there, the hiker climbs 1.7 miles up a steep trail with switchbacks. Moist air from the falls makes ideal habitat for several varieties of ferns, mosses, and wildflowers. Along the way, viewing platforms with benches enable hikers to catch their breath while enjoying views of the cascades, and children like to investigate the small cave on the trail. At the top, the trail continues 1.2 miles farther along Crabtree Creek to Crabtree Meadows parking lot on VA 826 (Crabtree Farm Road).

A .5-mile hike east on VA 826 from the upper parking lot will take you to a junction with the Appalachian Trail and Shoe Creek Trail. Just 1.2 miles east on the AT are rocky outcrops on the quiet summit of The Priest that overlook Rockfish Valley in Nelson County far below. The Shoe Creek Trail leads 3.5 miles south down the mountain to Piney River, a stocked trout stream on the Nelson County/Amherst County border. The trail can be reached from the bottom via VA 827 (Perkins Mill Road) west of Massies Mill and northwest of Piney River.

The state trout hatchery at Montebello is just 3 miles west on VA 56 from the lower parking area of Crabtree Falls. Visitors are invited to feed the trout and use the picnic facilities.

Directions: Lower trailhead: From the Blue Ridge Parkway, milepost 27.2, drive east on VA 56 for 6.6 miles to parking area, on right. Or from the east, at junction of US 29 and VA 56 at Colleen in southwestern Nelson County, follow VA 56 west about 19 miles (through Massies Mill) to parking area, on left. Upper trailhead (requires high-axle vehicle or four-wheel drive): Drive 2.7 miles west on VA 56 from lower parking area. Turn left (south) on VA 826 and go 3.7 miles to large parking area.

Activities: Hiking, primitive camping (and picnicking at nearby fish hatchery).

Facilities: Hiking trail, vault toilets, viewing platforms with benches.

Dates: Open daily, year-round.

Fees: None.

Closest town: Massies Mill is 9 miles southeast.

For more information: Glenwood and Pedlar Ranger District, PO Box 10, Natural Bridge, VA 24579. Phone (540) 291-2188.

MOUNT PLEASANT NATIONAL SCENIC AREA

[Fig. 40(5)] The 7,580-acre Mount Pleasant National Scenic Area was designated by Congress in 1994 as one of only seven such areas in the country. Here, the 6.2-mile Henry Lanum Trail forms a loop connecting the summits of the two highest mountains of the Pedlar Ranger District. Mount Pompey is 4,032 feet high and Mount Pleasant is 4,021 feet high.

Multitiered flat outcroppings of pre-Cambrian granite typical of the Blue Ridge Mountains provide breathtaking panoramic views of the valleys formed by the Piney River and Buffalo River.

Chestnut oak, yellow birch, and pignut hickory are in the hardwood canopy, while mountain laurel, rhododendron, wild hydrangea, mountain ash, highbush blueberries, and witch-hazel can be found in the understory. Wildflowers to look for include starry campion, tiger lily, bloodroot, and Indian pipe.

The forested mountain slopes provide acorns, hickory nuts, grapes, and blueberries, staples in the diets of black bear. White-tailed deer come into the high mountain fields and meadows to browse at dusk. Bobcats, wild turkeys, red and gray squirrels, gray foxes, and cottontail rabbits also inhabit the woods. The high peaks are perfect places to observe the annual fall hawk migration.

The 3-mile Hotel Trail, completed in 1989, makes a 7.5-mile loop using part of the Appalachian Trail (AT). This trail takes off from the right of the parking lot as you enter from FR 48. It winds through open fields and meadows, along Little Cove Creek, and intersects with the AT at Cow Camp Gap. A three-sided AT shelter is located nearby. Hikers can then hike to the northeast on the AT about 2 miles to Hog Camp Gap. From there, it's a 10-minute hike back to the parking lot on FR 48.

In early summer, hikers along the trails in the Mount Pleasant National Scenic Area may notice trees losing their leaves. They may also hear the constant sound of something raining from above. What they're seeing and hearing is an infestation of the fall cankerworm, which covers about 500 acres of the Pedlar Ranger District, extending southward to US 60 (*see* Ghost Forests, page 11).

Directions: From Buena Vista in eastern Rockbridge County, take US 60 east about 10 miles. Turn left and follow VA 634 for 2 miles. Go right on Wiggin Springs Road and drive 2.2 miles, where road becomes FR 48. Continue 2 miles on FR 48 to parking area.

Activities: Hiking, primitive camping, seasonal hunting.

Facilities: Shelter on Hotel Trail/AT loop.

Dates: Trails are open year-round, though winter weather may make access impossible.

Fees: None.

Closest town: Buena Vista is 16 miles southwest.

For more information: Glenwood and Pedlar Ranger District, PO Box 10, Natural Bridge, VA 24579. Phone (540) 291-2188.

Trails: Henry Lanum Trail (formerly Pompey and Mount Pleasant Loop Trail) is 6.2-mile loop connecting two mountain summits (combined with .5-mile spur to summit of Mount Pleasant). Hotel Trail combines with Appalachian Trail to form 7.5-mile mountainous loop.

Elevation: Henry Lanum Trail: 3,400 feet to 4,032 feet on Pompey Mountain. Hotel Trail: 3,000 feet to 4,022 feet on Cold Mountain.

Degree of difficulty: Moderate, with difficult steep sections.

Surface: Natural forest floor with rocky sections.

Wintergreen

[Fig. 40(1)] On the eastern slope of the Blue Ridge in Nelson County, partly surrounded by National Forest and bordering the Blue Ridge Parkway and Appalachian Trail, is a year-round resort called Wintergreen.

In the lofty headwaters of Stoney Creek, spreading into Rockfish Valley below, Wintergreen offers 17 ski trails, a 30-mile network of hiking trails, 25 tennis courts, equestrian center, six swimming pools, fly-fishing stream, and two championship golf courses—one the highest course in the state, the other selected as a favorite by *Golf Digest*. Facilities at the resort are clustered in two areas: one with a mountain entrance and one with a valley entrance.

Wintergreen, however, is more than a sports resort. Wintergreen's original planners committed a major portion of its 11,000 acres to wilderness, and today over 6,000 acres remain as undisturbed forest with a rich mosaic of natural wildflower gardens, waterfalls, and rock formations called Old Appalachia, dating back as far as 1,100 million years.

When a high-altitude spring seepage was found to have an unusual boreal wildflower garden growing beneath a canopy of yellow birch, the land was set aside as Shamokin Springs Nature Preserve. Protected are such treasures as the speckled wood lily (*Lilium philadelphicum*), wild lily-of-the-valley (*Maianthemum*), spotted coralroot (*Corallorhiza maculata*), monkshood (*Aconitum*), and Turk's cap lily (*Lilium superbum*). Among the ferns that also thrive here are cinnamon, shield, New York, silvery athyrium, and Christmas.

The Wintergreen Nature Foundation, a nonprofit charitable organization, delves into the land's natural heritage annually with two events—a Spring Wildflower Symposium and, in fall, the Virginia Natural History Weekend Retreat. The spring event is conducted by well-known botanists, photographers, and artists. The fall retreat is cosponsored by the Virginia Museum of Natural History. Some of the state's finest field scientists offer hikes, lectures, and workshops on such topics as birding, geology, paleontology, mammalogy, herpetology, and botany.

Directions: From the Blue Ridge Parkway at Reeds Gap (mile 13.7), go east on VA 664 down the mountain for about 1 mile. Go left at entrance to Wintergreen mountain village. From Nellysford in Nelson County, go about 3 miles southwest on VA 151. Go right on VA 664 and drive about 5 miles to mountain village entrance, on right. (Entrance to valley facilities is just east of Nellysford.)

Activities: Hiking, mountain biking, skiing, snowboarding, golf, tennis, horseback riding, swimming, interpretive programs, children's programs, children's nature camps.

Facilities: Outdoor center, hiking/mountain biking trails, lodging, restaurants, ski slopes, tennis courts, equestrian center, golf courses, swimming pools, fishing/canoeing/swimming lake, trout stream, spa, indoor/outdoor sports facility.

Dates: Open year-round. Skiing, approximately mid-Dec.–Mar. Spring Wildflower Symposium, mid-May; Natural History Weekend, mid-Sept.

Fees: For resort guests, there is no charge for some outdoor activities such as hiking and bird walks. There is a charge for the Spring Wildflower Symposium and Virginia Natural History Weekend Retreat.

Closest town: Nellysford is about 10 miles east of Mountain Village and 1 mile southeast of valley facilities.

For more information: For outdoor events or programs: The Wintergreen Nature Foundation, PO Box 468, Wintergreen, VA 22958. Phone (804) 325-8172. For other activities or information: Wintergreen, Wintergreen, VA 22958. Phone (804) 325-2200 or (800) 325-2200. For ski report: (804) 325-2100.

Black Bears in Virginia

What are the chances of seeing a black bear in the Virginia mountains? That depends. The time of year makes a difference. So does the area of the state in which one is traveling. Both Native American and white settlers hunted the black bear *(Ursus americanus)* for its hide, meat, teeth, and claws and for sport. With no controls, populations dwindled, and in some areas the bear was completely wiped out. However, bear numbers are now expanding thanks to modern conservation management by the Virginia Department of Game and Inland Fisheries. Young bears that have been chased off by adult females are spotted these days in some unusual places, such as the suburbs of Richmond, the state capital. Virginia has one of the largest black bear populations in the East with an estimated 4,500 or more animals. Shenandoah National Park alone, serving as a 100-mile-long mountain refuge, has the highest black bear density in the country. A game department trapping and tagging program over a 10-year period estimated a bear population in excess of 1.5 bears per square mile. The park covers 300 square miles. According to the estimate, there were more than 450 bears in the park. In fact, the number of bears in Virginia has increased to the point that nuisance bears destroying corn or raiding rural trash cans are routinely trapped and moved to sections of the state such as southwest Virginia where the bear population is still small.

Late spring and early summer are good times to see rambling bears. The females are getting ready to mate again—bears reproduce every two years—so the overgrown youngsters are forced out on their own. Black bears are shy and prefer in almost every case to put as much distance as possible between themselves and humans. In Virginia, bears have no history of aggression. But they are big (up to 400 pounds) and truly wild and thus unpredictable, and the encounter can quickly become dangerous if one gets between a sow and her cubs. Hikers who see a bear should give it plenty of room, watch from a safe distance, and store the incident in the archives of memory.

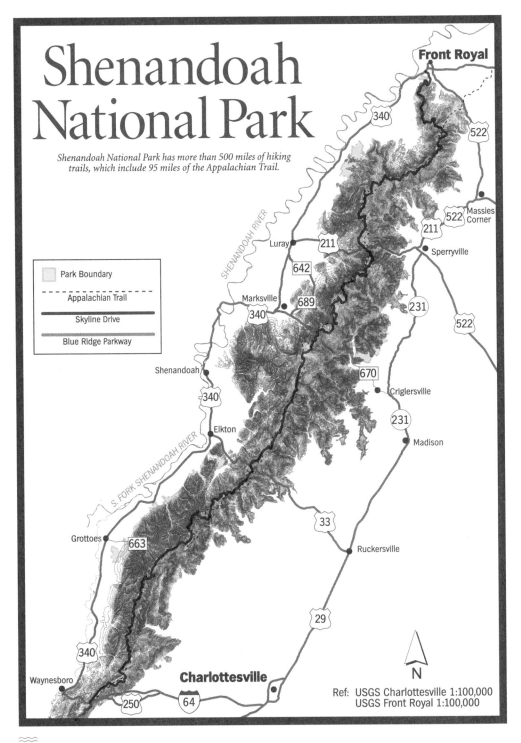

Shenandoah National Park

Shenandoah National Park has more than 500 miles of hiking trails, which include 95 miles of the Appalachian Trail.

Front Royal

340

522

SHENANDOAH RIVER

522 Massies Corner

211

Luray 211

Sperryville

642

Marksville 689

231

340

522

Shenandoah

670

340

Criglersville

231

Elkton

Madison

S. FORK SHENANDOAH RIVER

33

Grottoes 663

Ruckersville

29

340

Waynesboro

Charlottesville

250 64

Park Boundary

- - - Appalachian Trail

———— Skyline Drive

———— Blue Ridge Parkway

N

Ref: USGS Charlottesville 1:100,000
USGS Front Royal 1:100,000

Shenandoah National Park & Skyline Drive

[Fig. 43, Fig. 44] When President Franklin D. Roosevelt dedicated Shenandoah National Park in 1936, a novel experiment in public land use was begun. At the time, most national parks were being set aside to protect already-existing natural beauty, wildlife, and wilderness. Shenandoah National Park was an attempt to determine if 196,466 acres of damaged mountain land would revert to a pristine state if set aside and protected from further human alteration.

The land-use experiment would run counter to the traditional precept that land was to be used in ways most beneficial to man and that nature and wilderness were little more than impediments to be conquered. Long, narrow Shenandoah National Park—100 miles in length and ranging from 13.2 miles to less than 1 mile in width—was formed from mountain land that had been the subject of hard human use since the first settlers began trickling into the area in the early to mid-1700s.

By the beginning of the twentieth century, farmers had established agriculture, orchards, and grazing land. Loggers increased the cutting of the mighty oaks and chestnuts and dragged them off the mountains. Sheep and cattle grazed where bear, elk, and wolves once roamed. The thin soil was wearing out along the crest of the Blue Ridge range where Shenandoah National Park was to be located.

Weary of the hard scrabble life in the mountains, people were beginning to move out. More than half the residents had left by the mid-1920s. The rest sold their land for establishment of the park, or they were relocated with federal assistance.

Not everyone was ready to leave the mountains. The people whose farms and homesteads were condemned fought the legal seizure by the Commonwealth of Virginia for a dozen years. Though the federal government permitted a few residents to live in their homes for the remainder of their lives, among the descendants of the mountain families, resentment still simmers in little towns such as Elkton, Luray, Sperryville, and Stanardsville in the Shenandoah Valley and Piedmont Virginia.

Land acquisition for the park would take years. But a 100-foot right-of-way for the Skyline Drive was acquired quicker through gifts and special purchases. The highway along the ridge was planned as the park's outstanding feature. President Herbert Hoover, who had a vacation cabin on the nearby Rapidan River, urged the approval of funding for road construction. Local crews began work in 1931, and on August 29, 1939, Skyline Drive [Fig. 44] was opened.

Meanwhile, President Roosevelt had taken office in 1932 and immediately established the Civilian Conservation Corps (CCC). Almost 1,000 unemployed young men came to live in camps at what was to become Shenandoah National Park. Called Roosevelt's Tree Army, these men built overlooks, guard walls, and log comfort stations, put in water and septic systems, cleared trails, created picnic areas and campgrounds, and landscaped the roadsides.

Located just 75 miles west of Washington, D.C., Shenandoah National Park today attracts nearly 2 million visitors a year. Between Front Royal in northern Virginia and Afton Mountain at Waynesboro, the park drapes across the crest of the Blue Ridge mountains, which form the eastern rampart of the Appalachian Mountains. These mountains are lower than the lofty peaks of Virginia's Blue Ridge Highlands south of Roanoke. Hawksbill, the highest peak in the park, is just 4,050 feet, compared to Mount Rogers's 5,729 feet in the southern section of the Blue Ridge.

Skyline Drive, the winding two-lane federal highway, divides the park as it extends 105 miles from Front Royal to Waynesboro. Some 75 overlooks provide visitors with expansive views of the Shenandoah Valley to the west and the rolling Piedmont country to the east. At the posted speed of 35 miles per hour, it takes three to five hours to drive the entire length, stopping at some of the overlooks. It is also permissible to stop wherever there is room to pull 6 to 12 feet off the road. The Drive is numbered from north to south with concrete mileposts from milepost 0 through milepost 105.

More than 95 percent of the once-abused land on both sides of the Drive is now covered with eastern deciduous forest with about 100 species of trees. To further protect the mountains, Congress in 1976 designated two-fifths of Shenandoah National Park as wilderness. In recent years, damage from ice storms, hurricane winds, flooding, and diseases and pests such as the gypsy moth have taken another toll.

Elk and wolves may be gone, but other animals that were once rare—white-tailed deer, black bear, wild turkey, bobcats—have now returned. Deer are common along Skyline Drive in early morning and late afternoon. As dusk falls, the eyes of numerous white-tailed deer grazing the roadsides reflect car headlights along the entire length of the Skyline Drive. (Because of problems with poaching, it is illegal to stop and shine a light—even car headlights—on deer.) Bears tend to stay in the backcountry, but the population is so large in the park that it isn't unusual to see a bear wander across a meadow or even the mountain highway.

Raccoons, opossums, and skunks sometimes poke around campgrounds at night, searching for morsels left by campers. (It's not only dangerous but illegal to feed wildlife in the park.) Chipmunks entertain by day as they scurry across a campsite to a burrow under a fallen tree. More than 200 species of birds have been identified in the park, including 35 varieties of warblers.

Some 1,200 flowering plants grow in the park. In spring and early summer, a few examples to look for are spring beauty (*Claytonia caroliniana*), foam flower (*Tiarella cordifolia*), wild geranium (*Geranium maculatum*), solomon's seal (*Polyganatum biflorum*), New Jersey tea (*Ceanothus americanus*), and bowman's root (*Gillenia trifoliata*). In later summer, there's fragrant thimbleberry (*Rubus odoratus*), beard-tongue (*Penstemon*), sundrop (*Oenothera fruticosa*), and butterfly weed (*Asclepias tuberosa*).

The park has more than 500 miles of footpaths ranging from easy leg-stretchers to a 101-mile segment of the Appalachian Trail, which runs the length of the park. Several developed campgrounds along Skyline Drive provide car campers with places to hear ruffed grouse drumming or barred owls calling or to take part in day and evening interpretive programs. Primitive backcountry camping is also an option but requires a free permit.

Hunting is off-limits in Shenandoah National Park, but fishing for native brook trout is available year-round for those willing to walk to remote streams that tumble down both sides of the Blue Ridge. Only artificial lures may be used. On designated streams, the creel limit is six trout per day with a 9-inch minimum size. On all other streams open to fishing, catch-and-release regulations apply. A Virginia fishing license is required. A free brochure listing trout streams and regulations is available at entrance stations and visitor centers or by calling the park.

The park and Skyline Drive are most crowded in mid-October when fall foliage is at its colorful peak. Summer weekends will also find favored trails clogged with elbow-to-elbow walkers. One alternative is to plan visits for weekdays or, better yet, the off-season. But even at the peak of fall foliage, when the park may have 50,000 visitors in a single day, hikers who desire solitude can find it on the lesser-known trails. There's personal adventure in finding a waterfall or greenstone formation or identifying a wildflower that's not on a nature trail.

RED-TAILED HAWK
(Buteo jamaicensis)
This hawk hunts for small animals from the air or from exposed perches.

Besides interpretive programs conducted by park rangers, interested persons are invited to sign up for special workshops and activities from time to time. Examples include a wildflower weekend (usually the second weekend in May), a Fourth of July weekend butterfly count (nationwide program modeled after the National Audubon Society's Christmas Bird Count), and the Christmas Bird Count.

The park remains open year-round. The Skyline Drive, however—the only road through the park—is sometimes closed from dusk to early morning during hunting season to discourage illegal hunting, and it is closed when it's covered with snow or ice. Cross-country skiers sometimes use the park roads when they are closed to traffic. All facilities—lodging, campgrounds, waysides, visitor centers, gas stations— close in late fall and reopen in mid-spring.

The Shenandoah Natural History Association is a nonprofit organization that sells books, maps, and related items at the two visitor centers. Income is used to support the interpretive and educational programs of the park. Lodging, groceries, and all items for sale in the park are provided by private concessionaires. ARAMARK Virginia Sky-line Company, Inc., operates the lodges, restaurants, waysides, gift shops, shower/laundry, and gas stations. The Potomac Appalachian Trail Club is an association of hikers that maintains the Appalachian Trail and six rental cabins in the park.

Directions: The north entrance is at the southern edge of Front Royal on US 340. The south entrance is on US 250 on the Augusta County/Nelson County border, 4 miles east of Waynesboro and just east of I-64 Exit 99. Or, from Luray, drive 8 miles east on US 211 to access the drive at mile 31.5. From Elkton, drive 5 miles east on US 33 to access the drive at mile 65.5.

Activities: Hiking, picnicking, camping, scenic drive, horseback riding, native trout fishing, interpretive programs, cross-country skiing.

Facilities: 2 lodge facilities, 2 visitor information centers, limited-housekeeping cabins, 4 campgrounds, 7 picnic areas, 3 restaurants, 3 snack bars, 4 campstores, 5 gas stations (1 outside park at each end, others open mid-spring to late fall at mile 24, mile 51.2, and mile 79.5). Several trail shelters, cabins, and huts (contact Potomac Appalachian Trail Club for details). Many hiking trails and interpretive trails. Restrooms and drinking water at restaurants, waysides, visitor centers, campgrounds, picnic areas.

Dates: The park is open year-round, but some portions of Skyline Drive, which is the only road through Shenandoah National Park, close during hunting season from dusk to early morning. For safety reasons this road also closes in inclement weather. All park facilities are usually open mid-spring to late fall. Call for exact dates.

Fees: There is a charge for entrance to Skyline Drive, lodging, and campsites.

Closest town: Waynesboro, in Augusta County, is 4 miles west of southern end. Front Royal is at northern end. Luray is about 5 miles west of the Skyline Drive entrance on US 211 (mile 31.5), and Elkton is about 5 miles west of the park on US 33 (mile 65.5).

For more information: Shenandoah National Park, 3655 US Highway 211 East, Luray, VA 22835-9036. Phone (540) 999-3500. Shenandoah Natural History Association, 3655 US Highway 211 East, Luray, VA 22835. Phone (540) 999-3582. ARAMARK Virginia Sky-line Company, Inc., PO Box 727, Luray, VA 22835. Phone (800) 999-4714. Potomac Appalachian Trail Club (PATC), 118 Park Street SE, Vienna, VA 22180.

BIG MEADOWS

[Fig. 44(9)] One of the most fascinating places in the park also happens to be one of the most accessible. At mile 51.2—near the halfway point of the Skyline Drive—is Big Meadows. Its 150 open acres cover a bowl-shaped depression underlain by solid Catoctin greenstone rock. Springs and precipitation keep the nearly impermeable ground swampy through most of the year.

Just before dusk, deer materialize from the surrounding woods in the shrubby meadow to browse. Just as predictably, park visitors appear to wander the meadows and watch the nearly tame deer. But there's much more to see. In the sun-washed meadow thrive some 270 species of plants, including several varieties of ferns and the park's largest collection of wildflowers. Among the flower varieties are northern evening primrose (*Oenothera biennis*), Turk's cap lily (*Lilium superbum*), beard-tongue (*Penstemon*), and stiff gentian (*Gentiana quinquefolia*) with its lovely lilac-blue open petals. The gentian grows about 1 to 2 feet tall and has a whorl of leaves just below the flower cluster.

Scientists say that Big Meadows was once much bigger—extending 1.5 miles north and south of its present 150 acres. But they can only speculate about its reason for being. Perhaps Indians set fire to the land regularly to keep it clear for hunting. The park now burns and mows the land to preserve its open character for nesting birds, deer, and other wildlife and for historical significance since the meadow has existed for several hundred years.

LODGING IN SHENANDOAH NATIONAL PARK

Motel-type units and rustic cabins are available from early April through November at Skyland (mile 41.7) and Big Meadows (mile 51.2). A few rental housekeeping cabins are available from early May to late October at Lewis Mountain (mile 57.5). Make reservations well in advance.

Reservations or Information: ARAMARK Virginia Sky-line Company, Inc., PO Box 727, Luray, VA 22835. Phone (800) 999-4714.

CAMPING IN SHENANDOAH NATIONAL PARK

Four campgrounds with spacious, shaded sites operate from May through October. These campgrounds include Mathews Arm (mile 22.2, 186 sites), Big Meadows (mile 51.2, 227 sites), Lewis Mountain (mile 57.5, 32 sites), and Loft Mountain (mile 79.5, 221 sites). A fee is charged. Handicapped-accessible sites are available at each campground. Only Big Meadows Campground takes reservations either at the gate or by calling (800) 365-CAMP and using SHEN as four-letter designator when asked.

There are no trailer hookups. All but Lewis Mountain have a trailer sewage disposal site. Shower and laundry facilities are at Big Meadows, Lewis Mountain, and Loft Mountain. Primitive facilities (reservation required) for organized youth groups are at mile 83.7 at Dundo Campground.

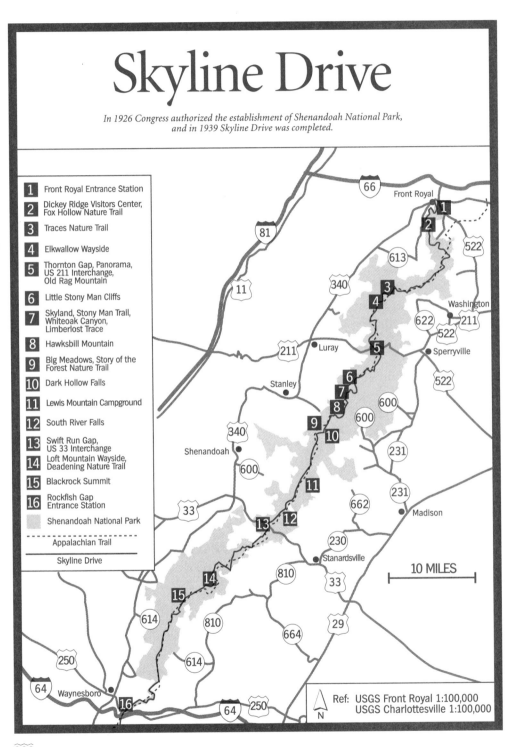

Skyline Drive

*In 1926 Congress authorized the establishment of Shenandoah National Park,
and in 1939 Skyline Drive was completed.*

1   Front Royal Entrance Station

2   Dickey Ridge Visitors Center, Fox Hollow Nature Trail

3   Traces Nature Trail

4   Elkwallow Wayside

5   Thornton Gap, Panorama, US 211 Interchange, Old Rag Mountain

6   Little Stony Man Cliffs

7   Skyland, Stony Man Trail, Whiteoak Canyon, Limberlost Trace

8   Hawksbill Mountain

9   Big Meadows, Story of the Forest Nature Trail

10   Dark Hollow Falls

11   Lewis Mountain Campground

12   South River Falls

13   Swift Run Gap, US 33 Interchange

14   Loft Mountain Wayside, Deadening Nature Trail

15   Blackrock Summit

16   Rockfish Gap Entrance Station

    Shenandoah National Park

- - - - - Appalachian Trail

───── Skyline Drive

10 MILES

Ref: USGS Front Royal 1:100,000
USGS Charlottesville 1:100,000

Free backcountry camping is allowed by permits. They are available at park headquarters, visitor centers, entrance stations, and self-registration stations at Rockfish Gap (mile 104.4 at the south end), Swift Run Gap (mile 65.5 at US 33 interchange), and the Tom Floyd Wayside (on the AT just outside the park's North District). Self-registration for overnighters near Old Rag Mountain is at the Weakley Hollow access.

Although it would seem such a large area would have plenty of backcountry campsites, that's not necessarily the case. Remember: Shenandoah has more backcountry campers per square mile than any other national park. Camping is not permitted within sight of a trail, road, another camping party, or a sign that says "No Camping." Because of the steep terrain, flat spots to pitch a tent are in short supply during peak seasons. Hikers who can arrange their visits on weekdays or during the off-season are not as likely to be disappointed or to be tempted to camp illegally.

PICNICKING IN SHENANDOAH NATIONAL PARK

Seven picnic areas, all with picnic tables, fireplaces, drinking fountains, and restrooms, are at the following locations: Dickey Ridge (mile 4.7), Elkwallow (mile 24.1), Pinnacles (mile 36.7), Big Meadows (mile 51.2), Lewis Mountain (mile 57.5), South River (mile 62.8), and Loft Mountain (mile 79.5). Picnic tables are also on the lower level at Skyland and scattered along the Drive. Sites accessible to the disabled and the elderly are available at all park picnic areas, and restrooms are accessible with assistance.

IMPORTANT MILEPOSTS ON SKYLINE DRIVE

Mile .6: Front Royal entrance station. [Fig. 44(1)]

Mile 4.6: Dickey Ridge Visitor Center. [Fig. 44(2)] Information, exhibits, slide show, phone, restrooms, water, self-guided trail, access to Dickey Ridge Trail, adjacent picnic area.

Mile 24: Elkwallow Wayside. [Fig. 44(4)] Snack bar, campstore, gifts, gas, water, toilets, phone, adjacent picnic area.

Mile 31.5: Thornton Gap, US 211 interchange. [Fig. 44(5)] Access from Luray, Warrenton, and Washington, D.C. Exit here for Old Rag Mountain trailhead (See hiking section).

Mile 31.6: Panorama. [Fig. 44(1)] Restaurant, phone, gift shop, information, AT access, hiking trails, restrooms.

Miles 41.7–42.5: Skyland. [Fig. 44(7)] Restaurant, lodging, gifts, taproom, horseback riding, restrooms, self-guided trail, interpretive programs, hikes.

Mile 51.2: Big Meadows. [Fig. 44(9)] Gas, restaurants, lodging, picnicking, camping, interpretive programs, hiking trails, restrooms, visitor center, phone.

Mile 57.5: Lewis Mountain Campground. [Fig. 44(11)] Picnic area, cabins, interpretive programs, campstore, phone, campground, showers, AT access, hiking trails.

Mile 65.5: Swift Run Gap, US 33 interchange. [Fig. 44(13)] AT and US 33 crossing.

Mile 79.5: Loft Mountain Wayside. [Fig. 44(14)] Food, gas, water, restrooms, information center (seasonal), gifts, campground, picnic area, amphitheater, camp store, laundry, showers, trailer disposal station, interpretive programs, hiking trails.

Mile 104.6: Rockfish Gap entrance station. [Fig. 44(16)] Operated seasonally. Park information available.

HIKING SHENANDOAH NATIONAL PARK

Shenandoah National Park is a Mecca for hikers. Some 500 miles of trails lead to waterfalls, deep canyons, old-growth forests, remains of early settlements, and rocky outcrops with sweeping views of the Piedmont to the east and Shenandoah Valley to the west. Trail blazes are blue for foot travel and yellow for horses. In addition, about 101 miles of the white-blazed Appalachian Trail (AT) pass through the park, roughly paralleling the Skyline Drive. The trail was constructed with gentle grades so it is rarely steep. An infinite variety of hikes is possible by combining portions of the AT and park trails to make loops.

On June 27, 1995, an intense rainstorm caused major flooding in many park streams, altering the course of some of them. Then Tropical Storm Fran blew down thousands of trees across park trails and roads on September 6, 1996. Hikers will come upon numerous reminders of both events in the park for many years, as personnel struggle with limited funding to repair the damage.

Hikes to some of the park's most popular waterfalls are at the following mileposts. Three of these (Whiteoak Canyon, Dark Hollow, and South River falls) are further described in the sampling of park hikes below. Overall Run Falls (miles 21.1 and 22.2), Whiteoak Canyon Falls (mile 42.6), Cedar Run Falls (mile 45.6), Rose River Falls (mile 49.4), Dark Hollow Falls (mile 50.7), Lewis Falls (mile 51.2), South River Falls (mile 62.8), Doyles River Falls (mile 81.1), Jones Run Falls (mile 84.1). Tip: Take a flashlight to trails with west views so you can watch the sunset and have light for the return trip.

Here are a few examples of park hikes:

FOX HOLLOW NATURE TRAIL (MILE 4.6). [Fig. 44(2)] Easy, 1.2-mile, self-guided circuit to mountaineer homesites. Climb from 1,940 feet at trailhead across road from Dickey Ridge Visitor Center to 2,250 feet.

TRACES NATURE TRAIL (MILE 22.2). [Fig. 44(3)] Easy, 1.7-mile, self-guided loop showing "traces" of old homesites, beginning at Mathews Arm Campground amphitheater parking area and climbing 335 feet.

OLD RAG MOUNTAIN (EXIT SKYLINE DRIVE AT THORNTON GAP, MILE 31.5). [Fig. 44(5)] The tough, steep climb to the summit of Old Rag Mountain is one of the most popular hikes in Shenandoah National Park and in Virginia. Unlike most hikes in the park, this one begins at the bottom of the mountain instead of from the Skyline Drive.

Old Rag is a roundish mountain in the northern tip of Madison County, east of White Oak Canyon. The circuit hike from Weakley Hollow on the northeastern slope is a 7.2-mile, blue-blazed loop that climbs a grueling 2,380 feet to the 3,291-foot summit where the hiker is rewarded with beautiful views of the surrounding mountains and valleys. Take the Ridge Trail south out of the parking area to the summit and descend on the Saddle Trail on the northwest slope. Then use the Weakley Hollow fire road to return to the starting point.

Along the trail, hikers pass between vertical granite walls less than 3 feet apart. Underfoot is a rocky stairstep formation. The rocks are what is left of an ancient dike formed when molten lava poured out of a fissure in the granite. An early start is necessary to allow ample time to rest between stretches of boulder climbing and treks up steep slopes. (Overnight trips are not allowed.) Despite the terrain, on a summer weekend the summit may be filled with hikers enjoying the outstanding views. Hikers over the age of 16 now pay a fee to climb Old Rag. A collection box is at the trailhead.

Each June, nearby Graves Mountain Lodge hosts a popular three-day bluegrass music festival on the grounds beside the Rose River. The picturesque river valley and the Blue Ridge mountains make the perfect background for the bluegrass, including some of the country's best-known bands. Graves Lodge is noted for its home-cooked food served at long tables, family style. Camping is available during the festival, but lodge rooms are reserved for the bands. Contact the lodge at (540) 923-4231 for festival tickets or meal reservations, which are required.

Directions: To reach the parking area and trailhead for the circuit hike, exit the Skyline Drive at Thornton Gap (mile 31.5) and go east on US 211 for 7 miles. Go south on US 522 for .6 mile. Turn right on VA 231 and go about 7 miles. Turn right on VA 601 and go about 4 miles (road becomes VA 707 and then VA 600). Go left at a sharp left turn (small private road goes straight) and continue .3 mile to parking area and trailhead. For alternative hikes up Old Rag, consult park maps.

LITTLE STONY MAN CLIFFS (MILE 39.1). [Fig. 44(6)] Moderate .9-mile round trip, climbing 270 feet to cliffs with outstanding views of Stony Man, Marys Rock, and the Pinnacle. The Little Stony Man cliffs are composed of greenstone formed in ancient times from what is called the Catoctin lava flows. With each new eruption (there were at least a dozen in the park), the lava reached higher and higher on granite hillsides, eventually covering all but the highest peaks.

STONY MAN NATURE TRAIL (MILE 41.7). [Fig. 44(7)] Self-guided, 1.6-mile round trip that climbs gradually from 3,670 feet at the trailhead to panoramic views on the summit of Stony Man Mountain (elevation 4,010 feet), the second highest point in the park. Hike is mostly easy, with strenuous sections. American mountain-ash grows near the summit. Squirrels, ruffed grouse, and many songbirds eat the tree's bright red berries in late summer and early fall. A small copper mine was also located near the summit in the early 1800s.

WHITEOAK CANYON (MILE 42.6). [Fig. 44(7)] One of the most beautiful and sought-after areas of Shenandoah National Park is this deep gorge with its six waterfalls, sheer cliffs, giant boulders, old hemlocks, and floor of ferns and mosses. A round trip to the first and tallest of the falls is 4.6 miles. This trail passes through the giant hemlocks of the Limberlost (see Limberlost Trail below). To reach the first falls, descend from 3,510 feet at trailhead parking to 2,470 feet. Park naturalists have identified false helibore (*Veratrum viride*) on the trail.

Below the first falls, the trail is steep. It's another 2.7 miles and 1,110 feet down to the last waterfall. Tip: Come on weekdays or, better yet, in the off-season. Whiteoak Canyon can be a busy place on summer weekends and during fall foliage.

LIMBERLOST TRAIL (MILE 43). [Fig. 44(7)] Easy, gently sloping, 1.3-mile loop (handicapped accessible) through ancient hemlocks, from 350 to 400 years old. Trail is improved with frequent benches, a 65-foot bridge and 150-foot wooden board-walk, and hard-packed crushed greenstone walkway. The acidic soil formed by decaying evergreen needles and the low light combine to make impossible conditions for all but the most shade-loving understory plants such as mosses, ferns, and lichens. An obvious question is why the hemlocks were spared when everything around them was logged. Credit goes to the founder of Skyland, a recreation area here even before the park was created. George Freeman Pollock paid lumbermen $10 a tree to leave the hemlocks standing. Incidentally, Pollock is also credited with influencing a study commission in 1924 to recommend to Congress that the Blue Ridge be the site of a national park.

HAWKSBILL MOUNTAIN (MILE 45.6). [Fig. 44(8)] Difficult 1.7-mile round trip from 3,365 feet to Hawksbill summit (elevation 4,050 feet), the highest point in the park. The trail crosses talus slopes, or boulderfields, beneath sheer cliffs of Catoctin greenstone. With repeated freezing and thawing, the rock broke from the cliffs thousands of years ago and tumbled down the slopes. Note the lichens, mosses, ferns, and hardy plants such as yellow clintonia (*Clintonia borealis)*, Alleghany stonecrop (*Penthorum*), flowering spurge (*Euphorbia corollata*), and sedums that have adapted to the scant soil.

The Shenandoah salamander (*Plethodon shenandoah*) is found here and two other places in the park (Stony Man Mountain and the Pinnacles). The body is dark brown. In one color phase the salamander has a narrow red-to-yellow stripe down the center of the back. In a second phase, the back is uniformly dark brown with scattered gold-colored flecks. The amphibian dwells in the soil that has collected among the rocks of north- and northwest-facing slopes above 2,900 feet.

On the summit is an observation platform with panoramic view, Byrds Nest Shelter No. 2, and picnic table. This is the best place in the park for watching the fall migration of hawks and other birds of prey.

DARK HOLLOW FALLS (MILE 50.7). [Fig. 44(10)] Moderate, 1.4-mile, heavily used trail from 3,425 feet at parking area down to beautiful waterfalls at 3,130 feet.

Stay on the trail to avoid slippery, dangerous rocks at top. Falls drop 70 feet over greenstone remaining from ancient lava flow. Trail goes below falls to Rose River fire road at 2,985 feet.

STORY OF THE FOREST NATURE TRAIL (MILE 51). [Fig. 44(9)] Easy, 1.8-mile, self-guided circuit featuring succession from meadow to forest. Elevation change is from 3,510 feet at Byrd Visitor Center trailhead to 3,800 feet.

SOUTH RIVER FALLS (MILE 62.8). [Fig. 44(12)] Easy-to-moderate, 2.6-mile round trip (steady climb of 850 feet on return) along old stone walls and old fields and down to gorge with view of falls and Saddleback Mountain. Flowering spurge (*Euphorbia corolata*) grows 1 to 3 feet high along the trail. Like its relative, the Christmas poinsettia (*E. pulcherrima*), the tiny true flowers are surrounded by what look like petals (white on the flowering spurge, red on the poinsettia) but are actually petal-like bracts.

DEADENING NATURE TRAIL (MILE 79.4). [Fig. 44(14)] 1.4-mile self-guided circuit from pastureland to mature forest. Chestnut stumps show evidence of girdling or "deadening" once practiced by mountain people to allow sunlight through canopy for crops or pasturelands. At the top is a spectacular view of Big Run watershed to the west.

BLACKROCK SUMMIT (MILE 84.8). [Fig. 44(15)] 1-mile, easy round trip along talus slopes (boulderfields) of Hampton quartzite. Spectacular view.

Sky Meadows State Park

[Fig. 45] Just an hour's drive from the nation's capital, Sky Meadows State Park provides a natural respite of pleasant pastures, hiking trails, rolling woodlands, old stone fences, and distant views from the eastern slopes of the Blue Ridge Mountains.

This is a low-key park, designed for those who like natural history, quiet woodland walks or rides on horseback, birdwatching, wildflower identification, deer watching, and the savoring of pastoral views that have changed little since the Civil War raged across these valleys and mountains. Sky Meadows is aptly named. A former owner, Sir Robert Hadow, thought the mix of hills and meadows looked a lot like his native Scotland. Hadow called the property Skye Farm. The land changed hands several times over the years. When philanthropist Paul Mellon donated a total of 1,618 acres for development of the state park in the 1970s and 1980s, his contributions brought the total land area to its present 1,862 acres.

Sky Meadows State Park is a place of unusual beauty, but it doesn't have many of the developed facilities that attract large crowds. There are no big lakes, only a children's fishing pond. The 12 campsites are primitive, and to reach them one has to hike .75 mile from the visitor center. But the park offers hiking trails and a horse trail, equine facilities, picnicking, fascinating interpretive programs, and a farm-

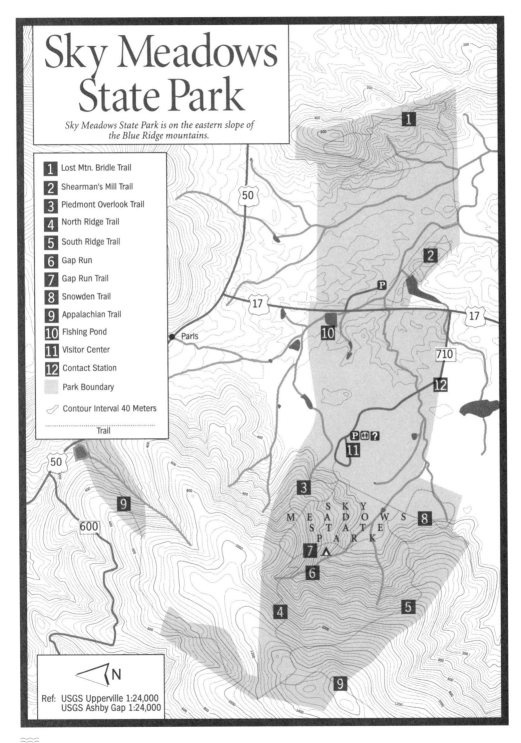

Sky Meadows State Park

Sky Meadows State Park is on the eastern slope of the Blue Ridge mountains.

1 Lost Mtn. Bridle Trail
2 Shearman's Mill Trail
3 Piedmont Overlook Trail
4 North Ridge Trail
5 South Ridge Trail
6 Gap Run
7 Gap Run Trail
8 Snowden Trail
9 Appalachian Trail
10 Fishing Pond
11 Visitor Center
12 Contact Station

Park Boundary

Contour Interval 40 Meters

Trail

Paris

SKY MEADOWS STATE PARK

N

Ref: USGS Upperville 1:24,000
USGS Ashby Gap 1:24,000

house/visitor center that is more than 150 years old. In May, Sky Meadows makes a great base camp for exploring the trillium-covered slopes of bordering Thompson Wildlife Management Area (WMA). The two are connected by the Appalachian Trail.

Sky Meadows is a beautiful place to walk or to sit and think about mountains, wildflowers, wildlife, and Virginia history.

Directions: From I-66 in northern Fauquier County, take Exit 23 and go north on US 17 for 7 miles to park entrance at VA 710, on left.

Activities: Primitive camping, picnicking, horseback riding, hiking, fishing, interpretive programs.

Facilities: 12 primitive campsites (accessible by .75-mile trail), 6 hiking trails and AT access, 4.6-mile bridle trail, 11-stall barn with corral, children's fishing pond, 1-mile nature trail. Visitor center in historical Mount Bleak house. Picnic area with drinking water, grills, restroom.

Dates: Day use and camping permitted year-round. Visitor center open daily during summer and on weekends in spring and fall. Tours presented on weekends and holidays (weekdays by request).

Fees: There is a charge for admission.

Closest town: Paris, near the Fauquier/Loudoun/Clarke county border, is 1.2 miles north at the junction of US 17 and US 50. Front Royal is about 21 miles southwest.

For more information: Sky Meadows State Park, 11012 Edmonds Lane, Delaplane, VA 20144. Phone (540) 592-3556.

TRAILS OF SKY MEADOWS STATE PARK

Six hiking trails, plus a 3.6-mile stretch of the Georgia-to-Maine Appalachian Trail (white blaze), climb the high meadows and ridges of the park. By combining portions of the trails, several loops are possible. From a service road at the west end of the visitor center, the red-blazed Piedmont Overlook Trail [Fig. 45(3)] climbs .7 mile through a field of wildflowers to connect with the blue-blazed North Ridge Trail [Fig. 45(4)]. Hikers can use this trail to descend and make a circuit, or continue uphill another .3 mile on the North Ridge Trail to the orange-blazed Gap Run Trail. Go left on Gap Run Trail [Fig. 45(7)] to descend to the primitive campground or continue along the North Ridge Trail .6 mile to a .3-mile spur climbing steeply to the AT.

For a picturesque return trip, at the junction with the North Ridge Trail [Fig. 45(4)] and the AT spur, take the yellow-blazed South Ridge Trail [Fig. 45(5)]. This path leads 1.6 miles first along an old road in the woods, then through grass pastures with expansive views to a connection with the lower end of the Gap Run Trail [Fig. 45(7)]. Go right to return to the visitor center. On the way back, the Gap Run Trail passes by a connection with the 1.1-mile interpretive loop of the Snowden Trail [Fig. 45(8)]. Equestrians have exclusive rights to the challenging and scenic Lost Mountain Bridle Trail [Fig. 45(1)]—a 4.6-mile loop that includes an .8-mile access trail.

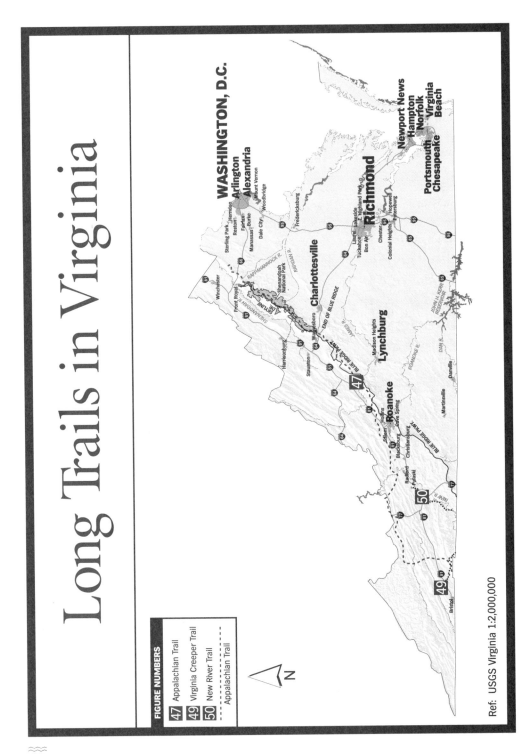

Long Trails in Virginia

FIGURE NUMBERS

47 Appalachian Trail
49 Virginia Creeper Trail
50 New River Trail
- - - - Appalachian Trail

Ref: USGS Virginia 1:2,000,000

Long Trails & River Valleys

V irginia has several outstanding long trails that provide hikers with many wonderful opportunities to enjoy the state's natural beauty. Whether you are a novice or an expert, there are many long trails to sample: the Appalachian Trail, the Virginia Creeper, the New River Trail, and the Big Blue and Tuscarora trails. The 545 miles of the Appalachian Trail offer many unforgettable hiking and camping opportunities. The Virginia Creeper, in the southwest corner of the state, is a 33-mile hike that testifies to the wisdom of rails-to-trails conversions. The New River Trail, a hike along what may be the second oldest river in the world, is another beautiful 57-mile jaunt on an old railroad bed that has been converted through a rails-to-trails program. Claytor Lake State Park is an impoundment on the New River. These two parks are included here because they cut across physiographic provinces, as does the James River which is also in this chapter.

[*Above*: New River Trail State Park]

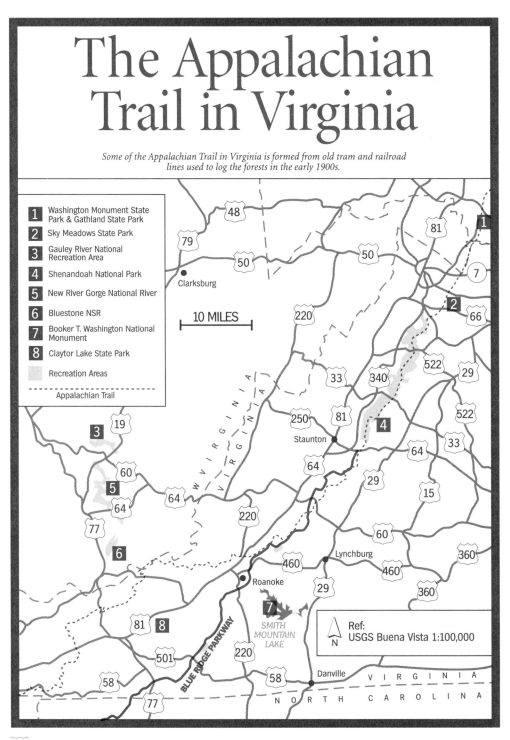

The Appalachian Trail in Virginia

Some of the Appalachian Trail in Virginia is formed from old tram and railroad lines used to log the forests in the early 1900s.

1. Washington Monument State Park & Gathland State Park
2. Sky Meadows State Park
3. Gauley River National Recreation Area
4. Shenandoah National Park
5. New River Gorge National River
6. Bluestone NSR
7. Booker T. Washington National Monument
8. Claytor Lake State Park

Recreation Areas

Appalachian Trail

10 MILES

Clarksburg

Staunton

Lynchburg

Roanoke

SMITH MOUNTAIN LAKE

Danville

BLUE RIDGE PARKWAY

VIRGINIA
NORTH CAROLINA

VIRGINIA / VIRGINIA

Ref:
USGS Buena Vista 1:100,000

N

The Appalachian Trail in Virginia

[Fig. 46(47), Fig. 47, Fig. 48] The Appalachian Trail is a footpath of more than 2,150 miles, stretching along the Appalachian Mountains and across great river valleys from Springer Mountain, Georgia, to Mount Katahdin, Maine. It's the longest footpath in the world, passing through 14 states.

Developing the AT took an enormous creative effort, requiring the cooperation of volunteers with federal, state, and local agencies. The trail was first proposed in an inspired magazine article by U.S. Forest Service planner Benton MacKaye of Massachusetts in 1921. His idea was to link Mount Washington in New Hampshire—the highest peak in the northern Appalachians—with Mount Mitchell in North Carolina—the highest peak in the southern Appalachians. Plans for the northern terminus extended the trail to Mount Katahdin. The southern terminus was first Lookout Mountain near Chattanooga, Tennessee, then changed to Mount Oglethorpe, Georgia, and then to its current location at Springer Mountain, Georgia.

In 1925, workers organized the Appalachian Trail Conference (ATC), a private nonprofit organization that today still oversees trail maintenance and management. The ATC chose the route; flagged it; built sections of trail, bridges, and steps where necessary; built shelters for hikers and backpackers; wrote guidebooks; and erected signs to aid hikers. In 1937, MacKaye's dream became reality with the dedication of the verdant pathway from New England across the Mason-Dixon Line to the Deep South.

In 1968, Congress passed the National Trails System Act, making the Appalachian Trail (AT) on the East Coast and the Canada-to-Mexico Pacific Crest Trail on the West Coast the first National Scenic Trails.

Although 14 states claim parts of the white-blazed AT, no state comes anywhere close to the 545 miles—more than a fourth of the total milage—that pass through Virginia. As it runs northeast/southwest up the Appalachians, the trail crosses back and forth across the Great Valley of Virginia to take in parts of all three mountainous portions of Virginia's five physiographic provinces—Plateau, Valley and Ridge, and Blue Ridge. It varies in altitude from just 660 feet above sea level at the James River crossing to well over 1 mile high atop Mount Rogers (5,729 feet).

Those who hike the complete AT through the state will travel through many sites covered in this book. Circuit hikes can be arranged to suit the individual by combining sections of the AT with connecting trails in various state parks, national forest districts, Shenandoah National Park, and along the Blue Ridge Parkway. Otherwise, hiking a stretch of the trail requires doubling back or leaving a second car at the finish.

The AT comes into Virginia from North Carolina at Damascus, in southeastern Washington County. A rugged but scenic 54.6 miles of the AT wind along the Iron Mountains of Mount Rogers National Recreation Area in the Blue Ridge Highlands. Then the footpath heads northward in southwest Virginia, zigzagging its way across the Valley and Ridge province. The trail runs the ridge above the amazing bowl of

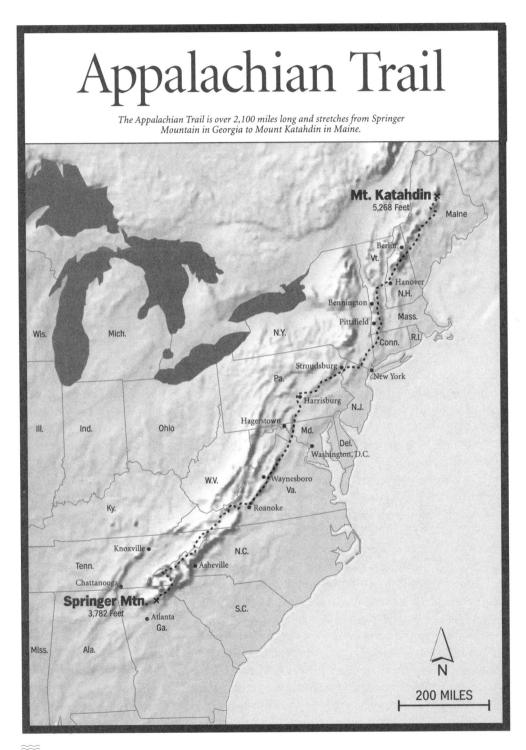

Appalachian Trail

The Appalachian Trail is over 2,100 miles long and stretches from Springer Mountain in Georgia to Mount Katahdin in Maine.

Burkes Garden on the Bland/Tazewell county line. It angles northeast to cross the New River and trace the edge of the Plateau province through Peters Mountain Wilderness along the West Virginia border for a few miles. Like a meandering river, it then wanders lazily south, east, and northeast across the Great Valley again to rejoin the Blue Ridge mountains north of Roanoke.

From mile 103 on the Blue Ridge Parkway, it plays tag with the Parkway and then the Skyline Drive along the mountain crests. North of Skyline Drive, it leads through acre upon acre of trillium carpeting the slopes of Thompson Wildlife Management Area as it heads for the confluence of the Shenandoah and Potomac rivers at Harpers Ferry, West Virginia, where the parent ATC organization is located. A crossing of the Shenandoah on the West Virginia line leaves hikers heading north with a last reminder of Virginia's gentle beauty.

Those who have become familiar with those 545 miles of AT have seen hemlock-lined ravines where rhododendrons bloom and jack-in-the-pulpits hide along stream edges. They've delighted in damp spring mornings after a rain when the fields are fragrant with honeysuckle. They've seen soaring cliffs of granite and greenstone that intrigue geologists and watched the turning of the heavens in the night sky over their campsites. The pool of a waterfall has cooled weary feet, the stump of an old chestnut has supported an achy back, and a sun-warmed handful of blackberries has served as breakfast.

If they're lucky, a black bear or two has crossed their path, an eagle has soared the ridgeline beside them, and a whip-poor-will has sung them a wilderness lullaby. They've also learned something of their own nature as they cope with loneliness, overcrowded shelters, heat rash, wet clothing, a leaking tent, a bee sting, blisters, and boredom. The trail is rarely easy, but the rewards are great. Like a river valley, the green corridor of the AT is largely hidden and unknown to all but the relatively few who follow it.

Many hikers who spend a lot of time on the trail become so appreciative of the never-ending job of volunteers from local ATC groups, they end up joining a chapter. These volunteers build bridges and shelters, identify rare species along the trail that need protection, remove debris after storms, and work to protect the rights of bordering landowners while keeping the trail open for everyone to enjoy.

The white, 2-by-6-inch, rectangular trail markers are painted on trees and rocks. A double blaze—one above the other—warns of turns, junctions, or other places where the hiker should be alert. Blue blazes mark AT side trails. Usually, these lead to shelters, a water supply, or viewpoints.

For more information: For guidebooks, maps, and other publications or to find out the closest affiliated AT club, contact the Appalachian Trail Conference, PO Box 807, Washington and Jackson Streets, Harpers Ferry, WV 25425-0807. Phone (304) 535-6331.

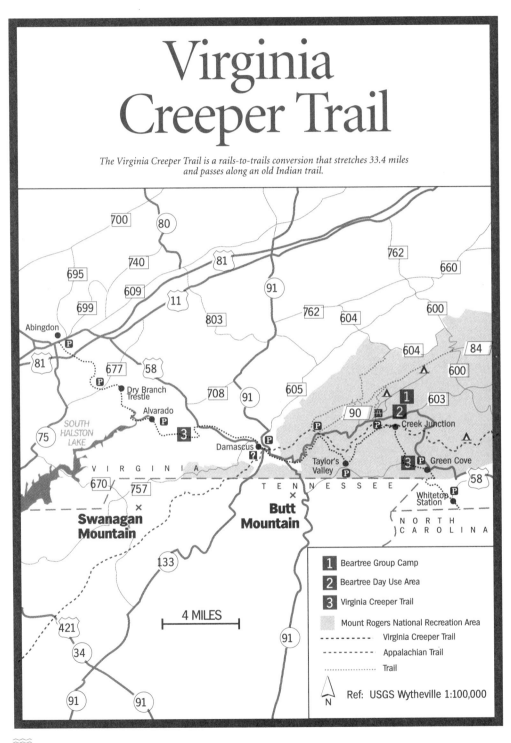

Virginia Creeper Trail

The Virginia Creeper Trail is a rails-to-trails conversion that stretches 33.4 miles and passes along an old Indian trail.

1 Beartree Group Camp

2 Beartree Day Use Area

3 Virginia Creeper Trail

Mount Rogers National Recreation Area

‑ ‑ ‑ ‑ ‑ ‑ ‑ ‑ ‑ ‑ Virginia Creeper Trail

‑ ‑ ‑ ‑ ‑ ‑ ‑ Appalachian Trail

················· Trail

N Ref: USGS Wytheville 1:100,000

4 MILES

The Virginia Creeper Trail

[Fig. 49, Fig. 46(49)] The Virginia Creeper Trail is a rails-to-trails conversion that stretches 33.4 miles from Abingdon in Washington County to the North Carolina line in western Grayson County. As with most trails that follow old railroad beds, this one links nature with history as it passes along an old Indian trail through some of southwest Virginia's best countryside and most splendid mountain scenery.

With humor, local folks referred to the mountain train that climbed eastward into the Iron Mountains as the Virginia Creeper, a name taken from the plant that grew abundantly beside the tracks. A steam engine laboring up mountain grades with heavy loads of lumber, iron ore, supplies, and passengers was also a "creeper" in every sense of the word.

Before the rails were laid, Indians followed animal trails out of the Blue Ridge to create a footpath northwestward. The path went through The Breaks of Dickenson County into Kentucky and on to the Big Sandy River and the Ohio River. Daniel Boone also camped along the trail, according to early records. In 1887, when iron mining became profitable, a railroad was constructed along the path from Abingdon east to the southern slope of Whitetop Mountain to bring products from the mountains to market.

By 1918, when lumber had become a more important resource, the line stretched 75 miles to Elkland, North Carolina, and included more than 100 trestles. Villagers out picking blackberries or elderberries along the tracks watched as stacks of red spruce, freshly cut from virgin forests high atop Mount Rogers, rumbled by on flatbed cars. Although beset by flood damage as well as economic problems associated with the Great Depression, a train ran at least weekly until 1976.

RAILS-TO-TRAILS PROGRAM

Walking the Virginia Creeper Trail confirms what a great idea the first person had who looked at an abandoned railroad and said: "Hiking trail!" Because of the extremely heavy loads hauled by steam engines, railroad beds were constructed with minimal grades. When a railroad bed is converted to a hiking trail, people in average physical condition gain access to beautiful countryside, pristine mountain streams, and exciting mountain passes. Anywhere the nearly extinct "iron horse" once tooted its whistle, there's trail potential.

Between 1800 and 1916, the federal government laid more than 300,000 miles of track. By the 1970s, many railroads were abandoned for other forms of transportation. Since 1986, a nonprofit group called the Rails-to-Trails Conservancy (RTC) has been the largest advocate for converting those tracks to trail systems. Who benefits? Anyone who wants to hike, bike, jog, ride a horse, fish a stream, or watch a bird along green corridors that lead through our country's towns, prairies, pasture lands, river valleys, and mountains.

HIKING AND BIKING THE VIRGINIA CREEPER TRAIL

The trail is wide, smooth, and well kept. Signs are clear and easy to locate at access points. The west half of the trail, from Abingdon to Damascus, is level and mostly open or it skirts the edge of fields and pastures. Signs along the first 1.5 miles provide a guided nature walk. At mile 7.2, the Middle and South forks of the Holston River converge at a trestle. The elevation is 1,900 feet, the lowest on the trail. Then the path climbs through dense forest into Mount Rogers National Recreation Area (NRA), rising 2,000 feet to grassy balds on Whitetop Mountain.

Because the railroad grade was never more than 5 percent, even going uphill is not difficult. Nevertheless, the trail is heavily used by mountain bikers who take a shuttle to the top, then ride downhill to Abingdon. Walkers do well to stay alert for careening bicyclists to come whizzing by.

It's hard to find a bicycle trail more user-friendly than the 18 miles between Whitetop and Damascus. The Creeper Trail combines downhill coasting with spectacular mountain scenery. Rental bikes and skis are available at Abingdon and at Damascus on a seasonal basis. Bikers should ring a bell or toot a horn to alert hikers before passing.

Although no facilities are available on the trail, the many access points and small towns along the way make it easy to walk sections of the trail without carrying gear. Be prepared for sudden changes in weather, especially at higher elevations. Cold wind, rain, fog, or snow can arrive unexpectedly. When temperatures near the freezing mark on a damp day, ice can form in a hurry.

TRAIL WILDLIFE

The Virginia Creeper Trail is an excellent place to observe wildlife, especially on weekdays or the off-season when human usage is light. Where the path parallels streams, you may find the chewed stumps that beavers leave where they have felled trees. Near mile 2, look for a beaver lodge in the pond. If there are fresh cuttings about, there's a good chance you could sit very quietly here at dusk or early morning and see the nocturnal rodents at work.

On warm spring evenings, when the temperature rises above 50 degrees, spring peepers (*Hyla crucifer*)—they're really thumbnail-size frogs—gather in damp areas to chirp their loud mating chorus. The marshy upper end of the pond is a favorite habitat of pond dwellers.

Cottontail rabbits and gray squirrels are abundant along the trail. Larger and somewhat rare fox squirrels inhabit small woodlands, stream corridors, and field borders. Both red and gray foxes are in the area. This is not the best place to find black bear, but visitors may get lucky and spot one. On the other hand, chances are good hikers might round a bend and startle a doe crossing the path with her fawns. Hikers, however, may be the ones to jump if they stop to sip from their canteen and a ruffed grouse or woodcock beside the trail suddenly explodes into flight. On rapid wing beats, ducks are likely to rise ahead from the South Fork of the Holston to settle farther upriver. In fact, one bird watcher estimates as many as 40 different species of birds can be seen per day. Where there are open fields, look for colorful bluebirds, goldfinches, and meadowlarks. In woodlands, the ovenbird, Carolina chickadee, nuthatch, and wood thrush proclaim their territories.

TRAIL VEGETATION

Along the 1.5-mile nature trail on the west end, there are two trees prized for their flexible wood. The Osage orange (*Maclure pomifera*) takes its name from the Osage Indians, who put the wood's flexibility to use in their bows. The mockernut hickory (*Carva tomentosa*) has been widely used for wagon parts, tool handles, and barrel hoops. The mockernut's wood will take a great deal of strain before breaking.

A sprinkling of the many wildflowers to look for includes bloodroot (*Sanguinaria canadensis*), spring beauty (*Claytonia virginica*), large-flowered bellwort (*Uvularia grandiflora*), solomon's-seal (*Polygonatum biflorum*), Virginia dayflower (*Commelina virginica*), and ditch stonecrop (*Penthorum sedoides*). Wildflowers bloom late in the spring at higher elevations past Taylors Valley (mile 21).

Impressive stands of Catawba rhododendron (*Rhododendron catawbiense*) hang out over streambanks in mountainous sections of the trail. A foggy, drippy day along the cascading waters of Whitetop Laurel Creek when the lush, purplish pink flowers are blooming offers a soft beauty for those who enjoy rainy-day hikes. Redbud, dogwood, wild cherry, and shadbush add their fragrance and color to spring on the trail.

FISHING ON THE VIRGINIA CREEPER TRAIL

At mile 8, the trail passes the north end of South Holston Lake, known for its smallmouth bass. The big reservoir, most of which lies in Tennessee, also provides excellent crappie fishing, along with largemouth bass, channel catfish, flathead catfish, and bluegill. In spring, white bass, and recently, walleye, run out of the lake and up the South Fork of the Holston, which parallels the trail to mile 13. However, access is limited, and visitors must obtain landowner permission if they have to cross private property to reach the water.

East of Damascus, the trail parallels Whitetop Laurel Creek, one of the state's best streams for stocked trout. Above the Straight Branch tributary, Whitetop Laurel is a native trout stream. Special regulations apply. Check the fishing regulations booklet available wherever licenses are sold.

For more information: Virginia Department of Game and Inland Fisheries, 4010 West Broad Street, Richmond, VA 23230-1104. Phone (804) 367-1000.

Directions: Trail access with parking is available at (from east to west) Abingdon, Watauga, Alvarado, Damascus, Iron Bridge, Straight Branch, Taylors Valley, Creek Junction, Callahan's Crossing, Green Cove Station, and Whitetop Station. Here are directions to the most popular points:

Abingdon (mile 0): Located in center of downtown near corner of A Street SE and Green Springs Road. Turn south off East Main Street onto Pecan Street. Go .2 mile. Look on left for the steam locomotive on permanent display at the trailhead. Parking is on the right.

Alvarado (mile 8.5): Take Exit 19 from I-81, go 5 miles east on US 58, turn right on VA 722 to 710 and parking area.

Damascus (mile 15.5): Trail parallels Main Street (US 58). Parking is where Main Street crosses Beaverdam Creek Bridge. Damascus, once a Daniel Boone campsite, is a nationally recognized welcome center for hikers on the Appalachian Trail (AT) and the Virginia Creeper Trail. An AT hostel is located here.

Creek Junction (mile 25): From Damascus, take US 58 east 10.1 miles to right on gravel VA 728 and go 1.5 miles to parking at trestle.

Whitetop Station (mile 32.3): From Damascus, take US 58 east 17 miles to right on VA 755. Go 2 miles to parking.

Activities: Hiking, jogging, mountain biking, horseback riding, cross-country skiing, fishing, interpretive walk. Camping is permitted in portion of trail that lies in Mount Rogers NRA, but campers should choose sites 100 feet off trail and away from streams. Between Abingdon and Damascus, where the trail passes through private property, landowners' permission must be obtained to camp. Contact Virginia Creeper Trail Club for private land campsite information. Wheelchairs with large tires can travel downhill from Creek Junction (mile 25) to Damascus (mile 15.5). No motorized vehicles.

Facilities: None on trail. Carry enough water to get from town to town. Forest service information centers, as well as water, toilets, and pay phones, are at Damascus and Green Cove trailheads.

Dates: Open year-round.

Closest town: Western trailhead is in Abingdon in southern Washington County. Damascus is near center of trail. Whitetop Station in southwestern Grayson County is 1.1 miles from trail's end at the North Carolina border.

For more information: Abingdon Convention and Visitors Bureau, Cummings Street, Abingdon, VA 24210. Phone (540) 676-2282 or (800) 435-3440. Virginia Creeper Trail Club, PO Box 2382, Abingdon, VA 24210. Mount Rogers National Recreation Area, Route 1, Box 303, Marion, VA 24354. Phone (540) 783-5196.

For bike or ski rental: Highlands Bike Rentals (at trailhead in Abingdon), phone (540) 628-9672. Highlands Ski and Outdoor Center, West Main Street, Abingdon, VA 24210. Phone (540) 682-1329. Blue Blaze Bike and Shuttle Service, Damascus, VA 24236. Phone (540) 575-5095. Mount Rogers Outfitters, 100 Laurel Avenue, Damascus, VA 24236. Phone (540) 475-5416.

Trail: 33.4-mile, linear, rails-to-trails footpath from Abingdon to VA/NC line. From Damascus to Creek Junction, several connections with Appalachian Trail make loop hikes possible.

Elevation: 1,900 feet at South Holston Trestle (mile 7.2) to 3,577 at VA/NC line (mile 34.3).

Degree of difficulty: Abingdon to Damascus (west half), easy. Damascus to Whitetop Station, easy to moderate.

Surface: Cinder, natural, crushed gravel, wooden trestles.

▓ ABINGDON

[Fig. 49] The Virginia Highlands Arts and Crafts Festival, held in historic Abingdon in Washington County during the first two weeks in August each year, is the town's way of celebrating the revival in old-time arts and crafts. The streets are filled with booths of some of the area's finest artists and craftspeople.

Visitors also browse the colorful shops in a town known for its own mountain crafts. A must-see is the Cave House Craft Shop housed in a 1958 Victorian home at 279 East Main Street, and run by a 140-member cooperative. Visitors can also take in a play at Barter Theater, America's longest-running repertory theater (at the corner of Main and College streets), but they are no longer required to barter corn or sweet potatoes for admission. Cash is accepted. The historic Martha Washington Inn with its wide front porch and famous rocking chairs beckons the weary traveler to come sit and watch the world pass. This elegantly restored inn predates the Civil War, and was once known as Martha Washington College, a school for young women. Typhoid fever and the Great Depression forced the school to close in the early twentieth century.

For more information: Abingdon Convention and Visitors Bureau, Cummings Street, Abingdon, VA 24210. Phone (540) 676-2282 or (800) 435-3440.

The Big Blue and Tuscarora Trails

The 143-mile Big Blue Trail (named for its blue blazes) takes off westward from the Appalachian Trail on Hogback Mountain in Shenandoah National Park. After crossing Massanutten Mountain and the Shenandoah Valley, it veers north and heads for Hancock, Maryland. There, it becomes the Tuscarora Trail and continues another 80 miles in a broad arc back to the AT near Duncannon, Pennsylvania.

Originally, the Big Blue and Tuscarora trails were planned as a westward rerouting of the Appalachian Trail to bypass growing population areas in northern Virginia and Maryland. However, the AT gained the permanent protection it needed with the National Scenic Trails Act in 1968. So the Big Blue–Tuscarora route became an alternate for hikers who prefer the more rural and rugged scenery of the Massanutten and Allegheny mountains. It can also be used as a giant loop hike when combined with the AT.

For more information: Appalachian Trail Conference, PO Box 807, Washington and Jackson Streets, Harpers Ferry, WV 25425-0807. Phone (304) 535-6331.

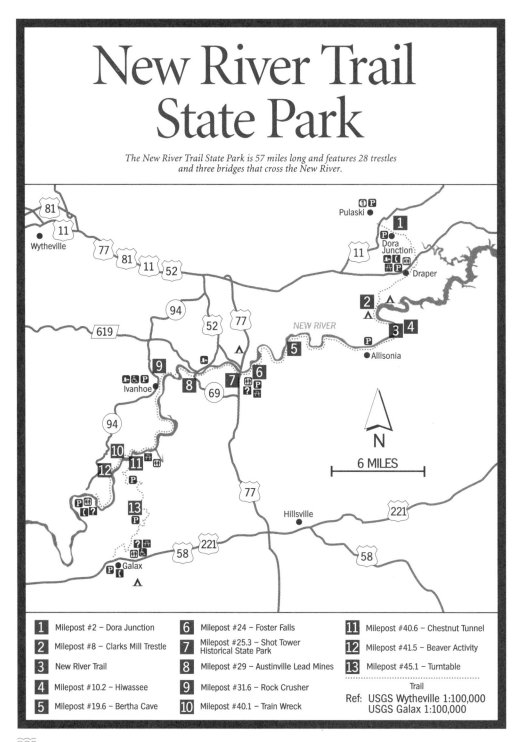

New River Trail State Park

The New River Trail State Park is 57 miles long and features 28 trestles and three bridges that cross the New River.

Pulaski
Dora Junction
Draper
Allisonia
Wytheville
NEW RIVER
Ivanhoe
Hillsville
Galax

N

6 MILES

Ref: USGS Wytheville 1:100,000
USGS Galax 1:100,000

1 Milepost #2 – Dora Junction	**6** Milepost #24 – Foster Falls	**11** Milepost #40.6 – Chestnut Tunnel
2 Milepost #8 – Clarks Mill Trestle	**7** Milepost #25.3 – Shot Tower Historical State Park	**12** Milepost #41.5 – Beaver Activity
3 New River Trail	**8** Milepost #29 – Austinville Lead Mines	**13** Milepost #45.1 – Turntable
4 Milepost #10.2 – Hiwassee	**9** Milepost #31.6 – Rock Crusher	Trail
5 Milepost #19.6 – Bertha Cave	**10** Milepost #40.1 – Train Wreck	

River Valleys: New River

[Fig. 50, Fig. 46(50)] At 350 million years old, the New River is hardly "new" at all. In fact, many geologists believe the New is second only to the Nile as the oldest river in the world. In prehistoric times, the river flowed north to the St. Lawrence River on the United States border with Canada.

During the Ice Age, glaciers carved up the New River, diverting it into the Ohio and eventually the Mississippi. The New River is also one of the few major rivers in the world to flow north. All other major waterways in this section of Virginia flow either south, east, or west, and thus take a more direct path to the Chesapeake Bay or the Gulf of Mexico. The New River is on of the few rivers in North America to flow south to north, and the only river to cut through the entire width of the Appalachian Mountains.

Because of the outstanding mountain and pastoral backdrops and the uncommonly clear waters that support a healthy ecosystem, the New River is ideal for boating, fishing, swimming, and snorkeling. Besides several varieties of fishes, the river teems with freshwater mussels and sponges, crayfish, salamanders, and snails. Raccoons leave little piles of shells where they've eaten mussels at water's edge. Ducks nest in roots and tree hollows along the banks and up in grassy creeks and marshes. Red-winged blackbirds make nests where there are cattails and reeds.

The North and South forks of the river converge on the Ashe and Alleghany county line in North Carolina, just south of Grayson County, Virginia. The river flows into Virginia near a tiny community called Mouth of Wilson, a southern gateway to some of Virginia's most spectacular mountain scenery in Mount Rogers National Recreation Area and Grayson Highlands State Park. The ancient New then begins its extraordinary 160-mile journey through Virginia and into West Virginia.

As it flows north, the river alternates between wild forests and languid farmlands. In keeping with the habit of rivers, the New follows a scenic path seldom seen by travelers on highways and byways. In passing through the Blue Ridge Mountains, it picks up New River Trail State Park, which follows it from Fries at the Grayson-Carroll county line north to the backwaters of Claytor Lake.

Claytor Dam, south of Interstate 81 and Radford, temporarily holds back the river while the Appalachian Power Company harnesses its energy. Then the New meanders north on the second half of its passage through Virginia, slips under Interstate 81, and forges through several mountain ranges of the Valley and Ridge province.

The river adds its beauty to the George Washington and Jefferson National Forests, squeezing between Walker and Sinking Creek mountains at the corner of Giles, Pulaski, and Montgomery counties. The New cools the feet of hikers on the Appalachian Trail west of Pearisburg, passes through a gap called the Narrows, and hails Peters Mountain Wilderness to the northeast as it leaves the state in the western tip of Giles County.

▒ HISTORY OF THE NEW RIVER VALLEY

Native American tools and artifacts found in the New River Valley suggest that hunting forays took the Indians throughout much of this naturally rich country as far back as 10,000 years ago, though evidence of permanent Indian settlements in the area is inconclusive.

European settlers, however, came, liked what they saw, and made themselves at home. In the last half of the 1700s, immigrants from Scotland, Ireland, England, and Germany walked or rode wagons and ox carts down the Great Valley. They came upon the mountains and streams and rich farmland and foggy mornings, and decided this area resembled the Old Country, so the settlers began spreading out, establishing homesteads and then forts to run to for safety.

Shawnee and Cherokee raiding parties regularly attacked the Europeans and tried to drive them out. Such dangers on the frontier reduced European immigration to a trickle during the French and Indian War and the American Revolution, but once peace could be assured, the wagons, horses, livestock, and people began a steady stream into the New River Valley. There was much to do and see.

Abundant food and fresh water were available. The New River and hundreds of nearby tributaries offered an additional source of food and a cheap and dependable supply of water-related energy for floating cut timber, grinding grains, making charcoal, tanning hides, and mining lead and iron. Mining and milling would all but disappear in the New River Valley in the early and mid-1900s, but manufacturing and service industries—and especially tourism—would fill the vacuum created when the rustic tanning of hides and the mining of saltpeter were no longer in demand.

▒ BOATING AND FLOATING THE NEW RIVER

The largest whitewater river in Virginia, the New offers challenges for all skill levels. However, until it enters West Virginia, it is mostly suited to those who enjoy a leisurely float through mountain passages and pastoral countryside. With many put-in sites, the river is ideal for those who like to leave a second car at a take-out point downriver and float the river in sections, perhaps camping along the way. Portages are required at Mouth of Wilson, Fries, Byllesby, and Buck dams.

There are numerous riffles and Class II and III rapids that will make an angler put down his rod and pick up a paddle in the upper section. In the lower river, north of Claytor Lake, some stretches are flat and require considerable paddling. Except during periods of high water, though, the river is best suited for novices and intermediate paddlers until it enters West Virginia, where its whitewater is renowned. There, the river changes character as it tumbles through the canyons of New River Gorge, creating serious rapids of Class III to Class V.

Outfitters in Virginia and West Virginia are ready to take visitors fishing, canoeing, tubing, or whitewater rafting. Some are listed here, or travelers can call local chambers of commerce for more information. For visitors who have their own craft, a state gazetteer will help locate the many boat landings spread along the river. Visitors should be prepared for sudden rises in water level when dam releases occur.

For more information: New River Trail State Park (canoe and inner tube rentals), Route 2, Box 126 F, Foster Falls, VA 24360. Phone (540) 699-6778 or (540) 236-8889. New River Adventures (based at Foster Falls), 1007 North Fourth Street, Wytheville, VA 24382. Phone (540) 228-8311. Allisonia Trading Post, HCO2 Box 15 B, Allisonia, VA 24347. Phone (540) 980-2051. Cliffview Trading Post, Route 4, Box 163, Galax, VA 24333. Phone (540) 238-1530. New River Canoe Livery, Pembroke, VA. Phone (540) 626-7189.

FISHING THE NEW RIVER

The largest smallmouth bass, walleye, and muskellunge ever caught in Virginia came from the New River. The bass weighed 7 pounds, 7 ounces; the walleye was 14 pounds, 2 ounces; and the muskie weighed 45 pounds. The New has a deserved reputation for producing citation (trophy) smallmouth, especially in the spring. In early 1997, a four-year-old (with Granddad's help) reeled in a 7-pound, 2-ounce smallmouth from the Giles County portion of the river.

In 1995, more trophy muskie—including one 36-pounder—came from the New than from any other body of water in the state. The fish are stocked from the North Carolina line to Fries Dam (southern trailheads for New River Trail State Park) and from Claytor Dam to the West Virginia line. Most are caught below Claytor Dam and downstream. Walleye run up the river out of Claytor Lake as early as January, as do white bass in April and May. Below Claytor Dam, look for walleye, stripers, white bass, catfish, largemouth bass, and rock bass.

Other varieties of fish that may hit your bait include redbreast sunfish, spotted bass, log perch, common carp, whitetail shiner, and channel catfish. Anglers or boaters below Claytor Dam must watch for water releases from the dam when electricity is being generated. The river level can rise dramatically and trap those riding in boats, fishing from rocks, or wading.

For more information: Virginia Department of Game and Inland Fisheries, 4010 West Broad Street, Richmond, VA 23230-1104. Phone (804) 367-1000.

SHOT TOWER HISTORICAL STATE PARK

[Fig. 17(2), Fig. 50(7)] Almost 200 years old, this fortresslike stone tower provided a complex but effective way to make lead shot for frontier hunters and adventurers and for the Confederacy during America's Civil War. The problem was how to make the shot perfectly round. Designers figured they could drop bits of hot lead from a height and it would cool into round balls as it fell. But two problems arose. One, wind currents could make the balls spin and cool unevenly. And two, the cooling lead would flatten when it hit bottom.

Thus the Shot Tower, which stands 75 feet high, with stone walls that are 2.5 feet thick. Beneath the floor of the tower, another 75-foot shaft was dug straight down by hand. The lower vertical shaft stopped just above river level, with a horizontal tunnel that led to the river.

In the top of the tower, 150 feet above the river level, molten lead was poured through porous sieves that shaped the projectiles. Tiny globs of hot lead in a 150-foot free-fall cooled uniformly, and were cushioned by a kettle of water at the bottom. Few of these old shot towers have survived wars, floods, and the ravages of time. Following renovation in 1968, the New River Shot Tower was designated a National Historic Mechanical Engineering Landmark by the American Society of Mechanical Engineers.

NEW RIVER TRAIL STATE PARK

[Fig. 50, Fig. 32(50)] From the beginning, rivers have fascinated people. They settle beside them and plant crops, yet harbor a yearning to check out a river's receding twists and turns and to find out what might lie beyond the next canyon.

Few places offer as much opportunity to hike, bike, or ride horseback alongside a major river as does the stretch of abandoned railroad bed that is now New River Trail State Park. Keeping perfect contact with the sinuous journey of the ancient New River and Chestnut Creek and the upper end of Claytor Lake, New River Trail State Park is 57 miles long, but only 80 feet wide. The path itself is 10 to 12 feet wide.

Several descriptive names are used to describe these long, skinny parks, including "linear park," "greenway," and "rails-to-trails park." The New River Trail is another example of the rails-to-trails plan to convert abandoned railroad to trail systems (*see* Rails-to-Trails Program, page 307). This one, created in 1987, features 28 former railroad trestles (now resurfaced to accommodate trail users) across tributary streams, three bridges that span the New River, and two 200-foot-long tunnels. With the unusual geologic features and history along the trail, not to mention the many opportunities for recreation, wildlife watching, and good fishing, the 55 miles of trail now open attract an increasing number of visitors each year.

Resident waterfowl along the park include mallards, wood ducks, American coots, Canada geese, great egrets, great blue herons, and little green herons. White-tailed deer drink from the river and its tributaries. Wild turkeys scratch in leaves along the banks. Beaver cuttings can be seen along the trail. Gray squirrels that live in trees along the river are not as wild—or wary—as those less accustomed to people.

Rivers are habitat for various reptiles and amphibians. A water snake may swim out from the edge as hikers pass, and head for the opposite bank. An occasional prehistoric-looking snapping turtle will watch with beady eyes from a safe distance.

Where tall weeds grow in a sunny field by the river, American goldfinches pick seeds from dried thistle stalks. The bright yellow males with black cap and wings are easy to spot. As evening settles on the riverbank, listen for the quiet call of robins in tall sycamores.

The east end of the expansive Mount Rogers National Recreation Area (NRA) borders the river on its west bank between Buck and Byllesby dams. Camping is available at New River Campground and Picnic Area here. This part of Mount Rogers NRA is not well known and therefore offers a better chance for solitude. A 2-mile stretch of the New River Trail between Lone Ash and Barren Springs in Wythe County is closed indefinitely.

The New River Trail also offers public access points for canoeing, kayaking, and fishing. Check park headquarters at Foster Falls for a free map listing access points and features along the riverside trail. The park rents canoes, bicycles, and inner tubes.

MILEPOSTS FROM SOUTH TO NORTH

Theoretically, following the New River north in the direction of its flow means walking downhill. For all practical purposes, however, the walk is level where it follows the river. At the northern end (milepost 8), the trail leaves the river and follows the old railroad bed, which heads on a more uphill course for Pulaski.

Starting from the two separate southern trailheads—the first at Galax on the Chestnut Creek tributary and the other at Fries on the river—here are a few highlights and the mileage as it relates to the old railroad mileposts (many still in place):

Mile 45.1: (at Chestnut Yard entrance). [Fig. 50(13)] Turntable. Look for the remains of the old platform turntable half buried in the clearing. Turntables were used to switch an engine from one direction to another.

Mile 41.5: (north of Fries entrance). [Fig. 50(12)] Beaver sign. Look along the river bank for trees felled by beavers. The cone-shaped stumps have the telltale grooves of the rodent's strong teeth. Large denning holes may also be found among the sycamore roots along the bank.

Mile 40.6: (north of Gambetta entrance) Chestnut Tunnel. [Fig. 50(11)] This 195-foot tunnel carved from rock is one of two on the trail.

Mile 40.1: (north of Fries entrance and just south of connection with Galax Trail). [Fig. 50(10)] Train wreck. In 1928, a passenger train and freight train collided at this spot, killing 3 and injuring 7 of 11 people aboard.

Mile 31.6: Rock crusher. [Fig. 50(9)] The 1901, 40,000-pound Allis-Chalmers rock crusher here once ground large slabs of limestone into smaller pieces for a local quarry.

Mile 29: Austinville Lead Mines. [Fig. 50(8)] Once lead was discovered here in 1756, the mining of minerals began in earnest. Most of the lead for the Revolutionary War and later for the Civil War came from the Austinville Lead Mines. Later the mine produced zinc, then limestone. When the mines closed in 1981, after operating continuously for over 200 years, they were among the oldest in the nation.

Mile 25.3: Shot Tower Historical State Park. [Fig. 50(7)] Built about 1807, the shot tower provided a method of dropping lead mined from the Austinville mines a distance great enough to cool it as it formed a round shape.

Mile 24: Foster Falls (Park Headquarters). [Fig. 50(6)] Foster Falls is being developed as the park headquarters and central recreation area for the park. The historic Foster Falls village includes a depot, hotel, sawmill/gristmill, and iron furnace. The Foster Falls Depot next to the trail and the abandoned Foster Falls Hotel off the trail are visible reminders of the now-defunct community and Hematite Iron Company that once depended on the railroad. Hematite is an important iron ore. In fact, the small mountain across the river from the trail is named Hematite Mountain and is an extension of the Iron Mountains to the west. The mountain to the east on the trail side of the river is Foster Falls Mountain, named for the impressive rapids here and for early landholder William Foster.

Mile 19.6: Bertha Cave. [Fig. 50(5)] Resist the temptation to disturb this 100-foot-deep cave, where a colony of bats depends on isolation from humans. Water percolating through porous limestone rock formed this and thousands of other Valley and Ridge caves.

Mile 10.2: Hiwassee. On the east side of the river near the Hiwassee Bridge is the town of Hiwassee, once a busy mining town. Hoover Mining Company, started in 1920, is the only remaining mining company in Pulaski County. The company still mines three natural iron oxide ores—ochre, umber, and sienna, used to make 300 different pigments.

Mile 8: Clarks Mill Trestle. [Fig. 50(2)] Underneath the trestle—and under the water backed up by the Claytor Lake Dam—are the remains of an old mill. The railroad bed leaves the New River at this point and heads for Pulaski.

Mile 2: Dora Junction. [Fig. 50(1)] Named for nearby remains of Dora Furnace, this junction is the northern trailhead for New River Trail State Park.

ENTRANCES TO NEW RIVER TRAIL STATE PARK

The trail is accessible at Hiwassee, Allisonia, Austinville, and Lone Ash, where there are no developed parking areas. Listed below are access points with parking areas:

Fries trailhead and boat launch (eastern Grayson County near Carroll County line): In Galax, from US 58 bridge over Chestnut Creek, go east approximately .5 mile and turn left (north) on VA 887. Go about .5 mile and turn left on Cliffview Road (VA 721). Go 5.8 miles to Fries. Parking is available near the town park and caboose.

Galax trailhead (on Carroll and Grayson county line): Park where US 58 crosses Chestnut Creek, just south of junction with VA 97.

Cliffview: In Galax, from US 58 bridge over Chestnut Creek, go east approximately .5 mile and turn left (north) on VA 887. Go about .5 mile and turn left on Cliffview Road (VA 721). Parking area is on left, across from Cliffview Mansion and Cliffview Trading Post.

Gambetta and Chestnut Yard: Follow directions to Cliffview and continue along VA 721. Turn right on VA 607 and go about 3 miles to Chestnut Yard. Or, after right turn on VA 607, go 1.5 miles and turn left on VA 743, continuing about 2 miles to Gambetta.

Byllesby Dam: From VA 94 in western corner of Carroll County, take VA 602 east about 3 miles to river.

Buck Dam: Follow above directions to Byllesby. Take VA 737 north to Buck Dam.

Ivanhoe: At Ivanhoe, in Wythe County, next to western corner of Carroll County, from VA 94, take VA 639 1 block east to river.

Shot Tower Historical State Park: From I-77 in southeastern Wythe County, take Exit 24 and go east .2 mile on VA 69 to VA 52. Go left and travel 1.5 miles on VA 52 to Shot Tower entrance, on left.

Foster Falls (Park Headquarters): Follow directions to Shot Tower, above. From VA 52, turn right on VA 608 and follow signs 2 miles to park.

Draper: From I-81, take Exit 92 and follow VA 658 east through Draper. Park across from Bryson's Store, less than 1 mile from interstate.

Pulaski/Xaloy trailhead: From I-81, take Exit 94B and go north 1.9 miles on VA 99 to Xaloy Drive. Turn right and go 100 yards to trailhead.

Other Directions: New River Campground and Picnic Area (U.S. Forest Service): From Ivanhoe, in southern Wythe County, go south on VA 94 about 4.5 miles. Look for Byllesby Dam sign and go left on VA 602. Go 3.6 miles and go left on gravel VA 737 (Buck Dam Road). Campground is 2 miles, on right.

Activities: Hiking, biking, horseback riding, boating, floating, fishing, picnicking. Tours at Shot Tower. Camping at nearby private campgrounds. Semiannual van tours for seniors.

Facilities: Benches scattered along trail. Picnic tables at Fries, Cliffview, Brush Creek near Byllesby Dam, New River Campground and Picnic Area (U.S. Forest Service) between Byllesby and Buck dams (shelter also), Shot Tower (grills also), Foster Falls (shelter also), and Draper. Convenience stores on VA 721 near Fries, in Galax, on VA 94 in Ivanhoe, about .5 mile off trail in Austinville, and just off the trail in Draper. Water fountains at Shot Tower and Cliffview. Restrooms at Fries, Cliffview, Brush Creek near Byllesby Dam, Buck Dam, Shot Tower, Foster Falls, and Draper. Access for the handicapped is possible at all entrances. Bicycle, canoe, and inner-tube rental available from park service at Foster Falls. New River Campground and Picnic Area has 16 campsites, drinking water, and vault toilets. Equestrian campground at private Horseshoe Campground at Draper. Plans include U.S. Forest Service campground near Buck Dam in Carroll County about 2 miles south of Wythe County line, and several primitive campsites. Parking for horse trailers at Fries, Cliffview, Foster Falls, and Draper entrances only.

Dates: Trail and New River Campground and Picnic Area open year-round. Shot Tower grounds open Apr. 1–Nov. 1, tower open Memorial Day–Labor Day and holidays. Seniors van tours in early May and early Oct.

Fees: Walking trail is free; a fee is charged for parking at Shot Tower and Foster Falls, Shot Tower tours, van tours for seniors, campsites at New River Campground.

Closest town: 2 southern trailheads are at Fries and Galax, both on the border of

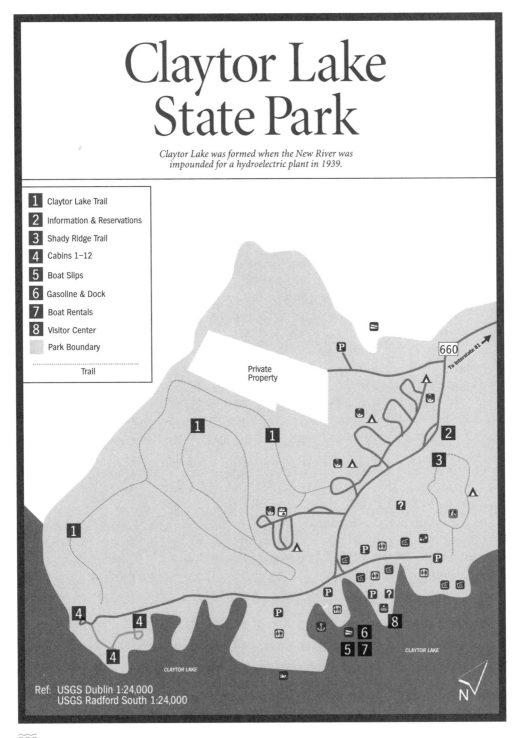

Claytor Lake State Park

Claytor Lake was formed when the New River was impounded for a hydroelectric plant in 1939.

1 Claytor Lake Trail
2 Information & Reservations
3 Shady Ridge Trail
4 Cabins 1–12
5 Boat Slips
6 Gasoline & Dock
7 Boat Rentals
8 Visitor Center
Park Boundary
Trail

Private Property

660
To Interstate 81

CLAYTOR LAKE

CLAYTOR LAKE

Ref: USGS Dublin 1:24,000
    USGS Radford South 1:24,000

N

Grayson and Carroll counties. Northern end is at Pulaski in Pulaski County. Shot Tower is 1.5 miles north of Poplar Camp in southeast Wythe County.

For more information: New River Trail State Park and Shot Tower Historical State Park, Route 1, Box 81X, Austinville, VA 24312-9801. Phone (540) 699-6778 or (540) 236-8889 (Cliffview office). New River Bicycles, Ltd., Route 1, Box 175, Draper, VA 24324. Phone (540) 980-1741.

Trail: 57-mile converted railroad bed along the New River through Grayson, Carroll, Wythe, and Pulaski counties.

Elevation: 2,150 at Fries to 1,950 at Pulaski.

Degree of difficulty: Easy.

Surface: Cinder and ballast stone, wooden trestles.

CLAYTOR LAKE AND CLAYTOR LAKE STATE PARK

CLAYTOR LAKE. [Fig. 51)] If the bottom of clear, cold, deep, 21-mile-long Claytor Lake was visible, visitors would get a glimpse of one link on the chain of history connecting white settlement along the frontier area known as southwest Virginia. The 4,475-acre impoundment of the New River lies south of Radford and east of Pulaski in Pulaski County, an easy jump from Interstate 81.

The nearby interstate and US 11 follow closely the old Wilderness Road, a foot-path and wagon trail for settlers traveling south down the Shenandoah and Roanoke valleys from Pennsylvania. Thousands of years before European pioneers started streaming down the valley in the mid-1700s, the road was a well-traveled hunting and raiding route used by southern Cherokee and Catawba tribes, as well as members of the northern Iroquois Confederacy of Five Nations. A mystic German sect called the Ephrata Brethren—later to be known as Dunkards—decided the land now covered by Claytor Lake was the place they wanted to stop. When the New River was dammed to form Claytor Lake for the generating of electric power in 1939, the community known as Dunkard's Bottom was swallowed by the rising waters.

FISHING AT CLAYTOR LAKE. Fishing is good but challenging in the narrow, winding waters of the lake. Claytor's steep shorelines make excellent habitat for smallmouth and spotted bass. In 1993, a 3-pound, 10-ounce spotted bass caught in the lake took the state record.

Good-sized largemouth bass come from Peak Creek, which branches off the upper river due east of Pulaski. Schools of striped bass in the 8- to 14-pound range occasionally produce a fish exceeding 20 pounds. Muskie, walleye, crappie, white bass, and catfish also bend anglers' rods at Claytor. Because there's so much water to cover, electronic fish-finding equipment can be a welcome aid.

CLAYTOR LAKE STATE PARK. With 472 acres of mostly hardwoods and pines, Claytor Lake State Park is now the centerpiece of 21-mile-long Claytor Lake. The park is a magnet to some 300,000 people a year whose primary recreational interests are waterbased.

Spotted Bass

Take a second look at what first appears to be a striped bass caught at Claytor Lake. It could be a spotted bass (*Micropterus punctulatus*). This feisty sport fish with the elongated body has a telltale tooth patch on the tongue. Also, instead of dark gray stripes on a silver-white side, it has small rows of black spots on its lower side.

Actually, the park and lake can get quite crowded on summer weekends. Much of the park property, however, is woodland, so getting away from the whine of bass boats and jet skies is no difficult matter.

As sought-after as this park is on a hot summer day, winter visitors have it mostly to themselves. An occasional hiker or runner and maybe a couple reminiscing about last summer's family reunion at the park will be there to give them a smile and a nod.

The park's visitor center [Fig. 51(8)]—a handsome, old, brick home located beside Claytor Lake—is historic. Haven Howe, a prominent Pulaski County citizen and Civil War cavalryman, built the home in 1879 using logs cut and dragged from the surrounding forests and bricks kiln-dried on the site. Howe was also a master craftsman. Visitors today still admire the freestanding staircase Howe built inside the house, the hardwood moulding he designed, and the wide pine floor he laid more than 100 years ago. Howe was also an environmentalist before the word was coined. He spent a great deal of time trying to reduce or halt tailings dumped in his beloved New River by iron-ore smelting plants in the region. The hard existence of early settlers is one topic of the visitor center exhibits. New exhibits focus on the lake's fish and water quality, and the park's animal life.

In summer, a full-service marina sells bait and tackle and manages a boat launch, motorboat and rowboat rental, and boat mooring at a floating dock. Evening programs draw guests to the lakeside amphitheater, The Gazebo.

Accommodations include four campground loops varying from densely wooded to sparsely shaded, to more open sites. There are also 12 lakefront rental cabins. Reservations, especially for peak season, should be made well in advance. A family fishing tournament and lake cleanup is held in June. On Labor Day weekend, patrons of the Claytor Lake Arts and Crafts Festival stroll among canopied booths shopping for baskets, pottery, handcrafted musical instruments, and oil paintings.

Before making a trip solely to take a luncheon or dinner cruise on the *Pioneer Maid*, travelers should call the office. The cruise is no longer available, but the state is investigating alternatives for this once-popular attraction. The double-deck, 600-foot boat sank, and protecting the clear lake waters from its diesel fuel became an expensive undertaking for the owners.

Directions: From I-81 in Pulaski County near Dublin, take Exit 101. Go southeast 2 miles on VA 660 (State Park Road) to park.

Activities: Camping, boating, fishing, swimming, hiking, picnicking, bird watching, lake cruising, interpretive programs, and, in late fall and early winter, a strictly controlled deer hunt.

Facilities: 129 campsites with picnic tables and grills in 4 campgrounds, electric and water at 43 sites, bathhouses; 12 lakefront cabins with fireplaces, electric appliances. Full-service marina with floating mooring docks, boat launch, boat rentals. Swimming beach, renovated bathhouse, diving tower, concession area. 3 hiking trails. Lakeside amphitheater.

Dates: Day use: open year-round. Campgrounds and cabins: open first weekend in May–Dec. 1. Swimming and marina: open in the summer.

Fees: A fee is charged for parking, camping, cabins, launch ramp, swimming. Fishing is free (must have Virginia fishing license).

Closest town: Dublin, in central Pulaski County, is 3 miles to the northwest.

For more information: Claytor Lake State Park, 4400 State Park Road, Dublin, VA 24084. Phone (540) 674-5492. Campsite or cabin reservations, phone (800) 933-PARK.

HIKING TRAILS AT CLAYTOR LAKE STATE PARK

Three trails totaling 4 miles wind through the oak-hickory forest and conifer stands of the park. The former horse trail was regraded and is now a hiking trail.

SHADY RIDGE NATURE TRAIL. [Fig. 51(3)] Beginning at the picnic area with a brief steep climb, the red-blazed trail then levels off for an easy .6-mile guided loop. Tall pines and cedars alternate with shrubby fields. A stand of large Carolina hemlocks is a highlight. Where old trees lie decaying on the ground, life replenishes itself. Bacteria, insects, and woodpeckers help the process along, until finally the tree is fully decomposed. Mushrooms, mosses, and new sprouts thrive in soil enriched by the decay.

Trail: .6-mile guided loop.

Elevation: 1,970 feet.

Degree of difficulty: Easy, after steep beginning.

CLAYTOR LAKE TRAIL. [Fig. 51(1)] Tulip poplar, hickory, red and white oak, black locust, and sycamore shade this blue-blazed, 1.6-mile trek through Claytor Lake's hardwood forest. The trail includes several lake views and is accessible across the road from the marina parking lot, from campground loops C and D, and across the road from the cabins.

Trail: 1.6-mile branching path, connecting campground loops C and D and cabins.

Elevation: 1,900 feet.

Degree of difficulty: Easy.

VIRGINIA
CREEPER
(Parthenocissus quinquefolia)

River Valleys: The James River

[Fig. 40] The headwaters of major rivers—the origin of so much water, so much life—have cast a spell over restless mankind for centuries. The Nile, for example, took the lives of several adventurers before the river's origin was eventually discovered in the mid-1800s. The headwaters of the James, Virginia's mightiest river, are more accessible, although it is still a moving experience to stand at the exact point in the Alleghaeny Mountains a mile below the community of Iron Gate where two smaller rivers—the Jackson and the Cowpasture—merge to become the state's longest and most hallowed ribbon of water. The James is not only one of the longest rivers in America lying completely within the borders of a single state, but its drainage base takes in nearly one-fourth of Virginia's total land mass.

The James River is the third largest tributary of the Chesapeake Bay. Beginning in the Allegheny Mountains in the northwestern part of Virginia, the river rushes, twists, and eventually glides a total of 343 miles through four of the state's five physiographic provinces—the Valley and Ridge, Blue Ridge, Piedmont Plateau, and Atlantic Coastal Plain.

The James's claim to fame is well documented.

In 1607, the boats of Englishmen crunched ashore a few miles upriver from the mouth of the James. There the James joins the Chesapeake Bay at Hampton Roads, and eventually, the Atlantic Ocean. The village was called Jamestown. It would become the first permanent English settlement in America. Traveling up the treacherous James was one way the mountains and valleys of Virginia got first a trickle, then a torrent of European farmers, trappers, missionaries, and adventurers.

To European settlers and eventually those who would call themselves Americans, the mighty James, like the Oregon Trail, beckoned as a logical route for westward expansion. Winding toward the setting sun through the fertile Piedmont above the fall line at Richmond then northwest into unexplored mountains, the river captivated the imaginations of both president and river rat.

President George Washington was intrigued by the use of canals for expansion and commerce. This was, after all, pre–Industrial Revolution America. Water seemed a logical way to transport goods and people. If a powerful river had already carved a major path through mountains 3,000 feet high—as the James had done in the Blue Ridge Mountains—then why not take advantage of it? Washington's dream was to connect East and West by a dependable system of river travel from Richmond through the mountains, on to the Kanawha and Ohio rivers, then eventually to the Mississippi and beyond. The system would become known as the James River & Kanawha Canal. Washington was the system's first president.

The canal was a project of immense scope. In the early 1800s, 3,300 people—mostly Irish immigrants—worked on construction of the canal with pick ax, mules, and black powder (dynamite hadn't been invented). Eventually there would be 23 low-level wing dams to divert river water into the canal system, a total of 98 locks to lift and lower boats at rapids and falls, 12 stone aqueducts, and 199 stone culverts to handle creeks and rivers flowing into the James. The canal that snaked alongside the James River and into the mountains was Virginia's largest public works project at the time and one of the most ambitious undertakings in the country.

By 1851, the great ditch with its elevated dirt towpath for horses and mules to pull barges and boats was complete to Buchanan in the mountains, 197 miles upriver from Richmond. Sections of the canal were used for some 80 years, but the James River & Kanawha Canal was completed only as far as Buchanan. Goods and people were then loaded on horses and wagons to travel the rest of the way through the Alleghaenies to Kentucky along the 208-mile-long James River & Kanawha Turnpike.

The simultaneous arrival of the steam engine and the coming of the Civil War doomed the ambitious canal system from Richmond through the mountains. By then, however, even the whitewater gorge called Balcony Falls through the Blue Ridge range near Glasgow—a barrier to river travel since the earliest explorers—had been mastered.

It is at Balcony Falls that the James has carved its route through the Blue Ridge range. Constricted by mountain walls that contain a series of Class III and IV whitewater rapids, the river speeds up at Balcony Falls, dropping nearly 200 feet through this section. The James roars over boulders and ledges of sandstone, limestone, and shale for a total of 7 miles as it carves a swath through the Blue Ridge. Federally designated James River Face Wilderness is on the south side.

Canoeists and kayakers love the area, but shooting Balcony Falls is a challenge best reserved for whitewater canoeists and kayakers of at least intermediate ability. A livery near Lexington, where the Maury River joins the James, rents river equipment and operates a shuttle service for those who want to float this portion of the river. For more information, contact James River Basin Canoe Livery, Ltd., Route 4, Box 109-A, Lexington, VA 24450. Phone (540) 261-7334.

A set of restored locks from the James River & Kanawha Canal are open for public inspection at Otter Creek where the Blue Ridge Parkway spans the river. The old canal locks, preserved by the U.S. Park Service, still have original pine planking. The stonework created by Irish and Italian stonemasons using rock quarried from the nearby mountains remains as beautiful today as when the locks were built in 1848.

FISHING THE JAMES

The James River is Virginia's best smallmouth bass river. Smallmouth prefer clean water that's richly oxygenated by riffles and rapids. If the fast water is broken up by deep, cool pools, so much the better. The upper regions of the James have it all.

Muskie have been stocked in the upper James, though these northern fish tend to come as a bonus when fishing for redbreast sunfish, bass, or catfish. The state Department of Game and Inland Fisheries has also stocked flathead catfish in the upper section of the James, but that fishery has not yet fully developed.

Public access points along the river are maintained by the state game department with license money. A free list of access points along the length of the James is available from the department office at Richmond (*see* below).

Fishing the James usually means float-fishing in a canoe or johnboat. The best method is to launch at a public ramp, drift with the current and cast while drifting, then take out at a public ramp downriver. Highway bridge crossings in Virginia are also access points to public waters. Another very effective and inexpensive lure is the 4-inch grub in various colors. Fly-fishermen also love the way smallmouth bass and sunfish take after Wooly Buggers and other flies that represent bottom-dwelling food.

For more information: Virginia Department of Game and Inland Fisheries, 4010 W. Broad Street, Richmond, VA 23230. Phone (804) 367-1000.

FLOATING THE JAMES

For sweeping views of the Allegheny and Blue Ridge mountains, of wilderness areas and river islands along the way, of stonework done by master craftsmen on riverside canals long abandoned, day-long float trips on the upper James offer the best way of seeing it all. Here are several trips recommended by the Virginia game department:

EAGLE ROCK TO HORSESHOE BEND. Paddling time, 4–6 hours. Numerous Class I–II riffles. Exceptional mountain scenery and vistas.

HORSESHOE BEND TO SPRINGWOOD. Paddling time, 2–4 hours. Outstanding mountain scenery, numerous Class I–II riffles. Take-out on right side of river beneath VA 630 bridge.

SPRINGWOOD TO BUCHANAN. Paddling time, 3–5 hours. Best muskie fishing in the James. Take-out on right side of river at public boat ramp in the town of Buchanan.

BUCHANAN TO GLASGOW. Paddling time, 8–10 hours. Many Class I–II riffles and mountain vistas. Primitive U.S. Forest Service canoe-in campsites on the right side of the river some 13 miles below Buchanan. James River Recreation Area (privately owned campground) on the right side of the river 3 miles upstream from Glasgow. General stores in Smallwood and Buchanan.

GLASGOW TO SNOWDEN. Paddling time, 2–3 hours. Though it is treacherous in places, this is possibly the most beautiful reach of the entire upper river. Here the James River cuts through the Blue Ridge mountain range. In addition to numerous Class I–II riffles, a major Class III–IV rapid of some 4 miles called Balcony Falls creates crashing stairsteps and runs through boulderfields as the river picks up speed and strength. Balcony Falls should be scouted carefully before running. James River Face Wilderness Area is on the right side of the river. There's a general store at Snowden. Take-out is on the left side up Rocky Row Run underneath the VA 501/VA 130 bridge.

For more information: Virginia Department of Game and Inland Fisheries, 4010 W. Broad Street, Richmond, VA 23230. Phone (804) 367-1000.

A. Books and References

The books and resources below are more than just a list. Taken as a whole, the resources represent a tremendous wealth of information to help the wanderer in Virginia's mountains piece together a fascinating puzzle.

Birds of the Blue Ridge Mountains by Marcus B. Simpson Jr., University of North Carolina Press, Chapel Hill, NC 1992.

Blue Ridge Parkway Guide by William G. Lord, Menasha Ridge Press, Birmingham, AL 1981.

Classic Virginia Rivers by Ed Grove, Eddy Out Press, Arlington, VA 1992.

A Cyclist's Guide to the Shenandoah Valley by Randy Porter and Nancy Sorrells, Shenandoah Odysseys, Staunton, VA 1995.

Endangered and Threatened Species in Virginia by Karen Terwilliger and John R. Tate, McDonald & Woodward Publishing, Blacksburg, VA 1995.

Fall Wildflowers of the Blue Ridge and Great Smoky Mountains by Oscar W. Gupton and Fred C. Swope, University Press of Virginia, Charlottesville, VA 1987.

Geology and Virginia by Richard V. Dietrich, University Press of Virginia, Charlottesville, VA 1970.

Going Underground: Your Guide to Caves in the Mid-Atlantic by Sharon Hernes Silverman, Camino Books, Inc., Philadelphia, PA 1991.

Guide to Shenandoah National Park and Skyline Drive by Henry Heatwole, Shenandoah Natural History Association, Luray, VA 1997.

A Guide to Virginia's Wildlife Management Areas, Virginia Department of Game and Inland Fisheries, Richmond, VA 1996.

Hikes to Waterfalls in Shenandoah National Park by Shenandoah Natural History Association, Luray, VA 1997.

Hiking Virginia by Randy Johnson, Falcon Press Publishing Co., Inc., Helena MT 1992.

Mountains of the Heart: A Natural History of the Appalachians by Scott Weidensaul, Fulcrum Publishing, Golden, CO 1994.

A Naturalist's Blue Ridge Parkway by David T. Catlin, University of Tennessee Press, Knoxville, TN 1984.

Natural Wonders of Virginia: A Guide to Parks, Preserves & Wild Places by Garvey and Deane Winegar, Country Roads Press, Brecksville, OH 1994.

Out There Virginia: A Guide to Backcountry Travel & Adventure by James Bannon, Out There Press, Asheville, NC 1997.

Roadside Geology of Virginia by Dr. Keith Frye, Mountain Press Publishing Co., Missoula, MT 1986.

Short Hikes in Shenandoah National Park by Shenandoah Natural History Association, Luray, VA 1994.

Trails of Virginia: Hiking the Old Dominion by Allen De Hart, University of North Carolina Press, Chapel Hill, NC 1995.

Trout Fishing in the Shenandoah National Park by Harry W. Murray, Shenandoah Publishing Company, Edinburg 1989.

Virginia Atlas and Gazetteer by DeLorme Mapping Company, Freeport, ME 1995.

Virginia Fishing Guide by Bob Gooch, University of Virginia Press, Charlottesville, VA 1988.

Virginia Outdoors: The Official Outdoor Recreation Guide by Virginia Tourism Corporation, Richmond, VA (Issued annually).

Virginia State Parks by Bill Bailey, Glovebox Guidebooks of America, Saginaw, MI 1996.

Walking the Blue Ridge: A Guide to the Trails of the Blue Ridge Parkway by Leonard Adkins, University of North Carolina Press, Chapel Hill, 1991.

Wildflowers of the Shenandoah Valley and Blue Ridge Mountains by Oscar W. Gupton and Fred C. Swope, University Press of Virginia, Charlottesville, VA 1979.

B. Conservation & Outdoor Organizations

The following are nonprofit organizations dedicated to the preservation and/or enjoyment of the rich natural heritage of Virginia's mountains.

Appalachian Trail Conference, National Office. PO Box 807, Harpers Ferry, WV 25425. Phone (304) 535-6331. Parent organization of trail clubs that maintain Appalachian Trail. Publishes guidebooks and maps, and is involved in many conservation activities; mountaineering; ski-touring; and construction and maintenance of shelters, cabins, and trails.

Blue Ridge Parkway Foundation. PO Box 10427, Salem Station, Winston-Salem, NC 27103. Encourages bequests for purchase of land and conservation easements along the Parkway.

Float Fishermen of Virginia. PO Box 1750, Roanoke, VA 24008. Phone (540) 366-2228 (a member's home phone). Statewide organization of canoeists, kayakers, rafters, and boaters dedicated to the conservation and protection of Virginia's rivers.

Fly-Fishers of Virginia. PO Box 29477, Richmond, VA 23242. Promotes fly-fishing, sportsmanship, conservation, and the enjoyment of angling.

Friends of the Blue Ridge Parkway. Virginia Office, PO Box 20986, Roanoke, VA 24018. Phone (800) 228-7275. Volunteers dedicated to preserving and protecting the highway as a national treasure. Programs focus on conservation, preservation, education, and advocacy.

Friends of the Rivers of Virginia. PO Box 1750, Roanoke, VA 24008. Phone (540) 343-3696. Statewide coalition dedicated to protecting and restoring rivers of Virginia.

Hawk Migration Association of North America. 377 Loomis Street, Southwick, MA 01077. Volunteers keep records on migrations and publish newsletter.

Izaak Walton League of America, Inc., Virginia Division. 506 Stonegate Drive, Blacksburg, VA 24060. Phone (540) 231-5610. Dedicated to wise stewardship and preservation of land and resources.

National Speleological Society. 2813 Cave Avenue, Huntsville, AL 35810-4431. Web site nss@caves.org; phone (205) 852-1300. Nonprofit organization affiliated with the American Association for the Advancement of Science. Members in local chapters or "grottoes" conduct regular meetings to bring cavers together within their general area and coordinate activities which may include mapping, cleaning, and gating sensitive caves.

The Nature Conservancy, Virginia Chapter. 1233A Cedars Court, Charlottesville, VA 22903. Phone (804) 295-6106. Preserves rare and endangered plants, animals, and natural communities by protecting the ecosystems that sustain them.

Potomac Appalachian Trail Club. 118 Park Street, SE, Vienna, VA 22180. Phone (703) 242-0693. Maintains 240 miles of Appalachian Trail and additional 750 miles of other trails. Publishes guidebooks and maps, and is involved in many conservation activities; mountaineering; ski-touring; and construction and maintenance of shelters, cabins, and trails.

Rails-to-Trails Conservancy. 1100 Seventeenth Street, NW, 10th Floor, Washington, DC 20036. Phone (202) 331-9696. Spearheads the effort to convert old railroad beds to trail systems.

Resource-Use Education Council. PO Box 1009, Richmond, VA 23240. Phone (804) 698-4442 or (804) 367-0188. Volunteers from state and federal government, colleges, and private industry promote environmental education. Conducts conservation education workshops for educators.

Shenandoah Natural History Association. 3655 US Highway 211 East, Luray, VA 22835. Phone (540) 999-3582. Supports interpretive and educational programs of the park through sale of books, maps, and related items at visitor centers.

Trout Unlimited, Virginia Council. 302 Danray Drive, Richmond, VA 23227. Phone (804) 264-6941. Statewide organization with 16 chapters working to protect and enhance cold-water fisheries.

Virginia Conservation Network. 1001 East Broad Street, Suite 410, Richmond, VA 23219. Phone (804) 644-0283. Network of organizations devoted to advancing an environmentally sound vision for Virginia.

Virginia Department of Conservation and Recreation. 203 Governor Street, Suite 302, Richmond, VA 23219. Phone (804) 786-2121. Conserves, protects, enriches, and advocates wise use of state's natural, recreational, and scenic resources. Department's Division of Natural Heritage attempts to identify significant natural areas and other features that are exemplary, rare, or endangered on a global or statewide basis.

Virginia Department of Game and Inland Fisheries. 4010 West Broad Street, Richmond, VA 23230. Phone (804) 367-1000. Manages a diversity of fish and wildlife species; provides environmental protection; enhances hunting, fishing, and boating programs; provides wildlife-related recreation opportunities. Runs Nongame and Endangered Wildlife Program.

Virginia Federation of Garden Clubs. Conducts Operation Wildflower in cooperation with Virginia Department of Transportation, seeding hundreds of acres along Virginia highways. Wildflower research assistance provided by Virginia Polytechnic Institute and State University, Blacksburg. To contribute seeds or learn more about program, call (800) PRIDE-VA.

Virginia Museum of Natural History. 1001 Douglas Avenue, Martinsville, VA 24112. Phone (540) 666-8600. Preserves, studies, and interprets Virginia's natural and cultural heritage. Statewide system of museum facilities, research sites, and educational programs.

Virginia Native Plant Society. PO Box 844, Annandale, VA 22003. Phone (804) 332-5757. Seeks to further appreciate and conserve Virginia's wild plants and habitats. Emphasizes public education, protection of endangered species, preservation of habitat, appropriate landscape use of native plants.

Virginia Outdoors Foundation. PO Box 322, Aldie, VA 22001. Phone (703) 327-6118. Strives to preserve Virginia's natural scenic, historic, scientific, and recreational areas by means of private philanthropy.

Virginia Outdoor Writers Association. 7286 Harvest Lane, Mechanicsville, VA 23111. Association of writers dedicated to disseminating information about Virginia's outdoors.

Virginia Society of Ornithology. 7451 Little River Turnpike, #202, Annandale, VA 22003. Phone (703) 305-5611. Dedicated to all aspects of birds of Virginia, including conservation, field research, education, and dissemination of information.

Virginia Wilderness Committee. Route 1, Box 156, Swoope, VA 22479. Phone (540) 337-8000. Preservation of outstanding roadless areas on federal land through congressional wilderness designation. Publishes *Virginia Wilderness* newsletter.

Virginia Wildlife Federation. 1001 East Broad Street, LL5, Richmond, VA 23219. Phone (804) 648-3136. Affiliated with the National Wildlife Federation. Devoted to the wise use, conservation, aesthetic appreciation, and restoration of wildlife and other natural resources.

The Wildlife Center of Virginia. PO Box 1557, Waynesboro, VA 22980. Phone (540) 942-9453. Professionally staffed veterinary hospital providing care to sick, injured, or orphaned wildlife.

Wildlife Society, Virginia Chapter. 4792 Anderson Highway, Powhatan, VA 23139. Phone (804) 598-3706. Strives to develop and promote sound stewardship of wildlife resources and prevent human-induced environmental degradation.

Wintergreen Nature Foundation. PO Box 468, Wintergreen, VA 22958. Phone (804) 325-8172. Encourages the understanding, appreciation, and conservation of the natural resources of the Blue Ridge mountains of central Virginia. Research and education facility for members and visitors and host site for regional and national conservation efforts.

C. Special Events, Fairs and Festivals

GENERAL

Friday Nite Jamboree—Traditional weekly barn dance at Cockram's General Store in Floyd. Phone (540) 745-4563.

Galax Mountain Music Jamboree—Traditional mountain music and dance, third Saturday night each month in Galax. Phone (540) 236-0668 or (540) 236-2184.

Virginia Horse Festival—Competitions in various styles of horseback riding held throughout the year at Lexington Equestrian Center, Lexington. Phone (540) 463-4300.

JANUARY

Virginia Special Olympics—With the help of volunteers, Wintergreen resort in Nelson County hosts this annual snow-skiing competition for mentally challenged athletes. January. Phone (804) 325-2200.

FEBRUARY

African-American Heritage Month—The Museum of American Frontier Culture hosts this examination of black contributions to early American growth. Held in February in Staunton. Phone (540) 332-7850.

MARCH

Highland Maple Festival—Tours to maple sugar camps to see both old and new methods of syrupmaking, Maple Museum, pancake breakfasts with maple syrup, craft show. March. Highland County Chamber of Commerce, PO Box 223, Monterey, VA 24465. Phone (540) 468-2550.

Mountain Empire Fly-Fishing School—Three-day school for beginners on fly-fishing tackle, entomology, knots, wading, artificial flies, stream lore, and casting techniques. Held at Hungry Mother State Park in March. Phone (540) 783-3422.

Whitetop Mountain Maple Festival—Festive event at Mount Rogers National Recreation Area features live country and western music, tours of maple tree tapping areas, pancake breakfasts where visitors can sample homemade syrups, arts and crafts, storytelling. Two weekends in late March. Sponsored by Mount Rogers Volunteer Fire Department and Rescue Squad. Phone (540) 773-3711.

APRIL

Kids Fishing Day—Stocked trout fishing for children at Elkhorn Lake, near Bridgewater. Sponsored by Dry River Ranger District, George Washington National Forest. April. Phone (540) 828-2591.

River Run and Bicycle Ride—Athletes face-off against the rugged terrain near Breaks Interstate Park on the Virginia/Kentucky border. April. Phone (540) 921-1544.

Shenandoah Valley Apple Blossom Festival—Dances, circus, luncheons, parades, band competitions, arts and crafts show in Winchester. April–May. Phone (540) 662-3863.

MAY

Appalachian Trail Days—Hikers are invited to Damascus, "the friendliest town on the Appalachian Trail," during May festivities, including square dancing, mountain music, costumed town folk, hiker talent show, rubber duck races, barbecue, and parade. Phone (540) 637-6766 or (800) 446-9670.

Delaplane Strawberry Festival—Celebrate the region's strawberry season at Sky Meadows State Park with strawberry sundaes, eighteenth-century dancing demonstration, Civil War brass band, crafts, hayrides, clowns, children's games, pony rides, and petting zoo. May. Phone (540) 592-3556.

Mount Rogers Naturalist Rally—Participants study natural history and wildlife of southwest Virginia during workshops and interpretive hikes at weekend retreat at Mount Rogers National Recreation Area. Talks by naturalists, hikes led by college professors. Sponsored by Mount Rogers Interpretive Association, usually coinciding with Mount Rogers Ramp Festival, third weekend in May. Phone (540) 783-2125 or (800) 446-9670.

Southwestern Virginia Pioneer Festival—Learn how southwest Virginia was colonized and developed at the Crab Orchard Museum and Pioneer Park. Demonstrations include basket weaving, wool spinning, and blacksmithing. Held at Tazewell in May. Phone (540) 988-6755.

Wildflower Weekend—Wildflower hikes into the surrounding Blue Ridge mountains originate at the Hotel Strasburg. First weekend in May in Strasburg. Phone (540) 253-9622.

Wildflower Weekend—Shenandoah National Park celebrates the arrival of spring with guided walks, exhibits, slide programs, and workshops during the third weekend in May. Park headquarters is at Luray. Phone (540) 999-3482

Wintergreen Wildflower Symposium—Experts in botany, geology, herpetology, etc., conduct seminars and lead wildflower and bird walks at Wintergreen in Nelson County. Mid-May. Phone (800) 282-8223 or (800) 325-2200.

JUNE

Bluegrass Festival—Open-air concerts in June at Graves Mountain Lodge on scenic Robinson River in Virginia's northern Blue Ridge mountains featuring some of the nation's finest musicians. Lodge is near Syria in Madison County. Phone (540) 923-4231.

Grayson County Fiddlers Convention—Music jamboree held at Elk Creek last weekend in June. Free camping. Sponsored by Elk Creek Valley Volunteer Fire Department. Phone (540) 773-3711.

Wayne C. Henderson Festival—Music festival and guitar competition at Grayson Highlands State Park with prize of Wayne Henderson guitar. Sponsored by Rugby Volunteer Fire Department and Rescue Squad. Third Saturday in June. Phone (540) 773-3711.

JUNE–JULY

Appalachian Trail Conference—Activities include hikes, workshops, children's activities, and evening entertainment. The conference is held at James Madison University, Harrisonburg, for a week in late June or early July. Phone (540) 981-0693.

JUNE–JULY–AUGUST

Bluemont Concert Series—This free outdoor concert series draws hundreds to the lawn of the old Frederick County Courthouse in Old Town Winchester. Features folk, Cajun, bluegrass, and other music under the stars on Friday evenings in June, July, and part of August. Phone (540) 665-0079.

The Shenandoah Valley Music Festival—Long-running series of high-quality summer and fall concerts in rustic open-air pavilion at historic mineral springs resort hotel at Orkney Springs. Phone (800) 459-3396

Theater at Lime Kiln—Memorial Day begins the summer season at Lime Kiln, an outdoor theater that is nationally recognized for presenting original plays and musicals relating to Virginia's culture and history. Plays and concerts take place under the stars in an enchanting setting: the ruins of an actual lime kiln built in the 1800s. Plays are performed Monday through Saturday until Labor Day. On Sunday nights, some of the best and brightest in the music business perform jazz, blues, folk, and bluegrass music. Lexington. Phone (540) 463-3074.

JULY

Blue Ridge Heritage Festival—southwest Virginia's 19 counties celebrate mountain music, arts and crafts, and attractions of the Blue Ridge Highlands. Held at Fort Chiswell in July. Phone (540) 228-3111.

Hungry Mother Arts and Crafts Festival—Longest-running state park art and crafts festival in Virginia featuring more than 125 artisans, musical programs, and children's programs at Hungry Mother State Park. Third weekend in July. Phone (540) 828-2591 or (540) 783-3161.

Riverfest—Celebrate the great outdoors with a raft race down the New River. Other highlights are a barbecue cooking contest, craft show, and live music. Held at Radford on second Saturday following the Fourth of July. Phone (540) 639-2202.

Shenandoah Valley Bicycle Festival—Bikers of all levels compete at Bridgewater in races ranging from 5 to 100 miles. Bridgewater College hosts the event, usually at end of July. Phone (540) 434-3862.

AUGUST

Natural Chimneys Jousting Tournament—Horseback jousting where riders at full gallop attempt to spear series of tiny hanging rings. Event started in 1821. Third Saturday in August at Mount Solon. Phone (540) 350-2510 or (540) 249-5729.

Old Fiddlers Convention—Oldest and largest in the world, the four-day Old Fiddlers Convention is held at Felts Park in Galax on second week in August, sponsored by Galax Moose Lodge. Phone (540) 236-2184 or (540) 773-3711.

Riverfest—Sponsored by the Friends of the Shenandoah, this August festival takes place at the confluence of the north and south branches of the Shenandoah River at Front Royal. Activities include canoe races, fishing tournament, river rodeo with tug of war, centipede canoe race, obstacle course, and blindfolded canoe race. On shore are crafts, food, and live music. Phone (540) 636-4948.

The Virginia Highlands Arts and Crafts Festival—Celebrates revival in old-time arts and crafts, streets filled with items by the area's finest artists and craftspeople. Held in historic Abingdon in Washington County, first two weeks in August. Phone (540) 676-2282 or (800) 435-3440.

SEPTEMBER

Apple Harvest Arts and Crafts Festival—Held at Jim Barnett Park in Winchester, festival features apple-butter making and pie contests, live music, arts and crafts. September. Phone (540) 662-4135.

Claytor Lake Arts and Crafts Fair—Family Labor Day celebration with many artisans displaying handmade articles under the park trees. Held Labor Day weekend. Claytor Lake State Park, Pulaski County. Phone (540) 980-7363.

Henry Street African-American Heritage Festival—Celebration of African-American culture in neighborhood close to downtown Roanoke. Ethnic food, music, entertainment, children's activities. September. Phone (540) 345-4818.

"Spirit of the Indian" Pow Wow—Learn about the past and present culture of Virginia's Native Americans at this gathering at Claudius Crozet Park, 12 miles west of Charlottesville. Held in Crozet in early September. Phone (804) 929-0334.

Taste of the Mountains Main Street Festival—Artisans demonstrate basket weaving, woodcarving, glass blowing, chair caning, furniture making, quilting, spinning, bark-basket making, and beekeeping. Hear Appalachian tunes on dulcimers and harps and watch the footwork of clog dancers. Petting zoo, mountain-inspired food. Held in Madison in September. Phone (540) 948-3645 or 948-4455.

OCTOBER

Blue Ridge Folklife Festival—Ferrum College hosts this popular event the last Saturday in October. Widely attended, the festival showcases regional traditions, with crafts workers showing time-honored skills, old-time musicians, and traditional Appalachian competitions. Ferrum. Phone (540) 365-4416.

Mountain Foliage Festival—Celebrates humor of mountain folk with Grand Privy Race, the only outhouse race in Virginia. Contestants race privies on wheels down Main Street of Independence, sending winner to national event. Held second Saturday in October, sponsored by Town of Independence and 1908 Courthouse. Phone (540) 773-3711.

Oktoberfest—German beer, Virginia wine, food, and an oompah band playing traditional German music make this a special festival. There's also a Bach Bash presented by the Mid-Atlantic Chamber Orchestra as well as arts and crafts displays. Held in Staunton in October. Phone (540) 886-2351.

Virginia Fall Foliage Festival—Two October weekends of fine arts and crafts, apple-butter making, gem and mineral show, food booths, chili cook-off. Held in Waynesboro since 1973. Phone (540) 949-8513.

DECEMBER

Monticello Holiday Open House—In early December, at the former home of Thomas Jefferson, visitors are treated to candlelight tours of the mansion, which is decorated in period ornaments. Traditional music nightly. Refreshments in the gift shop. Charlottesville. Phone (804) 984-9828.

D. Outfitters, Guides, and Suppliers

Virginia Mountains from North Carolina to Roanoke

Allisonia Trading Post. Outfitting on New River Trail State Park. HCO2 Box 15 B, Allisonia, VA 24347. Phone (540) 980-2051.

Blue Blaze Bike and Shuttle Service. Shuttle service for high country trails, Virginia Creeper Trail and Appalachian Trail. P. O. Box 982, 227 West Laurel Avenue, Damascus, VA 24236. Phone (800) 475-5095 or (540) 475-5095.

Cliffview Trading Post. Bicycle and horse rental on New River Trail State Park. Route 4, Box 163, Galax, VA 24333. Phone (540) 238-1530.

Land, Air, & Water. Canoe scenic rivers, bike backroads and trails, fish, cave, ride horseback, raft, and more. P. O. Box 1210, St. Paul, VA 24283. Phone (540) 762-7500 or E-mail: outdoor@compunet.net.

Mount Rogers High Country Outdoor Center. Wilderness adventures, sightseeing, pack trips, and wagon rides. Trips originate at livery base camp on VA 603 in Troutdale. P. O. Box 151, Troutdale, VA 24378. Phone (540) 677-3900.

New River Adventures. Canoe and bike rental and shuttle service along New River and New River Trail State Park. Easy access to New River at small boat ramp at Foster Falls. 1007 North 4th Street, Wytheville, VA 24382. Phone (540) 228-8311.

The Outpost. Rental fly fishing equipment, information, maps, permits to fish four-mile-long stocked Cascades Stream at The Homestead, state licenses, clothing. Guides for trout fishing Cascades Stream, Back Creek, Little Back Creek, upper and lower Jackson River. 2 Cottage Row, Box 943, Hot Springs, VA 24445. (540) 839-5442.

Virginia Highlands Llamas. Outfitter cooks gourmet meals and provides llamas to carry the gear. Route 1, Box 41, Bland, VA 24315. Phone (540) 688-4464.

Virginia Wilderness Co. Guided backpacking, fly fishing trips into southwest Virginia backcountry. Gourmet cooking. All camping, fishing equipment provided. 10468 Fortune Ridge Road, Bent Mountain, VA 24059. Phone (800) 683-1831, ext. 3461. (540) 929-4025.

Wilderness Road Tours. Van and bus tours of Cumberland Gap area. 224 Greenwood Road, Middlesboro, KY 40965. Phone (606) 248-2626.

Virginia Mountains—North of Roanoke

Downriver Canoe Co. Shenandoah River outfitting and guide service. P. O. Box 10, Bentonville, VA 22610. Phone (800) 338-1963.

Highland Adventures. Variety of mountain bike excursions, rock climbing and caving tours in western Virginia and West Virginia. Shuttle and meals. P. O. Box 151, Monterey, VA 24465. Phone (540) 468-2722.

James River Basin Canoe Livery, Ltd. Outfitter with 10 mapped trips of varying difficulty. RFD #6, Box 125, Lexington, VA 24450. E-mail: CanoeVa@Rockbridge.net. Phone (540) 261-7334.

Murray's Fly Shop. Fly rods, 50,000 flies, schools, guides. P. O. Box 156, Edinburg, VA 22824. Phone (540) 984-4212.

Rockbridge Outfitters, Ltd. Mountain bike rental, retail outlet for camping, bike supplies. 112 West Washington Street, Lexington, VA 24450. Phone (540) 463-1947.

Shenandoah River Outfitters. Outfitting and guide services on scenic South Fork of Shenandoah River. Canoe, kayak, tube, fish. Tent campground, cabins available. 6502 South Page Valley Road, Luray, VA 22835. (540) 743-4159 or (800) 6CANOE2.

Wilderness Voyagers. Canoe and camping rental; shuttle service, hiking trips; retail outlet. 1544 East Market Street, Harrisonburg, VA 22801. Phone (540) 434-7234.

Woodstone Meadows Equine Center. Trail rides in Massanutten Mountains. Route 1, Box 110-L, McGaheysville, VA 22840. Phone (540) 289-6152.

E. Glossary

Anticline—Arching rock fold that is closed at the top and open at bottom. Oldest formation occurs in the center of an anticline.

Basement—Complex of igneous and metamorphic rock that underlies the sedimentary rocks of a region.

Biotic—Pertaining to plants and animals.

Boreal—Relating to the northern biotic area characterized by the dominance of coniferous forests.

Carbonate rock—Collective term including limestone and dolomite.

Coniferous—Describing the cone-bearing trees of the pine family; usually evergreen.

Continental drift—Theory that the continental land masses drift across the earth as the earth's plates move and interact in a process called plate tectonics.

Deciduous—Plants that shed their leaves seasonally and are leafless for part of the year.

Endemic—Having originated in and being restricted to one particular environment.

Escarpment—Cliff or steep rock face formed by faulting that separates two comparatively level land surfaces.

Extinct—No longer existing.

Extirpated—Extinct in a particular area.

Feldspar—Complex of silicates that make up bulk of the earth's crust.

Fold—Warped rock including synclines and anticlines.

Gneiss—Metamorphic granitelike rock showing layers.

Granite—Igneous rock composed predominantly of visible grains of feldspar and quartz. Used in building.

Igneous—Rock formed by cooled and hardened magma within the crust or lava on the surface.

Karst—Area of land lying over limestone and characterized by sinkholes, caves, and sinking streams.

Lava—Magma which reaches the surface of the earth.

Magma—Molten rock within the earth's crust.

Metamorphic—Rock which has been changed into present state after being subjected to heat and pressure from the crust, or chemical alteration.

Monadnock—Land that contains more erosion-resistant rock than surrounding area and therefore is higher.

Orogeny—A geologic process which results in the formation of mountain belts.

Outcrop—Exposed bedrock.

Overthrust belt—An area where older rock has been thrust over younger rock.

Rapids—Fast-moving water that flows around rocks and boulders in rivers; classified from I to VI according to degree of difficulty navigating.

Schist—Flaky, metamorphic rock containing parallel layers of minerals such as mica.

Sedimentary—Rocks formed by the accumulation of sediments (sandstone, shale) or the remains of products of animals or plants (limestone, coal).

Shale—Sedimentary rock composed of clay, mud, and silt grains which easily splits into layers.

Syncline—A rock fold shaped like a U that is closed at the bottom and open at the top. The youngest rock is at the center of a syncline.

Talus—Rock debris and boulders that accumulate at the base of a cliff.

Watershed—The area drained by a river and all its tributaries.

Index